Śrī Caitanya-caritāmṛta

BOOKS by
His Divine Grace A.C. Bhaktivedanta Swami Prabhupāda

Bhagavad-gītā As It Is
Śrīmad-Bhāgavatam, Cantos 1-5 (15 Vols.)
Śrī Caitanya-caritāmṛta (17 Vols.)
Teachings of Lord Caitanya
The Nectar of Devotion
Śrī Īśopaniṣad
Easy Journey to Other Planets
Kṛṣṇa Consciousness: The Topmost Yoga System
Kṛṣṇa, The Supreme Personality of Godhead (3 Vols.)
Transcendental Teachings of Prahlād Mahārāja
Kṛṣṇa, the Reservoir of Pleasure
The Perfection of Yoga
Beyond Birth and Death
On the Way to Kṛṣṇa
Rāja-vidyā: The King of Knowledge
Elevation to Kṛṣṇa Consciousness
Kṛṣṇa Consciousness: The Matchless Gift
Back to Godhead Magazine (Founder)

A complete catalogue is available upon request

International Society for Krishna Consciousness
3764 Watseka Avenue
Los Angeles, California 90034

All Glory to Śrī Guru and Gaurāṅga

ŚRĪ CAITANYA-CARITĀMṚTA

of Kṛṣṇadāsa Kavirāja Gosvāmī

Madhya-līlā
Volume Three

"The Lord's Tour of South India"

with the original Bengali text, Roman transliterations, synonyms, translation and elaborate purports

by

HIS DIVINE GRACE
A.C. Bhaktivedanta Swami Prabhupāda
Founder-Ācārya of the International Society for Krishna Consciousness

THE BHAKTIVEDANTA BOOK TRUST
New York · Los Angeles · London · Bombay

Readers interested in the subject matter of this book
are invited by the International Society for Krishna Consciousness
to correspond with its Secretary.

International Society for Krishna Consciousness
3764 Watseka Avenue
Los Angeles, California 90034

Library of Congress Catalogue Card Number: 73-93206
International Standard Book Number: 0-912776-65-x

Printed in the United States of America

Contents

Introduction

Śrī Caitanya-caritāmṛta is the principal work on the life and teachings of Śrī Kṛṣṇa Caitanya. Śrī Caitanya is the pioneer of a great social and religious movement which began in India a little less than five hundred years ago and which has directly and indirectly influenced the subsequent course of religious and philosophical thinking not only in India but in the recent West as well.

Caitanya Mahāprabhu is regarded as a figure of great historical significance. However, our conventional method of historical analysis—that of seeing a man as a product of his times—fails here. Śrī Caitanya is a personality who transcends the limited scope of historical settings.

At a time when, in the West, man was directing his explorative spirit toward studying the structure of the physical universe and circumnavigating the world in search of new oceans and continents, Śrī Kṛṣṇa Caitanya, in the East, was inaugurating and masterminding a revolution directed inward, toward a scientific understanding of the highest knowledge of man's spiritual nature.

The chief historical sources for the life of Śrī Kṛṣṇa Caitanya are the *kaḍacās* (diaries) kept by Murāri Gupta and Svarūpa Dāmodara Gosvāmī. Murāri Gupta, a physician and close associate of Śrī Caitanya's, recorded extensive notes on the first twenty-four years of Śrī Caitanya's life, culminating in his initiation into the renounced order, *sannyāsa*. The events of the rest of Caitanya Mahāprabhu's forty-eight years are recorded in the diary of Svarūpa Dāmodora Gosvāmī, another of Caitanya Mahāprabhu's intimate associates.

Śrī Caitanya-caritāmṛta is divided into three sections called *līlās,* which literally means "pastimes"—*Ādi-līlā* (the early period), *Madhya-līlā* (the middle period) and *Antya-līlā* (the final period). The notes of Murāri Gupta form the basis of the *Ādi-līlā,* and Svarūpa Dāmodara's diary provides the details for the *Madhya-* and *Antya-līlās.*

The first twelve of the seventeen chapters of *Ādi-līlā* constitute the preface for the entire work. By referring to Vedic scriptural evidence, this preface establishes Śrī Caitanya as the *avatāra* (incarnation) of Kṛṣṇa (God) for the age of Kali—the current epoch, beginning five thousand years ago and characterized by materialism, hypocrisy and dissension. In these descriptions, Caitanya Mahāprabhu, who is identical with Lord Kṛṣṇa, descends to liberally grant pure love of God to the fallen souls of this degraded age by propagating *saṅkīrtana*—literally, "congregational glorification of God"—especially by organizing massive public chanting of the *mahā-mantra* (Great Chant for Deliverance). The esoteric purpose of Lord Caitanya's appearance in the world is revealed, his co-*avatāras* and principal devotees are described and his teachings are summarized. The remaining portion of *Ādi-līlā,* chapters thirteen through seventeen, briefly recounts his divine birth and his life until he accepted the renounced order. This includes his childhood miracles, schooling, marriage and early philosophical confrontations, as well as his organization of a widespread *saṅkīrtana* movement and his civil disobedience against the repression of the Mohammedan government.

The subject of *Madhya-līlā,* the longest of the three divisions, is a detailed narration of Lord Caitanya's extensive and eventful travels throughout India as a renounced mendicant, teacher, philosopher, spiritual preceptor and mystic. During this period of six years, Śrī Caitanya transmits his teachings to his principal disciples. He debates and converts many of the most renowned philosophers and theologians of his time, including Śaṅkarites, Buddhists and Muslims, and incorporates their many thousands of followers and disciples into his own burgeoning numbers. A dramatic account of Caitanya Mahāprabhu's miraculous activities at the giant Jagannātha Cart Festival in Orissa is also included in this section.

Antya-līlā concerns the last eighteen years of Śrī Caitanya's manifest presence, spent in semiseclusion near the famous Jagannātha temple at Jagannātha Purī in Orissa. During these final years, Śrī Caitanya drifted deeper and deeper into trances of spiritual ecstasy unparalleled in all of religious and literary history, Eastern or Western. Śrī Caitanya's perpetual and ever-increasing religious beatitude, graphically described in the eyewitness accounts of Svarūpa Dāmodara Gosvāmī, his constant companion during this period, clearly defy the investigative and descriptive abilities of modern psychologists and phenomenologists of religious experience.

The author of this great classic, Kṛṣṇadāsa Kavirāja Gosvāmī, born in the year 1507, was a disciple of Raghunātha dāsa Gosvāmī, a confidential follower of Caitanya Mahāprabhu. Raghunātha dāsa, a renowned ascetic saint, heard and memorized all the activities of Caitanya Mahāprabhu told to him by Svarūpa Dāmodara. After the passing away of Śrī Caitanya and Svarūpa Dāmodara, Raghunātha dāsa, unable to bear the pain of separation from these objects of his complete devotion, traveled to Vṛndāvana, intending to commit suicide by jumping from Govardhana Hill. In Vṛndāvana, however, he encountered Rūpa Gosvāmī and Sanātana Gosvāmī, the most confidential disciples of Caitanya Mahāprabhu. They convinced him to give up his plan of suicide and impelled him to reveal to them the spiritually inspiring events of Lord Caitanya's later life. Kṛṣṇadāsa Kavirāja Gosvāmī was also residing in Vṛndāvana at this time, and Raghunātha dāsa Gosvāmī endowed him with a full comprehension of the transcendental life of Śrī Caitanya.

By this time, several biographical works had already been written on the life of Śrī Caitanya by contemporary and near-contemporary scholars and devotees. These included *Śrī Caitanya-carita* by Murāri Gupta, *Caitanya-maṅgala* by Locana dāsa Ṭhākura and *Caitanya-bhāgavata.* This latter text, a work by Vṛndāvana dāsa Ṭhākura, who was then considered the principal authority on Śrī Caitanya's life, was highly revered. While composing his important work, Vṛndāvana dāsa, fearing that it would become too voluminous, avoided elaborately describing many of the events of Śrī Caitanya's life, particulary the later ones. Anxious to hear of these later pastimes, the devotees of Vṛndāvana requested Kṛṣṇadāsa Kavirāja Gosvāmī, whom they respected as a great saint, to compose a book to narrate these episodes in detail. Upon this request, and with the permission and blessings of the Madana-mohana Deity of Vṛndāvana, he began compiling *Śrī Caitanya-caritāmṛta,* which, due to its biographical excellence and thorough exposition of Lord Caitanya's profound philosophy and teachings, is regarded as the most significant of biographical works on Śrī Caitanya.

He commenced work on the text while in his late nineties and in failing health, as he vividly describes in the text itself: "I have now become too old and disturbed in invalidity. While writing, my hands tremble. I cannot remember anything, nor can I see or hear properly. Still I write, and this is a great wonder." That he nevertheless completed, under such debilitating conditions, the greatest literary gem of medieval India is surely one of the wonders of literary history.

This English translation and commentary is the work of His Divine Grace A. C. Bhaktivedanta Swami Prabhupāda, the world's most distinguished teacher of Indian religious and philosophical thought. His commentary is based upon two Bengali commentaries, one by his teacher Śrīla Bhaktisiddhānta Sarasvatī Gosvāmī, the eminent Vedic scholar who predicted, "The time will come when the people of the world will learn Bengali to read *Śrī Caitanya-caritāmṛta,*" and the other by Śrīla Bhaktisiddhānta's father, Bhaktivinoda Ṭhākura.

His Divine Grace A. C. Bhaktivedanta Swami Prabhupāda is himself a disciplic descendant of Śrī Caitanya Mahāprabhu, and he is the first scholar to execute systematic English translations of the major works of Śrī Caitanya's followers. His consummate Bengali and Sanskrit scholarship and intimate familiarity with the precepts of Śrī Kṛṣṇa Caitanya are a fitting combination that eminently qualifies him to present this important classic to the English-speaking world. The ease and clarity with which he expounds upon difficult philosophical concepts lures even a reader totally unfamiliar with Indian religious tradition into a genuine understanding and appreciation of this profound and monumental work.

The entire text, with commentary, presented in seventeen lavishly illustrated volumes by the Bhaktivedanta Book Trust, represents a contribution of major importance to the intellectual, cultural and spiritual life of contemporary man.

His Divine Grace
A. C. Bhaktivedanta Swami Prabhupāda
Founder-Ācārya of the International Society for Krishna Consciousness

At the site where Lord Caitanya Mahāprabhu met Śrī Rāmānanda Rāya, an altar displaying the Lord's footprints has been erected.

MAHAPRAVU VISITED MANGALGIRI IN 1512.A.D.
CHAITANYA-FOOT-PRINTS INSTALLED BY
PARAMHANSA
BHAKTI SIDDHANTA SARASWATI GOSWAMI
IN 1930

ABOVE: The temple of Pānā-nṛsiṁha, located in the hills known as Maṅgalagiri.
BELOW: A plaque commemorating the installation of Lord Caitanya's footprints at Maṅgalagiri in 1930 by Śrīla Bhaktisiddhānta Sarasvatī Gosvāmī Mahārāja Prabhupāda, the spiritual master of His Divine Grace A. C. Bhaktivedanta Swami Prabhupāda. (*p. 328*)

The temple of Cidāmbaram, which was visited by Śrī Caitanya Mahāprabhu on His tour of South India. (*p.* 332)

LEFT: The Tirupati temple, a famous holy place of pilgrimage in South India.
RIGHT: Vyeṅkaṭeśvara, the four-handed Deity of Lord Viṣṇu, located about eight miles from Tirupati. (*p. 327*)

The Bṛhatīśvara-śiva-mandira, situated near the great lake known as Śiva-gaṅgā. (*p. 335*)

Śrī Raṅga-kṣetra, the largest temple in India, where Lord Caitanya Mahāprahbu chanted and danced in ecstatic love of Godhead. (*pp. 335-337*)

PLATE ONE

"Seeing Lord Jagannātha, Śrī Caitanya Mahāprabhu also begged His permission to depart for South India. The priest then immediately delivered *prasāda* and a garland to Lord Caitanya. Thus receiving Lord Jagannātha's permission in the form of a garland, Śrī Caitanya Mahāprabhu offered obeisances, and in great jubilation prepared to depart for South India. Accompanied by His personal associates and Sārvabhauma Bhaṭṭācārya, Śrī Caitanya Mahāprabhu circumambulated the altar of Jagannātha. The Lord then departed on His South Indian tour." *(p. 27)*

PLATE TWO

"There was also one *brāhmaṇa* named Vāsudeva, who was a great person but was suffering from leprosy. Although suffering from leprosy, Vāsudeva was enlightened. When he came to Kūrma's house to see Caitanya Mahāprabhu, he was informed that the Lord had already left. The leper then fell to the ground unconscious. When Vāsudeva, the leper *brāhmaṇa,* was lamenting due to not being able to see Caitanya Mahāprabhu, the Lord immediately returned to that spot and embraced him. When Śrī Caitanya Mahāprabhu touched him, both the leprosy and his distress went to a distant place. Indeed, Vāsudeva's body became very beautiful, to his great happiness." (*pp. 69-71*)

PLATE THREE

"Śrī Caitanya Mahāprabhu could understand that the person who had come to bathe in the river was Rāmānanda Rāya. The Lord wanted so much to meet him that His mind immediately began running after him. Although Śrī Caitanya Mahāprabhu was running after him mentally, He patiently remained sitting. Rāmānanda Rāya, seeing the wonderful *sannyāsī,* then came to see Him. Śrīla Rāmānanda Rāya then saw Śrī Caitanya Mahāprabhu as brilliant as a hundred suns. The Lord was covered by a saffron garment. He was large in body and very strongly built, and His eyes were like lotus petals. Śrī Caitanya Mahāprabhu then embraced Śrī Rāmānanda Rāya very firmly. Indeed, both the master and the servant almost lost consciousness due to ecstatic love." (*pp. 88-91*)

PLATE FOUR

"Then Gāyatrī, mother of the *Vedas,* having been manifested by the divine sound of Śrī Kṛṣṇa's flute, entered the lotus mouth of Brahmā, the self-born, through his eight earholes. The lotus-born Brahmā received the *gāyatrī-mantra,* which had sprung from the song of Śrī Kṛṣṇa's flute. Thus he attained twice-born status, having been initiated by the supreme spiritual preceptor, Godhead Himself. Enlightened by the recollection of that *gāyatrī,* which embodies the three *Vedas,* Brahmā became acquainted with the expanse of the ocean of truth. Then he worshiped Śrī Kṛṣṇa, the essence of all the *Vedas,* with a hymn." (*p. 172*)

PLATE FIVE

"Addressing Kṛṣṇa and Arjuna, Lord Mahā-Viṣṇu [the Mahāpuruṣa] said, 'I wanted to see both of you, and therefore I have brought the sons of the *brāhmaṇa* here. Both of you have appeared in the material world to reestablish religious principles, and you have both appeared here with all your potencies. After killing all the demons, please quickly return to the spiritual world.' " (*pp. 180-181*)

PLATE SIX

"The pastimes of Śrī Rādhā and Kṛṣṇa are self-effulgent. They are happiness personified, unlimited and all-powerful. Even so, the spiritual humors of such pastimes are never complete without the *gopīs,* the Lord's personal friends. The Supreme Personality of Godhead is never complete without His spiritual potencies; therefore unless one takes shelter of the *gopīs,* one cannot enter into the company of Rādhā and Kṛṣṇa. Who can be interested in Their spiritual pastimes without taking Their shelter? There is an inexplicable fact about the natural inclinations of the *gopīs.* The *gopīs* never want to enjoy themselves with Kṛṣṇa personally. The happiness of the *gopīs* increases ten million times when they serve to engage Śrī Śrī Rādhā and Kṛṣṇa in Their transcendental pastimes." (*pp. 218-219*)

PLATE SEVEN

"Lord Śrī Kṛṣṇa is the reservoir of all pleasure, and Śrīmatī Rādhārāṇī is the personification of ecstatic love of Godhead. These two forms combined as one in Śrī Caitanya Mahāprabhu. This being the case, Lord Śrī Caitanya Mahāprabhu revealed His real form to Rāmānanda Rāya. Upon seeing this form, Rāmānanda Rāya almost lost consciousness in transcendental bliss. Unable to remain standing, he fell to the ground." (*pp. 270-271*)

PLATE EIGHT

"The Buddhists could understand that Lord Śrī Caitanya Mahāprabhu was a Vaiṣṇava, and they returned home very unhappy. Later, however, they began to plot against the Lord. Having made their plot, the Buddhists brought a plate of untouchable food before Lord Śrī Caitanya Mahāprabhu and called it *mahā-prasāda.* When the contaminated food was offered to Śrī Caitanya Mahāprabhu, a very large bird appeared on the spot, picked up the plate in its beak, and flew away. Indeed, the untouchable food fell upon the Buddhists, and the large bird dropped the plate on the head of the chief Buddhist teacher. When it fell on his head, it made a big sound and cut him, and the teacher immediately fell to the ground unconscious." (*pp. 320-323*)

CHAPTER 7

The Lord's Tour of South India

In his *Amṛta-pravāha-bhāṣya,* Śrīla Bhaktivinoda Ṭhākura summarizes the Seventh Chapter as follows. Śrī Caitanya Mahāprabhu accepted the renounced order of life in the month of Māgha (January-February) and went to Jagannātha Purī in the month of Phālguna (February-March). He saw the Dola-yātrā festival during the month of Phālguna, and in the month of Caitra He liberated Sārvabhauma Bhaṭṭācārya. During the month of Vaiśākha, He began to tour South India. When He proposed to travel to South India alone, Śrī Nityānanda Prabhu gave Him a *brāhmaṇa* assistant named Kṛṣṇadāsa. When Śrī Caitanya Mahāprabhu was beginning His tour, Sārvabhauma Bhaṭṭācārya gave Him four sets of clothes and requested Him to see Rāmānanda Rāya, who was residing at that time on the bank of the River Godāvarī. Along with other devotees, Nityānanda Prabhu accompanied the Lord to Ālālanātha, but there Lord Caitanya left them all behind and went ahead with the *brāhmaṇa* Kṛṣṇadāsa. The Lord began chanting the *mantra* "*kṛṣṇa kṛṣṇa kṛṣṇa kṛṣṇa kṛṣṇa kṛṣṇa kṛṣṇa he.*" In whatever village He spent the night, whenever a person came to see Him in His shelter, the Lord implored him to preach the Kṛṣṇa consciousness movement. After teaching the people of one village, the Lord proceeded to other villages to increase devotees. In this way He finally reached Kūrma-sthāna. While there, He bestowed His causeless mercy upon a *brāhmaṇa* called Kūrma and cured another *brāhmaṇa,* named Vāsudeva, who was suffering from leprosy. After curing this *brāhmaṇa* leper, Śrī Caitanya Mahāprabhu received the title Vāsudevāmṛta-prada, meaning "one who delivered nectar to the leper Vāsudeva."

TEXT 1

ধন্যং তং নৌমি চৈতন্যং বাসুদেবং দয়ার্দ্রঃধী ।
নষ্টকুষ্ঠং রূপপুষ্টং ভক্তিতুষ্টং চকার যঃ ॥ ১ ॥

dhanyaṁ taṁ naumi caitanyaṁ
vāsudevaṁ dayārdraḥ-dhī
naṣṭa-kuṣṭhaṁ rūpa-puṣṭaṁ
bhakti-tuṣṭaṁ cakāra yaḥ

SYNONYMS

dhanyam—auspicious; *tam*—unto Him; *naumi*—I offer obeisances; *caitanyam*—Śrī Caitanya Mahāprabhu; *vāsudevam*—unto the *brāhmaṇa* Vāsudeva; *dayā-ārdraḥ-dhī*—being compassionate; *naṣṭa-kuṣṭham*—cured the leprosy; *rūpa-puṣṭam*—beautiful; *bhakti-tuṣṭam*—satisfied in devotional service; *cakāra*—made; *yaḥ*—the Supreme Personality of Godhead.

TRANSLATION

Lord Caitanya Mahāprabhu, being very compassionate toward a brāhmaṇa named Vāsudeva, cured him of leprosy. He transformed him into a beautiful man satisfied with devotional service. I offer my respectful obeisances unto the glorious Lord Śrī Caitanya Mahāprabhu.

TEXT 2

জয় জয় শ্রীচৈতন্য জয় নিত্যানন্দ ।
জয়াদ্বৈতচন্দ্র জয় গৌরভক্তবৃন্দ ॥ ২ ॥

jaya jaya śrī-caitanya jaya nityānanda
jayādvaita-candra jaya gaura-bhakta-vṛnda

SYNONYMS

jaya jaya—all glories; *śrī-caitanya*—to Lord Caitanya Mahāprabhu; *jaya*—all glories; *nityānanda*—to Lord Nityānanda Prabhu; *jaya advaita-candra*—all glories to Advaita Ācārya; *jaya gaura-bhakta-vṛnda*—all glories to the devotees of Lord Caitanya.

TRANSLATION

All glories to Lord Caitanya Mahāprabhu! All glories to Lord Nityānanda Prabhu! All glories to Advaita Ācārya! And all glories to the devotees of Lord Caitanya!

TEXT 3

এইমতে সার্বভৌমের নিস্তার করিল ।
দক্ষিণ-গমনে প্রভুর ইচ্ছা উপজিল ॥ ৩ ॥

ei-mate sārvabhaumera nistāra karila
dakṣiṇa-gamane prabhura icchā upajila

SYNONYMS

ei-mate—in this way; *sārvabhaumera*—of Sārvabhauma Bhaṭṭācārya; *nistāra*—the liberation; *karila*—was executed; *dakṣiṇa-gamane*—in going to South India; *prabhura*—of the Lord; *icchā*—a desire; *upajila*—arose.

TRANSLATION

After delivering Sārvabhauma Bhaṭṭācārya, the Lord desired to go to South India to preach.

TEXT 4

মাঘ-শুক্লপক্ষে প্রভু করিল সন্ন্যাস ।
ফাল্গুনে আসিয়া কৈল নীলাচলে বাস ॥ ৪ ॥

māgha-śukla-pakṣe prabhu karila sannyāsa
phālgune āsiyā kaila nīlācale vāsa

SYNONYMS

māgha-śukla-pakṣe—in the waxing fortnight of the month of Māgha; *prabhu*—the Lord; *karila*—accepted; *sannyāsa*—the renounced order of life; *phālgune*—in the next month, Phālguna; *āsiyā*—coming; *kaila*—did; *nīlācale*—at Jagannātha Purī; *vāsa*—residence.

TRANSLATION

Śrī Caitanya Mahāprabhu accepted the renounced order during the waxing fortnight of the month of Māgha. During the following month, Phālguna, He went to Jagannātha Purī and resided there.

TEXT 5

ফাল্গুনের শেষে দোলযাত্রা সে দেখিল ।
প্রেমাবেশে তাঁহা বহু নৃত্যগীত কৈল ॥ ৫ ॥

phālgunera śeṣe dola-yātrā se dekhila
premāveśe tāṅhā bahu nṛtya-gīta kaila

SYNONYMS

phālgunera—of the month of Phālguna; *śeṣe*—at the end; *dola-yātra*—the Dola-yātrā festival; *se*—that; *dekhila*—saw; *prema-āveśe*—in the ecstasy of love of Godhead; *tāṅhā*—there; *bahu*—much; *nṛtya-gīta*—chanting and dancing; *kaila*—performed.

TRANSLATION

At the end of the month of Phālguna, He witnessed the Dola-yātrā ceremony, and in His usual ecstatic love of God, He chanted and danced in various ways on the occasion.

TEXT 6

চৈত্রে রহি' কৈল সার্বভৌম-বিমোচন ।
বৈশাখের প্রথমে দক্ষিণ যাইতে হৈল মন ॥ ৬ ॥

caitre rahi' kaila sārvabhauma-vimocana
vaiśākhera prathame dakṣiṇa yāite haila mana

SYNONYMS

caitre—in the month of Caitra (March-April); *rahi'*—residing there; *kaila*—did; *sārvabhauma-vimocana*—liberation of Sārvabhauma Bhaṭṭācārya; *vaiśākhera*—of the month of Vaiśākha; *prathame*—in the beginning; *dakṣiṇa*—to South India; *yāite*—to go; *haila*—it was; *mana*—the mind.

TRANSLATION

During the month of Caitra, while living at Jagannātha Purī, the Lord delivered Sārvabhauma Bhaṭṭācārya, and in the beginning of the next month (Vaiśākha), He decided to go to South India.

TEXTS 7-8

নিজগণ আনি' কহে বিনয় করিয়া ।
আলিঙ্গন করি' সবায় শ্রীহস্তে ধরিয়া ॥ ৭ ॥
তোমা-সবা জানি আমি প্রাণাধিক করি' ।
প্রাণ ছাড়া যায়, তোমা-সবা ছাড়িতে না পারি ॥ ৮ ॥

nija-gaṇa āni' kahe vinaya kariyā
āliṅgana kari' sabāya śrī-haste dhariyā

tomā-sabā jāni āmi prāṇādhika kari'
prāṇa chāḍā yāya, tomā-sabā chāḍite nā pāri

SYNONYMS

nija-gaṇa āni'—calling all the devotees; *kahe*—said; *vinaya*—humbleness; *kariyā*—showing; *āliṅgana kari'*—embracing; *sabāya*—all of them; *śrī-haste*—

with His hands; *dhariyā*—catching them; *tomā-sabā*—all of you; *jāni*—I know; *āmi*—I; *prāṇa-adhika*—more than My life; *kari'*—taking; *prāṇa chāḍā*—giving up life; *yāya*—is possible; *tomā-sabā*—all of you; *chāḍite*—to give up; *nā pāri*—I am not able.

TRANSLATION

Śrī Caitanya Mahāprabhu called all His devotees together and holding them by the hand humbly informed them: "You are all more dear to Me than My life. I can give up My life, but to give up you is difficult for Me.

TEXT 9

তুমি-সব বন্ধু মোর বন্ধুকৃত্য কৈলে ।
ইহাঁ আনি' মোরে জগন্নাথ দেখাইলে ॥ ৯ ॥

tumi-saba bandhu mora bandhu-kṛtya kaile
ihāṅ āni' more jagannātha dekhāile

SYNONYMS

tumi-saba—all of you; *bandhu*—friends; *mora*—My; *bandhu-kṛtya*—duties of a friend; *kaile*—you have executed; *ihāṅ*—here; *āni'*—bringing; *more*—to Me; *jagannātha*—Lord Jagannātha; *dekhāile*—you have shown.

TRANSLATION

"You are all My friends, and you have properly executed the duties of friends by bringing Me here to Jagannātha Purī and giving Me the chance to see Lord Jagannātha in the temple.

TEXT 10

এবে সবা-স্থানে মুঞি মাগোঁ এক দানে ।
সবে মেলি' আজ্ঞা দেহ, যাইব দক্ষিণে ॥ ১০ ॥

ebe sabā-sthāne muñi māgoṅ eka dāne
sabe meli' ājñā deha, yāiba dakṣiṇe

SYNONYMS

ebe—now; *sabā-sthāne*—from all of you; *muñi*—I; *māgoṅ*—beg; *eka dāne*—one gift; *sabe meli'*—all combining together; *ājñā deha*—give permission; *yāiba*—I shall go; *dakṣiṇe*—to South India.

TRANSLATION

"I now beg all of you for one bit of charity. Please give Me permission to leave for a tour of South India.

TEXT 11

বিশ্বরূপ-উদ্দেশে অবশ্য আমি যাব ।
একাকী যাইব, কাহো সঙ্গে না লইব ॥ ১১ ॥

viśvarūpa-uddeśe avaśya āmi yāba
ekākī yāiba, kāho saṅge nā la-iba

SYNONYMS

viśva-rūpa-uddeśe—to find Viśvarūpa; *avaśya*—certainly; *āmi*—I; *yāba*—shall go; *ekākī*—alone; *yāiba*—I shall go; *kāho*—someone; *saṅge*—in association; *nā*—not; *la-iba*—I shall take.

TRANSLATION

"I shall go to search out Viśvarūpa. Please forgive Me, but I want to go alone; I do not wish to take anyone with Me.

TEXT 12

সেতুবন্ধ হৈতে আমি না আসি যাবৎ ।
নীলাচলে তুমি সব রহিবে তাবৎ ॥ ১২ ॥

setubandha haite āmi nā āsi yāvat
nīlācale tumi saba rahibe tāvat

SYNONYMS

setu-bandha—the extreme southern point of India; *haite*—from; *āmi*—I; *nā*—not; *āsi*—returning; *yāvat*—as long as; *nīlācale*—in Jagannātha Purī; *tumi*—you; *saba*—all; *rahibe*—should stay; *tāvat*—that long.

TRANSLATION

"Until I return from Setubandha, all of you dear friends should remain at Jagannātha Purī."

TEXT 13

বিশ্বরূপ-সিদ্ধি-প্রাপ্তি জানেন সকল ।
দক্ষিণ-দেশ উদ্ধারিতে করেন এই ছল ॥ ১৩ ॥

viśvarūpa-siddhi-prāpti jānena sakala
dakṣiṇa-deśa uddhārite karena ei chala

SYNONYMS

viśva-rūpa—of Viśvarūpa; *siddhi*—of perfection; *prāpti*—achievement; *jānena*—the Lord knows; *sakala*—everything; *dakṣiṇa-deśa*—South India; *uddhārite*—just to liberate; *karena*—makes; *ei*—this; *chala*—pretense.

TRANSLATION

Knowing everything, Śrī Caitanya Mahāprabhu was aware that Viśvarūpa had already passed away. A pretense of ignorance was necessary, however, so that He could go to South India and liberate the people there.

TEXT 14

শুনিয়া সবার মনে হৈল মহাদুঃখ ।
নিঃশব্দ হইলা, সবার শুকাইল মুখ ॥ ১৪ ॥

śuniyā sabāra mane haila mahā-duḥkha
niḥśabda ha-ilā, sabāra śukāila mukha

SYNONYMS

śuniyā—hearing this; *sabāra*—of all the devotees; *mane*—in the minds; *haila*—there was; *mahā-duḥkha*—great unhappiness; *niḥśabda*—silent; *ha-ilā*—became; *sabāra*—of everyone; *śukāila*—dried up; *mukha*—the faces.

TRANSLATION

Upon hearing this message from Śrī Caitanya Mahāprabhu, all the devotees became very unhappy and remained silent with sullen faces.

TEXT 15

নিত্যানন্দপ্রভু কহে,—'ঐছে কৈছে হয় ।
একাকী যাইবে তুমি, কে ইহা সহয় ॥ ১৫ ॥

nityānanda-prabhu kahe,—"aiche kaiche haya
ekākī yāibe tumi, ke ihā sahaya

SYNONYMS

nityānanda-prabhu kahe—Lord Nityānanda Prabhu replied; *aiche kaiche haya*—how is this possible; *ekākī*—alone; *yāibe*—shall go; *tumi*—You; *ke*—who; *ihā*—this; *sahaya*—can tolerate.

TRANSLATION

Nityānanda Prabhu then said: "How is it possible for You to go alone? Who can tolerate this?

TEXT 16

দুই-এক সঙ্গে চলুক, না পড় হঠ-রঙ্গে ।
যারে কহ সেই দুই চলুক্ তোমার সঙ্গে ॥ ১৬ ॥

dui-eka saṅge caluka, nā paḍa haṭha-raṅge
yāre kaha sei dui caluk tomāra saṅge

SYNONYMS

dui—two; *eka*—or one; *saṅge*—with You; *caluka*—let go; *nā*—do not; *paḍa*—fall; *haṭha-raṅge*—in the clutches of thieves and rogues; *yāre*—whoever; *kaha*—You say; *sei*—those; *dui*—two; *caluk*—let go; *tomāra*—You; *saṅge*—along with.

TRANSLATION

"Let one or two of us go with You, otherwise You may fall into the clutches of thieves and rogues along the way. They may be whomever You like, but two persons should go with You.

TEXT 17

দক্ষিণের তীর্থপথ আমি সব জানি ।
আমি সঙ্গে যাই, প্রভু, আজ্ঞা দেহ তুমি ॥" ১৭ ॥

dakṣiṇera tīrtha-patha āmi saba jāni
āmi saṅge yāi, prabhu, ājñā deha tumi"

SYNONYMS

dakṣiṇera—of South India; *tīrtha-patha*—the ways to different places of pilgrimage; *āmi*—I; *saba*—all; *jāni*—know; *āmi*—I; *saṅge*—with You; *yāi*—go; *prabhu*—O My Lord; *ājñā*—order; *deha*—give; *tumi*—You.

TRANSLATION

"Indeed, I know all the paths to the different places of pilgrimage in South India. Just order Me, and I shall go with You."

TEXT 18

প্রভু কহে, "আমি—নর্তক, তুমি—সূত্রধার ।
তুমি যৈছে নাচাও, তৈছে নর্তন আমার ॥ ১৮ ॥

prabhu kahe, "āmi——nartaka, tumi——sūtra-dhāra
tumi yaiche nācāo, taiche nartana āmāra

SYNONYMS

prabhu kahe—the Lord replied; *āmi*—I; *nartaka*—a dancer; *tumi*—You; *sūtra-dhāra*—wire-puller; *tumi*—You; *yaiche*—just as; *nācāo*—make dance; *taiche*—in that way; *nartana*—dancing; *āmāra*—My.

TRANSLATION

The Lord replied: "I am simply a dancer, and You are the wire-puller. However You pull the wires to make Me dance, I shall dance in that way.

TEXT 19

সন্ন্যাস করিয়া আমি চলিলাঙ বৃন্দাবন ।
তুমি আমা লঞা আইলে অদ্বৈত-ভবন ॥ ১৯ ॥

sannyāsa kariyā āmi calilāṅ vṛndāvana
tumi āmā lañā āile advaita-bhavana

SYNONYMS

sannyāsa kariyā—after accepting the renounced order; *āmi*—I; *calilāṅ*—went; *vṛndāvana*—toward Vṛndāvana; *tumi*—You; *āmā*—Me; *lañā*—taking; *āile*—went; *advaita-bhavana*—to the house of Advaita Prabhu.

TRANSLATION

"After accepting the sannyāsa order, I decided to go to Vṛndāvana, but You took Me instead to the house of Advaita Prabhu.

TEXT 20

নীলাচল আসিতে পথে ভাঙ্গিলা মোর দণ্ড ।
তোমা-সবার গাঢ়-স্নেহে আমার কার্য-ভঙ্গ ॥ ২০ ॥

nīlācala āsite pathe bhāṅgilā mora daṇḍa
tomā-sabāra gāḍha-snehe āmāra kārya-bhaṅga

SYNONYMS

nīlācala—to Jagannātha Purī; *āsite*—going there; *pathe*—on the road; *bhāṅgilā*—You broke; *mora*—My; *daṇḍa*—*sannyāsa* staff; *tomā-sabāra*—of all of you; *gāḍha-snehe*—on account of the deep affection; *āmāra*—My; *kārya-bhaṅga*—disturbance of activities.

TRANSLATION

"While on the way to Jagannātha Purī, You broke My sannyāsa staff. I know that all of you have great affection for Me, but such things disturb My activities.

TEXT 21

জগদানন্দ চাহে আমা বিষয় ভুঞ্জাইতে।
যেই কহে সেই ভয়ে চাহিয়ে করিতে ॥ ২১ ॥

jagadānanda cāhe āmā viṣaya bhuñjāite
yei kahe sei bhaye cāhiye karite

SYNONYMS

jagadānanda—Jagadānanda; *cāhe*—wants; *āmā*—Me; *viṣaya*—sense gratification; *bhuñjāite*—to cause to enjoy; *yei kahe*—whatever he says; *sei*—that; *bhaye*—out of fear; *cāhiye*—I want; *karite*—to do.

TRANSLATION

"Jagadānanda wants Me to enjoy bodily sense gratification, and out of fear I do whatever he tells Me.

TEXT 22

কভু যদি ইঁহার বাক্য করিয়ে অন্যথা।
ক্রোধে তিন দিন মোরে নাহি কহে কথা ॥ ২২ ॥

kabhu yadi iṅhāra vākya kariye anyathā
krodhe tina dina more nāhi kahe kathā

SYNONYMS

kabhu—sometimes; *yadi*—if; *iṅhāra*—of Jagadānanda; *vākya*—the words; *kariye*—I do; *anyathā*—other than; *krodhe*—in anger; *tina dina*—for three days; *more*—to Me; *nāhi*—not; *kahe*—speaks; *kathā*—words.

TRANSLATION

"If I sometimes do something against his desire, out of anger he will not talk to Me for three days.

TEXT 23

মুকুন্দ হয়েন দুঃখী দেখি' সন্ন্যাস-ধর্ম ।
তিনবারে শীতে স্নান, ভূমিতে শয়ন ॥ ২৩ ॥

mukunda hayena duḥkhī dekhi' sannyāsa-dharma
tinabāre śīte snāna, bhūmite śayana

SYNONYMS

mukunda—Mukunda; *hayena*—becomes; *duḥkhī*—unhappy; *dekhi'*—seeing; *sannyāsa-dharma*—My regulative principles in the renounced order; *tina-bāre*—three times; *śīte*—in the winter; *snāna*—bath; *bhūmite*—on the ground; *śayana*—lying down.

TRANSLATION

"Being a sannyāsī, it is My duty to lie down on the ground and take a bath three times a day, even during the winter. But Mukunda becomes very unhappy when he sees My severe austerities.

TEXT 24

অন্তরে দুঃখী মুকুন্দ, নাহি কহে মুখে ।
ইহার দুঃখ দেখি' মোর দ্বিগুণ হয়ে দুঃখে ॥ ২৪ ॥

antare duḥkhī mukunda, nāhi kahe mukhe
ihāra duḥkha dekhi' mora dvi-guṇa haye duḥkhe

SYNONYMS

antare—within himself; *duḥkhī*—unhappy; *mukunda*—Mukunda; *nāhi*—not; *kahe*—says; *mukhe*—in the mouth; *ihāra*—of him; *duḥkha*—the unhappiness; *dekhi'*—seeing; *mora*—My; *dvi-guṇa*—twice; *haye*—there is; *duḥkhe*—the unhappiness.

TRANSLATION

"Of course, Mukunda does not say anything, but I know that he is very unhappy within, and upon seeing him unhappy, I become twice as unhappy.

TEXT 25

আমি ত'—সন্ন্যাসী, দামোদর—ব্রহ্মচারী ।
সদা রহে আমার উপর শিক্ষা-দণ্ড ধরি' ॥ ২৫ ॥

āmi ta'——sannyāsī, dāmodara——brahmacārī
sadā rahe āmāra upara śikṣā-daṇḍa dhari'

SYNONYMS

āmi ta'—I indeed; *sannyāsī*—in the renounced order of life; *dāmodara*—of the name Dāmodara; *brahmacārī*—in a stage of complete celibacy; *sadā*—always; *rahe*—remains; *āmāra upara*—on Me; *śikṣā-daṇḍa*—a stick for My education; *dhari'*—keeping.

TRANSLATION

"Although I am in the renounced order of life and Dāmodara is a brahmacārī, he still keeps a stick in his hand just to educate Me.

TEXT 26

ইঁহার আগে আমি না জানি ব্যবহার।
ইঁহারে না ভায় স্বতন্ত্র চরিত্র আমার ॥ ২৬ ॥

iṅhāra āge āmi nā jāni vyavahāra
iṅhāre nā bhāya svatantra caritra āmāra

SYNONYMS

iṅhāra āge—in front of him; *āmi*—I; *nā*--not; *jāni*—know; *vyavahāra*—social etiquette; *iṅhāre*—for him; *nā*—not; *bhāya*—exists; *sva-tantra*—independent; *caritra*—character; *āmāra*—My.

TRANSLATION

"According to Dāmodara, I am still a neophyte as far as social etiquette is concerned; therefore he does not like My independent nature.

TEXT 27

লোকাপেক্ষা নাহি ইঁহার কৃষ্ণকৃপা হৈতে।
আমি লোকাপেক্ষা কভু না পারি ছাড়িতে ॥ ২৭ ॥

lokāpekṣā nāhi iṅhāra kṛṣṇa-kṛpā haite
āmi lokāpekṣā kabhu nā pāri chāḍite

SYNONYMS

loka-apekṣā—care for society; *nāhi*—there is none; *iṅhāra*—of Dāmodara; *kṛṣṇa-kṛpā*—the mercy of the Lord; *haite*—from; *āmi*—I; *loka-apekṣā*—dependence on public opinion; *kabhu*—at any time; *nā*—not; *pāri*—able; *chāḍite*—to give up.

TRANSLATION

"Dāmodara Paṇḍita and others are more advanced in receiving the mercy of Lord Kṛṣṇa; therefore they are independent of public opinion. As such, they want Me to enjoy sense gratification, even though it be unethical. But since I am a poor sannyāsī, I cannot abandon the duties of the renounced order, and therefore I follow them strictly.

PURPORT

A *brahmacārī* is supposed to assist a *sannyāsī;* therefore a *brahmacārī* should not try to instruct a *sannyāsī.* That is the etiquette. Consequently Dāmodara should not have advised Caitanya Mahāprabhu of His duty.

TEXT 28

অতএব তুমি সব রহ নীলাচলে ।
দিন কত আমি তীর্থ ভ্রমিব একলে ॥" ২৮ ॥

ataeva tumi saba raha nīlācale
dina kata āmi tīrtha bhramiba ekale"

SYNONYMS

ataeva—therefore; *tumi*—you; *saba*—all; *raha*—remain; *nīlācale*—at Jagannātha Purī; *dina*—days; *kata*—some; *āmi*—I; *tīrtha*—the sacred places of pilgrimage; *bhramiba*—I shall tour; *ekale*—alone.

TRANSLATION

"You should all therefore remain here in Nīlācala for some days while I tour the sacred places of pilgrimage alone."

TEXT 29

ইঁহা-সবার বশ প্রভু হয়ে যে যে গুণে ।
দোষারোপ-চ্ছলে করে গুণ আস্বাদনে ॥ ২৯ ॥

iṅhā-sabāra vaśa prabhu haye ye ye guṇe
doṣāropa-cchale kare guṇa āsvādane

SYNONYMS

iṅhā-sabāra—of all the devotees; *vaśa*—controlled; *prabhu*—the Lord; *haye*—is; *ye ye*—whatever; *guṇe*—by the qualities; *doṣa-āropa-chale*—on the plea of attributing faults; *kare*—does; *guṇa*—high qualities; *āsvādane*—tasting.

TRANSLATION

Actually the Lord is controlled by the good qualities of all His devotees. On the pretense of attributing faults, He tastes all these qualities.

PURPORT

All the accusations made by Śrī Caitanya Mahāprabhu against His beloved devotees actually showed His great appreciation of their intense love for Him. Yet He mentioned these faults one after another as if He were offended by their intense affection. The personal associates of Śrī Caitanya Mahāprabhu sometimes behaved contrary to regulative principles out of intense love for the Lord, and because of their love Śrī Caitanya Mahāprabhu Himself sometimes violated the regulative principles of a *sannyāsī*. In the eyes of the public, such violations are not good, but Śrī Caitanya Mahāprabhu was so controlled by His devotees' love that He was obliged to break some of the rules. Although accusing them, Śrī Caitanya Mahāprabhu was indirectly indicating that He was very satisfied with their behavior in pure love of Godhead. Therefore in verse twenty-seven He mentions that His devotees and associates place more importance on love of Kṛṣṇa than on social etiquette. There are many instances of devotional service rendered by previous *ācāryas* who did not care about social behavior when intensely absorbed in love for Kṛṣṇa. Unfortunately, as long as we are within this material world, we must observe social customs to avoid criticism by the general populace. This is Śrī Caitanya Mahāprabhu's desire.

TEXT 30

চৈতন্যের ভক্ত-বাৎসল্য—অকথ্য-কথন ।
আপনে বৈরাগ্য-দুঃখ করেন সহন ॥ ৩০ ॥

caitanyera bhakta-vātsalya——akathya-kathana
āpane vairāgya-duḥkha karena sahana

SYNONYMS

caitanyera—of Lord Śrī Caitanya Mahāprabhu; *bhakta-vātsalya*—the love for His devotees; *akathya-kathana*—indescribable by words; *āpane*—personally; *vairāgya*—of the renounced order; *duḥkha*—unhappiness; *karena*—does; *sahana*—toleration.

TRANSLATION

No one can properly describe Lord Śrī Caitanya Mahāprabhu's affection for His devotees. He always tolerated all kinds of personal unhappiness resulting from His acceptance of the renounced order of life.

TEXT 31

সেই দুঃখ দেখি' যেই ভক্ত দুঃখ পায়।
সেই দুঃখ তাঁর শক্ত্যে সহন না যায় ॥ ৩১ ॥

sei duḥkha dekhi' yei bhakta duḥkha pāya
sei duḥkha tāṅra śaktye sahana nā yāya

SYNONYMS

sei duḥkha—that unhappiness; *dekhi'*—seeing; *yei*—whatever; *bhakta*—the devotees; *duḥkha*—unhappiness; *pāya*—get; *sei duḥkha*—that unhappiness; *tāṅra*—His; *śaktye*—by the power; *sahana*—toleration; *nā*—not; *yāya*—possible.

TRANSLATION

The regulative principles observed by Caitanya Mahāprabhu were sometimes intolerable, and all the devotees became greatly affected by them. Although strictly observing the regulative principles, Caitanya Mahāprabhu could not tolerate the unhappiness felt by His devotees.

TEXT 32

গুণে দোষোদ্গার-চ্ছলে সবা নিষেধিয়া।
একাকী ভ্রমিবেন তীর্থ বৈরাগ্য করিয়া ॥ ৩২ ॥

guṇe doṣodgāra-cchale sabā niṣedhiyā
ekākī bhramibena tīrtha vairāgya kariyā

SYNONYMS

guṇe—in the good qualities; *doṣa-udgāra-chale*—on the plea of attributing faults; *sabā*—all of them; *niṣedhiyā*—forbidding; *ekākī*—alone; *bhramibena*—will tour; *tīrtha*—the sacred places of pilgrimage; *vairāgya*—regulative principles of the renounced order of life; *kariyā*—observing.

TRANSLATION

Therefore, to prevent them from accompanying Him and becoming unhappy, Śrī Caitanya Mahāprabhu declared their good qualities to be faults.

The Lord wanted to tour all the places of pilgrimage alone and strictly observe the duties of the renounced order.

TEXT 33

তবে চারিজন বহু মিনতি করিল ।
স্বতন্ত্র ঈশ্বর প্রভু কভু না মানিল ॥ ৩৩ ॥

tabe cāri-jana bahu minati karila
svatantra īśvara prabhu kabhu nā mānila

SYNONYMS

tabe—thereafter; *cāri-jana*—four men; *bahu*—many; *minati*—petitions; *karila*—submitted; *sva-tantra*—independent; *īśvara*—the Supreme Personality of Godhead; *prabhu*—Śrī Caitanya Mahāprabhu; *kabhu*—at any time; *nā*—not; *mānila*—accepted.

TRANSLATION

Four devotees then humbly insisted that they go with the Lord, but Śrī Caitanya Mahāprabhu, being the independent Supreme Personality of Godhead, did not accept their request.

TEXT 34

তবে নিত্যানন্দ কহে,—যে আজ্ঞা তোমার ।
দুঃখ সুখ যে হউক্ কর্তব্য আমার ॥ ৩৪ ॥

tabe nityānanda kahe,——ye ājñā tomāra
duḥkha sukha ye ha-uk kartavya āmāra

SYNONYMS

tabe—thereupon; *nityānanda*—Lord Nityānanda Prabhu; *kahe*—says; *ye ājñā*—whatever order; *tomāra*—Your; *duḥkha sukha*—distress or happiness; *ye*—whatever; *ha-uk*—let there be; *kartavya*—the duty; *āmāra*—My.

TRANSLATION

Thereupon Lord Nityānanda said: "Whatever You order is My duty, regardless of whether it results in happiness or unhappiness.

TEXT 35

কিন্তু এক নিবেদন করোঁ আর বার ।
বিচার করিয়া তাহা কর অঙ্গীকার ॥ ৩৫ ॥

kintu eka nivedana karoṅ āra bāra
vicāra kariyā tāhā kara aṅgīkāra

SYNONYMS

kintu—but; *eka*—one; *nivedana*—petition; *karoṅ*—I do; *āra bāra*—again; *vicāra*—consideration; *kariyā*—giving; *tāhā*—that; *kara*—do; *aṅgīkāra*—acceptance.

TRANSLATION

"Yet I still submit one petition to You. Please consider it, and if You think it proper, please accept it.

TEXT 36

কৌপীন, বহির্বাস আর জলপাত্র ।
আর কিছু নাহি যাবে, সবে এই মাত্র ॥ ৩৬ ॥

kaupīna, bahir-vāsa āra jala-pātra
āra kichu nāhi yābe, sabe ei mātra

SYNONYMS

kaupīna—loincloth; *bahir-vāsa*—outer garments; *āra*—and; *jala-pātra*—water pot; *āra kichu*—anything else; *nāhi*—not; *yābe*—will go; *sabe*—all; *ei*—this; *mātra*—only.

TRANSLATION

"You must take with You a loincloth, external clothes and a water pot. You should take nothing more than this.

TEXT 37

তোমার দুই হস্ত বদ্ধ নাম-গণনে ।
জলপাত্র-বহির্বাস বহিবে কেমনে ॥ ৩৭ ॥

tomāra dui hasta baddha nāma-gaṇane
jala-pātra-bahirvāsa vahibe kemane

SYNONYMS

tomāra—Your; *dui*—two; *hasta*—hands; *baddha*—engaged; *nāma*—the holy name; *gaṇane*—in counting; *jala-pātra*—water pot; *bahir-vāsa*—external garments; *vahibe*—will carry; *kemane*—how.

TRANSLATION

"Since Your two hands will always be engaged in chanting and counting the holy names, how will You be able to carry the water pot and external garments?

PURPORT

From this verse it is clear that Caitanya Mahāprabhu was chanting the holy names a fixed number of times daily. The Gosvāmīs used to follow in the footsteps of Śrī Caitanya Mahāprabhu, and Haridāsa Ṭhākura also followed this principle. Concerning the Gosvāmīs—Śrīla Rūpa Gosvāmī, Śrīla Sanātana Gosvāmī, Śrīla Raghunātha Bhaṭṭa Gosvāmī, Śrīla Jīva Gosvāmī, Śrīla Gopāla Bhaṭṭa Gosvāmī and Śrīla Raghunātha dāsa Gosvāmī—Śrīnivāsa Ācārya confirms: *saṅkhyā-pūrvaka-nāma-gāna-natibhiḥ.* (*Ṣaḍ-gosvāmy-aṣṭaka,* 6) In addition to other duties, Śrī Caitanya Mahāprabhu introduced the system of chanting the holy name of the Lord a fixed number of times daily, as confirmed in this verse (*tomāra dui hasta baddha nāma-gaṇane*). Caitanya Mahāprabhu used to count on His fingers. While one hand was engaged in chanting, the other hand kept the number of rounds. This is corroborated in the *Caitanya-candrāmṛta* and also in Śrīla Rūpa Gosvāmī's *Stava-mālā:*

badhnan prema-bhara-prakampita-karo granthīn kaṭīḍorakaiḥ
saṅkhyātuṁ nija-loka-maṅgala-hare-kṛṣṇeti nāmnāṁ japan
(*Caitanya-candrāmṛta,* 9)

hare kṛṣṇety uccaiḥ sphurita-rasano nāma-gaṇanā-
kṛta-granthi-śreṇī-subhaga-kaṭi-sūtrojjvala-karaḥ
(*Caitanyāṣṭaka,* 5)

Therefore devotees in the line of Śrī Caitanya Mahāprabhu must chant at least sixteen rounds daily, and this is the number prescribed by the International Society for Krishna Consciousness. Haridāsa Ṭhākura daily chanted 300,000 names. Sixteen rounds is about 28,000 names. There is no need to imitate Haridāsa Ṭhākura or the other Gosvāmīs, but chanting the holy name a fixed number of times daily is essential for every devotee.

TEXT 38

প্রেমাবেশে পথে তুমি হবে অচেতন ।
এ-সব সামগ্রী তোমার কে করে রক্ষণ ॥ ৩৮ ॥

premāveśe pathe tumi habe acetana
e-saba sāmagrī tomāra ke kare rakṣaṇa

SYNONYMS

prema-āveśe—in ecstatic love of God; *pathe*—on the way; *tumi*—You; *habe*—will be; *acetana*—unconscious; *e-saba*—all this; *sāmagrī*—paraphernalia; *tomāra*—Your; *ke*—who; *kare*—does; *rakṣaṇa*—protection.

TRANSLATION

"When, along the way, You fall unconscious in ecstatic love of Godhead, who will protect Your belongings—the water pot, garments and so forth?"

TEXT 39

'কৃষ্ণদাস'-নামে এই সরল ব্রাহ্মণ ।
ইঁহো সঙ্গে করি' লহ, ধর নিবেদন ॥ ৩৯ ॥

'kṛṣṇadāsa'-nāme ei sarala brāhmaṇa
iṅho saṅge kari' laha, dhara nivedana

SYNONYMS

kṛṣṇa-dāsa-nāme—named Kṛṣṇadāsa; *ei*—this; *sarala*—simple; *brāhmaṇa*—brāhmaṇa; *iṅho*—he; *saṅge*—with You; *kari'*—accepting; *laha*—take; *dhara*—just catch; *nivedana*—the petition.

TRANSLATION

Śrī Nityānanda Prabhu continued: "Here is a simple brāhmaṇa named Kṛṣṇadāsa. Please accept him and take him with You. That is My request.

PURPORT

This Kṛṣṇadāsa, known as Kālā Kṛṣṇadāsa, is not the Kālā Kṛṣṇadāsa mentioned in the Eleventh Chapter, verse 37, of *Ādi-līlā*. The Kālā Kṛṣṇadāsa mentioned in the Eleventh Chapter is one of the twelve *gopālas* (cowherd boys) who appeared to substantiate the pastimes of Lord Caitanya Mahāprabhu. He is known as a great devotee of Lord Nityānanda Prabhu. The *brāhmaṇa* named Kālā Kṛṣṇadāsa who went with Śrī Caitanya to South India and later to Bengal is mentioned in the *Madhya-līlā,* Tenth Chapter, verses 62-74. One should not take these two to be the same person.

TEXT 40

জলপাত্র-বস্ত্র বহি' তোমা-সঙ্গে যাবে ।
যে তোমার ইচ্ছা, কর, কিছু না বলিবে ॥ ৪০ ॥

jala-pātra-vastra vahi' tomā-saṅge yābe
ye tomāra icchā, kara, kichu nā balibe

SYNONYMS

jala-pātra—water pot; *vastra*—and garments; *vahi'*—carrying; *tomā-saṅge*—with You; *yābe*—will go; *ye*—whatever; *tomāra icchā*—Your desire; *kara*—You do; *kichu nā balibe*—he will not say anything.

TRANSLATION

"He will carry Your water pot and garments. You may do whatever You like; he will not say a word."

TEXT 41

তবে তাঁর বাক্য প্রভু করি' অঙ্গীকারে ।
তাহা-সবা লঞা গেলা সার্বভৌম-ঘরে ॥ ৪১ ॥

tabe tāṅra vākya prabhu kari' aṅgīkāre
tāhā-sabā lañā gelā sārvabhauma-ghare

SYNONYMS

tabe—thereupon; *tāṅra*—of Lord Nityānanda Prabhu; *vākya*—the words; *prabhu*—Lord Caitanya Mahāprabhu; *kari'*—doing; *aṅgīkāre*—acceptance; *tāhā-sabā*—all of them; *lañā*—taking; *gelā*—went; *sārvabhauma-ghare*—to the house of Sārvabhauma Bhaṭṭācārya.

TRANSLATION

Accepting the request of Lord Nityānanda Prabhu, Lord Caitanya took all His devotees and went to the house of Sārvabhauma Bhaṭṭācārya.

TEXT 42

নমস্করি' সার্বভৌম আসন নিবেদিল ।
সবাকারে মিলি' তবে আসনে বসিল ॥ ৪২ ॥

namaskari' sārvabhauma āsana nivedila
sabākāre mili' tabe āsane vasila

SYNONYMS

namaskari'—offering obeisances; *sārvabhauma*—Sārvabhauma Bhaṭṭācārya; *āsana*—sitting places; *nivedila*—offered; *sabākāre*—all of them; *mili'*—meeting; *tabe*—after that; *āsane vasila*—he took his seat.

TRANSLATION

As soon as they entered his house, Sārvabhauma Bhaṭṭācārya offered the Lord obeisances and a place to sit. After seating all the others, the Bhaṭṭācārya took his seat.

TEXT 43

নানা কৃষ্ণবার্তা কহি' কহিল তাঁহারে ।
'তোমার ঠাঞি আইলাঙ আজ্ঞা মাগিবারে ॥ ৪৩ ॥

nānā kṛṣṇa-vārtā kahi' kahila tāṅhāre
'tomāra ṭhāñi āilāṅ ājñā māgibāre

SYNONYMS

nānā—various; *kṛṣṇa-vārtā*—topics on Lord Kṛṣṇa; *kahi'*—discussing; *kahila*—He informed; *tāṅhāre*—Sārvabhauma Bhaṭṭācārya; *tomāra ṭhāñi*—to your place; *āilāṅ*—I have come; *ājñā*—order; *māgibāre*—to beg.

TRANSLATION

After they had discussed various topics about Lord Kṛṣṇa, Śrī Caitanya Mahāprabhu informed Sārvabhauma Bhaṭṭācārya: "I have come to your place just to receive your order.

TEXT 44

সন্ন্যাস করি' বিশ্বরূপ গিয়াছে দক্ষিণে ।
অবশ্য করিব আমি তাঁর অন্বেষণে ॥ ৪৪ ॥

sannyāsa kari' viśvarūpa giyāche dakṣiṇe
avaśya kariba āmi tāṅra anveṣaṇe

SYNONYMS

sannyāsa kari'—after accepting the *sannyāsa* order; *viśva-rūpa*—Viśvarūpa (the elder brother of Śrī Caitanya Mahāprabhu); *giyāche*—has gone; *dakṣiṇe*—to South India; *avaśya*—certainly; *kariba*—shall do; *āmi*—I; *tāṅra*—of Him; *anveṣaṇe*—searching for.

TRANSLATION

"My elder brother, Viśvarūpa, has taken sannyāsa and gone to South India. Now I must go search for Him.

TEXT 45

আজ্ঞা দেহ, অবশ্য আমি দক্ষিণে চলিব ।
তোমার আজ্ঞাতে সুখে লেউটি' আসিব ॥" ৪৫ ॥

ājñā deha, avaśya āmi dakṣiṇe caliba
tomāra ājñāte sukhe leuṭi' āsiba'

SYNONYMS

ājñā deha—please give permission; *avaśya*—certainly; *āmi*—I; *dakṣiṇe*—in South India; *caliba*—shall go; *tomāra*—your; *ājñāte*—by the order; *sukhe*—in happiness; *leuṭi'*—returning; *āsiba*—I shall come.

TRANSLATION

"Please permit Me to go, for I must tour South India. With your permission, I shall soon return very happily."

TEXT 46

শুনি' সার্বভৌম হৈলা অত্যন্ত কাতর ।
চরণে ধরিয়া কহে বিষাদ-উত্তর ॥ ৪৬ ॥

śuni' sārvabhauma hailā atyanta kātara
caraṇe dhariyā kahe viṣāda-uttara

SYNONYMS

śuni'—hearing this; *sārvabhauma*—Sārvabhauma Bhaṭṭācārya; *hailā*—became; *atyanta*—greatly; *kātara*—agitated; *caraṇe*—the lotus feet; *dhariyā*—taking; *kahe*—says; *viṣāda*—of lamentation; *uttara*—a reply.

TRANSLATION

Upon hearing this, Sārvabhauma Bhaṭṭācārya became very agitated. Catching hold of the lotus feet of Caitanya Mahāprabhu, he gave this sorrowful reply.

TEXT 47

'বহুজন্মের পুণ্যফলে পাইনু তোমার সঙ্গ ।
হেন-সঙ্গ বিধি মোর করিলেক ভঙ্গ ॥ ৪৭ ॥

'bahu-janmera puṇya-phale pāinu tomāra saṅga
hena-saṅga vidhi mora karileka bhaṅga

SYNONYMS

bahu-janmera—of many births; *puṇya-phale*—as the fruit of pious activities; *pāinu*—I got; *tomāra*—Your; *saṅga*—association; *hena-saṅga*—such association; *vidhi*—providence; *mora*—my; *karileka*—has done; *bhaṅga*—breaking.

TRANSLATION

"After many births, due to some pious activity, I got Your association. Now providence is breaking this invaluable association.

TEXT 48

শিরে বজ্র পড়ে যদি, পুত্র মরি' যায় ।
তাহা সহি, তোমার বিচ্ছেদ সহন না যায় ॥ ৪৮ ॥

śire vajra paḍe yadi, putra mari' yāya
tāhā sahi, tomāra viccheda sahana nā yāya

SYNONYMS

śire—on the head; *vajra*—a thunderbolt; *paḍe*—falls; *yadi*—if; *putra*—son; *mari'*—dying; *yāya*—goes; *tāhā*—that; *sahi*—I can tolerate; *tomāra*—Your; *viccheda*—separation; *sahana*—enduring; *nā yāya*—cannot be done.

TRANSLATION

"If a thunderbolt falls on my head or if my son dies, I can tolerate it. But I cannot endure the unhappiness of Your separation.

TEXT 49

স্বতন্ত্র-ঈশ্বর তুমি করিবে গমন ।
দিন কথো রহ, দেখি তোমার চরণ' ॥ ৪৯ ॥

svatantra-īśvara tumi karibe gamana
dina katho raha, dekhi tomāra caraṇa'

SYNONYMS

svatantra-īśvara—the independent Supreme Personality of Godhead; *tumi*—You; *karibe*—will make; *gamana*—departure; *dina*—days; *katho*—some; *raha*—please stay; *dekhi*—I may see; *tomāra caraṇa*—Your lotus feet.

TRANSLATION

"My dear Lord, You are the independent Supreme Personality of Godhead. Certainly You will depart. I know that. Still, I ask You to stay here a few days more so that I can see Your lotus feet."

TEXT 50

তাহার বিনয়ে প্রভুর শিথিল হৈল মন।
রহিল দিবস কথো, না কৈল গমন ॥ ৫০ ॥

tāhāra vinaye prabhura śithila haila mana
rahila divasa katho, nā kaila gamana

SYNONYMS

tāhāra—of Sārvabhauma Bhaṭṭācārya; *vinaye*—on the request; *prabhura*—of Lord Śrī Caitanya Mahāprabhu; *śithila*—slackened; *haila*—became; *mana*—the mind; *rahila*—stayed; *divasa*—days; *katho*—a few; *nā*—not; *kaila*—did; *gamana*—departure.

TRANSLATION

Upon hearing Sārvabhauma Bhaṭṭācārya's request, Caitanya Mahāprabhu relented. He stayed a few days longer and did not depart.

TEXT 51

ভট্টাচার্য আগ্রহ করি' করেন নিমন্ত্রণ।
গৃহে পাক করি' প্রভুকে করা'ন ভোজন ॥ ৫১ ॥

bhaṭṭācārya āgraha kari' karena nimantraṇa
gṛhe pāka kari' prabhuke karā'na bhojana

SYNONYMS

bhaṭṭācārya—Sārvabhauma Bhaṭṭācārya; *āgraha*—eagerness; *kari'*—showing; *karena*—did; *nimantraṇa*—invitation; *gṛhe*—at home; *pāka*—cooking; *kari'*—doing; *prabhuke*—Lord Śrī Caitanya Mahāprabhu; *karā'na*—made; *bhojana*—eating.

TRANSLATION

The Bhaṭṭācārya eagerly invited Lord Caitanya Mahāprabhu to his home and fed Him very nicely.

TEXT 52

তাঁহার ব্রাহ্মণী, তাঁর নাম—'ষাঠীর মাতা'।
রান্ধি' ভিক্ষা দেন তেঁহো, আশ্চর্য তাঁর কথা ॥৫২॥

tāṅhāra brāhmaṇī, tāṅra nāma——'ṣāṭhīra mātā'
rāndhi' bhikṣā dena teṅho, āścarya tāṅra kathā

SYNONYMS

tāṅhāra brāhmaṇī—his wife; *tāṅra nāma*—her name; *ṣāṭhīra mātā*—the mother of Ṣāṭhī; *rāndhi'*—cooking; *bhikṣā dena*—offers food; *teṅho*—she; *āścarya*—wonderful; *tāṅra*—her; *kathā*—narration.

TRANSLATION

The Bhaṭṭācārya's wife, whose name was Ṣāṭhīmātā (the mother of Ṣāṭhī), did the cooking. The narrations of these pastimes are very wonderful.

TEXT 53

আগে ত' কহিব তাহা করিয়া বিস্তার।
এবে কহি প্রভুর দক্ষিণ-যাত্রা-সমাচার ॥ ৫৩ ॥

āge ta' kahiba tāhā kariyā vistāra
ebe kahi prabhura dakṣiṇa-yātrā-samācāra

SYNONYMS

āge—later; *ta'*—indeed; *kahiba*—I shall speak; *tāhā*—all those incidents; *kariyā*—doing; *vistāra*—elaboration; *ebe*—now; *kahi*—let me describe; *prabhura*—of Lord Caitanya Mahāprabhu; *dakṣiṇa*—in South India; *yātrā*—of the touring; *samācāra*—the narration.

TRANSLATION

Later I shall tell about this in elaborate detail, but at present I wish to describe Śrī Caitanya Mahāprabhu's South Indian tour.

TEXT 54

দিন পাঁচ রহি' প্রভু ভট্টাচার্য-স্থানে।
চলিবার লাগি' আজ্ঞা মাগিলা আপনে ॥ ৫৪ ॥

dina pāṅca rahi' prabhu bhaṭṭācārya-sthāne
calibāra lāgi' ājñā māgilā āpane

SYNONYMS

dina pāṅca—five days; *rahi'*—staying; *prabhu*—Lord Śrī Caitanya Mahāprabhu; *bhaṭṭācārya-sthāne*—at Sārvabhauma Bhaṭṭācārya's place; *calibāra lāgi'*—for starting; *ājñā*—order; *māgilā*—begged; *āpane*—personally.

TRANSLATION

After staying five days at the home of Sārvabhauma Bhaṭṭācārya, Śrī Caitanya Mahāprabhu personally asked his permission to depart for South India.

TEXT 55

প্রভুর আগ্রহে ভট্টাচার্য সম্মত হইলা ।
প্রভু তাঁরে লঞা জগন্নাথ-মন্দিরে গেলা ॥ ৫৫ ॥

prabhura āgrahe bhaṭṭācārya sammata ha-ilā
prabhu tāṅre lañā jagannātha-mandire gelā

SYNONYMS

prabhura āgrahe—by the eagerness of Śrī Caitanya Mahāprabhu; *bhaṭṭācārya*—Sārvabhauma Bhaṭṭācārya; *sammata ha-ilā*—became agreeable; *prabhu*—Lord Śrī Caitanya Mahāprabhu; *tāṅre*—him (Sārvabhauma Bhaṭṭācārya); *lañā*—taking; *jagannātha-mandire*—to the temple of Lord Jagannātha; *gelā*—went.

TRANSLATION

After receiving the Bhaṭṭācārya's permission, Lord Caitanya Mahāprabhu went to see Lord Jagannātha in the temple. He took the Bhaṭṭācārya with Him.

TEXT 56

দর্শন করি' ঠাকুর-পাশ আজ্ঞা মাগিলা ।
পূজারী প্রভুরে মালা-প্রসাদ আনি' দিলা ॥ ৫৬ ॥

darśana kari' ṭhākura-pāśa ājñā māgilā
pūjārī prabhure mālā-prasāda āni' dilā

SYNONYMS

darśana kari'—visiting the Lord; *ṭhākura-pāśa*—from the Lord; *ājñā māgilā*—begged permission; *pūjārī*—the priest; *prabhure*—unto Lord Śrī Caitanya Mahāprabhu; *mālā*—garland; *prasāda*—remnants of food; *āni'*—bringing; *dilā*—delivered.

TRANSLATION

Seeing Lord Jagannātha, Śrī Caitanya Mahāprabhu also begged His permission. The priest then immediately delivered prasāda and a garland to Lord Caitanya.

TEXT 57

আজ্ঞা-মালা পাঞা হর্ষে নমস্কার করি' ।
আনন্দে দক্ষিণ-দেশে চলে গৌরহরি ॥ ৫৭ ॥

ājñā-mālā pāñā harṣe namaskāra kari'
ānande dakṣiṇa-deśe cale gaurahari

SYNONYMS

ājñā-mālā—the garland of permission; *pāñā*—getting; *harṣe*—in great jubilation; *namaskāra*—obeisances; *kari'*—offering; *ānande*—with great pleasure; *dakṣiṇa-deśe*—to South India; *cale*—goes; *gaurahari*—Lord Śrī Caitanya Mahāprabhu.

TRANSLATION

Thus receiving Lord Jagannātha's permission in the form of a garland, Śrī Caitanya Mahāprabhu offered obeisances, and in great jubilation prepared to depart for South India.

TEXT 58

ভট্টাচার্য-সঙ্গে আর যত নিজগণ ।
জগন্নাথ প্রদক্ষিণ করি' করিলা গমন ॥ ৫৮ ॥

bhaṭṭācārya-saṅge āra yata nija-gaṇa
jagannātha pradakṣiṇa kari' karilā gamana

SYNONYMS

bhaṭṭācārya-saṅge—with Sārvabhauma Bhaṭṭācārya; *āra*—and; *yata*—all; *nija-gaṇa*—personal devotees; *jagannātha*—Lord Jagannātha; *pradakṣiṇa*—circumambulation; *kari'*—finishing; *karilā*—made; *gamana*—departure.

TRANSLATION

Accompanied by His personal associates and Sārvabhauma Bhaṭṭācārya, Śrī Caitanya Mahāprabhu circumambulated the altar of Jagannātha. The Lord then departed on His South Indian tour.

TEXT 59

সমুদ্র-তীরে তীরে আলালনাথ-পথে ।
সার্বভৌম কহিলেন আচার্য-গোপীনাথে ॥ ৫৯ ॥

samudra-tīre tīre ālālanātha-pathe
sārvabhauma kahilena ācārya-gopīnāthe

SYNONYMS

samudra-tīre—on the shore of the sea; *tīre*—on the shore; *ālālanātha-pathe*—on the path to the temple of Ālālanātha; *sārvabhauma*—Sārvabhauma Bhaṭṭācārya; *kahilena*—said; *ācārya-gopīnāthe*—to Gopīnātha Ācārya.

TRANSLATION

While the Lord was going along the path to Ālālanātha, which was located on the seashore, Sārvabhauma Bhaṭṭācārya gave the following orders to Gopīnātha Ācārya.

TEXT 60

চারি কোপীন-বহির্বাস রাখিয়াছি ঘরে ।
তাহা, প্রসাদান্ন, লঞা আইস বিপ্রদ্বারে ॥ ৬০ ॥

cāri kopīna-bahirvāsa rākhiyāchi ghare
tāhā, prasādānna, lañā āisa vipra-dvāre

SYNONYMS

cāri kopīna-bahirvāsa—four sets of loincloths and external clothing; *rākhiyāchi*—I have kept; *ghare*—at home; *tāhā*—that; *prasāda-anna*—remnants of food of Lord Jagannātha; *lañā*—taking; *āisa*—come here; *vipra-dvāre*—by means of some *brāhmaṇa.*

TRANSLATION

"Bring the four sets of loincloths and outer garments I keep at home, and also some prasāda of Lord Jagannātha's. You may carry these things with the help of some brāhmaṇa."

TEXT 61

তবে সার্বভৌম কহে প্রভুর চরণে ।
অবশ্য পালিবে, প্রভু, মোর নিবেদনে ॥ ৬১ ॥

tabe sārvabhauma kahe prabhura caraṇe
avaśya pālibe, prabhu, mora nivedane

SYNONYMS

tabe—thereafter; *sārvabhauma*—Sārvabhauma Bhaṭṭācārya; *kahe*—said; *prabhura caraṇe*—unto the lotus feet of the Lord; *avaśya*—certainly; *pālibe*—You will keep; *prabhu*—my Lord; *mora*—my; *nivedane*—request.

TRANSLATION

While Lord Śrī Caitanya Mahāprabhu was departing, Sārvabhauma Bhaṭṭācārya submitted the following at His lotus feet: "My Lord, I have one final request that I hope You will kindly fulfill.

TEXT 62

'রামানন্দ রায়' আছে গোদাবরী-তীরে ।
অধিকারী হয়েন তেঁহো বিদ্যানগরে ॥ ৬২ ॥

'rāmānanda rāya' āche godāvarī-tīre
adhikārī hayena teṅho vidyānagare

SYNONYMS

rāmānanda rāya—Rāmānanda Rāya; *āche*—there is; *godāvarī-tīre*—on the bank of River Godāvarī; *adhikārī*—a responsible officer; *hayena*—is; *teṅho*—he; *vidyānagare*—in the town known as Vidyānagara.

TRANSLATION

"In the town of Vidyānagara, on the bank of the Godāvarī, there is a responsible government officer named Rāmānanda Rāya.

PURPORT

In the *Amṛta-pravāha-bhāṣya,* Bhaktivinoda Ṭhākura states that Vidyānagara is today known as Poravandara. There is another Poravandara in western India in the province of Gujarat.

TEXT 63

শূদ্র বিষয়ি-জ্ঞানে উপেক্ষা না করিবে ।
আমার বচনে তাঁরে অবশ্য মিলিবে ॥ ৬৩ ॥

śūdra viṣayi-jñāne upekṣā nā karibe
āmāra vacane tāṅre avaśya milibe

SYNONYMS

śūdra—the fourth social division; *viṣayi-jñāne*—by the impression of being a worldly man; *upekṣā*—negligence; *nā karibe*—should not do; *āmāra*—my;

vacane—on the request; *tāṅre*—him; *avaśya*—certainly; *milibe*—You should meet.

TRANSLATION

"Please do not neglect him, thinking he belongs to a śūdra family engaged in material activities. It is my request that You meet him without fail."

PURPORT

In the *varṇāśrama-dharma,* the *śūdra* is the fourth division in the social status. *Paricaryātmakaṁ karma śūdrasyāpi svabhāva-jam* (Bg. 18.44). *Śūdras* are meant to engage in the service of the three higher classes—*brāhmaṇas, kṣatriyas* and *vaiśyas.* Śrī Rāmānanda Rāya belonged to the *karaṇa* class, which is the equivalent of the *kāyastha* class in Bengal. This class is regarded all over India as *śūdra.* It is said that the Bengali *kāyasthas* were originally engaged as servants of *brāhmaṇas* who came from North India to Bengal. Later, the clerical class became the *kāyasthas* in Bengal. Now there are many mixed classes known as *kāyastha.* Sometimes it is said in Bengal that those who cannot claim any particular class belong to the *kāyastha* class. Although these *kāyasthas* or *karaṇas* are considered *śūdras,* they are very intelligent and highly educated. Most of them are professionals such as lawyers or politicians. Thus in Bengal the *kāyasthas* are sometimes considered *kṣatriyas.* In Orissa, however, the *kāyastha* class, which includes the *karaṇas,* is considered in the *śūdra* category. Śrīla Rāmānanda Rāya belonged to this *karaṇa* class; therefore he was considered a *śūdra.* He was also the governor of South India under the regime of Mahārāja Pratāparudra of Orissa. In other words, Sārvabhauma Bhaṭṭācārya informed Lord Caitanya Mahāprabhu that Rāmānanda Rāya, although belonging to the *śūdra* class, was a highly responsible government officer. As far as spiritual advancement is concerned, materialists, politicians and *śūdras* are generally disqualified. Sārvabhauma Bhaṭṭācārya therefore requested that Lord Caitanya Mahāprabhu not neglect Rāmānanda Rāya, who was highly advanced spiritually although he was born a *śūdra* and a materialist.

A *viṣayī* is one who is attached to family life and is interested only in wife, children and worldly sense gratification. The senses can be engaged either in worldly enjoyment or in the service of the Lord. Those who are not engaged in the service of the Lord and are interested only in material sense gratification are called *viṣayī.* Śrīla Rāmānanda Rāya was engaged in government service, and he belonged to the *karaṇa* class. He was certainly not a *sannyāsī* in saffron cloth, yet he was in the transcendental position of a *paramahaṁsa* householder. Before becoming Caitanya Mahāprabhu's disciple, Sārvabhauma Bhaṭṭācārya considered Rāmānanda Rāya an ordinary *viṣayī* because he was a householder engaged in government service. However, when the Bhaṭṭācārya was actually enlightened in Vaiṣṇava philosophy, he could understand the exalted transcendental position of Śrī Rāmānanda Rāya; therefore he referred to him as *adhikārī.* An *adhikārī* is one who knows the transcendental science of Kṛṣṇa and is engaged in His service; therefore all *gṛhastha* devotees are designated as *dāsa adhikārī.*

TEXT 64

তোমার সঙ্গের যোগ্য তেঁহো এক জন।
পৃথিবীতে রসিক ভক্ত নাহি তাঁর সম ॥ ৬৪ ॥

tomāra saṅgera yogya teṅho eka jana
pṛthivīte rasika bhakta nāhi tāṅra sama

SYNONYMS

tomāra—Your; *saṅgera*—of association; *yogya*—fit; *teṅho*—he (Rāmānanda Rāya); *eka*—one; *jana*—person; *pṛthivīte*—in the world; *rasika*—expert in transcendental mellows; *bhakta*—devotee; *nāhi*—there is none; *tāṅra sama*—like him.

TRANSLATION

Sārvabhauma Bhaṭṭācārya continued: "Rāmānanda Rāya is a fit person to associate with You; no other devotee can compare with him in knowledge of the transcendental mellows.

TEXT 65

পাণ্ডিত্য আর ভক্তিরস,—দুঁহের তেঁহো সীমা।
সম্ভাষিলে জানিবে তুমি তাঁহার মহিমা ॥ ৬৫ ॥

pāṇḍitya āra bhakti-rasa,——duṅhera teṅho sīmā
sambhāṣile jānibe tumi tāṅhāra mahimā

SYNONYMS

pāṇḍitya—learning; *āra*—and; *bhakti-rasa*—the mellows of devotional service; *duṅhera*—of these two; *teṅho*—he; *sīmā*—the limit; *sambhāṣile*—when You talk with him; *jānibe*—will know; *tumi*—You; *tāṅhāra*—his; *mahimā*—glories.

TRANSLATION

"He is a most learned scholar as well as an expert in devotional mellows. Actually he is most exalted, and if You talk with him,You will see how glorious he is.

TEXT 66

অলৌকিক বাক্য চেষ্টা তাঁর না বুঝিয়া।
পরিহাস করিয়াছি তাঁরে 'বৈষ্ণব' বলিয়া ॥ ৬৬ ॥

alaukika vākya ceṣṭā tāṅra nā bujhiyā
parihāsa kariyāchi tāṅre 'vaiṣṇava' baliyā

SYNONYMS

alaukika—uncommon; *vākya*—words; *ceṣṭā*—endeavor; *tāṅra*—his; *nā*—without; *bujhiyā*—understanding; *parihāsa*—joking; *kariyāchi*—I have done; *tāṅre*—unto him; *vaiṣṇava*—a devotee of the Lord; *baliyā*—as.

TRANSLATION

"I could not realize when I first spoke with Rāmānanda Rāya that his topics and endeavors were all transcendentally uncommon. I made fun of him simply because he was a Vaiṣṇava."

PURPORT

Anyone who is a not a Vaiṣṇava or unalloyed devotee of the Supreme Lord must be a materialist. A Vaiṣṇava living according to Śrī Caitanya Mahāprabhu's injunctions is certainly not on the materialistic platform. Caitanya means "spiritual force." All of Śrī Caitanya Mahāprabhu's activities were carried out on the platform of spiritual understanding; therefore only those who are on the spiritual platform are able to understand the activities of Śrī Caitanya Mahāprabhu. Materialistic persons who cannot are generally known as *karmīs* or *jñānīs.* The *jñānīs* are mental speculators who simply try to understand what is spirit and what is soul. Their process is *neti neti:* "This is not spirit, this is not Brahman." The *jñānīs* are a little more advanced than the dull-headed *karmīs,* who are simply interested in sense gratification. Before becoming a Vaiṣṇava, Sārvabhauma Bhaṭṭācārya was a mental speculator (*jñānī*), and being such, he always cut jokes with Vaiṣṇavas. A Vaiṣṇava never agrees with the speculative system of the *jñānīs.* Both the *jñānīs* and *karmīs* depend on direct sense perception for their imperfect knowledge. The *karmīs* never agree to accept anything not directly perceived, and the *jñānīs* put forth only hypotheses. However, the Vaiṣṇavas, the unalloyed devotees of the Lord, do not follow the process of acquiring knowledge by direct sense perception or mental speculation. Because they are servants of the Supreme Lord, devotees receive knowledge directly from the Supreme Personality of Godhead as He speaks it in *Bhagavad-gītā,* or sometimes as He imparts it from within as *caitya-guru.* As stated in *Bhagavad-gītā:*

teṣāṁ satata-yuktānāṁ
bhajatāṁ prīti-pūrvakam
dadāmi buddhi-yogaṁ taṁ
yena mām upayānti te

"To those who are constantly devoted and worship Me with love, I give the understanding by which they can come to Me." (Bg. 10.10)

The *Vedas* are considered to have been spoken by the Supreme Lord. They were first realized by Brahmā, who is the first created being within the universe (*tene brahma hṛdā ya ādi-kavaye*). Our process is to receive knowledge through the *paramparā* system, from Kṛṣṇa to Brahmā, to Nārada, Vyāsa, Śrī Caitanya Mahāprabhu and the six Gosvāmīs. By disciplic succession, Lord Brahmā was enlightened from within by the original person, Kṛṣṇa. Our knowledge is fully perfect due to being handed from master to disciple. A Vaiṣṇava is always engaged in the transcendental loving service of the Lord, and as such neither *karmīs* nor *jñānīs* can understand the activities of a Vaiṣṇava. It is said, *vaiṣṇavera kriyā-mudrā vijñe nā bujhaya:* even the most learned man depending on direct perception of knowledge cannot understand the activities of a Vaiṣṇava. After being initiated into Vaiṣṇavism by Śrī Caitanya Mahāprabhu, Bhaṭṭācārya realized what a mistake he had made in trying to understand Rāmānanda Rāya, who was very learned and whose endeavors were all directed to rendering transcendental loving service to the Lord.

TEXT 67

তোমার প্রসাদে এবে জানিনু তাঁর তত্ত্ব ।
সম্ভাষিলে জানিবে তাঁর যেমন মহত্ত্ব ॥ ৬৭ ॥

tomāra prasāde ebe jāninu tāṅra tattva
sambhāṣile jānibe tāṅra yemana mahattva

SYNONYMS

tomāra prasāde—by Your mercy; *ebe*—now; *jāninu*—I have understood; *tāṅra*—of him (Rāmānanda Rāya); *tattva*—the truth; *sambhāṣile*—in talking together; *jānibe*—You will know; *tāṅra*—his; *yemana*—such; *mahattva*—greatness.

TRANSLATION

The Bhaṭṭācārya said: "By Your mercy I can now understand the truth about Rāmānanda Rāya. In talking with him, You also will acknowledge his greatness."

TEXT 68

অঙ্গীকার করি' প্রভু তাঁহার বচন ।
তাঁরে বিদায় দিতে তাঁরে কৈল আলিঙ্গন ॥ ৬৮ ॥

aṅgīkāra kari' prabhu tāṅhāra vacana
tāṅre vidāya dite tāṅre kaila āliṅgana

SYNONYMS

aṅgīkāra kari'—accepting this proposal; *prabhu*—Lord Caitanya Mahāprabhu; *tāṅhāra*—of him (Sārvabhauma Bhaṭṭācārya); *vacana*—the request; *tāṅre*—unto him; *vidāya dite*—to offer farewell; *tāṅre*—him; *kaila*—did; *āliṅgana*—embracing.

TRANSLATION

Lord Śrī Caitanya Mahāprabhu accepted Sārvabhauma Bhaṭṭācārya's request that He meet Rāmānanda Rāya. Bidding him farewell, the Lord embraced him.

TEXT 69

"ঘরে কৃষ্ণ ভজি' মোরে করিহ আশীর্বাদে ।
নীলাচলে আসি' যেন তোমার প্রসাদে ॥" ৬৯ ॥

"ghare kṛṣṇa bhaji' more kariha āśīrvāde
nīlācale āsi' yena tomāra prasāde"

SYNONYMS

ghare—at home; *kṛṣṇa*—Lord Kṛṣṇa; *bhaji'*—worshiping; *more*—unto Me; *kariha*—do; *āśīrvāde*—blessing; *nīlācale*—at Jagannātha Purī; *āsi'*—returning; *yena*—so that; *tomāra*—your; *prasāde*—by the mercy.

TRANSLATION

Śrī Caitanya Mahāprabhu asked the Bhaṭṭācārya's blessings while he was engaged in the devotional service of Lord Kṛṣṇa at home. The Lord wished to return again to Jagannātha Purī by his mercy.

PURPORT

The word *kariha āśīrvāde* means, "continue to bestow your blessings upon Me." Being a *sannyāsī,* Caitanya Mahāprabhu was on the highest platform of respect and adoration, whereas Sārvabhauma Bhaṭṭācārya, as a householder, was on the second platform. Therefore a *sannyāsī* is supposed to offer blessings to a *gṛhastha.* Now Śrī Caitanya Mahāprabhu by His practical behavior requested the blessings of a *gṛhastha.* This is the special significance of Śrī Caitanya Mahāprabhu's preaching. He gave equal status to everyone, regardless of material considerations. His movement is thoroughly spiritual. Although apparently a *gṛhastha* (householder), Sārvabhauma Bhaṭṭācārya was unlike the so-called *karmīs* interested in sense gratification. After being initiated by Śrī Caitanya Mahāprabhu, the Bhaṭṭācārya was perfectly situated in the spiritual order; therefore it was quite possible for him to offer blessings even to a *sannyāsī.* He was always engaged in the service of the

Lord even at home. In our disciplic line we have the example of a perfect householder *paramahaṁsa*—Śrīla Bhaktivinoda Ṭhākura. In his book *Śaraṇāgati,* Bhaktivinoda Ṭhākura stated: *ye dina gṛhe, bhajana dekhi', gṛhete goloka bhāya* (*Śaraṇāgati* 31.6). Whenever a householder glorifies the Supreme Lord in his home, his activities are immediately transformed into the activities of Goloka Vṛndāvana, spiritual activities taking place in the Goloka Vṛndāvana planet of Kṛṣṇa. Activities exhibited by Kṛṣṇa Himself at Bhauma Vṛndāvana, the Vṛndāvana-dhāma existing on this planet, are not different from His activities on the planet Goloka Vṛndāvana. This is proper realization of Vṛndāvana anywhere. In our Kṛṣṇa consciousness movement we inaugurated the New Vṛndāvana activities wherein devotees are always engaged in the transcendental loving service of the Lord, and this is not different from Goloka Vṛndāvana. The conclusion is that one who acts strictly in the line of Śrī Caitanya Mahāprabhu is competent to offer blessings to *sannyāsīs,* even though he be a *gṛhastha* householder. Although he is in an exalted position, a *sannyāsī* yet must elevate himself to the transcendental platform by rendering service to the Lord. By his actual behavior, Caitanya Mahāprabhu begged the blessings of Sārvabhauma Bhaṭṭācārya. He set the example of how one should expect blessings from a Vaiṣṇava, regardless of his social position.

TEXT 70

এত বলি' মহাপ্রভু করিলা গমন ।
মূর্চ্ছিত হঞা তাহাঁ পড়িলা সার্বভৌম ॥ ৭০ ॥

eta bali' mahāprabhu karilā gamana
mūrcchita hañā tāhāṅ paḍilā sārvabhauma

SYNONYMS

eta bali'—saying this; *mahā-prabhu*—Śrī Caitanya Mahāprabhu; *karilā*—made; *gamana*—departure; *mūrcchita*—fainted; *hañā*—becoming; *tāhāṅ*—there; *paḍilā*—fell down; *sārvabhauma*—Sārvabhauma Bhaṭṭācārya.

TRANSLATION

Saying this, Śrī Caitanya Mahāprabhu departed on His tour, and Sārvabhauma Bhaṭṭācārya immediately fainted and fell to the ground.

TEXT 71

তাঁরে উপেক্ষিয়া কৈল শীঘ্র গমন ।
কে বুঝিতে পারে মহাপ্রভুর চিত্ত-মন ॥ ৭১ ॥

tāṅre upekṣiyā kaila śīghra gamana
ke bujhite pāre mahāprabhura citta-mana

SYNONYMS

tāṅre—unto Sārvabhauma Bhaṭṭācārya; *upekṣiyā*—not paying serious attention; *kaila*—did; *śīghra*—very fast; *gamana*—walking; *ke*—who; *bujhite*—to understand; *pāre*—is able; *mahāprabhura*—of Śrī Caitanya Mahāprabhu; *citta-mana*—the mind and intention.

TRANSLATION

Although Sārvabhauma Bhaṭṭācārya fainted, Śrī Caitanya Mahāprabhu did not take notice of him. Rather, He left quickly. Who can understand the mind and intention of Śrī Caitanya Mahāprabhu?

PURPORT

It was naturally expected that when Sārvabhauma Bhaṭṭācārya fainted and fell to the ground Śrī Caitanya Mahāprabhu would have taken care of him and waited for him to regain consciousness, but He did not do so. Rather, Śrī Caitanya Mahāprabhu immediately started on His tour. It is therefore very difficult to understand the activities of a transcendental person. Sometimes they may seem rather odd, but a transcendental personality remains in his position, unaffected by material considerations.

TEXT 72

মহানুভাবের চিত্তের স্বভাব এই হয়।
পুষ্প-সম কোমল, কঠিন বজ্রময় ॥ ৭২ ॥

mahānubhāvera cittera svabhāva ei haya
puṣpa-sama komala, kaṭhina vajra-maya

SYNONYMS

mahā-anubhāvera—of a great personality; *cittera*—of the mind; *svabhāva*—the nature; *ei haya*—this is; *puṣpa-sama*—like a flower; *komala*—soft; *kaṭhina*—hard; *vajra-maya*—like a thunderbolt.

TRANSLATION

This is the nature of the mind of an uncommon personality. Sometimes it is soft like a flower, but sometimes it is as hard as a thunderbolt.

PURPORT

The softness of a flower and the hardness of a thunderbolt are reconciled in the behavior of a great personality. The following quotation from *Uttara-rāma-racita* (2.7) explains this behavior. One may also consult *Madhya-līlā*, Third Chapter, verse 212.

TEXT 73

বজ্রাদপি কঠোরাণি মৃদূনি কুসুমাদপি ।
লোকোত্তরাণাং চেতাংসি কো নু বিজ্ঞাতুমীশ্বরঃ ॥৭৩॥

vajrād api kaṭhorāṇi
mṛdūni kusumād api
lokottarāṇāṁ cetāṁsi
ko nu vijñātum īśvaraḥ

SYNONYMS

vajrāt api—than a thunderbolt; *kaṭhorāṇi*—harder; *mṛdūni*—softer; *kusumāt api*—than a flower; *loka-uttarāṇām*—persons above the human platform of behavior; *cetāṁsi*—the hearts; *kaḥ*—who; *nu*—but; *vijñātum*—to understand; *īśvaraḥ*—able.

TRANSLATION

"The hearts of those above common behavior are sometimes harder than a thunderbolt and sometimes softer than a flower. How can one accommodate such contradictions in great personalities?"

TEXT 74

নিত্যানন্দপ্রভু ভট্টাচার্যে উঠাইল ।
তাঁর লোকসঙ্গে তাঁরে ঘরে পাঠাইল ॥ ৭৪ ॥

nityānanda prabhu bhaṭṭācārye uṭhāila
tāṅra loka-saṅge tāṅre ghare pāṭhāila

SYNONYMS

nityānanda prabhu—Lord Śrī Nityānanda Prabhu; *bhaṭṭācārye*—Sārvabhauma Bhaṭṭācārya; *uṭhāila*—raised; *tāṅra*—His; *loka-saṅge*—along with associates; *tāṅre*—him (the Bhaṭṭācārya); *ghare*—to his home; *pāṭhāila*—sent.

TRANSLATION

Lord Nityānanda Prabhu raised Sārvabhauma Bhaṭṭācārya, and with the help of His men saw him to his home.

TEXT 75

ভক্তগণ শীঘ্র আসি' লৈল প্রভুর সাথ ।
বস্ত্র-প্রসাদ লঞা তবে আইলা গোপীনাথ ॥ ৭৫ ॥

bhakta-gaṇa śīghra āsi' laila prabhura sātha
vastra-prasāda lañā tabe āilā gopīnātha

SYNONYMS

bhakta-gaṇa—devotees; *śīghra*—very swiftly; *āsi'*—coming; *laila*—took; *prabhura*—of the Lord; *sātha*—the company; *vastra*—the garments; *prasāda*—and Lord Jagannātha's *prasāda; lañā*—with; *tabe*—thereafter; *āilā*—came; *gopīnātha*—Gopīnātha Ācārya.

TRANSLATION

Immediately all the devotees came and partook of Śrī Caitanya Mahāprabhu's company. Afterwards, Gopīnātha Ācārya came with the garments and prasāda.

TEXT 76

সবা-সঙ্গে প্রভু তবে আলালনাথ আইলা ।
নমস্কার করি' তারে বহুস্তুতি কৈলা ॥ ৭৬ ॥

sabā-saṅge prabhu tabe ālālanātha āilā
namaskāra kari' tāre bahu-stuti kailā

SYNONYMS

sabā-saṅge—with all of them; *prabhu*—Lord Śrī Caitanya Mahāprabhu; *tabe*—then; *ālālanātha*—the place named Ālālanātha; *āilā*—reached; *namaskāra kari'*—offering obeisances; *tāre*—Lord Śrī Caitanya Mahāprabhu; *bahu-stuti*—many prayers; *kailā*—offered.

TRANSLATION

All the devotees followed Śrī Caitanya Mahāprabhu to a place known as Ālālanātha. There they all offered respects and various prayers.

TEXT 77

প্রেমাবেশে নৃত্যগীত কৈল কতক্ষণ ।
দেখিতে আইলা তাহাঁ বৈসে যত জন ॥ ৭৭ ॥

premāveśe nṛtya-gīta kaila kata-kṣaṇa
dekhite āilā tāhāṅ vaise yata jana

SYNONYMS

prema-āveśe—in the great ecstasy of love of Godhead; *nṛtya-gīta*—dancing and chanting; *kaila*—performed; *kata-kṣaṇa*—for some time; *dekhite*—to see; *āilā*—came; *tāhāṅ*—there; *vaise*—who live; *yata jana*—all the men.

TRANSLATION

In great ecstasy, Śrī Caitanya Mahāprabhu danced and chanted for some time. Indeed, all the neighbors came to see Him.

TEXT 78

চৌদিকেতে সব লোক বলে 'হরি' 'হরি' ।
প্রেমাবেশে মধ্যে নৃত্য করে গৌরহরি ॥ ৭৮ ॥

caudikete saba loka bale 'hari' 'hari'
premāveśe madhye nṛtya kare gaurahari

SYNONYMS

caudikete—all around; *saba loka*—all persons; *bale*—shout; *hari hari*—the holy name of the Lord; *prema-āveśe*—in ecstatic love; *madhye*—in the middle; *nṛtya kare*—dances; *gaura-hari*—Śrī Caitanya Mahāprabhu.

TRANSLATION

All around Śrī Caitanya Mahāprabhu, who is also known as Gaurahari, people began to shout the holy name of Hari. Lord Caitanya, immersed in His usual ecstasy of love, danced in the midst of them.

TEXT 79

কাঞ্চন-সদৃশ দেহ, অরুণ বসন ।
পুলকাশ্রু-কম্প-স্বেদ তাহাতে ভূষণ ॥ ৭৯ ॥

kāñcana-sadṛśa deha, aruṇa vasana
pulakāśru-kampa-sveda tāhāte bhūṣaṇa

SYNONYMS

kāñcana-sadṛśa—like molten gold; *deha*—a body; *aruṇa*—saffron; *vasana*—garments; *pulaka-aśru*—standing of hair and crying; *kampa*—trembling; *sveda*—perspiration; *tāhāte*—therein; *bhūṣaṇa*—the ornaments.

TRANSLATION

The body of Śrī Caitanya Mahāprabhu was naturally very beautiful. It was like molten gold dressed in saffron cloth. Indeed, He was most beautiful for being ornamented with the ecstatic symptoms, which caused His hair to stand on end, tears to well in His eyes and His body to tremble and perspire all over.

TEXT 80

দেখিয়া লোকের মনে হৈল চমৎকার ।
যত লোক আইসে, কেহ নাহি যায় ঘর ॥ ৮০ ॥

dekhiyā lokera mane haila camatkāra
yata loka āise, keha nāhi yāya ghara

SYNONYMS

dekhiyā—seeing all this; *lokera*—of the people; *mane*—in the minds; *haila*—there was; *camatkāra*—astonishment; *yata*—all; *loka*—people; *āise*—came there; *keha*—anyone; *nāhi*—not; *yāya*—goes; *ghara*—home.

TRANSLATION

Everyone present was astonished to see Śrī Caitanya Mahāprabhu's dancing and His bodily transformations. Whoever came did not want to return home.

TEXT 81

কেহ নাচে, কেহ গায়, 'শ্রীকৃষ্ণ' 'গোপাল' ।
প্রেমেতে ভাসিল লোক,—স্ত্রী-বৃদ্ধ-আবাল ॥ ৮১ ॥

keha nāce, keha gāya, 'śrī-kṛṣṇa' 'gopāla'
premete bhāsila loka,——strī-vṛddha-ābāla

SYNONYMS

keha nāce—someone dances; *keha gāya*—someone chants; *śrī-kṛṣṇa*—Lord Śrī Kṛṣṇa's name; *gopāla*—Gopāla's name; *premete*—in love of Godhead; *bhāsila*—

floated; *loka*—all the people; *strī*—women; *vṛddha*—old men; *ā-bāla*—from the children.

TRANSLATION

Everyone—including children, old men and women—began to dance and chant the holy names of Śrī Kṛṣṇa and Gopāla. In this way they all floated in the ocean of love of Godhead.

TEXT 82

দেখি' নিত্যানন্দ প্রভু কহে ভক্তগণে ।
এইরূপে নৃত্য আগে হবে গ্রামে-গ্রামে ॥ ৮২ ॥

dekhi' nityānanda prabhu kahe bhakta-gaṇe
ei-rūpe nṛtya āge habe grāme-grāme

SYNONYMS

dekhi'—seeing this; *nityānanda*—Lord Nityānanda Prabhu; *prabhu*—the Lord; *kahe*—says; *bhakta-gaṇe*—unto the devotees; *ei-rūpe*—in this way; *nṛtya*—dancing; *āge*—ahead; *habe*—there will be; *grāme-grāme*—in every village.

TRANSLATION

Upon seeing the chanting and dancing of Lord Śrī Caitanya Mahāprabhu, Lord Nityānanda predicted that later there would be dancing and chanting in every village.

PURPORT

This prediction of Śrī Nityānanda Prabhu is applicable not only in India but also all over the world. That is now happening by His grace. The members of the International Society for Krishna Consciousness are now traveling from one village to another in the Western countries and are even carrying the Deity with them. These devotees distribute various literatures all over the world. We hope that these devotees who are preaching the message of Śrī Caitanya Mahāprabhu will very seriously follow strictly in His footsteps. If they follow the rules and regulations and chant sixteen rounds daily, their endeavor to preach the cult of Śrī Caitanya Mahāprabhu will certainly be successful.

TEXT 83

অতিকাল হৈল, লোক ছাড়িয়া না যায় ।
তবে নিত্যানন্দ-গোসাঞি স্বজিলা উপায় ॥ ৮৩ ॥

atikāla haila, loka chāḍiyā nā yāya
tabe nityānanda-gosāñi sṛjilā upāya

SYNONYMS

atikāla—very late; *haila*—it was; *loka*—the people in general; *chāḍiyā*—giving up; *nā yāya*—do not go; *tabe*—at that time; *nityānanda*—Śrīla Nityānanda Prabhu; *gosāñi*—the spiritual master; *sṛjilā*—invented; *upāya*—a means.

TRANSLATION

Seeing that it was already getting late, Lord Nityānanda Prabhu, the spiritual master, invented a means to disperse the crowd.

TEXT 84

মধ্যাহ্ন করিতে গেলা প্রভুকে লঞা ।
তাহা দেখি' লোক আইসে চৌদিকে ধাঞা ॥ ৮৪ ॥

madhyāhna karite gelā prabhuke lañā
tāhā dekhi' loka āise caudike dhāñā

SYNONYMS

madhyāhna karite—to take lunch at noon; *gelā*—went; *prabhuke*—Lord Śrī Caitanya Mahāprabhu; *lañā*—taking; *tāhā dekhi'*—seeing that; *loka*—the people in general; *āise*—came; *caudike*—all around; *dhāñā*—running.

TRANSLATION

When Lord Nityānanda Prabhu took Śrī Caitanya Mahāprabhu for lunch at noon, everyone came running around Them.

TEXT 85

মধ্যাহ্ন করিয়া আইলা দেবতা-মন্দিরে ।
নিজগণ প্রবেশি' কপাট দিল বহির্দ্বারে ॥ ৮৫ ॥.

madhyāhna kariyā āilā devatā-mandire
nija-gaṇa praveśi' kapāṭa dila bahir-dvāre

SYNONYMS

madhyāhna kariyā—performing bathing, etc; *āilā*—came back; *devatā-mandire*—to the temple of the Lord; *nija-gaṇa praveśi'*—allowing His own men; *kapāṭa dila*—shut; *bahir-dvāre*—the outside door.

TRANSLATION

After finishing Their baths, They returned at noon to the temple. Admitting His own men, Śrī Nityānanda Prabhu closed the outside door.

TEXT 86

তবে গোপীনাথ দুইপ্রভুরে ভিক্ষা করাইল ।
প্রভুর শেষ প্রসাদান্ন সবে বাঁটি' খাইল ॥ ৮৬ ॥

tabe gopīnātha dui-prabhure bhikṣā karāila
prabhura śeṣa prasādānna sabe bāṅṭi' khāila

SYNONYMS

tabe—thereupon; *gopīnātha*—Gopīnātha Ācārya; *dui-prabhure*—unto the two Lords Caitanya Mahāprabhu and Nityānanda Prabhu; *bhikṣā karāila*—gave *prasāda* to eat; *prabhura*—of the Lord; *śeṣa*—the remnants; *prasāda-anna*—food; *sabe*—all of them; *bāṅṭi'*—sharing; *khāila*—ate.

TRANSLATION

Gopīnātha Ācārya then brought prasāda for the two Lords to eat, and after They ate, the remnants of the food were distributed to all the devotees.

TEXT 87

শুনি' শুনি' লোক-সব আসি' বহির্দ্বারে ।
'হরি' 'হরি' বলি' লোক কোলাহল করে ॥ ৮৭ ॥

śuni' śuni' loka-saba āsi' bahir-dvāre
'hari' 'hari' bali' loka kolāhala kare

SYNONYMS

śuni' śuni'—hearing this; *loka-saba*—all the people; *āsi'*—coming there; *bahir-dvāre*—to the outside door; *hari hari*—the holy name of the Lord; *bali'*—chanted; *loka*—all the people; *kolāhala*—tumultuous sound; *kare*—made.

TRANSLATION

Hearing about this, everyone there came to the outside door and began chanting the holy name, "Hari! Hari!" Thus there was a tumultuous sound.

TEXT 88

তবে মহাপ্রভু দ্বার করাইল মোচন।
আনন্দে আসিয়া লোক পাইল দরশন ॥ ৮৮ ॥

tabe mahāprabhu dvāra karāila mocana
ānande āsiyā loka pāila daraśana

SYNONYMS

tabe—thereupon; *mahāprabhu*—Śrī Caitanya Mahāprabhu; *dvāra*—the door; *karāila*—made; *mocana*—opening; *ānande*—in great pleasure; *āsiyā*—coming; *loka*—all the people; *pāila*—got; *daraśana*—sight.

TRANSLATION

After lunch, Śrī Caitanya Mahāprabhu made them open the door. In this way everyone received His audience with great pleasure.

TEXT 89

এইমত সন্ধ্যা পর্যন্ত লোক আসে, যায়।
'বৈষ্ণব' হইল লোক, সবে নাচে, গায় ॥ ৮৯ ॥

ei-mata sandhyā paryanta loka āse, yāya
'vaiṣṇava' ha-ila loka, sabe nāce, gāya

SYNONYMS

ei-mata—in this way; *sandhyā paryanta*—until evening; *loka*—people; *āse yāya*—come and go; *vaiṣṇava*—devotees; *ha-ila*—became; *loka*—all the people; *sabe*—all of them; *nāce*—dance; *gāya*—and chant.

TRANSLATION

The people came and went until evening, and all of them became Vaiṣṇava devotees and began to chant and dance.

TEXT 90

এইরূপে সেই ঠাঞি ভক্তগণ-সঙ্গে।
সেই রাত্রি গোঙাইলা কৃষ্ণকথা-রঙ্গে ॥ ৯০ ॥

ei-rūpe sei ṭhāñi bhakta-gaṇa-saṅge
sei rātri goṅāilā kṛṣṇa-kathā-raṅge

SYNONYMS

ei-rūpe—in this way; *sei ṭhāñi*—in that place; *bhakta-gaṇa-saṅge*—with the devotees; *sei rātri*—that night; *goṅāilā*—passed; *kṛṣṇa-kathā-raṅge*—in great pleasure discussing Lord Kṛṣṇa.

TRANSLATION

Śrī Caitanya Mahāprabhu then passed the night there and discussed the pastimes of Lord Kṛṣṇa with His devotees with great pleasure.

TEXT 91

প্রাতঃকালে স্নান করি' করিলা গমন ।
ভক্তগণে বিদায় দিলা করি' আলিঙ্গন ॥ ৯১ ॥

prātaḥ-kāle snāna kari' karilā gamana
bhakta-gaṇe vidāya dilā kari' āliṅgana

SYNONYMS

prātaḥ-kāle—in the morning; *snāna*—bath; *kari'*—after taking; *karilā*—started; *gamana*—tour; *bhakta-gaṇe*—to all the devotees; *vidāya*—farewell; *dilā*—gave; *kari'*—doing; *āliṅgana*—embracing.

TRANSLATION

The next morning, after taking His bath, Śrī Caitanya Mahāprabhu started on His South Indian tour. He bade farewell to the devotees by embracing them.

TEXT 92

মূর্চ্ছিত হঞা সবে ভুমিতে পড়িলা ।
তাঁহা-সবা পানে প্রভু ফিরি' না চাহিলা ॥ ৯২ ॥

mūrcchita hañā sabe bhumite paḍilā
tāṅhā-sabā pāne prabhu phiri' nā cāhilā

SYNONYMS

mūrcchita hañā—becoming unconscious; *sabe*—all; *bhumite*—on the ground; *paḍilā*—fell down; *tāṅhā-sabā*—all of them; *pāne*—toward; *prabhu*—Lord Śrī Caitanya Mahāprabhu; *phiri'*—turning; *nā*—not; *cāhilā*—saw.

TRANSLATION

Although they all fell to the ground unconscious, the Lord did not turn to see them but proceeded onward.

TEXT 93

বিচ্ছেদে ব্যাকুল প্রভু চলিলা দুঃখী হঞা।
পাছে কৃষ্ণদাস যায় জলপাত্র লঞা॥ ৯৩॥

vicchede vyākula prabhu calilā duḥkhī hañā
pāche kṛṣṇadāsa yāya jala-pātra lañā

SYNONYMS

vicchede—in separation; *vyākula*—perturbed; *prabhu*—Lord Śrī Caitanya Mahāprabhu; *calilā*—went on; *duḥkhī*—unhappy; *hañā*—becoming; *pāche*—just behind; *kṛṣṇa-dāsa*—His servant named Kṛṣṇadāsa; *yāya*—went; *jala-pātra*—the water pot; *lañā*—taking.

TRANSLATION

In separation, the Lord became very perturbed and walked on unhappily. His servant, Kṛṣṇadāsa, who was carrying His water pot, followed behind.

TEXT 94

ভক্তগণ উপবাসী তাহাঁই রহিলা।
আর দিনে দুঃখী হঞা নীলাচলে আইলা॥ ৯৪॥

bhakta-gaṇa upavāsī tāhāṅi rahilā
āra dine duḥkhī hañā nīlācale āilā

SYNONYMS

bhakta-gaṇa—the devotees; *upavāsī*—fasting; *tāhāṅi*—there; *rahilā*—remained; *āra dine*—on the next day; *duḥkhī*—unhappy; *hañā*—becoming; *nīlācale*—to Jagannātha Purī; *āilā*—returned.

TRANSLATION

All the devotees remained there and fasted, but the next day they all unhappily returned to Jagannātha Purī.

TEXT 95

মত্তসিংহ-প্রায় প্রভু করিলা গমন।
প্রেমাবেশে যায় করি' নাম-সংকীর্তন॥ ৯৫॥

matta-siṁha-prāya prabhu karilā gamana
premāveśe yāya kari' nāma-saṅkīrtana

SYNONYMS

matta-siṁha—a mad lion; *prāya*—almost like; *prabhu*—Lord Śrī Caitanya Mahāprabhu; *karilā*—did; *gamana*—touring; *prema-āveśe*—in ecstatic love; *yāya*—goes; *kari'*—performing; *nāma-saṅkīrtana*—chanting Kṛṣṇa's name.

TRANSLATION

Almost like a mad lion, Lord Śrī Caitanya Mahāprabhu went on His tour filled with ecstatic love and performing saṅkīrtana, chanting Kṛṣṇa's names as follows.

TEXT 96

কৃষ্ণ ! কৃষ্ণ ! কৃষ্ণ ! কৃষ্ণ ! কৃষ্ণ ! কৃষ্ণ ! কৃষ্ণ ! হে ।
কৃষ্ণ ! কৃষ্ণ ! কৃষ্ণ ! কৃষ্ণ ! কৃষ্ণ ! কৃষ্ণ ! কৃষ্ণ ! হে ॥
কৃষ্ণ ! কৃষ্ণ ! কৃষ্ণ ! কৃষ্ণ ! কৃষ্ণ ! কৃষ্ণ ! রক্ষ মাম্ ।
কৃষ্ণ ! কৃষ্ণ ! কৃষ্ণ ! কৃষ্ণ ! কৃষ্ণ ! কৃষ্ণ ! পাহি মাম্ ॥
রাম ! রাঘব ! রাম ! রাঘব ! রাম ! রাঘব ! রক্ষ মাম্ ।
কৃষ্ণ ! কেশব ! কৃষ্ণ ! কেশব ! কৃষ্ণ ! কেশব ! পাহি মাম্ ॥

kṛṣṇa! kṛṣṇa! kṛṣṇa! kṛṣṇa! kṛṣṇa! kṛṣṇa! kṛṣṇa! he
kṛṣṇa! kṛṣṇa! kṛṣṇa! kṛṣṇa! kṛṣṇa! kṛṣṇa! kṛṣṇa! he
kṛṣṇa! kṛṣṇa! kṛṣṇa! kṛṣṇa! kṛṣṇa! kṛṣṇa! rakṣa mām
kṛṣṇa! kṛṣṇa! kṛṣṇa! kṛṣṇa! kṛṣṇa! kṛṣṇa! pāhi mām
rāma! rāghava! rāma! rāghava! rāma! rāghava! rakṣa mām
kṛṣṇa! keśava! kṛṣṇa! keśava! kṛṣṇa! keśava! pāhi mām

SYNONYMS

kṛṣṇa—Lord Kṛṣṇa; *he*—O; *rakṣa*—please protect; *mām*—me; *pāhi*—please maintain; *rāma*—Lord Rāma; *rāghava*—descendant of King Raghu; *keśava*—killer of the Keśī demon.

TRANSLATION

The Lord chanted:

Kṛṣṇa! Kṛṣṇa! Kṛṣṇa! Kṛṣṇa! Kṛṣṇa! Kṛṣṇa! Kṛṣṇa! he
Kṛṣṇa! Kṛṣṇa! Kṛṣṇa! Kṛṣṇa! Kṛṣṇa! Kṛṣṇa! Kṛṣṇa! he
Kṛṣṇa! Kṛṣṇa! Kṛṣṇa! Kṛṣṇa! Kṛṣṇa! Kṛṣṇa! rakṣa mām
Kṛṣṇa! Kṛṣṇa! Kṛṣṇa! Kṛṣṇa! Kṛṣṇa! Kṛṣṇa! pāhi mām

That is, "O Lord Kṛṣṇa, please protect Me and maintain Me." He also chanted:

Rāma! Rāghava! Rāma! Rāghava! Rāma! Rāghava! rakṣa mām
Kṛṣṇa! Keśava! Kṛṣṇa! Keśava! Kṛṣṇa! Keśava! pāhi mām

That is, "O Lord Rāma, descendant of King Raghu, please protect Me. O Kṛṣṇa, O Keśava, killer of the Keśī demon, please maintain Me."

TEXT 97

এই শ্লোক পড়ি' পথে চলিলা গৌরহরি ।
লোক দেখি' পথে কহে,— বল 'হরি' 'হরি' ॥ ৯৭ ॥

ei śloka paḍi' pathe calilā gaurahari
loka dekhi' pathe kahe,——bala 'hari' 'hari'

SYNONYMS

ei śloka paḍi'—reciting this verse *kṛṣṇa! kṛṣṇa!; pathe*—on the way; *calilā*—went; *gaura-hari*—Lord Śrī Caitanya Mahāprabhu; *loka dekhi'*—seeing other people; *pathe*—on the way; *kahe*—He says; *bala*—say; *hari hari*—the holy name of Lord Hari.

TRANSLATION

Chanting this verse, Lord Śrī Caitanya Mahāprabhu, known as Gaurahari, went on His way. As soon as He saw someone, He would request him to chant, "Hari! Hari!"

TEXT 98

সেই লোক প্রেমমত্ত হঞা বলে 'হরি' 'কৃষ্ণ' ।
প্রভুর পাছে সঙ্গে যায় দর্শন-সতৃষ্ণ ॥ ৯৮ ॥

sei loka prema-matta hañā bale 'hari' 'kṛṣṇa'
prabhura pāche saṅge yāya darśana-satṛṣṇa

SYNONYMS

sei loka—that person; *prema-matta*—maddened in love of Godhead; *hañā*—becoming; *bale*—says; *hari kṛṣṇa*—the holy name of Lord Hari and Lord Kṛṣṇa; *prabhura pāche*—behind the Lord; *saṅge*—with Him; *yāya*—goes; *darśana-satṛṣṇa*—being very eager to see Him.

TRANSLATION

Whoever heard Lord Caitanya Mahāprabhu chant, "Hari, Hari," also chanted the holy name of Lord Hari and Kṛṣṇa. In this way, they all followed the Lord, very eager to see Him.

TEXT 99

কতক্ষণে রহি' প্রভু তারে আলিঙ্গিয়া ।
বিদায় করিল তারে শক্তি সঞ্চারিয়া ॥ ৯৯ ॥

kata-kṣaṇe rahi' prabhu tāre āliṅgiyā
vidāya karila tāre śakti sañcāriyā

SYNONYMS

kata-kṣaṇe rahi'—after remaining for some time; *prabhu*—Lord Śrī Caitanya Mahāprabhu; *tāre*—them; *āliṅgiyā*—embracing; *vidāya karila*—bade farewell; *tāre*—in them; *śakti*—spiritual potency; *sañcāriyā*—investing.

TRANSLATION

After some time, the Lord would embrace these people and bid them to return home, after investing them with spiritual potency.

PURPORT

In his *Amṛta-pravāha-bhāṣya,* Śrīla Bhaktivinoda Ṭhākura explains that this spiritual potency is the essence of the pleasure potency and the eternity potency. By these two potencies, one is empowered with devotional service. Lord Kṛṣṇa Himself, or His representative, the unalloyed devotee, can mercifully bestow these combined potencies upon any man. Being thus endowed with such potencies, one can become an unalloyed devotee of the Lord. Anyone favored by Lord Śrī Caitanya Mahāprabhu was empowered with this *bhakti-śakti.* Thus the Lord's followers were able to preach Kṛṣṇa consciousness by divine grace.

TEXT 100

সেইজন নিজ-গ্রামে করিয়া গমন ।
'কৃষ্ণ' বলি' হাসে, কান্দে, নাচে অনুক্ষণ ॥ ১০০ ॥

sei-jana nija-grāme kariyā gamana
'kṛṣṇa' bali' hāse, kānde, nāce anukṣaṇa

SYNONYMS

sei-jana—that person; *nija-grāme*—to his own village; *kariyā gamana*—returning there; *kṛṣṇa bali'*—saying the holy name of Lord Kṛṣṇa; *hāse*—laughs; *kānde*—cries; *nāce*—dances; *anukṣaṇa*—always.

TRANSLATION

Being thus empowered, they would return to their own villages, always chanting the holy name of Kṛṣṇa and sometimes laughing, crying and dancing.

TEXT 101

যারে দেখে, তারে কহে,—কহ কৃষ্ণনাম।
এইমত 'বৈষ্ণব' কৈল সব নিজ-গ্রাম ॥ ১০১ ॥

yāre dekhe, tāre kahe,——kaha kṛṣṇa-nāma
ei-mata 'vaiṣṇava' kaila saba nija-grāma

SYNONYMS

yāre dekhe—whomever he meets; *tāre*—to him; *kahe*—he says; *kaha kṛṣṇa-nāma*—kindly chant the Hare Kṛṣṇa *mantra; ei-mata*—in this way; *vaiṣṇava*—devotees of the Supreme Personality of Godhead; *kaila*—made; *saba*—all; *nija-grāma*—his own village.

TRANSLATION

These empowered people used to request everyone and anyone—whomever they saw—to chant the holy name of Kṛṣṇa. In this way all the villagers would also become devotees of the Supreme Personality of Godhead.

PURPORT

In order to become an empowered preacher, one must be favored by Lord Śrī Caitanya Mahāprabhu or His devotee, the spiritual master. One must also request everyone to chant the *mahā-mantra*. In this way, such a person can convert others to Vaiṣṇavism, showing them how to become pure devotees of the Supreme Personality of Godhead.

TEXT 102

গ্রামান্তর হৈতে দেখিতে আইল যত জন।
তাঁর দর্শন-কৃপায় হয় তাঁর সম ॥ ১০২ ॥

grāmāntara haite dekhite āila yata jana
tāṅra darśana-kṛpāya haya tāṅra sama

SYNONYMS

grāma-antara haite—from different villages; *dekhite*—to see; *āila*—came; *yata jana*—all the persons; *tāṅra*—his; *darśana-kṛpāya*—by the mercy of seeing him; *haya*—become; *tāṅra sama*—similar Vaiṣṇavas.

TRANSLATION

Simply by seeing such empowered individuals, people from different villages would become like them by the mercy of their glance.

TEXT 103

সেই যাই' গ্রামের লোক বৈষ্ণব করয় ।
অন্যগ্রামী আসি' তাঁরে দেখি' বৈষ্ণব হয় ॥ ১০৩ ॥

sei yāi' grāmera loka vaiṣṇava karaya
anya-grāmī āsi' tāṅre dekhi' vaiṣṇava haya

SYNONYMS

sei—that Vaiṣṇava; *yāi'*—going to his own village; *grāmera loka*—all the people of the village; *vaiṣṇava*—devotees; *karaya*—makes; *anya-grāmī*—inhabitants from different villages; *āsi'*—coming there; *tāṅre dekhi'*—by seeing them; *vaiṣṇava haya*—become devotees.

TRANSLATION

When these individuals returned to their villages, they also converted others into devotees. When others came to see them, they also were converted.

TEXT 104

সেই যাই' আর গ্রামে করে উপদেশ ।
এইমত 'বৈষ্ণব' হৈল সব দক্ষিণ-দেশ ॥ ১০৪ ॥

sei yāi' āra grāme kare upadeśa
ei-mata 'vaiṣṇava' haila saba dakṣiṇa-deśa

SYNONYMS

sei—that man; *yāi'*—going; *āra*—different; *grāme*—to the villages; *kare*—gives; *upadeśa*—instruction; *ei-mata*—in this way; *vaiṣṇava*—devotees; *haila*—became; *saba*—all; *dakṣiṇa-deśa*—the people of South India.

TRANSLATION

In this way, as those men went from one village to another, all the people of South India became devotees.

TEXT 105

এইমত পথে যাইতে শত শত জন।
'বৈষ্ণব' করেন তাঁরে করি' আলিঙ্গন ॥ ১০৫ ॥

ei-mata pathe yāite śata śata jana
'vaiṣṇava' karena tāṅre kari' āliṅgana

SYNONYMS

ei-mata—in this way; *pathe*—on the way; *yāite*—while passing; *śata śata*—hundreds and hundreds; *jana*—persons; *vaiṣṇava*—devotees; *karena*—makes; *tāṅre*—Him; *kari'*—doing; *āliṅgana*—embracing.

TRANSLATION

Thus many hundreds of people became Vaiṣṇavas when they passed the Lord on the way and were embraced by Him.

TEXT 106

যেই গ্রামে রহি' ভিক্ষা করেন যাঁর ঘরে।
সেই গ্রামের যত লোক আইসে দেখিবারে ॥১০৬॥

yei grāme rahi' bhikṣā karena yāṅra ghare
sei grāmera yata loka āise dekhibāre

SYNONYMS

yei grāme—in whatever village; *rahi'*—staying; *bhikṣā*—alms; *karena*—accepts; *yāṅra*—whose; *ghare*—at home; *sei*—that; *grāmera*—of the village; *yata loka*—all the persons; *āise*—come; *dekhibāre*—to see.

TRANSLATION

In whatever village Śrī Caitanya Mahāprabhu stayed to accept alms, many people came to see Him.

TEXT 107

প্রভুর কৃপায় হয় মহাভাগবত।
সেই সব আচার্য হঞা তারিল জগৎ ॥ ১০৭ ॥

prabhura kṛpāya haya mahābhāgavata
sei saba ācārya hañā tārila jagat

SYNONYMS

prabhura kṛpāya—by the mercy of the Lord; *haya*—become; *mahā-bhāgavata*—first-class devotees; *sei saba*—all such persons; *ācārya*—teachers; *hañā*—becoming; *tārila*—liberated; *jagat*—the whole world.

TRANSLATION

By the mercy of the Supreme Lord, Śrī Caitanya Mahāprabhu, everyone became a first-class devotee. Later they became teachers or spiritual masters and liberated the entire world.

TEXT 108

এইমত কৈলা যাবৎ গেলা সেতুবন্ধে ।
সর্বদেশ 'বৈষ্ণব' হৈল প্রভুর সম্বন্ধে ॥ ১০৮ ॥

ei-mata kailā yāvat gelā setubandhe
sarva-deśa 'vaiṣṇava' haila prabhura sambandhe

SYNONYMS

ei-mata—in this way; *kailā*—performed; *yāvat*—until; *gelā*—went; *setu-bandhe*—to the southernmost part of India; *sarva-deśa*—all the countries; *vaiṣṇava*—devotees; *haila*—became; *prabhura*—Lord Śrī Caitanya Mahāprabhu; *sambandhe*—in connection with.

TRANSLATION

In this way the Lord went to the extreme southern part of India, and He converted all the provinces to Vaiṣṇavism.

TEXT 109

নবদ্বীপে যেই শক্তি না কৈলা প্রকাশে ।
সে শক্তি প্রকাশি' নিস্তারিল দক্ষিণদেশে ॥ ১০৯ ॥

navadvīpe yei śakti nā kailā prakāśe
se śakti prakāśi' nistārila dakṣiṇa-deśe

SYNONYMS

nava-dvīpe—at Navadvīpa; *yei*—that which; *śakti*—the potency; *nā*—not; *kailā*—did; *prakāśe*—manifestation; *se*—that; *śakti*—potency; *prakāśi'*—manifesting; *nistārila*—delivered; *dakṣiṇa-deśe*—South India.

TRANSLATION

Lord Śrī Caitanya Mahāprabhu did not manifest His spiritual potencies at Navadvīpa, but He did manifest them in South India and liberated all the people there.

PURPORT

At that time there were many *smārtas* (nondevotee followers of Vedic rituals) at the holy place of Navadvīpa, which was also the birthplace of Lord Śrī Caitanya Mahāprabhu. Followers of the *smṛti-śāstra* are called *smārtas*. Most of them are nondevotees, and their main business is following strictly the brahminical principles. However, they are not enlightened in devotional service. In Navadvīpa all the learned scholars are followers of the *smṛti-śāstra,* and Lord Caitanya Mahāprabhu did not attempt to convert them. Therefore the author has remarked that the spiritual potency Lord Śrī Caitanya Mahāprabhu did not manifest at Navadvīpa was by His grace manifest in South India. Thus everyone there became a Vaiṣṇava. By this it is to be understood that people are really interested in preaching in a favorable situation. If the candidates for conversion are too disturbing, a preacher may not attempt to spread Kṛṣṇa consciousness amongst them. It is better to go where the situation is more favorable. This Kṛṣṇa consciousness movement was first attempted in India, but the people of India, being absorbed in political thoughts, did not take to it. They were entranced by the political leaders. We preferred, therefore, to come to the West, following the order of our spiritual master, and by the grace of Lord Caitanya Mahāprabhu this movement is becoming successful.

TEXT 110

প্রভুকে যে ভজে, তারে তাঁর কৃপা হয়।
সেই সে এ-সব লীলা সত্য করি' লয় ॥ ১১০ ॥

prabhuke ye bhaje, tāre tāṅra kṛpā haya
sei se e-saba līlā satya kari' laya

SYNONYMS

prabhuke—Lord Śrī Caitanya Mahāprabhu; *ye*—anyone who; *bhaje*—worships; *tāre*—unto him; *tāṅra*—of Lord Caitanya Mahāprabhu; *kṛpā*—the mercy; *haya*—there is; *sei se*—such person; *e-saba*—all these; *līlā*—pastimes; *satya*—truth; *kari'*—accepting as; *laya*—takes.

TRANSLATION

Lord Śrī Caitanya Mahāprabhu's empowering of others can be understood by one who is actually a devotee of the Lord and who has received His mercy.

TEXT 111

অলৌকিক-লীলায় যার না হয় বিশ্বাস।
ইহলোক, পরলোক তার হয় নাশ ॥ ১১১ ॥

alaukika-līlāya yāra nā haya viśvāsa
iha-loka, para-loka tāra haya nāśa

SYNONYMS

alaukika—uncommon; *līlāya*—in the pastimes; *yāra*—of someone; *nā*—not; *haya*—there is; *viśvāsa*—faith; *iha-loka*—in this world; *para-loka*—in the next world; *tāra*—of him; *haya*—there is; *nāśa*—destruction.

TRANSLATION

If one does not believe in the uncommon, transcendental pastimes of the Lord, he is vanquished both in this world and in the next.

TEXT 112

প্রথমেই কহিল প্রভুর যেরূপে গমন।
এইমত জানিহ যাবৎ দক্ষিণ-ভ্রমণ ॥ ১১২ ॥

prathamei kahila prabhura ye-rūpe gamana
ei-mata jāniha yāvat dakṣiṇa-bhramaṇa

SYNONYMS

prathamei—at the beginning; *kahila*—I have explained; *prabhura*—of Lord Śrī Caitanya Mahāprabhu; *ye-rūpe*—as; *gamana*—the touring; *ei-mata*—in this way; *jāniha*—you should know; *yāvat*—as long as; *dakṣiṇa-bhramaṇa*—touring in South India.

TRANSLATION

Whatever I have stated about the beginning of the Lord's movement should also be understood to hold for as long as the Lord toured South India.

TEXT 113

এইমত যাইতে যাইতে গেলা কূর্মস্থানে।
কূর্ম দেখি' কৈল তাঁরে স্তবন-প্রণামে ॥ ১১৩ ॥

ei-mata yāite yāite gelā kūrma-sthāne
kūrma dekhi' kaila tāṅre stavana-praṇāme

SYNONYMS

ei-mata—in this way; *yāite yāite*—while passing; *gelā*—He went; *kūrma-sthāne*—to the place of pilgrimage known as Kūrma-kṣetra; *kūrma dekhi'*—seeing Lord Kūrma; *kaila*—offered; *tāṅre*—unto Him; *stavana*—prayers; *praṇāme*—and obeisances.

TRANSLATION

When Lord Śrī Caitanya Mahāprabhu came to the holy place known as Kūrma-kṣetra, He saw the Deity and offered prayers and obeisances.

PURPORT

This Kūrma-sthāna is a well-known place of pilgrimage. There is a temple there of Kūrmadeva. In the *Prapannāmṛta* it is said that Lord Jagannātha took Śrī Rāmānujācārya from Jagannātha Purī and one night threw him to Kūrma-kṣetra. This Kūrma-kṣetra is situated on the line of the southern railway in India. One has to go to the railway station known as Cikā Kola Road. From this station one goes eight miles to the east to reach the holy place known as Kūrmācala. Those who speak the Telugu language consider this holy place very important. This statement is reported in the government gazette known as *Gañjāma Manual.* There is the Deity of Kūrma there, and Śrīla Rāmānujācārya was thrown from Jagannātha Purī to this place. At that time he thought that the Deity of Kūrma was Lord Śiva's deity; therefore he was fasting there. Later, when he understood that the *kūrma-mūrti* was another form of Lord Viṣṇu, he instituted very gorgeous worship of Lord Kūrma. This statement is found in the *Prapannāmṛta* (Chapter Thirty-six). This holy place of Kūrma-kṣetra, or Kūrma-sthāna, was actually reestablished by Śrīpāda Rāmānujācārya under the influence of Lord Jagannātha-deva at Jagannātha Purī. Later the temple came under the jurisdiction of the king of Vijaya-nagara. The Deity was worshiped by the Vaiṣṇavas of the Madhvācārya-sampradāya. In the temple there are some inscriptions said to be written by Śrī Narahari Tīrtha, who was in the disciplic succession of Madhvācārya. Śrīla Bhaktisiddhānta Sarasvatī Ṭhākura explains those inscriptions as follows: (1) Śrī Puruṣottama Yati appeared as the instructor of many learned men. He was a very favorite devotee of Lord Viṣṇu. (2) His preaching was accepted throughout the world with great respect, and by his power he would liberate many nondevotees with strong reason and logic. (3) He initiated Ānanda Tīrtha and converted many foolish men to accept *sannyāsa* and punished them with his rod. (4) All his writings and words are very potent. He gave people devotional service to Lord Viṣṇu, and liberation for elevation to the spiritual world. (5) His instructions in devotional service were able to elevate any man to the lotus feet of the Lord. (6) Narahari Tīrtha was also initiated by him, and he became the ruler of the Kaliṅga Province. (7) Narahari Tīrtha fought with the Śavaras, who were *caṇḍālas,* or hunters, and thus saved the temple of Kūrma. (8) Narahari Tīrtha was a very religious and powerful king. (9) He died in the Śaka Era 1203, in the month of Vaiśākha in the fortnight of the moon's waxing period, on the day of Ekādaśī, after the temple was constructed and dedicated to the holy name of Yogānanda Nṛsiṁhadeva. The tablet is dated 1281 A.D., 29 March, Saturday.

TEXT 114

প্রেমাবেশে হাসি' কান্দি' নৃত্য-গীত কৈল ।
দেখি' সর্ব লোকের চিত্তে চমৎকার হৈল ॥ ১১৪ ॥

premāveśe hāsi' kāndi' nṛtya-gīta kaila
dekhi' sarva lokera citte camatkāra haila

SYNONYMS

prema-āveśe—in great ecstasy of love of Godhead; *hāsi'*—laughing; *kāndi'*—crying; *nṛtya-gīta*—dancing and chanting; *kaila*—performed; *dekhi'*—seeing; *sarva lokera*—of all the people there; *citte*—within the hearts; *camatkāra*—astonishment; *haila*—there was.

TRANSLATION

While at this place, Lord Śrī Caitanya Mahāprabhu was in His usual ecstasy of love of Godhead and was laughing, crying, dancing and chanting. Everyone who saw Him was astonished.

TEXT 115

আশ্চর্য শুনিয়া লোক আইল দেখিবারে ।
প্রভুর রূপ-প্রেম দেখি' হৈলা চমৎকারে ॥ ১১৫ ॥

āścarya śuniyā loka āila dekhibāre
prabhura rūpa-prema dekhi' hailā camatkāre

SYNONYMS

āścarya—wonderful occurrence, *śuniyā*—hearing; *loka*—people; *āila*—came; *dekhibāre*—to see; *prabhura*—of Lord Śrī Caitanya Mahāprabhu; *rūpa*—beauty; *prema*—and love of Godhead; *dekhi'*—seeing; *hailā*—there was; *camatkāre*—astonishment.

TRANSLATION

After hearing of these wonderful occurrences, everyone came to see Him there. When they saw the beauty of the Lord and His ecstatic condition, they were all struck with wonder.

TEXT 116

দর্শনে 'বৈষ্ণব' হৈল, বলে 'কৃষ্ণ' 'হরি' ।
প্রেমাবেশে নাচে লোক ঊর্ধ্ব বাহু করি' ॥ ১১৬ ॥

darśane 'vaiṣṇava' haila, bale 'kṛṣṇa' 'hari'
premāveśe nāce loka ūrdhva bāhu kari'

SYNONYMS

darśane—in seeing; *vaiṣṇava haila*—they became devotees; *bale*—started to say; *kṛṣṇa*—Lord Kṛṣṇa; *hari*—Lord Hari; *prema-āveśe*—in the great ecstasy of love of Godhead; *nāce*—dance; *loka*—all the people; *ūrdhva bāhu kari'*—raising the arms.

TRANSLATION

Just by seeing Lord Caitanya Mahāprabhu, everyone became a devotee. They began to chant Kṛṣṇa and Hari and all the holy names. They all were merged in a great ecstasy of love, and they began to dance, raising their arms.

TEXT 117

কৃষ্ণনাম লোকমুখে শুনি' অবিরাম ।
সেই লোক 'বৈষ্ণব' কৈল অন্য সব গ্রাম ॥ ১১৭ ॥

kṛṣṇa-nāma loka-mukhe śuni' avirāma
sei loka 'vaiṣṇava' kaila anya saba grāma

SYNONYMS

kṛṣṇa-nāma—the holy name of Lord Kṛṣṇa; *loka-mukhe*—from the mouth of those people; *śuni'*—hearing; *avirāma*—always; *sei loka*—those persons; *vaiṣṇava*—devotees; *kaila*—made; *anya*—other; *saba*—all; *grāma*—villages.

TRANSLATION

Always hearing them chant the holy names of Lord Kṛṣṇa, others also became Vaiṣṇavas in those villages.

TEXT 118

এইমত পরম্পরায় দেশ 'বৈষ্ণব' হৈল ।
কৃষ্ণনামামৃত-বন্যায় দেশ ভাসাইল ॥ ১১৮ ॥

ei-mata paramparāya deśa 'vaiṣṇava' haila
kṛṣṇa-nāmāmṛta-vanyāya deśa bhāsāila

SYNONYMS

ei-mata—in this way; *paramparāya*—by disciplic succession; *deśa*—the country; *vaiṣṇava haila*—became devotees; *kṛṣṇa-nāma-amṛta*—of the nectar of the holy name of Kṛṣṇa; *vanyāya*—in the inundation; *deśa*—the whole country; *bhāsāila*—overflooded.

TRANSLATION

By hearing the holy name of Kṛṣṇa, the entire country became Vaiṣṇava. It was as if the nectar of the holy name of Kṛṣṇa overflooded the entire country.

TEXT 119

কতক্ষণে প্রভু যদি বাহ্য প্রকাশিলা।
কূর্মের সেবক বহু সম্মান করিলা ॥ ১১৯ ॥

kata-kṣaṇe prabhu yadi bāhya prakāśilā
kūrmera sevaka bahu sammāna karilā

SYNONYMS

kata-kṣaṇe—after some time; *prabhu*—Lord Caitanya Mahāprabhu; *yadi*—when; *bāhya*—external consciousness; *prakāśilā*—manifested; *kūrmera*—of the Lord Kūrma Deity; *sevaka*—a servant; *bahu*—much; *sammāna*—respect; *karilā*—showed.

TRANSLATION

After some time, when Lord Śrī Caitanya Mahāprabhu manifested His external consciousness, a priest of the Lord Kūrma Deity gave Him various offerings.

TEXT 120

যেই গ্রামে যায় তাহাঁ এই ব্যবহার।
এক ঠাঞি কহিল, না কহিব আর বার ॥ ১২০ ॥

yei grāme yāya tāhāṅ ei vyavahāra
eka ṭhāñi kahila, nā kahiba āra bāra

SYNONYMS

yei grāme—to whichever village; *yāya*—He goes; *tāhāṅ*—there; *ei*—this; *vyavahāra*—behavior; *eka ṭhāñi*—one place; *kahila*—described; *nā*—not; *kahiba*—shall describe; *āra*—another; *bāra*—time.

TRANSLATION

Śrī Caitanya Mahāprabhu's mode of preaching has already been explained, and I shall not repeat the explanation. In whichever village the Lord entered, His behavior was the same.

TEXT 121

'কূর্ম'-নামে সেই গ্রামে বৈদিক ব্রাহ্মণ ।
বহু শ্রদ্ধা-ভক্ত্যে কৈল প্রভুর নিমন্ত্রণ ॥ ১২১ ॥

'kūrma'-nāme sei grāme vaidika brāhmaṇa
bahu śraddhā-bhaktye kaila prabhura nimantraṇa

SYNONYMS

kūrma-nāme—of the name Kūrma; *sei*—that; *grāme*—in the village; *vaidika brāhmaṇa*—a Vedic *brāhmaṇa; bahu*—much; *śraddhā-bhaktye*—with faith and devotion; *kaila*—made; *prabhura*—of Śrī Caitanya Mahāprabhu; *nimantraṇa*—invitation.

TRANSLATION

In one village there was a Vedic brāhmaṇa named Kūrma. He invited Lord Caitanya Mahāprabhu to his home with great respect and devotion.

TEXT 122

ঘরে আনি' প্রভুর কৈল পাদ প্রক্ষালন ।
সেই জল বংশ-সহিত করিল ভক্ষণ ॥ ১২২ ॥

ghare āni' prabhura kaila pāda prakṣālana
sei jala vaṁśa-sahita karila bhakṣaṇa

SYNONYMS

ghare āni'—after bringing Him home; *prabhura*—of Lord Śrī Caitanya Mahāprabhu; *kaila*—did; *pāda prakṣālana*—washing of the lotus feet; *sei jala*—that water; *vaṁśa-sahita*—with all the family members; *karila bhakṣaṇa*—drank.

TRANSLATION

This brāhmaṇa brought Lord Caitanya Mahāprabhu to his home, washed His lotus feet and, with his family members, drank that water.

TEXT 123

অনেকপ্রকার স্নেহে ভিক্ষা করাইল ।
গোসাঞির শেষান্ন সবংশে খাইল ॥ ১২৩ ॥

aneka-prakāra snehe bhikṣā karāila
gosāñira śeṣānna sa-vaṁśe khāila

SYNONYMS

aneka-prakāra—various kinds; *snehe*—in affection; *bhikṣā*—food; *karāila*—made Him eat; *gosāñira*—of Lord Caitanya Mahāprabhu; *śeṣa-anna*—remnants of food; *sa-vaṁśe*—with all the members of the family; *khāila*—ate.

TRANSLATION

That Kūrma brāhmaṇa with great affection and respect made Śrī Caitanya Mahāprabhu eat all kinds of food. After that, the remnants were shared by all the members of the family.

TEXT 124

'যেই পাদপদ্ম তোমার ব্রহ্মা ধ্যান করে ।
সেই পাদপদ্ম সাক্ষাৎ আইল মোর ঘরে ॥ ১২৪ ॥

'yei pāda-padma tomāra brahmā dhyāna kare
sei pāda-padma sākṣāt āila mora ghare

SYNONYMS

yei—those; *pāda-padma*—lotus feet; *tomāra*—Your; *brahmā*—Lord Brahmā; *dhyāna kare*—meditates on; *sei pāda-padma*—those lotus feet; *sākṣāt*—directly; *āila*—have come; *mora*—my; *ghare*—to the home.

TRANSLATION

The brāhmaṇa then began to pray: "O my Lord, Your lotus feet are meditated upon by Lord Brahmā, and these very lotus feet have come into my home.

TEXT 125

মোর ভাগ্যের সীমা না যায় কহন ।
আজি মোর শ্লাঘ্য হৈল জন্ম-কুল-ধন ॥ ১২৫ ॥

mora bhāgyera sīmā nā yāya kahana
āji mora ślāghya haila janma-kula-dhana

SYNONYMS

mora—my; *bhāgyera*—of the fortune; *sīmā*—the limit; *nā*—not; *yāya*—possible; *kahana*—describing; *āji*—today; *mora*—my; *ślāghya*—glorious; *haila*—became; *janma*—birth; *kula*—family; *dhana*—and wealth.

TRANSLATION

"My dear Lord, there is no limit to my great fortune. It cannot be described. Today my family, birth and riches have all been glorified."

TEXT 126

কৃপা কর, প্রভু, মোরে, যাঙ তোমা-সঙ্গে ।
সহিতে না পারি দুঃখ বিষয়-তরঙ্গে ॥' ১২৬ ॥

kṛpā kara, prabhu, more, yāṅ tomā-saṅge
sahite nā pāri duḥkha viṣaya-taraṅge'

SYNONYMS

kṛpā kara—kindly show favor; *prabhu*—O my Lord; *more*—unto me; *yāṅ*—I go; *tomā-saṅge*—with You; *sahite nā pāri*—I cannot tolerate; *duḥkha*—the troubles; *viṣaya-taraṅge*—in the waves of materialistic life.

TRANSLATION

The brāhmaṇa begged Lord Caitanya Mahāprabhu, "My dear Lord, kindly show me favor and let me go with You. I can no longer tolerate the waves of misery caused by materialistic life."

PURPORT

This statement is applicable for everyone, regardless of how rich or prosperous one may be. Narottama dāsa Ṭhākura has confirmed this statement: *saṁsāra-viṣānale, divā-niśi hiyā jvale.* He states that the materialistic way of life causes a burning in the heart. One cannot make any provisions for the troublesome life of the material world. It is a fact that one may be very happy as far as riches are concerned and one may be very opulent in every respect, yet one has to manage the *viṣayas* to meet the demands of the body and of so many family members and subordinates. One has to take so much trouble to minister to others. Narottama dāsa Ṭhākura therefore prays: *viṣaya chāḍiyā kabe śuddha ha'be mana.* Thus one must become freed from the materialistic way of life. One has to merge himself in the ocean of transcendental bliss. In other words, one cannot relish transcendental bliss without being freed from the materialistic way of life. It appears that the *brāhmaṇa* named Kūrma was materially very happy, for he expressed his family tradition as *janma-kula-dhana.* Now, being glorified, he wanted to leave all these material opulences. He wanted to travel with Śrī Caitanya Mahāprabhu. According to the Vedic way of civilization, one should leave his family after attaining fifty years of age and go to the forest of Vṛndāvana to devote the rest of his life to the service of the Lord.

TEXT 127

প্রভু কহে,—"ঐছে বাত্ কভু না কহিবা ।
গৃহে রহি' কৃষ্ণ-নাম নিরন্তর লৈবা ॥ ১২৭ ॥

prabhu kahe,——"aiche vāt kabhu nā kahibā
gṛhe rahi' kṛṣṇa-nāma nirantara laibā

SYNONYMS

prabhu kahe—Śrī Caitanya Mahāprabhu said; *aiche vāt*—such words; *kabhu*—at any time; *nā kahibā*—you should not speak; *gṛhe rahi'*—staying at home; *kṛṣṇa-nāma*—the holy name of the Lord; *nirantara*—always; *laibā*—you should chant.

TRANSLATION

Śrī Caitanya Mahāprabhu replied, "Don't speak like that again. Better to remain at home and chant the holy name of Kṛṣṇa always.

PURPORT

It is not advisable in this age of Kali to leave one's family suddenly, for people are not trained as proper *brahmacārīs* and *gṛhasthas.* Therefore Śrī Caitanya Mahāprabhu advised the *brāhmaṇa* not to be too eager to give up family life. It would be better to remain with his family and try to become purified by chanting the Hare Kṛṣṇa *mahā-mantra* regularly under the direction of a spiritual master. This is the instruction of Śrī Caitanya Mahāprabhu. If this principle is followed by everyone, there is no need to accept *sannyāsa*. In the next verse Śrī Caitanya Mahāprabhu advises everyone to become an ideal householder by offenselessly chanting the Hare Kṛṣṇa *mantra* and teaching the same principle to everyone he meets.

TEXT 128

যারে দেখ, তারে কহ 'কৃষ্ণ'-উপদেশ ।
আমার আজ্ঞায় গুরু হঞা তার' এই দেশ ॥ ১২৮ ॥

yāre dekha, tāre kaha 'kṛṣṇa'-upadeśa
āmāra ājñāya guru hañā tāra' ei deśa

SYNONYMS

yāre—whomever; *dekha*—you meet; *tāre*—him; *kaha*—tell; *kṛṣṇa-upadeśa*—the instruction of *Bhagavad-gītā* as it is spoken by the Lord or of *Śrīmad-Bhāgavatam,* which advises one to worship Śrī Kṛṣṇa; *āmāra ājñāya*—under My order; *guru hañā*—becoming a spiritual master; *tāra'*—deliver; *ei deśa*—this country.

TRANSLATION

"Instruct everyone to follow the orders of Lord Śrī Kṛṣṇa as they are given in Bhagavad-gītā and Śrīmad-Bhāgavatam. In this way become a spiritual master and try to liberate everyone in this land."

PURPORT

This is the sublime mission of the International Society for Krishna Consciousness. Many people come and inquire whether they have to give up family life to join the Society, but that is not our mission. One can remain comfortably in his residence. We simply request everyone to chant the *mahā-mantra:* Hare Kṛṣṇa, Hare Kṛṣṇa, Kṛṣṇa Kṛṣṇa, Hare Hare/ Hare Rāma, Hare Rāma, Rāma Rāma, Hare Hare. If one is a little literate and can read *Bhagavad-gītā As It Is* and *Śrīmad-Bhāgavatam,* that is so much the better. These works are now available in an English translation and are done very authoritatively to appeal to all classes of men. Instead of living engrossed in material activities, people throughout the world should take advantage of this movement and chant the Hare Kṛṣṇa *mahā-mantra* at home with their families. One should also refrain from sinful activities—illicit sex, meat-eating, gambling and intoxication. Out of these four items, illicit sex is very sinful. Every person must get married. Every woman especially must get married. If the women outnumber the men, some men can accept more than one wife. In that way there will be no prostitution in society. If men can marry more than one wife, illicit sex life will be stopped. One can also produce many nice preparations to offer Kṛṣṇa—grain, fruit, flowers and milk. Why should one indulge in unnecessary meat-eating and maintain horrible slaughterhouses? What is the use of smoking and drinking tea and coffee? People are already intoxicated by material enjoyment, and if they indulge in further intoxication, what chance is there for self-realization? Similarly, one should not partake in gambling and unnecessarily agitate the mind. The real purpose of human life is to attain the spiritual platform and return to Godhead. That is the *summum bonum* of spiritual realization. The Kṛṣṇa consciousness movement is trying to elevate human society to the perfection of life by pursuing the method described by Śrī Caitanya Mahāprabhu in His advice to the *brāhmaṇa* Kūrma. That is, one should stay at home, chant the Hare Kṛṣṇa *mantra* and preach the instructions of Kṛṣṇa as they are given in *Bhagavad-gītā* and *Śrīmad-Bhāgavatam.*

TEXT 129

কভু না বাধিবে তোমার বিষয়-তরঙ্গ ।
পুনরপি এই ঠাঞি পাবে মোর সঙ্গ ॥" ১২৯ ॥

kabhu nā vādhibe tomāra viṣaya-taraṅga
punarapi ei ṭhāñi pābe mora saṅga"

SYNONYMS

kabhu—at any time; *nā*—not; *vādhibe*—will obstruct; *tomāra*—your; *viṣaya-taraṅga*—materialistic way of life; *punarapi*—again; *ei ṭhāñi*—at this place; *pābe*—you will get; *mora*—My; *saṅga*—association.

TRANSLATION

Śrī Caitanya Mahāprabhu further advised the brāhmaṇa Kūrma, "If you follow this instruction, your materialistic life at home will not obstruct your spiritual advancement. Indeed, if you follow these regulative principles, we will again meet here, or, rather, you will never lose My company."

PURPORT

This is an opportunity for everyone. If one simply follows the instructions of Śrī Caitanya Mahāprabhu, under the guidance of His representative, and chants the Hare Kṛṣṇa *mantra,* teaching everyone as far as possible the same principle, the contamination of the materialistic way of life will not even touch him. It does not matter whether one lives in a holy place like Vṛndāvana, Navadvīpa or Jagannātha Purī or in the midst of European cities where the materialistic way of life is very prominent. If a devotee follows the instructions of Śrī Caitanya Mahāprabhu, he lives in the company of the Lord. Wherever he lives, he converts that place into Vṛndāvana and Navadvīpa. This means that materialism cannot touch him. This is the secret of success for one advancing in Kṛṣṇa consciousness.

TEXT 130

এই মত যাঁর ঘরে করে প্রভু ভিক্ষা।
সেই ঐছে কহে, তাঁরে করায় এই শিক্ষা॥ ১৩০॥

ei mata yāṅra ghare kare prabhu bhikṣā
sei aiche kahe, tāṅre karāya ei śikṣā

SYNONYMS

ei mata—in this way; *yāṅra*—of whom; *ghare*—at the home; *kare*—does; *prabhu*—Lord Śrī Caitanya Mahāprabhu; *bhikṣā*—accepting *prasāda; sei*—that man; *aiche*—similarly; *kahe*—says; *tāṅre*—unto him; *karāya*—does; *ei*—this; *śikṣā*—enlightenment.

TRANSLATION

At whosoever's house Śrī Caitanya accepted His alms by taking prasāda, He would convert the dwellers to His saṅkīrtana movement and advise them just as He advised the brāhmaṇa named Kūrma.

PURPORT

The cult of Śrī Caitanya Mahāprabhu is explained here very nicely. One who surrenders to Him and is ready to follow Him with heart and soul does not need to change his location. Nor is it necessary for one to change status. One may remain a householder, a medical practitioner, an engineer or whatever. It doesn't matter. One only has to follow the instruction of Śrī Caitanya Mahāprabhu, chant the Hare Kṛṣṇa *mahā-mantra* and instruct relatives and friends in the teachings of *Bhagavad-gītā* and *Śrīmad-Bhāgavatam.* One has to learn humility and meekness at home, following the instructions of Śrī Caitanya Mahāprabhu, and in that way one's life will be spiritually successful. One should not try to be an artificially advanced devotee, thinking, "I am a first-class devotee." Such thinking should be avoided. It is best not to accept any disciples. One has to become purified at home by chanting the Hare Kṛṣṇa *mahā-mantra* and preaching the principles enunciated by Śrī Caitanya Mahāprabhu. Thus one can become a spiritual master and be freed from the contamination of material life.

There are many *sahajiyās* who decry the activities of the six Gosvāmīs—Śrīla Rūpa, Sanātana, Raghunātha dāsa, Bhaṭṭa Raghunātha, Jīva and Gopāla Bhaṭṭa Gosvāmīs—who are the personal associates of Śrī Caitanya Mahāprabhu and who enlightened society by writing books on devotional service. Similarly, Narottama dāsa Ṭhākura and other great *ācāryas* like Madhvācārya, Rāmānujācārya and others accepted many thousands of disciples to induce them to render devotional service. However, there is a class of *sahajiyās* who think that these activities are opposed to the principles of devotional service. Indeed, they consider such activities simply another phase of materialism. Thus opposing the principles of Śrī Caitanya Mahāprabhu, they commit offenses at His lotus feet. They should better consider His instructions and, instead of seeking to be considered humble and meek, should refrain from criticizing the followers of Śrī Caitanya Mahāprabhu who engage in preaching. To protect His preachers, Śrī Caitanya Mahāprabhu has given much clear advice in these verses of *Caitanya-caritāmṛta.*

TEXTS 131-132

পথে যাইতে দেবালয়ে রহে যেই গ্রামে ।
যাঁর ঘরে ভিক্ষা করে, সেই মহাজনে ॥ ১৩১ ॥
কূর্মে যৈছে রীতি, তৈছে কৈল সর্ব ঠাঞি ।
নীলাচলে পুনঃ যাবৎ না আইলা গোসাঞি ॥ ১৩২॥

pathe yāite devālaye rahe yei grāme
yāṅra ghare bhikṣā kare, sei mahā-jane

kūrme yaiche rīti, taiche kaila sarva-ṭhāñi
nīlācale punaḥ yāvat nā āilā gosāñi

SYNONYMS

pathe yāite—while passing on the road; *devālaye*—in a temple; *rahe*—He stays; *yei grāme*—in any village; *yāṅra ghare*—at whose place; *bhikṣā kare*—takes alms or eats; *sei mahā-jane*—to such a great personality; *kūrme*—unto the *brāhmaṇa* Kūrma; *yaiche*—just as; *rīti*—the process; *taiche*—in the same way; *kaila*—did; *sarva-ṭhāñi*—in all places; *nīlācale*—to Jagannātha Purī; *punaḥ*—again; *yāvat*—until; *nā*—not; *āilā*—returned; *gosāñi*—the Lord.

TRANSLATION

While on His tour, Śrī Caitanya Mahāprabhu would spend the night at a temple or on the roadside. Whenever He accepted food from a person, He would give him the same advice He gave the brāhmaṇa named Kūrma. He adopted this process until He returned from His South Indian tour to Jagannātha Purī.

TEXT 133

অতএব ইহাঁ কহিলাঙ করিয়া বিস্তার ।
এইমত জানিবে প্রভুর সর্বত্র ব্যবহার ॥ ১৩৩ ॥

ataeva ihāṅ kahilāṅ kariyā vistāra
ei-mata jānibe prabhura sarvatra vyavahāra

SYNONYMS

ataeva—therefore; *ihāṅ*—here; *kahilāṅ*—I have described; *kariyā vistāra*—elaborately; *ei-mata*—in this way; *jānibe*—you will know; *prabhura*—of Śrī Caitanya Mahāprabhu; *sarvatra*—everywhere; *vyavahāra*—the behavior.

TRANSLATION

Thus I have described the Lord's behavior elaborately in the case of Kūrma. In this way, you will know Śrī Caitanya Mahāprabhu's dealings throughout South India.

TEXT 134

এইমত সেই রাত্রি তাহাঁই রহিলা ।
প্রাতঃকালে প্রভু স্নান করিয়া চলিলা ॥ ১৩৪ ॥

ei-mata sei rātri tāhāṅi rahilā
prātaḥ-kāle prabhu snāna kariyā calilā

SYNONYMS

ei-mata—in this way; *sei rātri*—that night; *tāhāṅi*—there; *rahilā*—stayed; *prātaḥ-kāle*—in the morning; *prabhu*—Śrī Caitanya Mahāprabhu; *snāna*—bath; *kariyā*—taking; *calilā*—again started.

TRANSLATION

Thus Lord Śrī Caitanya Mahāprabhu would remain at night in one place and the next morning, after bathing, start again.

TEXT 135

প্রভুর অনুব্রজি' কূর্ম বহু দূর আইলা ।
প্রভু তাঁরে যত্ন করি' ঘরে পাঠাইলা ॥ ১৩৫ ॥

prabhura anuvraji' kūrma bahu dūra āilā
prabhu tāṅre yatna kari' ghare pāṭhāilā

SYNONYMS

prabhura—Lord Śrī Caitanya Mahāprabhu; *anuvraji'*—following behind; *kūrma*—the *brāhmaṇa* named Kūrma; *bahu*—much; *dūra*—distance; *āilā*—came;

prabhu—Lord Śrī Caitanya Mahāprabhu; *tāṅre*—him; *yatna kari'*—taking much care; *ghare*—to his home; *pāṭhāilā*—sent.

TRANSLATION

When Śrī Caitanya Mahāprabhu left, the brāhmaṇa Kūrma followed Him a great distance, but eventually Lord Caitanya took care to send him back home.

TEXT 136

'বাসুদেব'-নাম এক দ্বিজ মহাশয়।
সর্বাঙ্গে গলিত কুষ্ঠ, তাতে কীড়াময়॥ ১৩৬॥

'vāsudeva'-nāma eka dvija mahāśaya
sarvāṅge galita kuṣṭha, tāte kīḍā-maya

SYNONYMS

vāsudeva-nāma—of the name Vāsudeva; *eka dvija*—one *brāhmaṇa; mahāśaya*—a great person; *sarva-aṅge*—all over his body; *galita*—acute; *kuṣṭha*—leprosy; *tāte*—in that; *kīḍā-maya*—full of living worms.

TRANSLATION

There was also one brāhmaṇa named Vāsudeva, who was a great person but was suffering from leprosy. Indeed, his body was filled with living worms.

TEXT 137

অঙ্গ হৈতে যেই কীড়া খসিয়া পড়য়।
উঠাঞা সেই কীড়া রাখে সেই ঠাঞ॥ ১৩৭॥

aṅga haite yei kīḍā khasiyā paḍaya
uṭhāñā sei kīḍā rākhe sei ṭhāña

SYNONYMS

aṅga haite—from his body; *yei*—which; *kīḍā*—a worm; *khasiyā*—drops; *paḍaya*—falling off; *uṭhāñā*—picking up; *sei*—that; *kīḍā*—worm; *rākhe*—places; *sei ṭhāña*—in the same place.

TRANSLATION

Although suffering from leprosy, the brāhmaṇa Vāsudeva was enlightened. As soon as one worm fell from his body, he would pick it up and place it back again in the same location.

TEXT 138

রাত্রিতে শুনিলা তেঁহো গোসাঞির আগমন ।
দেখিবারে আইলা প্রভাতে কূর্মের ভবন ॥ ১৩৮ ॥

rātrite śunilā teṅho gosāñira āgamana
dekhibāre āilā prabhāte kūrmera bhavana

SYNONYMS

rātrite—at night; *śunilā*—heard; *teṅho*—he; *gosāñira*—of Lord Śrī Caitanya Mahāprabhu; *āgamana*—the arrival; *dekhibāre*—to see Him; *āilā*—he came; *prabhāte*—in the morning; *kūrmera*—of the *brāhmaṇa* named Kūrma; *bhavana*—to the house.

TRANSLATION

Then one night Vāsudeva heard of Lord Caitanya Mahāprabhu's arrival, and in the morning he came to see the Lord at the house of Kūrma.

TEXT 139

প্রভুর গমন কূর্ম-মুখেতে শুনিঞা ।
ভূমিতে পড়িলা দুঃখে মূর্চ্ছিত হঞা ॥ ১৩৯ ॥

prabhura gamana kūrma-mukhete śuniñā
bhūmite paḍilā duḥkhe mūrcchita hañā

SYNONYMS

prabhura—of Lord Śrī Caitanya Mahāprabhu; *gamana*—the going; *kūrma-mukhete*—from the mouth of the *brāhmaṇa* Kūrma; *śuniñā*—hearing; *bhūmite*—on the ground; *paḍilā*—fell down; *duḥkhe*—in great distress; *mūrcchita*—unconsciousness; *hañā*—becoming.

TRANSLATION

When the leper Vāsudeva came to Kūrma's house to see Caitanya Mahāprabhu, he was informed that the Lord had already left. The leper then fell to the ground unconscious.

TEXT 140

অনেক প্রকার বিলাপ করিতে লাগিলা ।
সেইক্ষণে আসি' প্রভু তাঁরে আলিঙ্গিলা ॥ ১৪০ ॥

aneka prakāra vilāpa karite lāgilā
sei-kṣaṇe āsi' prabhu tāṅre āliṅgilā

SYNONYMS

aneka prakāra—various kinds; *vilāpa*—lamentation; *karite*—to do; *lāgilā*—began; *sei-kṣaṇe*—immediately; *āsi'*—coming back; *prabhu*—Śrī Caitanya Mahāprabhu; *tāṅre*—him; *āliṅgilā*—embraced.

TRANSLATION

When Vāsudeva, the leper brāhmaṇa, was lamenting due to not being able to see Caitanya Mahāprabhu, the Lord immediately returned to that spot and embraced him.

TEXT 141

প্রভু-স্পর্শে দুঃখ-সঙ্গে কুষ্ঠ দূরে গেল ।
আনন্দ সহিতে অঙ্গ সুন্দর হইল ॥ ১৪১ ॥

prabhu-sparśe duḥkha-saṅge kuṣṭha dūre gela
ānanda sahite aṅga sundara ha-ila

SYNONYMS

prabhu-sparśe—by the touch of Śrī Caitanya Mahāprabhu; *duḥkha-saṅge*—along with his unhappiness; *kuṣṭha*—the infection of leprosy; *dūre*—to a distant place; *gela*—went; *ānanda sahite*—with great pleasure; *aṅga*—whole body; *sundara*—beautiful; *ha-ila*—became.

TRANSLATION

When Śrī Caitanya Mahāprabhu touched him, both the leprosy and his distress went to a distant place. Indeed, Vāsudeva's body became very beautiful, to his great happiness.

TEXT 142

প্রভুর কৃপা দেখি' তাঁর বিস্ময় হৈল মন ।
শ্লোক পড়ি' পায়ে ধরি, করয়ে স্তবন ॥ ১৪২ ॥

prabhura kṛpā dekhi' tāṅra vismaya haila mana
śloka paḍi' pāye dhari, karaye stavana

SYNONYMS

prabhura—of Lord Śrī Caitanya Mahāprabhu; *kṛpā*—the mercy; *dekhi'*—seeing; *tāṅra*—of the *brāhmaṇa* Vāsudeva; *vismaya haila mana*—there was astonishment in his mind; *śloka paḍi'*—reciting a verse; *pāye dhari*—touching His lotus feet; *karaye stavana*—offers prayers.

TRANSLATION

The brāhmaṇa Vāsudeva was astonished to behold the wonderful mercy of Śrī Caitanya Mahāprabhu, and he began to recite a verse from Śrīmad-Bhāgavatam, touching the Lord's lotus feet.

TEXT 143

ক্বাহং দরিদ্রঃ পাপীয়ান্ ক্ব কৃষ্ণঃ শ্রীনিকেতনঃ ।
ব্রহ্মবন্ধুরিতি স্মাহং বাহুভ্যাং পরিরম্ভিতঃ ॥ ১৪৩ ॥

kvāhaṁ daridraḥ pāpīyān
kva kṛṣṇaḥ śrī-niketanaḥ
brahma-bandhur iti smāhaṁ
bāhubhyāṁ parirambhitaḥ

SYNONYMS

kva—who; *aham*—I; *daridraḥ*—poor; *pāpīyān*—sinful; *kva*—who; *kṛṣṇaḥ*—the Supreme Personality of Godhead; *śrī-niketanaḥ*—the transcendental form of all opulence; *brahma-bandhuḥ*—the friend of a *brāhmaṇa,* not fit even to be called a *brāhmaṇa; iti*—thus; *sma*—certainly; *aham*—I; *bāhubhyām*—by the arms; *parirambhitaḥ*—embraced.

TRANSLATION

He said, " 'Who am I? A sinful, poor friend of a brāhmaṇa. And who is Kṛṣṇa? The Supreme Personality of Godhead full in six opulences. Nonetheless, He has embraced me with His two arms.' "

PURPORT

This verse was spoken by Sudāmā Brāhmaṇa in *Śrīmad-Bhāgavatam* (10.81.16) in connection with his meeting Lord Kṛṣṇa.

TEXTS 144-145

বহু স্তুতি করি' কহে,—শুন, দয়াময় ।
জীবে এই গুণ নাহি, তোমাতে এই হয় ॥ ১৪৪ ॥
মোরে দেখি' মোর গন্ধে পলায় পামর ।
হেন-মোরে স্পর্শ' তুমি,—স্বতন্ত্র ঈশ্বর ॥ ১৪৫ ॥

bahu stuti kari' kahe,——śuna, dayā-maya
jīve ei guṇa nāhi, tomāte ei haya

more dekhi' mora gandhe palāya pāmara
hena-more sparśa' tumi,——svatantra īśvara

SYNONYMS

bahu—many; *stuti*—prayers; *kari'*—presenting; *kahe*—says; *śuna*—kindly hear; *dayā-maya*—O greatly merciful Lord; *jīve*—in the living entity; *ei*—this; *guṇa*—quality; *nāhi*—there is not; *tomāte*—in You; *ei*—this; *haya*—is; *more dekhi'*—by seeing me; *mora gandhe*—from smelling my body; *palāya*—runs away; *pāmara*—even a sinful man; *hena-more*—such a person as me; *sparśa'*—touch; *tumi*—You; *sva-tantra*—fully independent; *īśvara*—the Supreme Personality of Godhead.

TRANSLATION

The brāhmaṇa Vāsudeva continued: "O my merciful Lord, such mercy is not possible for ordinary living entities. Such mercy can be found only in You. Upon seeing me, even a sinful person goes away due to my bad bodily odor. Yet You have touched me. Such is the independent behavior of the Supreme Personality of Godhead."

TEXT 146

কিন্তু আছিলাঙ ভাল অধম হঞা।
এবে অহঙ্কার মোর জন্মিবে আসিয়া ॥ ১৪৬ ॥

kintu āchilāṅ bhāla adhama hañā
ebe ahaṅkāra mora janmibe āsiyā

SYNONYMS

kintu—but; *āchilāṅ*—I was; *bhāla*—all right; *adhama*—the lowest of mankind; *hañā*—being; *ebe*—now; *ahaṅkāra*—pride; *mora*—my; *janmibe*—will appear; *āsiyā*—coming.

TRANSLATION

Being meek and humble, the brāhmaṇa Vāsudeva worried that he would become proud after being cured by the grace of Śrī Caitanya Mahāprabhu.

TEXT 147

প্রভু কহে,- "কভু তোমার না হবে অভিমান।
নিরন্তর কহ তুমি 'কৃষ্ণ' 'কৃষ্ণ' নাম ॥ ১৪৭ ॥

prabhu kahe,——"kabhu tomāra nā habe abhimāna
nirantara kaha tumi 'kṛṣṇa' 'kṛṣṇa' nāma

SYNONYMS

prabhu kahe—the Lord said; *kabhu*—at any time; *tomāra*—your; *nā*—not; *habe*—there will be; *abhimāna*—pride; *nirantara*—incessantly; *kaha*—chant; *tumi*—you; *kṛṣṇa kṛṣṇa nāma*—the holy name of Lord Kṛṣṇa.

TRANSLATION

To protect the brāhmaṇa, Śrī Caitanya Mahāprabhu advised him to chant the Hare Kṛṣṇa mantra incessantly. By doing so, he would never become unnecessarily proud.

TEXT 148

কৃষ্ণ উপদেশি' কর জীবের নিস্তার ।
অচিরাতে কৃষ্ণ তোমা করিবেন অঙ্গীকার ॥" ১৪৮ ॥

kṛṣṇa upadeśi' kara jīvera nistāra
acirāte kṛṣṇa tomā karibena aṅgīkāra"

SYNONYMS

kṛṣṇa upadeśi'—instructing about Kṛṣṇa; *kara*—just do; *jīvera*—of all living entities; *nistāra*—the liberation; *acirāte*—very soon; *kṛṣṇa*—Lord Kṛṣṇa; *tomā*—you; *karibena*—will make; *aṅgīkāra*—acceptance.

TRANSLATION

Śrī Caitanya Mahāprabhu also advised Vāsudeva to preach about Kṛṣṇa and thus liberate living entities. As a result, Kṛṣṇa would very soon accept him as His devotee.

PURPORT

Although Vāsudeva *vipra* was a leper and had suffered greatly, still Śrī Caitanya Mahāprabhu cured him. The only return the Lord wanted was that Vāsudeva preach the instructions of Kṛṣṇa and liberate all human beings. That is the process of the International Society for Krishna Consciousness. Each and every member of this Society was rescued from a very abominable condition, but now they are engaged in preaching the cult of Kṛṣṇa consciousness. They are not only cured of the disease called materialism but are also living a very happy life. Everyone accepts them as great devotees of Kṛṣṇa, and their qualities are manifest in their very faces. If one wants to be recognized as a devotee by Kṛṣṇa, he should take to preaching work, following the advice of Śrī Caitanya Mahāprabhu. Then one will undoubtedly attain the lotus feet of Śrī Kṛṣṇa Caitanya, Lord Kṛṣṇa Himself, without delay.

TEXT 149

এতেক কহিয়া প্রভু কৈল অন্তর্ধানে ।
দুই বিপ্র গলাগলি কান্দে প্রভুর গুণে ॥ ১৪৯ ॥

eteka kahiyā prabhu kaila antardhāne
dui vipra galāgali kānde prabhura guṇe

SYNONYMS

eteka—so much; *kahiyā*—speaking; *prabhu*—Lord Śrī Caitanya Mahāprabhu; *kaila*—made; *antardhāne*—disappearance; *dui vipra*—the two *brāhmaṇas,* Kūrma and Vāsudeva; *galāgali*—embracing one another; *kānde*—cry; *prabhura guṇe*—due to the mercy of Śrī Caitanya Mahāprabhu.

TRANSLATION

After thus instructing the brāhmaṇa Vāsudeva in that way, Śrī Caitanya Mahāprabhu disappeared from that place. Then the two brāhmaṇas, Kūrma and Vāsudeva, embraced one another and began to cry, remembering the transcendental qualities of Śrī Caitanya Mahāprabhu.

TEXT 150

‘বাসুদেবোদ্ধার’ এই কহিল আখ্যান ।
‘বাসুদেবামৃতপ্রদ’ হৈল প্রভুর নাম ॥ ১৫০ ॥

'vāsudevoddhāra' ei kahila ākhyāna
'vāsudevāmṛta-prada' haila prabhura nāma

SYNONYMS

vāsudeva-uddhāra—giving liberation to Vāsudeva; *ei*—this; *kahila*—is described; *ākhyāna*—narration; *vāsudeva-amṛta-prada*—the giver of nectar to Vāsudeva; *haila*—became; *prabhura nāma*—Lord Śrī Caitanya Mahāprabhu's holy name.

TRANSLATION

Thus I have described how Śrī Caitanya Mahāprabhu reclaimed the leper Vāsudeva and so received the name Vāsudevāmṛta-prada.

TEXT 151

এই ত' কহিল প্রভুর প্রথম গমন।
কূর্ম-দরশন, বাসুদেব-বিমোচন ॥ ১৫১ ॥

ei ta' kahila prabhura prathama gamana
kūrma-daraśana, vāsudeva-vimocana

SYNONYMS

ei ta' kahila—thus I have described; *prabhura*—of Lord Śrī Caitanya Mahāprabhu; *prathama gamana*—the first tour; *kūrma-daraśana*—visiting the temple of Kūrma; *vāsudeva-vimocana*—and liberating the leper *brāhmaṇa* of the name Vāsudeva.

TRANSLATION

Thus I end my description of the first tour of Śrī Caitanya Mahāprabhu, His visiting the temple of Kūrma and His liberating the leper brāhmaṇa Vāsudeva.

TEXT 152

শ্রদ্ধা করি' এই লীলা যে করে শ্রবণ।
অচিরাতে মিলয়ে তারে চৈতন্য-চরণ ॥ ১৫২ ॥

śraddhā kari' ei līlā ye kare śravaṇa
acirāte milaye tāre caitanya-caraṇa

SYNONYMS

śraddhā kari'—with great faith; *ei līlā*—this pastime; *ye*—anyone; *kare*—does; *śravaṇa*—hearing; *acirāte*—very soon; *milaye*—meets; *tāre*—him; *caitanya-caraṇa*—the lotus feet of Śrī Caitanya Mahāprabhu.

TRANSLATION

One who hears these pastimes of Śrī Caitanya Mahāprabhu with great faith will surely very soon attain the lotus feet of Lord Śrī Caitanya Mahāprabhu.

TEXT 153

চৈতন্যলীলার আদি-অন্ত নাহি জানি।
সেই লিখি, যেই মহান্তের মুখে শুনি ॥ ১৫৩ ॥

caitanya-līlāra ādi-anta nāhi jāni
sei likhi, yei mahāntera mukhe śuni

SYNONYMS

caitanya-līlāra—of the pastimes of Śrī Caitanya Mahāprabhu; *ādi*—beginning; *anta*—and end; *nāhi*—not; *jāni*—I know; *sei*—that; *likhi*—I write; *yei*—which; *mahā-antera*—of the great personalities; *mukhe*—from the mouths; *śuni*—I hear.

TRANSLATION

I admit that I do not know the beginning nor the end of Śrī Caitanya Mahāprabhu's pastimes. However, whatever I have written I have heard from the mouths of great personalities.

PURPORT

The name Vāsudevāmṛta-prada is mentioned in the verses composed by Sārvabhauma Bhaṭṭācārya. When a person actually revives his consciousness with thoughts of Kṛṣṇa by the mercy of Śrī Caitanya Mahāprabhu, he revives his spiritual life and becomes addicted to the service of the Lord. Only then can he act as an *ācārya*. In other words, everyone should engage in preaching, following in the footsteps of Śrī Caitanya Mahāprabhu. In this way one will be very much appreciated by Lord Kṛṣṇa and will quickly be recognized by Him. Actually a devotee of Śrī Caitanya Mahāprabhu must engage in preaching in order to increase the followers of the Lord. By thus preaching actual Vedic knowledge all over the world, one will benefit all mankind.

TEXT 154

ইথে অপরাধ মোর না লইও, ভক্তগণ ।
তোমা-সবার চরণ—মোর একান্ত শরণ ॥ ১৫৪ ॥

ithe aparādha mora nā la-io, bhakta-gaṇa
tomā-sabāra caraṇa——mora ekānta śaraṇa

SYNONYMS

ithe—in this; *aparādha*—offenses; *mora*—my; *nā la-io*—do not take; *bhakta-gaṇa*—O devotees; *tomā*—of your; *sabāra*—of all; *caraṇa*—the lotus feet; *mora*—my; *ekānta*—only; *śaraṇa*—shelter.

TRANSLATION

O devotees, please do not consider my offenses in this regard. Your lotus feet are my only shelter.

TEXT 155

শ্রীরূপ-রঘুনাথ-পদে যার আশ ।
চৈতন্যচরিতামৃত কহে কৃষ্ণদাস ॥ ১৫৫ ॥

śrī-rūpa-raghunātha-pade yāra āśa
caitanya-caritāmṛta kahe kṛṣṇadāsa

SYNONYMS

śrī-rūpa—Śrīla Rūpa Gosvāmī; *raghunātha*—Śrīla Raghunātha dāsa Gosvāmī; *pade*—at the lotus feet; *yāra*—whose; *āśa*—expectation; *caitanya-caritāmṛta*—the book named *Caitanya-caritāmṛta; kahe*—describes; *kṛṣṇa-dāsa*—Śrīla Kṛṣṇadāsa Kavirāja Gosvāmī.

TRANSLATION

Praying at the lotus feet of Śrī Rūpa and Śrī Raghunātha, always desiring their mercy, I, Kṛṣṇadāsa, narrate Śrī Caitanya-caritāmṛta, following in their footsteps.

Thus end the Bhaktivedanta purports to the Śrī Caitanya-caritāmṛta, Madhya-līlā, *Seventh Chapter, describing the liberation of the* brāhmaṇa *Vāsudeva and the Lord's tour of South India.*

CHAPTER 8

Talks Between Śrī Caitanya Mahāprabhu and Rāmānanda Rāya

The summary of the Eighth Chapter is given by Śrīla Bhaktivinoda Ṭhākura in the *Amṛta-pravāha-bhāṣya.*

After visiting the temple of Jiyaḍa-nṛsiṁha, Śrī Caitanya Mahāprabhu went to the banks of the River Godāvarī to a place known as Vidyānagara. When Śrīla Rāmānanda Rāya went there to take his bath, they both met. After being introduced, Śrī Rāmānanda Rāya requested Śrī Caitanya Mahāprabhu to remain in the village for some days. Honoring his request, Caitanya Mahāprabhu stayed there in the home of some Vedic *brāhmaṇas.* In the evening, Śrīla Rāmānanda Rāya used to come to see Śrī Caitanya Mahāprabhu. Rāmānanda Rāya, who was clothed in ordinary dress, offered the Lord respectful obeisances. Śrī Caitanya Mahāprabhu questioned him on the object and process of worship and also asked him to recite verses from Vedic literature.

First of all, Śrīla Rāmānanda Rāya enunciated the system of the *varṇāśrama* institution. He recited various verses about *karmārpaṇa,* stating that everything should be dedicated to the Lord. He then spoke of detached action, knowledge mixed with devotional service, and finally the spontaneous loving service of the Lord. After hearing Śrīla Rāmānanda Rāya recite some verses, Śrī Caitanya Mahāprabhu accepted the principle of pure devotional service devoid of all the kinds of speculation. After this, Śrī Caitanya Mahāprabhu asked Rāmānanda Rāya to explain the higher platform of devotional service. Then Śrīla Rāmānanda Rāya explained unalloyed devotional service, love of Godhead, serving the Lord with pure servitude as well as in fraternity and parental love. Finally he spoke of serving the Lord in conjugal love. He then spoke of how conjugal love can be developed in various ways. This conjugal love attains its highest perfection in Śrīmatī Rādhārāṇī's love for Kṛṣṇa. He next described the position of Śrīmatī Rādhārāṇī and the transcendental mellows of love of God. Śrīla Rāmānanda Rāya then recited one verse of his own concerning the platform of ecstatic vision, technically called *prema-vilāsa-vivarta.* Śrīla Rāmānanda Rāya also explained that all stages of conjugal love can be attained through the mercy of the residents of Vṛndāvana, especially by the mercy of the *gopīs.* All these subject matters were thus vividly described. Gradually Rāmānanda Rāya could understand the position of Śrī Caitanya Mahāprabhu, and when Śrī Caitanya Mahāprabhu exhibited His real form, Rāmānanda Rāya fell unconscious. After some days, Śrī Caitanya

Mahāprabhu asked Rāmānanda Rāya to retire from government service and come to Jagannātha Purī. These descriptions of the meetings between Rāmānanda Rāya and Śrī Caitanya Mahāprabhu are taken from the notebook of Svarūpa Dāmodara Gosvāmī.

TEXT 1

সঞ্চার্য রামাভিধ-ভক্তমেঘে
স্বভক্তিসিদ্ধান্তচয়ামৃতানি ।
গৌরাব্ধিরেতৈরমুনা বিতীর্ণৈ-
স্তজ্‌জ্ঞত্ব-রত্নালয়তাং প্রযাতি ॥ ১ ॥

sañcārya rāmābhidha-bhakta-meghe
sva-bhakti-siddhānta-cayāmṛtāni
gaurābdhir etair amunā vitīrṇais
taj-jñatva-ratnālayatāṁ prayāti

SYNONYMS

sañcārya—by empowering; *rāma-abhidha*—of the name Rāma; *bhakta-meghe*—in the cloudlike devotee Rāya; *sva-bhakti*—of His own devotional service; *siddhānta*—of conclusions; *caya*—all collections; *amṛtāni*—nectar; *gaura-abdhiḥ*—the ocean known as Śrī Caitanya Mahāprabhu; *etaiḥ*—by these; *amunā*—by the cloud known as Rāmānanda Rāya; *vitīrṇaiḥ*—distributed; *tat-jñatva*—of knowledge of devotional service; *ratna-ālayatām*—the quality of being an ocean containing valuable jewels; *prayāti*—achieved.

TRANSLATION

Śrī Caitanya Mahāprabhu, who is known as Gaurāṅga, is the reservoir of all conclusive knowledge in devotional service. He empowered Śrī Rāmānanda Rāya, who may be likened to a cloud of devotional service. This cloud was filled with all the conclusive purports of devotional service and was empowered by the ocean to spread this water over the sea. Śrī Caitanya Mahāprabhu Himself was the ocean of knowledge of pure devotional service.

TEXT 2

জয় জয় শ্রীচৈতন্য জয় নিত্যানন্দ ।
জয়াদ্বৈতচন্দ্র জয় গৌরভক্তবৃন্দ ॥ ২ ॥

jaya jaya śrī-caitanya jaya nityānanda
jayādvaita-candra jaya gaura-bhakta-vṛnda

SYNONYMS

jaya jaya—all glories; *śrī-caitanya*—Lord Śrī Caitanya Mahāprabhu; *jaya*—all glories; *nityānanda*—to Lord Nityānanda; *jaya advaita-candra*—all glories to Advaita Ācārya; *jaya gaura-bhakta-vṛnda*—all glories to the devotees of Śrī Caitanya Mahāprabhu.

TRANSLATION

All glories to Lord Śrī Caitanya Mahāprabhu! All glories to Lord Nityānanda! All glories to Advaita Ācārya! And all glories to all the devotees of Lord Śrī Caitanya Mahāprabhu!

TEXT 3

পূর্ব-রীতে প্রভু আগে গমন করিলা।
'জিয়ড়নৃসিংহ'-ক্ষেত্রে কতদিনে গেলা ॥ ৩ ॥

pūrva-rīte prabhu āge gamana karilā
'jiyaḍa-nṛsiṁha'-kṣetre kata-dine gelā

SYNONYMS

pūrva-rīte—according to His previous program; *prabhu*—Lord Śrī Caitanya Mahāprabhu; *āge*—ahead; *gamana*—going; *karilā*—did; *jiyaḍa-nṛsiṁha*—of the name Jiyaḍa-nṛsiṁha; *kṣetre*—at the place of pilgrimage; *kata-dine*—after some days; *gelā*—arrived.

TRANSLATION

According to His previous program, Lord Śrī Caitanya Mahāprabhu went forward on His tour and after some days arrived at the place of pilgrimage known as Jiyaḍa-nṛsiṁha.

PURPORT

The Jiyaḍa-nṛsiṁha temple is situated on the top of a hill about five miles away from Viśākhā-pattana. There is a railway station on the South Indian Railway known as Siṁhācala. The temple known as Siṁhācala is the best temple in the vicinity of Viśākhā-pattana. This temple is very affluent and is a typical example of the architecture of the area. In one stone tablet it is mentioned that formerly a queen covered the Deity with gold plate. This is mentioned in the *Viśākhā-pat-*

tana Gazetteer. About the temple, there are residential quarters for the priests and devotees. Indeed, at the present moment there are many residential quarters to accommodate visiting devotees. The original Deity is situated within the depths of the temple, but there is another Deity, a duplicate, known as the *vijaya-mūrti.* This smaller Deity can be moved from the temple and taken on public processions. Priests who generally belong to the Rāmānuja-sampradāya are in charge of the Deity worship.

TEXT 4

নৃসিংহ দেখিয়া কৈল দণ্ডবৎপ্রণতি ।
প্রেমাবেশে কৈল বহু নৃত্য-গীত-স্তুতি ॥ ৪ ॥

nṛsiṁha dekhiyā kaila daṇḍavat-praṇati
premāveśe kaila bahu nṛtya-gīta-stuti

SYNONYMS

nṛsiṁha dekhiyā—by seeing Lord Nṛsiṁha in the temple; *kaila*—did; *daṇḍavat-praṇati*—offering of obeisances, falling flat before the Deity; *premāveśe*—in ecstatic love; *kaila*—did; *bahu*—all kinds of; *nṛtya*—dancing; *gīta*—chanting; *stuti*—and offering of prayers.

TRANSLATION

After seeing the Deity Lord Nṛsiṁha in the temple, Śrī Caitanya Mahāprabhu offered His respectful obeisances by falling flat. Then, in ecstatic love, He performed various dances, chanted and offered prayers.

TEXT 5

“শ্রীনৃসিংহ, জয় নৃসিংহ, জয় জয় নৃসিংহ ।
প্রহ্লাদেশ জয় পদ্মামুখপদ্মভৃঙ্গ ॥” ৫ ॥

"śrī-nṛsiṁha, jaya nṛsiṁha, jaya jaya nṛsiṁha
prahlādeśa jaya padmā-mukha-padma-bhṛṅga"

SYNONYMS

śrī-nṛsiṁha—Lord Nṛsiṁha with Lakṣmī; *jaya nṛsiṁha*—all glories to Lord Nṛsiṁha; *jaya jaya*—again and again glories; *nṛsiṁha*—to Nṛsiṁhadeva; *prahlāda-īśa*—to the Lord of Prahlāda Mahārāja; *jaya*—all glories; *padmā*—of the goddess of fortune; *mukha-padma*—of the lotuslike face; *bhṛṅga*—the bee.

TRANSLATION

"All glories to Nṛsiṁhadeva! All glories to Nṛsiṁhadeva, who is the Lord of Prahlāda Mahārāja and, like the honeybee, is always engaged in beholding the lotuslike face of the goddess of fortune.

PURPORT

The goddess of fortune is always embraced by Lord Nṛsiṁhadeva. This is mentioned in *Śrīmad-Bhāgavatam* in the First and Tenth Cantos by the great commentator Śrīla Śrīdhara Svāmī. The following verse was composed by Śrīdhara Svāmī in his commentary on *Śrīmad-Bhāgavatam* (10.87.1).

vāg-īśā yasya vadane
lakṣmīr yasya ca vakṣasi
yasyāste hṛdaye samvit
taṁ nṛsiṁham ahaṁ bhaje

"Lord Nṛsiṁhadeva is always assisted by Sarasvatī, the goddess of learning, and He is always embracing to His chest the goddess of fortune. The Lord is always complete in knowledge within Himself. Let us offer obeisances unto Nṛsiṁhadeva."

Similarly, in his commentary on the First Canto of *Śrīmad-Bhāgavatam* (1.1.1), Śrīdhara Svāmī describes Lord Nṛsiṁhadeva in this way:

prahlāda-hṛdayāhlādaṁ
bhaktāvidyā-vidāraṇam
śarad-indu-ruciṁ vande
pārīndra-vadanaṁ harim

"Let me offer my obeisances unto Lord Nṛsiṁhadeva, who is always enlightening Prahlāda Mahārāja within his heart and who always kills the nescience that attacks the devotees. His mercy is distributed like moonshine, and His face is like that of a lion. Let me offer my obeisances unto Him again and again."

TEXT 6

উগ্রোঽপ্যনুগ্র এবায়ং স্বভক্তানাং নৃকেশরী।
কেশরীব স্বপোতানামন্যেষামুগ্রবিক্রমঃ ॥ ৬ ॥

ugro 'py anugra evāyaṁ
sva-bhaktānāṁ nṛ-keśarī
keśarīva sva-potānām
anyeṣāṁ ugra-vikramaḥ

SYNONYMS

ugraḥ—ferocious; *api*—although; *anugraḥ*—not ferocious; *eva*—certainly; *ayam*—this; *sva-bhaktānām*—to His pure devotees; *nṛ-keśarī*—having the body of a human being and a lion; *keśarī iva*—like a lioness; *sva-potānām*—to her young cubs; *anyeṣām*—to others; *ugra*—ferocious; *vikramaḥ*—whose strength.

TRANSLATION

"Although very ferocious, the lioness is very kind to her cubs. Similarly, although very ferocious to nondevotees like Hiraṇyakaśipu, Lord Nṛsiṁhadeva is very, very soft and kind to devotees like Prahlāda Mahārāja."

PURPORT

This verse was composed by Śrīdhara Svāmī in his commentary on *Śrīmad-Bhāgavatam* (7.9.1).

TEXT 7

এইমত নানা শ্লোক পড়ি' স্তুতি কৈল ।
নৃসিংহ-সেবক মালা-প্রসাদ আনি' দিল ॥ ৭ ॥

ei-mata nānā śloka paḍi' stuti kaila
nṛsiṁha-sevaka mālā-prasāda āni' dila

SYNONYMS

ei-mata—in this way; *nānā*—various; *śloka*—verses; *paḍi'*—reciting; *stuti*—prayers; *kaila*—offered; *nṛsiṁha-sevaka*—the priest of Lord Nṛsiṁhadeva in the temple; *mālā*—garlands; *prasāda*—and remnants of the food of Lord Nṛsiṁhadeva; *āni'*—bringing; *dila*—offered.

TRANSLATION

In this way Lord Śrī Caitanya Mahāprabhu recited different verses from the śāstra. The priest of Lord Nṛsiṁhadeva then brought garlands and the remnants of the Lord's food and offered them to Śrī Caitanya Mahāprabhu.

TEXT 8

পূর্ববৎ কোন বিপ্রে কৈল নিমন্ত্রণ ।
সেই রাত্রি তাহাঁ রহি' করিলা গমন ॥ ৮ ॥

pūrvavat kona vipre kaila nimantraṇa
sei rātri tāhāṅ rahi' karilā gamana

SYNONYMS

pūrva-vat—as previously; *kona*—some; *vipre*—*brāhmaṇa; kaila*—made; *nimantraṇa*—invitation; *sei rātri*—that night; *tāhāṅ*—there; *rahi'*—staying; *karilā*—did; *gamana*—touring.

TRANSLATION

As usual, a brāhmaṇa offered Śrī Caitanya Mahāprabhu an invitation. The Lord passed the night in the temple and then commenced His tour again.

TEXT 9

প্রভাতে উঠিয়া প্রভু চলিলা প্রেমাবেশে ।
দিগ্ বিদিক্ নাহি জ্ঞান রাত্রি-দিবসে ॥ ৯ ॥

prabhāte uṭhiyā prabhu calilā premāveśe
dig-vidik nāhi jñāna rātri-divase

SYNONYMS

prabhāte—in the morning; *uṭhiyā*—rising; *prabhu*—Lord Śrī Caitanya Mahāprabhu; *calilā*—went; *prema-āveśe*—in great ecstatic love; *dik-vidik*—the right or wrong direction; *nāhi*—there was not; *jñāna*—knowledge; *rātri-divase*—day and night.

TRANSLATION

The next morning, in the great ecstasy of love, Lord Śrī Caitanya Mahāprabhu started on His tour with no knowledge of the proper direction, and He continued the whole day and night.

TEXT 10

পূর্ববৎ 'বৈষ্ণব' করি' সর্ব লোকগণে ।
গোদাবরী-তীরে প্রভু আইলা কতদিনে ॥ ১০ ॥

pūrvavat 'vaiṣṇava' kari' sarva loka-gaṇe
godāvarī-tīre prabhu āilā kata-dine

SYNONYMS

pūrva-vat—as previously; *vaiṣṇava*—devotees; *kari'*—making; *sarva*—all; *loka-gaṇe*—the people; *godāvarī-tīre*—on the bank of the River Godāvarī; *prabhu*—the Lord; *āilā*—arrived; *kata-dine*—after some days.

TRANSLATION

As previously, Śrī Caitanya Mahāprabhu converted to Vaiṣṇavism many people He met on the road. After some days, the Lord reached the banks of the River Godāvarī.

TEXT 11

গোদাবরী দেখি' হইল 'যমুনা'-স্মরণ ।
তীরে বন দেখি' স্মৃতি হৈল বৃন্দাবন ॥ ১১ ॥

godāvarī dekhi' ha-ila 'yamunā'-smaraṇa
tīre vana dekhi' smṛti haila vṛndāvana

SYNONYMS

godāvarī—the River Godāvarī; *dekhi'*—seeing; *ha-ila*—there was; *yamunā-smaraṇa*—remembrance of the River Yamunā; *tīre*—on the banks; *vana*—the forests; *dekhi'*—seeing; *smṛti*—remembrance; *haila*—there was; *vṛndāvana*—Śrī Vṛndāvana.

TRANSLATION

When He saw the River Godāvarī, the Lord remembered the River Yamunā, and when He saw the forest on the banks of the river, He remembered Śrī Vṛndāvana-dhāma.

TEXT 12

সেই বনে কতক্ষণ করি' নৃত্য-গান ।
গোদাবরী পার হঞা তাহাঁ কৈল স্নান ॥ ১২ ॥

sei vane kata-kṣaṇa kari' nṛtya-gāna
godāvarī pāra hañā tāhāṅ kaila snāna

SYNONYMS

sei vane—in that forest; *kata-kṣaṇa*—for some time; *kari'*—performing; *nṛtya-gāna*—dancing and chanting; *godāvarī*—the river; *pāra hañā*—crossing; *tāhāṅ*—there; *kaila*—took; *snāna*—bath.

TRANSLATION

After performing His usual chanting and dancing for some time in this forest, the Lord crossed the river and took His bath on the other bank.

TEXT 13

ঘাট ছাড়ি' কতদূরে জল-সন্নিধানে ।
বসি' প্রভু করে কৃষ্ণনাম-সংকীর্তনে ॥ ১৩ ॥

ghāṭa chāḍi' kata-dūre jala-sannidhāne
vasi' prabhu kare kṛṣṇa-nāma-saṅkīrtane

SYNONYMS

ghāṭa chāḍi'—leaving the bathing place; *kata-dūre*—a short distance away; *jala-sannidhāne*—near the water; *vasi'*—sitting; *prabhu*—the Lord; *kare*—does; *kṛṣṇa-nāma-saṅkīrtane*—chanting of the holy name of Lord Kṛṣṇa.

TRANSLATION

After bathing in the river, the Lord walked a little distance from the bathing place and engaged in chanting the holy name of Kṛṣṇa.

TEXT 14

হেনকালে দোলায় চড়ি' রামানন্দ রায় ।
স্নান করিবারে আইলা, বাজনা বাজায় ॥ ১৪ ॥

hena-kāle dolāya caḍi' rāmānanda rāya
snāna karibāre āilā, bājanā bājāya

SYNONYMS

hena-kāle—at this time; *dolāya caḍi'*—riding on a palanquin; *rāmānanda rāya*—Śrīla Rāmānanda Rāya; *snāna*—bath; *karibāre*—to take; *āilā*—came there; *bājanā bājāya*—accompanied by a musical band.

TRANSLATION

At that time, accompanied by the sounds of music, Rāmānanda Rāya came there mounted on a palanquin to take his bath.

TEXT 15

তাঁর সঙ্গে বহু আইলা বৈদিক ব্রাহ্মণ ।
বিধিমতে কৈল তেঁহো স্নানাদি-তর্পণ ॥ ১৫ ॥

tāṅra saṅge bahu āilā vaidika brāhmaṇa
vidhi-mate kaila teṅho snānādi-tarpaṇa

SYNONYMS

tāṅra saṅge—with him; *bahu*—many; *āilā*—came; *vaidika*—following the Vedic principles; *brāhmaṇa*—*brāhmaṇas; vidhi-mate*—according to ritualistic ceremonies; *kaila*—did; *teṅho*—he, Śrīla Rāmānanda Rāya; *snāna-ādi-tarpaṇa*—bathing and offering oblations, etc.

TRANSLATION

Many brāhmaṇas, following the Vedic principles, accompanied Rāmānanda Rāya. According to the Vedic rituals, Rāmānanda Rāya took his bath and offered oblations to his forefathers.

TEXT 16

প্রভু তাঁরে দেখি' জানিল—এই রামরায়।
তাঁহারে মিলিতে প্রভুর মন উঠি' ধায়॥ ১৬॥

prabhu tāṅre dekhi' jānila——ei rāma-rāya
tāṅhāre milite prabhura mana uṭhi' dhāya

SYNONYMS

prabhu—Śrī Caitanya Mahāprabhu; *tāṅre*—him; *dekhi'*—seeing; *jānila*—could understand; *ei*—this; *rāma-rāya*—Śrīla Rāmānanda Rāya; *tāṅhāre*—him; *milite*—to meet; *prabhura*—of Lord Caitanya Mahāprabhu; *mana*—mind; *uṭhi'*—rising; *dhāya*—runs after.

TRANSLATION

Śrī Caitanya Mahāprabhu could understand that the person who had come to bathe in the river was Rāmānanda Rāya. The Lord wanted so much to meet him that His mind immediately began running after him.

TEXT 17

তথাপি ধৈর্য ধরি' প্রভু রহিলা বসিয়া।
রামানন্দ আইলা অপূর্ব সন্ন্যাসী দেখিয়া॥ ১৭॥

tathāpi dhairya dhari' prabhu rahilā vasiyā
rāmānanda āilā apūrva sannyāsī dekhiyā

SYNONYMS

tathāpi—still; *dhariya dhari'*—keeping patient; *prabhu*—Lord Śrī Caitanya Mahāprabhu; *rahilā*—remained; *vasiyā*—sitting; *rāmānanda*—Śrīla Rāmānanda Rāya; *āilā*—arrived; *apūrva*—wonderful; *sannyāsī*—renunciate; *dekhiyā*—seeing.

TRANSLATION

Although Śrī Caitanya Mahāprabhu was running after him mentally, He patiently remained sitting. Rāmānanda Rāya, seeing the wonderful sannyāsī, then came to see Him.

TEXT 18

সূর্যশত-সম কান্তি, অরুণ বসন ।
সুবলিত প্রকাণ্ড দেহ, কমল-লোচন ॥ ১৮ ॥

sūrya-śata-sama kānti, aruṇa vasana
subalita prakāṇḍa deha, kamala-locana

SYNONYMS

sūrya-śata—hundreds of suns; *sama*—like; *kānti*—luster; *aruṇa*—saffron; *vasana*—garments; *subalita*—very strongly built; *prakāṇḍa*—big; *deha*—body; *kamala-locana*—eyes like lotus petals.

TRANSLATION

Śrīla Rāmānanda Rāya then saw Śrī Caitanya Mahāprabhu as brilliant as a hundred suns. The Lord was covered by a saffron garment. He was large in body and very strongly built, and His eyes were like lotus petals.

TEXT 19

দেখিয়া তাঁহার মনে হৈল চমৎকার ।
আসিয়া করিল দণ্ডবৎ নমস্কার ॥ ১৯ ॥

dekhiyā tāṅhāra mane haila camatkāra
āsiyā karila daṇḍavat namaskāra

SYNONYMS

dekhiyā—seeing; *tāṅhāra*—his; *mane*—in the mind; *haila*—there was; *camatkāra*—wonder; *āsiyā*—coming there; *karila*—did; *daṇḍa-vat*—like a rod; *namaskāra*—obeisances.

TRANSLATION

When Rāmānanda Rāya saw the wonderful sannyāsī, he was struck with wonder. He went to Him and immediately offered his respectful obeisances, falling down flat like a rod.

TEXT 20

উঠি' প্রভু কহে,—উঠ, কহ 'কৃষ্ণ' 'কৃষ্ণ'।
তারে আলিঙ্গিতে প্রভুর হৃদয় সতৃষ্ণ ॥ ২০ ॥

uṭhi' prabhu kahe,——uṭha, kaha 'kṛṣṇa' 'kṛṣṇa'
tāre āliṅgite prabhura hṛdaya satṛṣṇa

SYNONYMS

uṭhi'—rising; *prabhu*—the Lord; *kahe*—said; *uṭha*—get up; *kaha*—chant; *kṛṣṇa kṛṣṇa*—the holy name of Lord Kṛṣṇa; *tāre*—him; *āliṅgite*—to embrace; *prabhura*—of Lord Śrī Caitanya Mahāprabhu; *hṛdaya*—the heart; *sa-tṛṣṇa*—very much eager.

TRANSLATION

The Lord stood up and asked Rāmānanda Rāya to arise and chant the holy name of Kṛṣṇa. Indeed, Śrī Caitanya Mahāprabhu was very eager to embrace him.

TEXT 21

তথাপি পুছিল,—তুমি রায় রামানন্দ ?
তেঁহো কহে,—সেই হঙ দাস শূদ্র মন্দ ॥ ২১ ॥

tathāpi puchila,——tumi rāya rāmānanda?
teṅho kahe,——sei haṅa dāsa śūdra manda

SYNONYMS

tathāpi—still; *puchila*—He inquired; *tumi*—you; *rāya rāmānanda*—Rāmānanda Rāya; *teṅho kahe*—he replied; *sei haṅa*—I am that; *dāsa*—servant; *śūdra*—belonging to the *śūdra* community; *manda*—very low.

TRANSLATION

Śrī Caitanya Mahāprabhu then inquired whether he was Rāmānanda Rāya, and he replied, "Yes, I am Your very low servant, and I belong to the śūdra community."

TEXT 22

তবে তারে কৈল প্রভু দৃঢ় আলিঙ্গন।
প্রেমাবেশে প্রভু-ভৃত্য দোঁহে অচেতন ॥ ২২ ॥

tabe tāre kaila prabhu dṛḍha āliṅgana
premāveśe prabhu-bhṛtya doṅhe acetana

SYNONYMS

tabe—thereafter; *tāre*—him; *kaila*—did; *prabhu*—Lord Śrī Caitanya Mahāprabhu; *dṛḍha*—firm; *āliṅgana*—embracing; *prema-āveśe*—in ecstatic love; *prabhu-bhṛtya*—the servant and the master; *doṅhe*—both; *acetana*—unconscious.

TRANSLATION

Śrī Caitanya Mahāprabhu then embraced Śrī Rāmānanda Rāya very firmly. Indeed, both the master and the servant almost lost consciousness due to ecstatic love.

TEXT 23

স্বাভাবিক প্রেম দোঁহার উদয় করিলা ।
দুঁহা আলিঙ্গিয়া দুঁহে ভূমিতে পড়িলা ॥ ২৩ ॥

svābhāvika prema doṅhāra udaya karilā
duṅhā āliṅgiyā duṅhe bhūmite paḍilā

SYNONYMS

svābhāvika—natural; *prema*—love; *doṅhāra*—of both of them; *udaya*—awakening; *karilā*—there was; *duṅhā*—both; *āliṅgiyā*—embracing; *duṅhe*—both of them; *bhūmite*—on the ground; *paḍilā*—fell down.

TRANSLATION

Their natural love for one another was awakened in them both, and they both embraced and fell down on the ground.

PURPORT

Śrīla Rāmānanda Rāya was an incarnation of the *gopī* Viśākhā. Since Śrī Caitanya Mahāprabhu was Lord Kṛṣṇa Himself, there was naturally an awakening of love between Viśākhā and Kṛṣṇa. Śrī Kṛṣṇa Caitanya Mahāprabhu is the combination of Śrīmatī Rādhārāṇī and Kṛṣṇa. The *gopī* Viśākhā is a principal *gopī* assisting Śrīmatī Rādhārāṇī. Rāmānanda Rāya and Śrī Caitanya Mahāprabhu embraced since their natural love also was awakened.

TEXT 24

স্তম্ভ, স্বেদ, অশ্রু, কম্প, পুলক, বৈবর্ণ্য ।
দুঁহার মুখেতে শুনি' গদগদ 'কৃষ্ণ'বর্ণ ॥ ২৪ ॥

stambha, sveda, aśru, kampa, pulaka, vaivarṇya
duṅhāra mukhete śuni' gadgada 'kṛṣṇa' varṇa

SYNONYMS

stambha—paralysis; *sveda*—perspiration; *aśru*—tears; *kampa*—shivering; *pulaka*—palpitations; *vaivarṇya*—paleness; *duṅhāra*—of both of them; *mukhete*—in the mouth; *śuni'*—hearing; *gadgada*—faltering; *kṛṣṇa varṇa*—Kṛṣṇa's name.

TRANSLATION

When they embraced one another, ecstatic symptoms—paralysis, perspiration, tears, shivering, palpitations and paleness—appeared. The word "Kṛṣṇa" came from their mouths falteringly.

TEXT 25

দেখিয়া ব্রাহ্মণগণের হৈল চমৎকার ।
বৈদিক ব্রাহ্মণ সব করেন বিচার ॥ ২৫ ॥

dekhiyā brāhmaṇa-gaṇera haila camatkāra
vaidika brāhmaṇa saba karena vicāra

SYNONYMS

dekhiyā—seeing this; *brāhmaṇa-gaṇera*—of the ritualistic *brāhmaṇas; haila*—there was; *camatkāra*—wonder; *vaidika*—followers of Vedic ritualistic ceremonies; *brāhmaṇa*—the *brāhmaṇas; saba*—all; *karena*—did; *vicāra*—consideration.

TRANSLATION

When the stereotyped, ritualistic brāhmaṇas who were following the Vedic principles saw this ecstatic manifestation of love, they were struck with wonder. All these brāhmaṇas began to reflect as follows.

TEXT 26

এই ত' সন্ন্যাসীর তেজ দেখি ব্রহ্মসম ।
শূদ্রে আলিঙ্গিয়া কেনে করেন ক্রন্দন ॥ ২৬ ॥

ei ta' sannyāsīra teja dekhi brahma-sama
śūdre āliṅgiyā kene karena krandana

SYNONYMS

ei ta'—this indeed; *sannyāsīra*—of the *sannyāsī,* Śrī Caitanya Mahāprabhu; *teja*—bodily effulgence; *dekhi*—we see; *brahma-sama*—exactly like Brahman; *śūdre*—a *śūdra,* or worker; *āliṅgiyā*—embracing; *kene*—why; *karena*—does; *krandana*—crying.

TRANSLATION

These brāhmaṇas began to think, "We can see that this sannyāsī has a luster like the effulgence of Brahman, but how is it He is crying upon embracing a śūdra, a member of the fourth caste in the social order?"

TEXT 27

এই মহারাজ—মহাপণ্ডিত, গম্ভীর ।
সন্ন্যাসীর স্পর্শে মত্ত হইলা অস্থির ॥ ২৭ ॥

ei mahārāja——mahā-paṇḍita, gambhīra
sannyāsīra sparśe matta ha-ilā asthira

SYNONYMS

ei mahārāja—this Rāmānanda Rāya, who is the Governor; *mahā-paṇḍita*—a very learned person; *gambhīra*—grave; *sannyāsīra sparśe*—by touching a *sannyāsī; matta*—mad; *ha-ilā*—became; *asthira*—restless.

TRANSLATION

They thought, "This Rāmānanda Rāya is the Governor of Madras, a highly learned and grave person, a mahā-paṇḍita, but upon touching this sannyāsī he has become restless like a madman."

TEXT 28

এইমত বিপ্রগণ ভাবে মনে মন ।
বিজাতীয় লোক দেখি, প্রভু কৈল সম্বরণ ॥ ২৮ ॥

ei-mata vipra-gaṇa bhāve mane mana
vijātīya loka dekhi, prabhu kaila saṁvaraṇa

SYNONYMS

ei-mata—in this way; *vipra-gaṇa*—all the *brāhmaṇas; bhāve*—think; *mane mana*—within their minds; *vijātīya loka*—outside people; *dekhi*—seeing; *prabhu*—Lord Caitanya Mahāprabhu; *kaila*—did; *saṁvaraṇa*—restraining.

TRANSLATION

While the brāhmaṇas were thinking in this way about the activities of Śrī Caitanya Mahāprabhu and Rāmānanda Rāya, Śrī Caitanya Mahāprabhu saw the brāhmaṇas and restrained His transcendental emotions.

PURPORT

Rāmānanda Rāya was intimately related to Śrī Caitanya Mahāprabhu; therefore he can be accepted as a *sajātīya,* a person within the intimate circle of the Lord. The *brāhmaṇas,* however, were followers of the Vedic rituals and were not able to have an intimate connection with Śrī Caitanya Mahāprabhu. Consequently they are called *vijātīya-loka.* In other words, they were not pure devotees. One may be a highly learned *brāhmaṇa,* but if he is not a pure devotee he is a *vijātīya,* an outcaste, one outside devotional service—in other words, a nondevotee. Although Śrī Caitanya Mahāprabhu and Rāmānanda Rāya were embracing in ecstasy, the Lord restrained His transcendental emotions upon seeing the outsider *brāhmaṇas.*

TEXT 29

সুস্থ হঞা দুঁহে সেই স্থানেতে বসিলা ।
তবে হাসি' মহাপ্রভু কহিতে লাগিলা ॥ ২৯ ॥

sustha hañā duṅhe sei sthānete vasilā
tabe hāsi' mahāprabhu kahite lāgilā

SYNONYMS

su-stha hañā—becoming steady; *duṅhe*—both of them; *sei*—that; *sthānete*—in the place; *vasilā*—sat down; *tabe*—then; *hāsi'*—smiling; *mahāprabhu*—Caitanya Mahāprabhu; *kahite*—to speak; *lāgilā*—began.

TRANSLATION

When they regained their sanity, they both sat down, and Śrī Caitanya Mahāprabhu began to smile and speak as follows.

TEXT 30

'সার্বভৌম ভট্টাচার্য কহিল তোমার গুণে ।
তোমারে মিলিতে মোরে করিল যতনে ॥ ৩০ ॥

'sarvabhauma bhaṭṭācārya kahila tomāra guṇe
tomāre milite more karila yatane

SYNONYMS

sārvabhauma bhaṭṭācārya—of the name Sārvabhauma Bhaṭṭācārya; *kahila*—has spoken; *tomāra*—your; *guṇe*—good qualities; *tomāre*—you; *milite*—to meet; *more*—Me; *karila*—made; *yatane*—endeavor.

TRANSLATION

"Sārvabhauma Bhaṭṭācārya has spoken of your good qualities, and he has made a great endeavor to convince Me to meet you.

TEXT 31

তোমা মিলিবারে মোর এথা আগমন।
ভাল হৈল, অনায়াসে পাইলুঁ দরশন॥' ৩১ ॥

tomā milibāre mora ethā āgamana
bhāla haila, anāyāse pāiluṅ daraśana'

SYNONYMS

tomā—you; *milibāre*—to meet; *mora*—My; *ethā*—here; *āgamana*—coming; *bhāla haila*—it was very good; *anāyāse*—without difficulty; *pāiluṅ*—I have gotten; *daraśana*—interview.

TRANSLATION

"Indeed, I have come here just to meet you. It is very good that even without making an effort I have gotten your interview here."

TEXT 32

রায় কহে,—সার্বভৌম করে ভৃত্যজ্ঞান।
পরোক্ষেহ মোর হিতে হয় সাবধান॥ ৩২ ॥

rāya kahe,——sārvabhauma kare bhṛtya-jñāna
parokṣeha mora hite haya sāvadhāna

SYNONYMS

rāya kahe—Rāmānanda Rāya replied; *sārvabhauma*—Sārvabhauma Bhaṭṭācārya; *kare*—does; *bhṛtya-jñāna*—thinks of me as his servant; *parokṣeha*—in my absence; *mora*—of me; *hite*—for the benefit; *haya*—is; *sāvadhāna*—always careful.

TRANSLATION

Rāmānanda Rāya replied, "Sārvabhauma Bhaṭṭācārya thinks of me as his servant. Even in my absence he is very careful to do me good.

TEXT 33

তাঁর কৃপায় পাইনু তোমার দরশন ।
আজি সফল হৈল মোর মনুষ্যজনম ॥ ৩৩ ॥

tāṅra kṛpāya pāinu tomāra daraśana
āji saphala haila mora manuṣya-janama

SYNONYMS

tāṅra kṛpāya—by his mercy; *pāinu*—I have gotten; *tomāra*—Your; *daraśana*—interview; *āji*—today; *sa-phala*—successful; *haila*—has become; *mora*—my; *manuṣya-janama*—birth as a human being.

TRANSLATION

"By his mercy I have received Your interview here. Consequently I consider that today I have become a successful human being.

TEXT 34

সার্বভৌমে তোমার কৃপা,—তার এই চিহ্ন ।
অস্পৃশ্য স্পর্শিলে হঞা তাঁর প্রেমাধীন ॥ ৩৪ ॥

sārvabhaume tomāra kṛpā,——tāra ei cihna
aspṛśya sparśile hañā tāṅra premādhīna

SYNONYMS

sārvabhaume—unto Sārvabhauma Bhaṭṭācārya; *tomāra*—Your; *kṛpā*—mercy; *tāra*—of such mercy; *ei*—this; *cihna*—the symptom; *aspṛśya*—untouchable; *sparśile*—You have touched; *hañā*—becoming; *tāṅra*—his; *prema-adhīna*—influenced by love.

TRANSLATION

"I can see that You have bestowed special mercy upon Sārvabhauma Bhaṭṭācārya. Therefore You have touched me, although I am untouchable. This is due only to his love for You.

TEXT 35

কাহাঁ তুমি—সাক্ষাৎ ঈশ্বর নারায়ণ ।
কাহাঁ মুঞি—রাজসেবী বিষয়ী শূদ্রাধম ॥ ৩৫ ॥

kāhāṅ tumi——sākṣāt īśvara nārāyaṇa
kāhāṅ muñi——rāja-sevī viṣayī śūdrādhama

SYNONYMS

kāhāṅ—whereas; *tumi*—You; *sākṣāt*—directly; *īśvara nārāyaṇa*—the Supreme Personality of Godhead; *kāhāṅ*—whereas; *muñi*—I; *rāja-sevī*—government servant; *viṣayī*—materialist; *śūdra-adhama*—worse than a *śūdra,* or fourth-class man.

TRANSLATION

"You are the Supreme Personality of Godhead, Nārāyaṇa Himself, and I am only a government servant interested in materialistic activities. Indeed, I am the lowest amongst men of the fourth caste.

TEXT 36

মোর স্পর্শে না করিলে ঘৃণা, বেদভয় ।
মোর দর্শন তোমা বেদে নিষেধয় ॥ ৩৬ ॥

mora sparśe nā karile ghṛṇā, veda-bhaya
mora darśana tomā vede niṣedhaya

SYNONYMS

mora—of me; *sparśe*—by the touch; *nā*—not; *karile*—You did; *ghṛṇā*—hatred; *veda-bhaya*—afraid of injunctions of the *Vedas; mora*—of me; *darśana*—seeing; *tomā*—You; *vede*—the Vedic injunctions; *niṣedhaya*—forbid.

TRANSLATION

"You do not fear the Vedic injunctions stating that You should not associate with a śūdra. You were not contemptuous of my touch, although in the Vedas You are forbidden to associate with śūdras.

PURPORT

In *Bhagavad-gītā* (9.32) the Lord says:

māṁ hi pārtha vyapāśritya
ye 'pi syuḥ pāpa-yonayaḥ
striyo vaiśyās tathā śūdrās
te 'pi yānti parāṁ gatim

"O son of Pṛthā, those who take shelter in Me, though they be of lower birth—women, *vaiśyas* [merchants], as well as *śūdras* [workers]—can approach the supreme destination."

The word *pāpa-yonayaḥ* means "born of lower caste women." The *vaiśyas* are merchants, and the *śūdras* or workers are servants. According to Vedic classifications, they belong to a lower social order. A low life means a life without Kṛṣṇa consciousness. High and low positions in society were calculated by considering a person's Kṛṣṇa consciousness. A *brāhmaṇa* is considered to be on the highest platform because he knows Brahman, the Absolute Truth. The second caste, the *kṣatriya* caste, also know Brahman, but not as well as the *brāhmaṇas*. The *vaiśyas* and *śūdras* do not clearly understand God consciousness, but if they take to Kṛṣṇa consciousness by the mercy of Kṛṣṇa and the spiritual master, they do not remain in the lower castes (*pāpa-yonayaḥ*). It is clearly stated: *te 'pi yānti parāṁ gatim.*

Unless one has attained the highest standard of life, one cannot return home, back to Godhead. One may be a *śūdra, vaiśya* or woman, but if he is situated in the service of the Lord in Kṛṣṇa consciousness, he should not be considered *strī, śūdra, vaiśya* or one lower than a *śūdra*. A person engaged in the Lord's service—though from a lowborn family—should never be considered to belong to a lowborn family. The *Padma Purāṇa* forbids: *vīkṣate jāti-sāmānyāt/ sa yāti narakaṁ dhruvam.* A person goes to hell quickly when he considers a devotee of the Lord in terms of birth. Although Śrī Rāmānanda Rāya supposedly took birth in a *śūdra* family, he is not to be considered a *śūdra,* for he was a great advanced devotee. Indeed, he was on the transcendental platform. Śrī Caitanya Mahāprabhu therefore embraced him. Out of spiritual humility, Śrī Rāmānanda Rāya presented himself as a *śūdra* (*rāja-sevī viṣayī śūdrādhama*). Even though one may engage in government service or in any other pound-shilling-pence business—in short, in materialistic life—he need only take to Kṛṣṇa consciousness. Kṛṣṇa consciousness is a very simple process. One need only chant the holy names of the Lord and strictly follow the principles forbidding sinful activity. In this way one can no longer be considered an untouchable, a *viṣayī* or a *śūdra*. One who is advanced in spiritual life should not associate with nondevotees—namely men in government service and men engaged in materialistic activity for sense gratification or in the service of others. Such men are considered *viṣayī,* materialistic. It is said:

niṣkiñcanasya bhagavad-bhajanonmukhasya
pāraṁ paraṁ jigamiṣor bhava-sāgarasya
sandarśanaṁ viṣayiṇām atha yoṣitāṁ ca
hā hanta hanta viṣa-bhakṣaṇato 'py asādhu

"A person who is very seriously engaged in cultivating devotional service with a view to crossing the ocean of nescience and who has completely abandoned all material activities should never see a *śūdra,* a *vaiśya* or a woman." (*Śrī Caitanya-candrodaya-nāṭaka* 8.23)

TEXT 37

তোমার কৃপায় তোমায় করায় নিন্দ্যকর্ম ।
সাক্ষাৎ ঈশ্বর তুমি, কে জানে তোমার মর্ম ॥ ৩৭ ॥

tomāra kṛpāya tomāya karāya nindya-karma
sākṣāt īśvara tumi, ke jāne tomāra marma

SYNONYMS

tomāra kṛpāya—Your mercy; *tomāya*—unto You; *karāya*—induces; *nindya-karma*—forbidden actions; *sākṣāt īśvara*—directly the Supreme Personality of Godhead; *tumi*—You; *ke jāne*—who can know; *tomāra*—Your; *marma*—purpose.

TRANSLATION

"You are the Supreme Personality of Godhead Himself; therefore no one can understand Your purpose. By Your mercy, You are touching me, although this is not sanctioned by the Vedas.

PURPORT

A *sannyāsī* is strictly forbidden to see the *viṣayīs* and materialistic people. However, Śrī Caitanya Mahāprabhu, out of His boundless and causeless mercy, could show favor to anyone, regardless of birth and position.

TEXT 38

আমা নিস্তারিতে তোমার ইহাঁ আগমন ।
পরম-দয়ালু তুমি পতিত-পাবন ॥ ৩৮ ॥

āmā nistārite tomāra ihāṅ āgamana
parama-dayālu tumi patita-pāvana

SYNONYMS

āmā nistārite—to deliver me; *tomāra*—Your; *ihāṅ*—here; *āgamana*—appearance; *parama-dayālu*—greatly merciful; *tumi*—You; *patita-pāvana*—the deliverer of all fallen souls.

TRANSLATION

"You have come here specifically to deliver me. You are so merciful that You alone can deliver all fallen souls.

PURPORT

Śrīla Narottama dāsa Ṭhākura sings in his *Prārthanā* (40):

śrī-kṛṣṇa-caitanya-prabhu dayā kara more,
tomā vinā ke dayālu jagat saṁsāre

patita-pāvana-hetu tava avatāra,
mo-sama patita prabhu nā pāibe āra

"My dear Lord, please be merciful to me. Who can be more merciful than Your Lordship within these three worlds? You appear as an incarnation just to reclaim the conditioned, fallen souls, but I assure You that You will not find a soul more fallen than me."

Śrī Caitanya Mahāprabhu's specific mission is to deliver fallen souls. Of course, in this age of Kali there is hardly anyone who is not fallen according to the calculations of Vedic behavior. In His instructions to Rūpa Gosvāmī, Śrī Caitanya Mahāprabhu described the so-called followers of Vedic religion in this way (*Madhya* 19.146):

veda-niṣṭha-madhye ardheka veda 'mukhe' māne
veda-niṣiddha pāpa kare, dharma nāhi gaṇe

So-called followers of Vedic principles simply accept the *Vedas* formally, but they act against Vedic principles. This is symptomatic of this age of Kali. People claim to follow a certain type of religion, saying formally, "I am Hindu, I am Muslim, I am Christian, I am this or that," but actually no one follows the principles enunciated in religious scriptures. This is the disease of this age. However, the merciful Śrī Caitanya Mahāprabhu has simply advised us to chant the Hare Kṛṣṇa *mahā-mantra: harer nāma harer nāma harer nāma eva kevalam.* The Lord can deliver anyone and everyone, even though one may have fallen from the injunctions of revealed scriptures. This is Śrī Caitanya Mahāprabhu's special mercy. Consequently He is known as *patita-pāvana,* the deliverer of all fallen souls.

TEXT 39

মহান্ত-স্বভাব এই তারিতে পামর ।
নিজ কার্য নাহি তবু যান তার ঘর ॥ ৩৯ ॥

mahānta-svabhāva ei tārite pāmara
nija kārya nāhi tabu yāna tāra ghara

SYNONYMS

mahānta-svabhāva—the nature of saintly persons; *ei*—this; *tārite*—to deliver; *pāmara*—fallen souls; *nija*—own; *kārya*—business; *nāhi*—there is not; *tabu*—still; *yāna*—goes; *tāra*—his; *ghara*—house.

TRANSLATION

"It is the general practice of all saintly people to deliver the fallen. Therefore they go to people's houses, although they have no personal business there.

PURPORT

A *sannyāsī* is supposed to beg from door to door. He does not beg simply because he is hungry. His real purpose is to enlighten the occupant of every house by preaching Kṛṣṇa consciousness. A *sannyāsī* does not abandon his superior position and become a beggar just for the sake of begging. Similarly, a person in householder life may be very important, but he may also voluntarily take to the mendicant way of life. Rūpa Gosvāmī and Sanātana Gosvāmī were ministers, but they voluntarily accepted the mendicant's life in order to humbly preach Śrī Caitanya Mahāprabhu's message. It is said about them: *tyaktvā tūrṇam aśeṣa-maṇḍala-pati-śreṇīṁ sadā tucchavat bhūtvā dīna-gaṇeśakau karuṇayā kaupīna-kanthāśritau.* Although the Gosvāmīs were very aristocratic, they became mendicants just to deliver the fallen souls according to the order of Śrī Caitanya Mahāprabhu. One should also consider that those who engage in the missionary activities of Kṛṣṇa consciousness are under the guidance of Śrī Caitanya Mahāprabhu. They are not actually beggars; their real business is to deliver fallen souls. Therefore they may go from door to door just to introduce a book about Kṛṣṇa consciousness so that people can become enlightened by reading. Formerly *brahmacārīs* and *sannyāsīs* used to beg from door to door. At the present moment, especially in the Western countries, a person may be handed over to the police if he begs from door to door. In Western countries, begging is considered criminal. Members of the Kṛṣṇa consciousness movement have no business begging. Instead, they work very hard to introduce some literatures about Kṛṣṇa consciousness so that people can read them and be benefited. However, if one gives some contribution to a Kṛṣṇa conscious man, he never refuses it.

TEXT 40

মহদ্বিচলনং নৃণাং গৃহিণাং দীনচেতসাম্ ।
নিঃশ্রেয়সায় ভগবন্নান্যথা কল্পতে ক্বচিৎ ॥ ৪০ ॥

mahad-vicalanaṁ nṛṇāṁ
gṛhiṇāṁ dīna-cetasām
niḥśreyasāya bhagavan
nānyathā kalpate kvacit

SYNONYMS

mahat-vicalanam—the wandering of saintly persons; *nṛṇām*—of human beings; *gṛhiṇām*—who are householders; *dīna-cetasām*—low-minded; *niḥśreyasāya*—for the ultimate benefit; *bhagavan*—O my Lord; *na anyathā*—not any other purpose; *kalpate*—one imagines; *kvacit*—at any time.

TRANSLATION

" 'My dear Lord, sometimes great saintly persons go to the homes of householders, although these householders are generally low-minded. When a saintly person visits their homes, one can understand that it is for no other purpose than to benefit the householders.'

PURPORT

This verse is from *Śrīmad-Bhāgavatam* (10.8.4).

TEXT 41

আমার সঙ্গে ব্রাহ্মণাদি সহস্রেক জন ।
তোমার দর্শনে সবার দ্রবীভূত মন ॥ ৪১ ॥

āmāra saṅge brāhmaṇādi sahasreka jana
tomāra darśane sabāra dravī-bhūta mana

SYNONYMS

āmāra saṅge—with me; *brāhmaṇa-ādi*—*brāhmaṇas* and others; *sahasreka*—more than one thousand; *jana*—persons; *tomāra*—of You; *darśane*—in seeing; *sabāra*—of all of them; *dravī-bhūta*—became melted; *mana*—the hearts.

TRANSLATION

"Along with me there are about a thousand men—including the brāhmaṇas—and all of them appear to have had their hearts melted simply by seeing You.

TEXT 42

'কৃষ্ণ' 'কৃষ্ণ' নাম শুনি সবার বদনে ।
সবার অঙ্গ—পুলকিত, অশ্রু—নয়নে ॥ ৪২ ॥

'kṛṣṇa' 'kṛṣṇa' nāma śuni sabāra vadane
sabāra aṅga——pulakita, aśru——nayane

SYNONYMS

kṛṣṇa kṛṣṇa—Kṛṣṇa, Kṛṣṇa; *nāma*—the holy name; *śuni*—I hear; *sabāra*—of everyone; *vadane*—in the mouths; *sabāra*—of all; *aṅga*—the bodies; *pulakita*—gladdened; *aśru*—tears; *nayane*—in the eyes.

TRANSLATION

"I hear everyone chanting the holy name of Kṛṣṇa. Everyone's body is thrilled with ecstasy, and there are tears in everyone's eyes.

TEXT 43

আকৃত্যে-প্রকৃত্যে তোমার ঈশ্বর-লক্ষণ ।
জীবে না সম্ভবে এই অপ্রাকৃত গুণ ॥ ৪৩ ॥

ākṛtye-prakṛtye tomāra īśvara-lakṣaṇa
jīve nā sambhave ei aprākṛta guṇa

SYNONYMS

ākṛtye—in bodily features; *prakṛtye*—in behavior; *tomāra*—of You; *īśvara*—of the Supreme Personality of Godhead; *lakṣaṇa*—the symptoms; *jīve*—in an ordinary living being; *nā*—not; *sambhave*—possible; *ei*—these; *aprākṛta*—transcendental; *guṇa*—qualities.

TRANSLATION

"My dear sir, according to Your bodily features and Your behavior, You are the Supreme Personality of Godhead. Such behavior and features are impossible for ordinary living beings, for they cannot possess such transcendental qualities."

PURPORT

Śrī Caitanya Mahāprabhu's bodily features were uncommon. Indeed, His body was extraordinary in its measurements. The measurement of His chest as well as the measurement of His forearms were the same length. This is called *nyagrodha-parimaṇḍala*. As far as His nature is concerned, He was kind to everyone. No one but the Supreme Personality of Godhead can be kind to everyone. Therefore the Lord's name is Kṛṣṇa, all-attractive. As stated in *Bhagavad-gītā* (14.4), Kṛṣṇa is kind to everyone. In every species of life (*sarva-yoniṣu*), He is the original father, the seed-giver (*bīja-pradaḥ pitā*). How, then, can He be unkind to any living entity?

One may be a man, an animal or even a tree, but the Lord is kind to everyone. That is God's qualification. He also says in *Bhagavad-gītā* (9.29), *samo 'ham sarva-bhūteṣu:* the Lord is equally kind to everyone. And He advises *sarva-dharmān parityajya mām ekaṁ śaraṇaṁ vraja.* This instruction is meant not only for Arjuna but for all living entities. Whoever takes advantage of this offer is immediately immune to all sinful activity and returns home, back to Godhead. While present on this planet, Śrī Caitanya Mahāprabhu made the same offer.

TEXT 44

প্রভু কহে,—তুমি মহা-ভাগবতোত্তম ।
তোমার দর্শনে সবার দ্রব হৈল মন ॥ ৪৪ ॥

prabhu kahe,——tumi mahā-bhāgavatottama
tomāra darśane sabāra drava haila mana

SYNONYMS

prabhu kahe—the Lord replied; *tumi*—you; *mahā-bhāgavata-uttama*—the best of the topmost devotees; *tomāra darśane*—by seeing you; *sabāra*—of everyone; *drava*—melted; *haila*—became; *mana*—the heart.

TRANSLATION

The Lord replied to Rāmānanda Rāya: "Sir, you are the best of the topmost devotees; therefore upon seeing you everyone's heart has melted.

PURPORT

Unless one is a first-class devotee, he cannot be a preacher. A preacher is generally a topmost devotee, but in order to meet the general populace, he has to come to distinguish between devotees and nondevotees. Otherwise, an advanced devotee makes no such distinctions. Indeed, he always sees everyone engaged in the service of the Lord. When one engages in preaching work, he must distinguish between people and understand that some people are not engaged in the devotional service of the Lord. The preacher then has to take compassion upon such innocent people who do not know how to worship the Lord. In *Śrīmad-Bhāgavatam* (11.2.45), the symptoms of a topmost devotee are described as follows:

sarva-bhūteṣu yaḥ paśyed
bhagavad-bhāvam ātmanaḥ
bhūtāni bhagavaty ātmany
eṣa bhāgavatottamaḥ

"The advanced devotee sees that all living entities are part and parcel of the Supreme Personality of Godhead. Everyone is in Kṛṣṇa, and Kṛṣṇa is also within everyone. Such a vision is possible only for a person who is very advanced in devotional service."

TEXT 45

অন্যের কি কথা, আমি—'মায়াবাদী সন্ন্যাসী'।
আমিহ তোমার স্পর্শে কৃষ্ণ-প্রেমে ভাসি ॥ ৪৫ ॥

anyera ki kathā, āmi——'māyāvādī sannyāsī'
āmiha tomāra sparśe kṛṣṇa-preme bhāsi

SYNONYMS

anyera—of others; *ki kathā*—what to speak; *āmi*—I; *māyāvādī sannyāsī*—a *sannyāsī* of the Māyāvādī sect; *āmiha*—I; *tomāra*—of you; *sparśe*—by the touch; *kṛṣṇa*—of Kṛṣṇa; *preme*—in love; *bhāsi*—float.

TRANSLATION

"Although I am a Māyāvādī sannyāsī, a nondevotee, I am also floating in the ocean of love of Kṛṣṇa simply by touching you. And what to speak of others?

TEXT 46

এই জানি' কঠিন মোর হৃদয় শোধিতে।
সার্বভৌম কহিলেন তোমারে মিলিতে ॥ ৪৬ ॥

ei jāni' kaṭhina mora hṛdaya śodhite
sārvabhauma kahilena tomāre milite

SYNONYMS

ei jāni'—knowing this; *kaṭhina*—very hard; *mora*—My; *hṛdaya*—heart; *śodhite*—to rectify; *sārvabhauma*—Sārvabhauma Bhaṭṭācārya; *kahilena*—asked; *tomāre*—you; *milite*—to meet.

TRANSLATION

"Knowing this, in order to rectify My heart, which is very hard, Sārvabhauma Bhaṭṭācārya asked Me to meet you."

TEXT 47

এইমত দুঁহে স্তুতি করে দুঁহার গুণ।
দুঁহে দুঁহার দরশনে আনন্দিত মন ॥ ৪৭ ॥

ei-mata duṅhe stuti kare duṅhāra guṇa
duṅhe duṅhāra daraśane ānandita mana

SYNONYMS

ei-mata—in this way; *duṅhe*—both of them; *stuti*—praise; *kare*—offer; *duṅhāra*—of both of them; *guṇa*—qualities; *duṅhe*—both of them; *duṅhāra*—of both of them; *daraśane*—by the seeing; *ānandita*—pleased; *mana*—the minds.

TRANSLATION

In this way each of them praised the qualities of the other, and both of them were pleased to see one another.

TEXT 48

হেনকালে বৈদিক এক বৈষ্ণব ব্রাহ্মণ ।
দণ্ডবৎ করি' কৈল প্রভুরে নিমন্ত্রণ ॥ ৪৮ ॥

hena-kāle vaidika eka vaiṣṇava brāhmaṇa
daṇḍavat kari' kaila prabhure nimantraṇa

SYNONYMS

hena-kāle—at this time; *vaidika*—a follower of the Vedic ritualistic ceremonies; *eka*—one; *vaiṣṇava brāhmaṇa*—a *brāhmaṇa* following Vaiṣṇava principles; *daṇḍavat*—obeisances offered by falling flat; *kari'*—offering; *kaila*—made; *prabhure*—unto Lord Śrī Caitanya Mahāprabhu; *nimantraṇa*—invitation.

TRANSLATION

At this time, one brāhmaṇa Vaiṣṇava, following the Vedic principles, came and offered obeisances. He fell flat before Śrī Caitanya Mahāprabhu and invited Him for lunch.

TEXT 49

নিমন্ত্রণ মানিল তাঁরে বৈষ্ণব জানিয়া ।
রামানন্দে কহে প্রভু ঈষৎ হাসিয়া ॥ ৪৯ ॥

nimantraṇa mānila tāṅre vaiṣṇava jāniyā
rāmānande kahe prabhu īṣat hāsiyā

SYNONYMS

nimantraṇa—the invitation; *mānila*—accepted; *tāṅre*—him (the *brāhmaṇa*); *vaiṣṇava*—a devotee; *jāniyā*—understanding; *rāmānande*—unto Rāmānanda; *kahe*—said; *prabhu*—Śrī Caitanya Mahāprabhu; *īṣat*—a little; *hāsiyā*—smiling.

TRANSLATION

Lord Śrī Caitanya Mahāprabhu accepted the brāhmaṇa's invitation, knowing him to be a devotee, and, slightly smiling, spoke as follows to Rāmānanda Rāya.

PURPORT

Śrī Caitanya Mahāprabhu accepted the invitation of the Vaiṣṇava *brāhmaṇa.* Even though one is a *brāhmaṇa* strictly following all the rules and regulations of brahminical culture, if he is not a devotee, a follower of Śrī Caitanya Mahāprabhu, one should not accept his invitation. At the present moment, people have become so degraded that they do not even follow the Vedic principles, to say nothing of Vaiṣṇava principles. They eat anything and everything—whatever they like—and therefore the members of this Kṛṣṇa consciousness movement should be very cautious about accepting invitations.

TEXT 50

তোমার মুখে কৃষ্ণকথা শুনিতে হয় মন।
পুনরপি পাই যেন তোমার দরশন ॥ ৫০ ॥

tomāra mukhe kṛṣṇa-kathā śunite haya mana
punarapi pāi yena tomāra daraśana

SYNONYMS

tomāra mukhe—in your mouth; *kṛṣṇa-kathā*—talks on Kṛṣṇa; *śunite*—to hear; *haya*—there is; *mana*—My mind; *punarapi*—again; *pāi*—I may get; *yena*—if possible; *tomāra*—your; *daraśana*—interview.

TRANSLATION

"I wish to hear from you about Lord Kṛṣṇa. Indeed, My mind is inclined to desire this; therefore I wish to see you again."

TEXTS 51-52

রায় কহে,—আইলা যদি পামর শোধিতে।
দর্শনমাত্রে শুদ্ধ নহে মোর দুষ্ট চিত্তে ॥ ৫১ ॥
দিন পাঁচ-সাত রহি' করহ মার্জন।
তবে শুদ্ধ হয় মোর এই দুষ্ট মন ॥ ৫২ ॥

rāya kahe,——āilā yadi pāmara śodhite
darśana-mātre śuddha nahe mora duṣṭa citte

dina pāṅca-sāta rahi' karaha mārjana
tabe śuddha haya mora ei duṣṭa mana

SYNONYMS

rāya kahe—Rāmānanda Rāya replied; *āilā*—You have come; *yadi*—although; *pāmara*—a fallen soul; *śodhite*—to rectify; *darśana-mātre*—simply seeing You; *śuddha nahe*—not purified; *mora*—my; *duṣṭa*—polluted; *citte*—consciousness; *dina*—days; *pāṅca-sāta*—five or seven; *rahi'*—staying; *karaha*—kindly do; *mārjana*—cleansing; *tabe*—then; *śuddha*—pure; *haya*—it is; *mora*—my; *ei*—this; *duṣṭa*—polluted; *mana*—mind.

TRANSLATION

Rāmānanda Rāya replied, "My Lord, although You have come to correct me, a fallen soul, my mind is not yet purified simply by seeing You. Please stay for five or seven days and kindly cleanse my polluted mind. After that much time, my mind will certainly be pure."

TEXT 53

যদ্যপি বিচ্ছেদ দোঁহার সহন না যায় ।
তথাপি দণ্ডবৎ করি' চলিলা রামরায় ॥ ৫৩ ॥

yadyapi viccheda doṅhāra sahana nā yāya
tathāpi daṇḍavat kari' calilā rāma-rāya

SYNONYMS

yadyapi—although; *viccheda*—separation; *doṅhāra*—of both of them; *sahana*—toleration; *nā*—not; *yāya*—possible; *tathāpi*—still; *daṇḍavat*—obeisances; *kari'*—offering; *calilā*—departed; *rāma-rāya*—Rāmānanda Rāya.

TRANSLATION

Although neither could tolerate the other's separation, Rāmānanda Rāya nonetheless offered his obeisances to Lord Śrī Caitanya Mahāprabhu and departed.

TEXT 54

প্রভু যাই' সেই বিপ্রঘরে ভিক্ষা কৈল ।
দুই জনার উৎকণ্ঠায় আসি' সন্ধ্যা হৈল ॥ ৫৪ ॥

prabhu yāi' sei vipra-ghare bhikṣā kaila
dui janāra utkaṇṭhāya āsi' sandhyā haila

SYNONYMS

prabhu—Lord Śrī Caitanya Mahāprabhu; *yāi'*—going; *sei*—that; *vipra-ghare*—to the house of the *brāhmaṇa; bhikṣā*—lunch; *kaila*—accepted; *dui*—two; *janāra*—of the persons; *utkaṇṭhāya*—in the impatience; *āsi'*—coming; *sandhyā*—evening; *haila*—appeared.

TRANSLATION

Lord Śrī Caitanya Mahāprabhu then went to the house of the brāhmaṇa who had invited Him and took His lunch there. When the evening of that day arrived, both Rāmānanda Rāya and the Lord were eager to meet one another again.

TEXT 55

প্রভু স্নান-কৃত্য করি' আছেন বসিয়া।
একভৃত্য-সঙ্গে রায় মিলিলা আসিয়া ॥ ৫৫ ॥

prabhu snāna-kṛtya kari' āchena vasiyā
eka-bhṛtya-saṅge rāya mililā āsiyā

SYNONYMS

prabhu—the Lord; *snāna-kṛtya*—the daily duty of bathing; *kari'*—finishing; *āchena*—was; *vasiyā*—sitting; *eka*—one; *bhṛtya*—servant; *saṅge*—with; *rāya*—Rāya Rāmānanda; *mililā*—met; *āsiyā*—coming.

TRANSLATION

After finishing His evening bath, Śrī Caitanya Mahāprabhu sat down and waited for Rāmānanda Rāya to come. Then Rāmānanda Rāya, accompanied by one servant, came to meet Him.

PURPORT

A Vaiṣṇava who is supposed to be advanced in spiritual understanding—be he a householder or *sannyāsī*—must bathe three times a day: morning, noon and evening. When one is engaged in the service of the Deity, he must especially follow the principles of *Padma Purāṇa* and take regular baths. He should also, after bathing, decorate his body with the twelve *tilakas*.

TEXT 56

নমস্কার কৈল রায়, প্রভু কৈল আলিঙ্গনে।
দুই জনে কৃষ্ণ-কথা কয় রহঃস্থানে ॥ ৫৬ ॥

namaskāra kaila rāya, prabhu kaila āliṅgane
dui jane kṛṣṇa-kathā kaya rahaḥ-sthāne

SYNONYMS

namaskāra—obeisances; *kaila*—offered; *rāya*—Rāmānanda Rāya; *prabhu*—Lord Śrī Caitanya Mahāprabhu; *kaila*—did; *āliṅgane*—embracing; *dui*—two; *jane*—the persons; *kṛṣṇa-kathā*—talks about Kṛṣṇa; *kaya*—discussed; *rahaḥ-sthāne*—in a secluded place.

TRANSLATION

Rāmānanda Rāya approached Lord Śrī Caitanya and offered his respectful obeisances, and the Lord embraced him. Then they both began to discuss Kṛṣṇa in a secluded place.

PURPORT

The word *rahaḥ-sthāne,* "in a secluded place," is very significant. Talks about Kṛṣṇa and His pastimes—especially His pastimes in Vṛndāvana and His dealings with the *gopīs*—are all very confidential. They are not subject matter for public discussion because those who have no understanding of the transcendental nature of Kṛṣṇa's pastimes always commit great offenses, thinking Kṛṣṇa to be an ordinary human being and the *gopīs* ordinary girls. Following the principle of Lord Śrī Caitanya Mahāprabhu, who never discussed the dealings between Kṛṣṇa and the *gopīs* publicly, devotees in the Kṛṣṇa consciousness movement are enjoined not to discuss the pastimes of Lord Kṛṣṇa in Vṛndāvana in public. For the general public, *saṅkīrtana* is the most effective method to awaken Kṛṣṇa consciousness. If possible, one should discuss the principles enunciated in *Bhagavad-gītā.* Śrī Caitanya Mahāprabhu followed this principle very strictly and discussed the philosophy of *Bhagavad-gītā* with learned scholars like Sārvabhauma Bhaṭṭācārya and Prakāśānanda Sarasvatī. However, He taught the principles of the *bhakti* cult to students like Sanātana Gosvāmī and Rūpa Gosvāmī, and He discussed with Śrī Rāmānanda Rāya the topmost devotional dealings between Kṛṣṇa and the *gopīs.* For the general populace, He performed *saṅkīrtana* very vigorously. We must also follow these principles in preaching Kṛṣṇa consciousness all over the world.

TEXT 57

প্রভু কহে,—"পড় শ্লোক সাধ্যের নির্ণয়।"
রায় কহে,—"স্বধর্মাচরণে বিষ্ণুভক্তি হয় ॥" ৫৭ ॥

prabhu kahe,—"paḍa śloka sādhyera nirṇaya"
rāya kahe,—"sva-dharmācaraṇe viṣṇu-bhakti haya"

SYNONYMS

prabhu kahe—Lord Śrī Caitanya Mahāprabhu said; *paḍa*—just recite; *śloka*—a verse from the revealed scriptures; *sādhyera*—of the aim of life; *nirṇaya*—an ascertainment; *rāya kahe*—Rāmānanda Rāya replied; *sva-dharma-ācaraṇe*—by executing one's occupational duty; *viṣṇu-bhakti*—devotional service to Lord Viṣṇu; *haya*—there is.

TRANSLATION

Śrī Caitanya Mahāprabhu ordered Rāmānanda Rāya to recite a verse from the revealed scriptures concerning the ultimate goal of life. Rāmānanda replied that if one executes the prescribed duties of his social position, he awakens his original Kṛṣṇa consciousness.

PURPORT

In this connection, Śrī Rāmānujācārya stated in the *Vedārtha-saṁgraha* that devotional service is naturally very dear to the living entity. Indeed, it is life's goal. This devotional service is supreme knowledge, or Kṛṣṇa consciousness, and it brings detachment from all material activity. In the transcendental position, a living being can perfectly acknowledge the superiority of serving the Supreme Lord. The devotees attain the Supreme Lord only by devotional service. Having such knowledge, one engages in his occupational duty, and that is called *bhakti-yoga*. By performing *bhakti-yoga,* one can rise to the platform of pure devotional service.

A great saint, the father of Śrīla Vyāsadeva, Parāśara Muni, has specifically mentioned that devotional service to the Lord can ultimately be awakened in human society by the discharge of duties in accordance with the *varṇāśrama*. The Supreme Personality of Godhead instituted *varṇāśrama-dharma* to give human beings a chance to return home, back to Godhead. The Supreme Personality of Godhead, Lord Śrī Kṛṣṇa, who is known in *Bhagavad-gītā* as Puruṣottama—the greatest of all personalities—personally came and declared that the institution of *varṇāśrama-dharma* was founded by Him. As stated in *Bhagavad-gītā* (4.13):

cāturvarṇyaṁ mayā sṛṣṭaṁ
guṇa-karma-vibhāgaśaḥ
tasya kartāram api māṁ
viddhy akartāram avyayam

Elsewhere in *Bhagavad-gītā* (18.45-46) the Lord says:

sve sve karmaṇy abhirataḥ
saṁsiddhiṁ labhate naraḥ

sva-karma-nirataḥ siddhiṁ
yathā vindati tac chṛṇu

yataḥ pravṛttir bhūtānāṁ
yena sarvam idaṁ tatam
sva-karmaṇā tam abhyarcya
siddhiṁ vindati mānavaḥ

Human society should be divided into four divisions—*brāhmaṇa, kṣatriya, vaiśya* and *śūdra*—and everyone should always engage in his occupational duty. The Lord says that those engaged in their occupational duty can attain perfection simply by rendering loving devotional service to the Lord while executing their particular duty. Actually the modern ideal of a classless society can be introduced only by Kṛṣṇa consciousness. Let men perform their occupational duty, and let them give their profits to the service of the Lord. In other words, one can attain the perfection of life by discharging one's occupational duty and employing the results in the service of the Lord. This method is confirmed by great personalities like Bodhāyana, Taṅka, Dramiḍa, Guhadeva, Kapardi and Bhāruci. It is also confirmed by *Vedānta-sūtra.*

TEXT 58

বর্ণাশ্রমাচারবতা পুরুষেণ পরঃ পুমান্ ।
বিষ্ণুরারাধ্যতে পন্থা নান্যত্তত্তোষকারণম্ ॥ ৫৮ ॥

varṇāśramācāravatā
puruṣeṇa paraḥ pumān
viṣṇur ārādhyate panthā
nānyat tat-toṣa-kāraṇam

SYNONYMS

varṇa-āśrama-ācāravatā—who behaves according to the system of four divisions of social order and four divisions of spiritual life; *puruṣeṇa*—by a man; *paraḥ*—the supreme; *pumān*—person; *viṣṇuḥ*—Lord Viṣṇu; *ārādhyate*—is worshiped; *panthā*—way; *na*—not; *anyat*—another; *tat-toṣa-kāraṇam*—cause of satisfying the Lord.

TRANSLATION

"The Supreme Personality of Godhead, Lord Viṣṇu, is worshiped by the proper execution of prescribed duties in the system of varṇa and āśrama. There is no other way to satisfy the Supreme Personality of Godhead. One must be situated in the institution of the four varṇas and āśramas."

PURPORT

This is a quotation from the *Viṣṇu Purāṇa* (3.8.9). As stated by Śrīla Bhaktivinoda Ṭhākura in his *Amṛta-pravāha-bhāṣya:* "The purport is that one can realize life's perfection simply by satisfying the Supreme Personality of Godhead." This is also confirmed in *Śrīmad-Bhāgavatam* (1.2.13):

ataḥ pumbhir dvija-śreṣṭhā
varṇāśrama-vibhāgaśaḥ
svanuṣṭhitasya dharmasya
saṁsiddhir hari-toṣaṇam

"O best among the twiceborn, it is therefore concluded that the highest perfection one can achieve, by discharging his prescribed duties [*dharma*] according to caste divisions and order of life, is to please the Lord Hari."

Every man should perform his occupational duty in the light of his particular tendency. According to his abilities, one should accept a position in the *varṇāśrama* institution. The divisions of *brāhmaṇa, kṣatriya, vaiśya* and *śūdra* are natural divisions within society. Indeed, everyone has a prescribed duty according to the *varṇāśrama-dharma.* Those who properly execute their prescribed duties live peacefully and are not disturbed by material conditions. The spiritual orders—*brahmacarya, gṛhastha, vānaprastha* and *sannyāsa*—are called *āśramas.* If one executes his prescribed duty in both the social and spiritual order, the Supreme Personality of Godhead is satisfied. If one neglects his duties, however, he becomes a transgressor and a candidate for a hellish condition. Actually we see that different people are engaged in different ways; therefore there must be divisions according to work. To attain perfection, one must make devotional service the center of life. In this way one can awaken his natural instincts by work, association and education. One should accept the *varṇāśrama* divisions by qualification, not by birth. Unless this system is introduced, human activities cannot be systematically executed.

The *brāhmaṇas* are the intellectuals who can understand the Supreme Personality of Godhead. They are always engaged in the cultivation of knowledge. It does not matter whether one is born in India or outside India. Those who are naturally very heroic and who tend to rule over others are called *kṣatriyas.* Those who tend to produce food by agricultural methods, protect cows and other animals and engage in trade are called *vaiśyas,* or merchants. Those who are not sufficiently intelligent to be *brāhmaṇas, kṣatriyas* or *vaiśyas* are required to serve a master and are called *śūdras.* Thus everyone can engage in the service of the Lord and Kṛṣṇa consciousness. If a society does not function according to such natural divisions, the social orders become degraded. The conclusion is that the scientific method of *varṇāśrama-dharma* should be adopted by society.

TEXT 59

প্রভু কহে,- "এহো বাহ্য, আগে কহ আর।"
রায় কহে, "কৃষ্ণে কর্মার্পণ--সর্বসাধ্য-সার॥" ৫৯ ॥

prabhu kahe,——"eho bāhya, āge kaha āra"
rāya kahe, "kṛṣṇe karmārpaṇa——sarva-sādhya-sāra"

SYNONYMS

prabhu kahe—the Lord said; *eho*—this; *bāhya*—external; *āge*—ahead; *kaha*—say; *āra*—more; *rāya kahe*—Śrī Rāmānanda Rāya said; *kṛṣṇe*—unto Kṛṣṇa; *karma-arpaṇa*—offering the results of activities; *sarva-sādhya-sāra*—the essence of all means of perfection.

TRANSLATION

The Lord replied, "This is external. You had better tell Me of some other means." Rāmānanda replied, "To offer the results of one's activities to Kṛṣṇa is the essence of all perfection."

TEXT 60

যৎ করোষি যদশ্নাসি যজ্জুহোষি দদাসি যৎ।
যত্তপস্যসি কৌন্তেয় তৎ কুরুষ্ব মদর্পণম্ ॥ ৬০ ॥

yat karoṣi yad aśnāsi
yaj juhoṣi dadāsi yat
yat tapasyasi kaunteya
tat kuruṣva mad-arpaṇam

SYNONYMS

yat—whatever; *karoṣi*—you do; *yat*—whatever; *aśnāsi*—you eat; *yat*—whatever; *juhoṣi*—you offer in sacrifice; *dadāsi*—you give in charity; *yat*—whatever; *yat*—whatever; *tapasyasi*—you perform as austerity; *kaunteya*—O son of Kuntī; *tat*—that; *kuruṣva*—just do; *mat*—unto Me; *arpaṇam*—offering.

TRANSLATION

Rāmānanda Rāya continued, " 'O son of Kuntī, all that you do, all that you eat, all that you offer and give away, as well as all austerities that you may perform, should be done as an offering unto Me.' "

PURPORT

The Lord has said that the *varṇāśrama-dharma* is not properly executed in this age of Kali; therefore He ordered Rāmānanda Rāya to go further into the matter.

Rāmānanda replied with this verse from *Bhagavad-gītā* (9.27) that while remaining in the system of *varṇāśrama-dharma,* one may offer the results of his activities to Lord Śrī Kṛṣṇa in loving service. Naturally Lord Śrī Caitanya Mahāprabhu was asking Rāmānanda Rāya about the execution of devotional service. Rāmānanda Rāya first enunciated the principle of *varṇāśrama-dharma* in consideration of materialistic people. However, this conception is not transcendental. As long as one is in the material world, he must follow the principles of *varṇāśrama-dharma,* but devotional service is transcendental. The system of *varṇāśrama-dharma* refers to the three modes of material nature, but transcendental devotional service is on the absolute platform. Śrī Caitanya Mahāprabhu belonged to the spiritual world, and His methods for propagating the *saṅkīrtana* movement were also imported from the spiritual world. Śrīla Narottama dāsa Ṭhākura has sung: *golokera prema-dhana, hari-nāma-saṅkīrtana, rati na janmila kene tāya.* This states that the *saṅkīrtana* movement has nothing to do with this material world. It is imported from the spiritual world, Goloka Vṛndāvana. Narottama dāsa Ṭhākura laments that mundane people do not take this *saṅkīrtana* movement seriously. Considering the position of devotional service and the *saṅkīrtana* movement, Śrī Caitanya Mahāprabhu deemed the system of *varṇāśrama-dharma* to be material, although it aims at elevation to the spiritual platform. However, the *saṅkīrtana* movement can raise one immediately to the spiritual platform. Consequently it is said that *varṇāśrama-dharma* is external, and Caitanya Mahāprabhu requested Rāmānanda Rāya to proceed deeper into the matter and uncover the spiritual platform.

Sometimes materialists consider Lord Viṣṇu a material conception. Impersonalists think that above Lord Viṣṇu is the impersonal Brahman. The impersonalists misunderstand the worship of Lord Viṣṇu. They worship Lord Viṣṇu to merge into His body. In order that *viṣṇu-ārādhana* not be misunderstood, Śrī Caitanya Mahāprabhu requested that Śrī Rāmānanda Rāya proceed further and clear up the issue. Rāmānanda Rāya quoted the verse from *Bhagavad-gītā* stating that the results of one's occupational duty may be offered to Lord Viṣṇu or Kṛṣṇa. In *Śrīmad-Bhāgavatam* (1.2.8) it is also said:

dharmaḥ svanuṣṭhitaḥ puṁsāṁ
viṣvaksena-kathāsu yaḥ
notpādayed yadi ratiṁ
śrama eva hi kevalam

"If one executes the occupational duties of *varṇāśrama-dharma* but does not cultivate his dormant Kṛṣṇa consciousness, his activities are futile. His occupation simply becomes unnecessary labor."

TEXT 61

প্রভু কহে,—"এহো বাহ্য,আগে কহ আর।"
রায় কহে, "স্বধর্ম-ত্যাগ,—এই সাধ্য-সার॥" ৬১ ॥

prabhu kahe,——"eho bāhya, āge kaha āra"
rāya kahe, "svadharma-tyāga,——ei sādhya-sāra"

SYNONYMS

prabhu kahe—the Lord replied; *eho*—this; *bāhya*—external; *āge*—ahead; *kaha*—speak; *āra*—more; *rāya kahe*—Rāmānanda Rāya replied; *sva-dharma-tyāga*—relinquishing one's occupational duties; *ei*—this; *sādhya-sāra*—the essence of all perfection.

TRANSLATION

"This is also external," Śrī Caitanya Mahāprabhu said. "Please proceed and speak further on this matter." Rāmānanda Rāya replied, "To give up one's occupational duties in the varṇāśrama is the essence of perfection."

PURPORT

A *brāhmaṇa* may renounce his family and accept *sannyāsa*. Others also—*kṣatriyas* and *vaiśyas*—may also give up their families and take to Kṛṣṇa consciousness. Such renunciation is called *karma-tyāga*. By such renunciation, the Supreme Personality of Godhead is satisfied. However, this renouncing of one's activities to Kṛṣṇa is not uncontaminated and is therefore on the material platform. Such activities are considered within the material universe because, according to Śrī Caitanya Mahāprabhu, they refer to the material universe and are therefore external. To correct this, Rāmānanda Rāya recommended that one take to the renounced order of life in order to transcend material activities. This is supported by the following verse from *Śrīmad-Bhāgavatam* (11.11.32).

TEXT 62

আজ্ঞায়ৈবং গুণান্ দোষান্ময়াদিষ্টানপি স্বকান্ ।
ধর্মান্ সংত্যজ্য যঃ সর্বান্ মাং ভজেৎ স চ সত্তমঃ ॥ ৬২ ॥

ājñāyaivaṁ guṇān doṣān
mayādiṣṭān api svakān
dharmān saṁtyajya yaḥ sarvān
māṁ bhajet sa ca sattamaḥ

SYNONYMS

ājñāya—knowing perfectly; *evam*—thus; *guṇān*—qualities; *doṣān*—faults; *mayā*—by Me; *ādiṣṭān*—instructed; *api*—although; *svakān*—own; *dharmān*—occupational duties; *saṁtyajya*—giving up; *yaḥ*—anyone who; *sarvān*—all; *mām*—unto Me; *bhajet*—may render service; *saḥ*—he; *ca*—and; *sattamaḥ*—a first-class person.

TRANSLATION

Rāmānanda Rāya continued, " 'Occupational duties are described in the religious scriptures. If one analyzes them, he can fully understand their qualities and faults and then give them up completely to render service unto the Supreme Personality of Godhead. Such a person is considered a first-class man.'

TEXT 63

সর্বধর্মান্ পরিত্যজ্য মামেকং শরণং ব্রজ ।
অহং ত্বাং সর্বপাপেভ্যো মোক্ষয়িষ্যামি মা শুচঃ ॥ ৬৩ ॥

sarva-dharmān parityajya
mām ekaṁ śaraṇaṁ vraja
ahaṁ tvāṁ sarva-pāpebhyo
mokṣayiṣyāmi mā śucaḥ

SYNONYMS

sarva-dharmān—all kinds of occupational duties; *parityajya*—giving up; *mām ekam*—unto Me only; *śaraṇam*—as shelter; *vraja*—go; *aham*—I; *tvām*—unto you; *sarva-pāpebhyaḥ*—from all the reactions of sinful life; *mokṣayiṣyāmi*—will give liberation; *mā*—don't; *śucaḥ*—worry.

TRANSLATION

"As stated in scripture [Bg. 18.66]: 'After giving up all kinds of religious and occupational duties, if you come to Me, the Supreme Personality of Godhead, and take shelter, I will give you protection from all of life's sinful reactions. Do not worry.' "

PURPORT

In this connection, Śrīla Raghunātha dāsa Gosvāmī instructs in his book *Manaḥ-śikṣā* (2):

na dharmaṁ nādharmaṁ śruti-gaṇa-niruktaṁ kila kuru
vraje rādhā-kṛṣṇa-pracura-paricaryām iha tanu

He has thus enjoined that we should not perform religious or irreligious activities as prescribed in the *Vedas*. The best course is to engage always in the service of Lord Kṛṣṇa and Rādhārāṇī. That is the perfection of everything in this life. Similarly, in *Śrīmad-Bhāgavatam* (4.29.46) it is said by Nārada Muni:

yadā yasyānugṛhṇāti
bhagavān ātma-bhāvitaḥ
sa jahāti matiṁ loke
vede ca pariniṣṭhitām

"When one actually takes to the loving service of the Supreme Personality of Godhead, he gives up all duties in the material world as well as all duties prescribed by Vedic literatures. In this way one is fixed in the service of the Lord."

TEXT 64

প্রভু কহে,—"এহো বাহ্য, আগে কহ আর।"
রায় কহে,—"জ্ঞানমিশ্রা ভক্তি—সাধ্যসার॥" ৬৪॥

prabhu kahe,—"eho bāhya, āge kaha āra"
rāya kahe,—"jñāna-miśrā bhakti—sādhya-sāra"

SYNONYMS

prabhu kahe—the Lord said; *eho*—this; *bāhya*—external; *āge*—ahead; *kaha*—say; *āra*—more; *rāya kahe*—Rāya replied; *jñāna-miśrā bhakti*—devotional service mixed with empiric knowledge; *sādhya-sāra*—is the essence of perfection.

TRANSLATION

After hearing Rāmānanda Rāya speak in this way, Lord Śrī Caitanya Mahāprabhu said, "Go ahead and say something more." Rāmānanda Rāya then replied, "Devotional service mixed with empiric knowledge is the essence of perfection."

PURPORT

Devotional service mixed with non-Vedic speculative knowledge is certainly not pure devotional service. Therefore Śrīla Bhaktisiddhānta Sarasvatī in his *Anubhāṣya* preached that self-realization following the execution of ritualistic ceremonies is in the neutral stage between liberation and conditional life. It is the place beyond this material world in the River Virajā, where the three modes of material nature are subdued or neutralized in the unmanifest stage. However, in the spiritual world is a manifestation of spiritual energy, known as Vaikuṇṭhaloka where there is no anxiety. The material world is known as *brahmāṇḍa*. The material universe is the creation of the external energy. Between the two creations—the material creation and the spiritual creation—is a river known as Virajā as well as a place known as Brahmaloka. Virajānadī and Brahmaloka are shelters for living entities disgusted with material life and inclined to impersonal existence by way of denying material variegatedness. Since these places are not situated in the Vaikuṇṭhalokas or the spiritual world, Śrī Caitanya Mahāprabhu proclaims them to be external. In the Brahmaloka and Virajānadī, one cannot conceive of the Vaikuṇṭhalokas. Brahmaloka and Virajānadī are also attained after difficult austerities, but in these realms there is no understanding of the Supreme Personality of Godhead and His transcendental loving service. Without such spiritual knowledge, simple detachment from material conditions is but another side of material existence. From the spiritual point of view, it is all external. When Śrī Caitanya Mahāprabhu rejected this proposal, Rāmānanda Rāya suggested that devotional service based on philosophy and logic is a more progressed position. He therefore quoted the following verse from *Bhagavad-gītā* (18.54).

TEXT 65

ব্রহ্মভূতঃ প্রসন্নাত্মা ন শোচতি ন কাঙ্ক্ষতি ।
সমঃ সর্বেষু ভূতেষু মদ্ভক্তিং লভতে পরাম্ ॥ ৬৫ ॥

brahma-bhūtaḥ prasannātmā
na śocati na kāṅkṣati
samaḥ sarveṣu bhūteṣu
mad-bhaktiṁ labhate parām

SYNONYMS

brahma-bhūtaḥ—freed from material conceptions of life but attached to an impersonal situation; *prasanna-ātmā*—fully joyful; *na śocati*—he does not lament; *na kāṅkṣati*—he does not hanker; *samaḥ*—equally disposed; *sarveṣu*—all; *bhūteṣu*—to the living entities; *mat-bhaktim*—My devotional service; *labhate*—achieves; *parām*—transcendental.

TRANSLATION

Rāmānanda Rāya continued, "According to Bhagavad-gītā: 'One who is thus transcendentally situated at once realizes the Supreme Brahman and becomes fully joyful. He never laments nor desires to have anything; he is equally disposed to every living entity. In that state he attains pure devotional service unto Me.' "

PURPORT

In *Bhagavad-gītā* it is said that a person who accepts the theory of monism—being always engaged in empiric philosophical discussions about spiritual life—becomes joyful and is relieved from all material lamentation and hankering. At that stage, one is equipoised. He sees all living entities as spiritual beings. After attaining this elevated stage, one can attain pure devotional service. The conclusion is that devotional service mixed with ritualistic fruitive activity is inferior to spiritual service based on empiric philosophic discussion.

TEXT 66

প্রভু কহে, "এহো বাহ্য, আগে কহ আর ।"
রায় কহে,—"জ্ঞানশূন্যা ভক্তি—সাধ্যসার ॥" ৬৬ ॥

prabhu kahe, "eho bāhya, āge kaha āra"
rāya kahe,——"jñāna-śūnyā bhakti——sādhya-sāra"

SYNONYMS

prabhu kahe—the Lord said; *eho*—this; *bāhya*—external; *āge*—ahead; *kaha*—speak; *āra*—further; *rāya kahe*—Rāmānanda Rāya replied; *jñāna-śūnyā bhakti*—devotional service independent of logic and empiric philosophy; *sādhya-sāra*—the essence of the perfection of life.

TRANSLATION

After hearing this, the Lord, as usual, rejected it, considering it to be external devotional service. He again asked Rāmānanda Rāya to speak further, and Rāmānanda Rāya replied, "Pure devotional service without any touch of speculative knowledge is the essence of perfection."

PURPORT

Śrīla Bhaktisiddhānta Sarasvatī Ṭhākura in his *Anubhāṣya* commentary says that this stage—devotional service mixed with speculative knowledge—is also external and not within the jurisdiction of pure devotional service as practiced in Vaikuṇṭhaloka. As soon as there is some conception of materialistic thought—be it positive or negative—the service is not spiritual. It may be free from material contamination, but because there is mental speculation the devotional service is not pure and freed from the contamination of material life. A living entity who wants to be completely pure must be above this material conception. The negation of material existence does not necessarily mean spiritual existence. After material existence is negated, spiritual existence—namely *sac-cid-ānanda*—still may not be manifest. Until one comes to the stage of actually understanding one's eternal relationship with the Supreme Lord, he cannot enter into spiritual life. Spiritual life means becoming detached from material life and engaging in the loving service of the Lord. Śrī Caitanya Mahāprabhu therefore asked Rāmānanda Rāya to explain something transcendental to devotional service mixed with speculative knowledge. A pure devotee is completely surrendered to the lotus feet of the Lord, and only by his love does he conquer Kṛṣṇa, who cannot be conquered by anyone. Kṛṣṇa always stands victorious over everything. No one can conquer Him. One can attain the stage of pure devotion simply by fully surrendering. This is next corroborated by *Śrīmad-Bhāgavatam* (10.14.3), wherein Lord Brahmā, defeated by the potency of Śrī Kṛṣṇa, fully surrendered unto the Lord.

TEXT 67

জ্ঞানে প্রয়াসমুদপাস্য নমন্ত এব
জীবন্তি সন্মুখরিতাং ভবদীয়বার্তাম্ ।

স্থানে স্থিতাঃ শ্রুতিগতাং তনুবাঙ্মনোভি-
র্যে প্রায়শোঽজিত জিতোঽপ্যসি তৈস্ত্রিলোক্যাম্ ॥ ৬৭ ॥

jñāne prayāsam udapāsya namanta eva
jīvanti san-mukharitāṁ bhavadīya-vārtām
sthāne sthitāḥ śruti-gatāṁ tanu-vāṅ-manobhir
ye prāyaśo 'jita jito 'py asi tais tri-lokyām

SYNONYMS

jñāne—in gaining knowledge; *prayāsam*—unnecessary endeavor; *udapāsya*—setting far aside; *namantaḥ*—completely surrendering; *eva*—certainly; *jīvanti*—live; *sat-mukharitām*—declared by great realized devotees; *bhavadīya-vārtām*—discussions about You, the Supreme Personality of Godhead; *sthāne sthitāḥ*—situated in their own positions; *śruti-gatām*—received aurally; *tanu-vāk-manobhiḥ*—by the body, words and mind; *ye*—those who; *prāyaśaḥ*—almost always; *ajita*—O my unconquerable Lord (beyond perception and unlimitedly independent); *jitaḥ*—conquered; *api*—indeed; *asi*—You are; *taiḥ*—by such pure devotees; *tri-lokyām*—within the three worlds.

TRANSLATION

Rāmānanda Rāya continued, "Lord Brahmā said, 'My dear Lord, those devotees who have thrown away the impersonal conception of the Absolute Truth and have therefore abandoned discussing empiric philosophical truths should hear from self-realized devotees about Your holy name, form, pastimes and qualities. They should completely follow the principles of devotional service and remain free from illicit sex, gambling, intoxication and animal slaughter. Surrendering themselves fully with body, words and mind, they can live in any āśrama or social status. Indeed, You are conquered by such persons, although You are always unconquerable.' "

TEXT 68

প্রভু কহে,—"এহো হয়, আগে কহ আর।"
রায় কহে,—"প্রেমভক্তি—সর্বসাধ্যসার॥" ৬৮ ॥

prabhu kahe,——"eho haya, āge kaha āra"
rāya kahe,——"prema-bhakti——sarva-sādhya-sāra"

SYNONYMS

prabhu kahe—the Lord said; *eho haya*—this is all right; *āge kaha āra*—speak something more; *rāya kahe*—Rāya replied; *prema-bhakti*—ecstatic love in devotional service to the Lord; *sarva-sādhya-sāra*—the essence of all perfection.

TRANSLATION

At this point, Śrī Caitanya Mahāprabhu replied, "This is all right, but still you can speak more on the subject." Rāmānanda Rāya then replied, "Ecstatic love for the Supreme Personality of Godhead is the essence of all perfection."

PURPORT

In this connection, Śrīla Bhaktivinoda Ṭhākura in his *Amṛta-pravāha-bhāṣya* says that after hearing Rāmānanda Rāya, Lord Caitanya Mahāprabhu said, *eho haya, āge kaha āra.* This means that this is the process accepted in devotional service, but there is something more than this. Therefore Lord Caitanya Mahāprabhu requested him to explain what was beyond. Simply executing the duties of all *varṇas* and *āśramas* is not as good as offering all the results of one's activities to the Lord. When one gives up all fruitive activity and fully surrenders to the Lord, he attains *sva-dharma-tyāga,* wherein he abandons the social order and takes to the renounced order. That is certainly better. However, better than the renounced order is cultivation of knowledge mixed with devotional service. Yet all these activities are external to the activities of the spiritual world. There is no touch of pure devotional service in them. Pure devotional service cannot be attained by empiric philosophy, nor can perfection be attained simply by good association. Devotional service by self-realization is a different subject matter. It is untouched by fruitive activity, for one surrenders the results of activities to the Lord, abandons prescribed duties and accepts the renounced order of life. Such devotional service is situated on a higher platform than that of empiric philosophical speculation with a mixture of *bhakti.* This is verified by Śrīla Rūpa Gosvāmī in his *Bhakti-rasāmṛta-sindhu* (1.1.11):

anyābhilāṣitā-śūnyaṁ
jñāna-karmādy-anāvṛtam
ānukūlyena kṛṣṇānu-
śīlanaṁ bhaktir uttamā

"One should render transcendental loving service to the Supreme Lord Kṛṣṇa favorably and without desire for material profit or gain through fruitive activities or philosophical speculation. That is called pure devotional service."

Devotional activities, however, sometimes appear to be impure in the neophyte stage, but in the mature stage they are completely pure from material activity. Therefore Rāmānanda Rāya replied after hearing the last statement of Śrī Caitanya Mahāprabhu: *prema-bhakti—sarva-sādhya-sāra.* Śrī Caitanya Mahāprabhu actually accepted this verse (*jñāne prayāsam*) as the basic principle of perfection. One has to practice this principle in order to make further progress. When further progress is actually made, one comes to the platform of ecstatic loving service to the Lord. This first stage is technically called *sādhana-bhakti,* or devotional service in practice. The result of *sādhana-bhakti* must be ecstatic love, attachment for the Supreme Personality of Godhead, which is also called *prema-bhakti*. In the neophyte stage, *sādhana-bhakti* includes faith, association with devotees, and practicing devotional service. Thus one is freed from all unwanted things. One then becomes fixed in devotional service and increases his desire to act in devotional service. Thus one becomes attached to the Lord and His devotional service.

TEXT 69

নানোপচার-কৃতপূজনমার্তবন্ধোঃ
প্রেম্ণৈব ভক্তহৃদয়ং সুখবিদ্রুতং স্যাৎ ।
যাবৎ ক্ষুদস্তি জঠরে জরঠা পিপাসা
তাবৎ সুখায় ভবতো নমু ভক্ষ্য-পেয়ে ॥ ৬৯ ॥

nānopacāra-kṛta-pūjanam ārta-bandhoḥ
premṇaiva bhakta-hṛdayaṁ sukha-vidrutaṁ syāt
yāvat kṣud asti jaṭhare jaraṭhā pipāsā
tāvat sukhāya bhavato nanu bhakṣya-peye

SYNONYMS

nānā-upacāra—by varieties of ingredients; *kṛta*—performed; *pūjanam*—worshiping; *ārta-bandhoḥ*—of the Supreme Personality of Godhead, who is the friend of all distressed persons; *premṇā*—by ecstatic love; *eva*—indeed; *bhakta-hṛdayam*—the heart of a devotee; *sukha-vidrutam*—melted in transcendental bliss; *syāt*—becomes; *yāvat*—as long as; *kṣut*—appetite; *asti*—there is; *jaṭhare*—in the stomach; *jaraṭhā*—strong; *pipāsā*—thirst; *tāvat*—so long; *sukhāya*—for happiness; *bhavataḥ*—are; *nanu*—indeed; *bhakṣya*—eatables; *peye*—and drinkables.

TRANSLATION

Rāmānanda Rāya continued, " 'As long as there is hunger and thirst, eating and drinking make one feel very happy. When the Lord is worshiped with pure love, transcendental bliss is awakened in the heart of the devotee.'

TEXT 70

কৃষ্ণভক্তিরসভাবিতা মতিঃ
ক্রীয়তাং যদি কুতোঽপি লভ্যতে।
তত্র লৌল্যমপি মূল্যমেকলং
জন্মকোটিসুকৃতৈর্ন লভ্যতে॥ ৭০ ॥

kṛṣṇa-bhakti-rasa-bhāvitā matiḥ
krīyatāṁ yadi kuto 'pi labhyate
tatra laulyam api mūlyam ekalaṁ
janma-koṭi-sukṛtair na labhyate

SYNONYMS

kṛṣṇa-bhakti-rasa-bhāvitā—absorbed in the mellows of executing devotional service to Kṛṣṇa; *matiḥ*—intelligence; *krīyatām*—let it be purchased; *yadi*—if; *kutaḥ api*—somewhere; *labhyate*—is available; *tatra*—there; *laulyam*—greed; *api*—indeed; *mūlyam*—price; *ekalam*—only; *janma-koṭi*—of millions of births; *sukṛtaiḥ*—by pious activities; *na*—not; *labhyate*—is obtained.

TRANSLATION

" 'Pure devotional service in Kṛṣṇa consciousness cannot be had even by pious activity in hundreds and thousands of lives. It can be attained only by paying one price—that is, intense greed to obtain it. If it is available somewhere, one must purchase it without delay.' "

PURPORT

The previous two verses are included in the *Padyāvalī* (13,14) by Śrīla Rūpa Gosvāmī. Verse sixty-nine refers to devotional service in faith, and verse seventy refers to devotional service rendered out of intense greed. The first is devotional service rendered in accordance to the regulative principles, and the second refers to spontaneous loving service of the Lord without extraneous endeavor. Henceforward the basic principle underlying the talks between Śrī Caitanya Mahāprabhu and Rāmānanda Rāya will be spontaneous loving service to the Lord. The regulative principles according to the injunctions of the *śāstras* are necessary insofar as one's original dormant Kṛṣṇa consciousness is not spontaneously awakened. An example of spontaneous action is the flowing of rivers into the ocean. Nothing can stop this flow of water. Similarly, when one's dormant Kṛṣṇa consciousness is awakened, it spontaneously flows to the lotus feet of Kṛṣṇa without impediment. Whatever will be spoken henceforth by Rāmānanda Rāya based on spontaneous love will be agreeable to Śrī Caitanya Mahāprabhu, and the Lord will ask him more and more about this subject.

TEXT 71

প্রভু কহে,—"এহো হয়, আগে কহ আর।"
রায় কহে, "দাস্য-প্রেম - সর্বসাধ্যসার ॥" ৭১ ॥

prabhu kahe,——"eho haya, āge kaha āra"
rāya kahe, "dāsya-prema——sarva-sādhya-sāra"

SYNONYMS

prabhu kahe—the Lord said; *eho haya*—this is all right; *āge kaha āra*—please speak more; *rāya kahe*—Rāmānanda Rāya replied; *dāsya-prema*—spontaneous love in the humor of servitude; *sarva-sādhya-sāra*—the essence of perfection.

TRANSLATION

Hearing up to the point of spontaneous love, the Lord said, "This is all right, but if you know more, please tell Me." In reply, Rāmānanda Rāya said, "Spontaneous loving service in servitude—as exchanged by master and servant—is the highest perfection.

PURPORT

Spontaneous loving service to the Lord is called devotional service with an intimate attachment between the servitor and the served. This intimacy is called *mamatā.* Between the servitor and the served, there is a feeling of oneness. This *mamatā* begins with *dāsya-prema,* service rendered to the master by the servant. Unless there is such a relationship, the loving affairs between the Lord and His devotee are not actually fixed. When the devotee feels, "The Lord is my master" and renders service unto Him, Kṛṣṇa consciousness is awakened. This fixed consciousness is on a higher platform than simple cognizance of love of Godhead.

TEXT 72

যন্নামশ্রুতিমাত্রেণ পুমান্ ভবতি নির্মলঃ ।
তস্য তীর্থপদঃ কিংবা দাসানামবশিষ্যতে ॥ ৭২ ॥

yan-nāma-śruti-mātreṇa
pumān bhavati nirmalaḥ
tasya tīrtha-padaḥ kiṁ vā
dāsānām avaśiṣyate

SYNONYMS

yat—of whom; *nāma*—of the name; *śruti-mātreṇa*—simply by hearing; *pumān*—a person; *bhavati*—becomes; *nirmalaḥ*—pure; *tasya*—of Him; *tīrtha-padaḥ*—of the Supreme Personality of Godhead, at whose lotus feet are all places of pilgrimage; *kim*—what; *vā*—more; *dāsānām*—of the servants; *avaśiṣyate*—is remaining.

TRANSLATION

" 'A man becomes purified simply by hearing the holy name of the Supreme Personality of Godhead, whose lotus feet create the holy places of pilgrimage. Therefore what remains to be attained by those who have become His servants?'

PURPORT

This is a quotation from *Śrīmad-Bhāgavatam* (9.5.16) and is an admission by the great sage Durvāsā Muni. Durvāsā Muni, a caste *brāhmaṇa* and great *yogī,* used to hate Mahārāja Ambarīṣa. When he decided to chastise Mahārāja Ambarīṣa through his yogic powers, he was chased by the Sudarśana *cakra* of the Supreme Personality of Godhead. When things were settled, he said, "When the holy name of the Supreme Personality of Godhead is heard by any person, that person is immediately sanctified. The Supreme Lord is master of the devotees, and the devotees, under His shelter, naturally come to own His opulences."

TEXT 73

ভবন্তমেবানুচরন্নিরন্তরঃ
প্রশান্তনিঃশেষমনোরথান্তরঃ ।
কদাহমৈকান্তিকনিত্যকিঙ্করঃ
প্রহর্ষয়িষ্যামি স-নাথ-জীবিতম্ ॥ ৭৩ ॥

bhavantam evānucaran nirantaraḥ
praśānta-niḥśeṣa-mano-rathāntaraḥ
kadāham aikāntika-nitya-kiṅkaraḥ
praharṣayiṣyāmi sa-nātha-jīvitam

SYNONYMS

bhavantam—You; *eva*—certainly; *anucaran*—serving; *nirantaraḥ*—always; *praśānta*—pacified; *niḥśeṣa*—all; *manaḥ-ratha*—desires; *antaraḥ*—other; *kadā*—when; *aham*—I; *aikāntika*—exclusive; *nitya*—eternal; *kiṅkaraḥ*—servant; *praharṣayiṣyāmi*—I shall become joyful; *sa-nātha*—with a fitting master; *jīvitam*—living.

TRANSLATION

" 'By serving You constantly, one is freed from all material desires and is completely pacified. When shall we engage as Your permanent eternal servants and always feel joyful to have such a perfect master?' "

PURPORT

This is a statement made by the great saintly devotee Yāmunācārya in his *Stotra-ratna* (43).

TEXT 74

প্রভু কহে,—"এহো হয়, কিছু আগে আর ।"
রায় কহে,—"সখ্য-প্রেম - সর্বসাধ্যসার ॥" ৭৪ ॥

prabhu kahe,——"eho haya, kichu āge āra"
rāya kahe,——"sakhya-prema——sarva-sādhya-sāra"

SYNONYMS

prabhu kahe—the Lord said; *eho haya*—this is also right; *kichu*—something; *āge*—ahead; *āra*—more; *rāya kahe*—Rāmānanda Rāya replied; *sakhya-prema*—transcendental loving service in fraternity; *sarva-sādhya-sāra*—the highest perfectional stage.

TRANSLATION

Hearing this from Rāmānanda Rāya, the Lord again requested him to go a step further. In reply, Rāmānanda Rāya said, "Loving service to Kṛṣṇa rendered in fraternity is the highest perfection.

PURPORT

As long as loving service is rendered to the Lord in the master-servant relationship, there is some fear, for the servant is always afraid of the master, despite the intimacy of self-interest. In this stage the servant is always afraid of the master and respectful of Him. When the devotee is further advanced, he has nothing to fear. He considers the Lord and himself on an equal level. At such a time, the devotee is fully convinced that Lord Kṛṣṇa is a friend and cannot at all be dissatisfied if the devotee lives with Him on an equal level. This understanding is called *viśrambha,* that is, devoid of a respectful attitude. When this attitude is chosen, it becomes *sakhya-prema,* or love of Godhead in friendship. On this stage there is developed consciousness of equality between the Lord and the devotee.

TEXT 75

ইত্থং সতাং ব্রহ্মসুখানুভূত্যা দাস্যং গতানাং পরদৈবতেন ।
মায়াশ্রিতানাং নরদারকেণ সার্ধং বিজহ্রুঃ কৃতপুণ্যপুঞ্জাঃ॥৭৫॥

ittham satāṁ brahma-sukhānubhūtyā
dāsyaṁ gatānāṁ para-daivatena
māyāśritānāṁ nara-dārakeṇa
sārdhaṁ vijahruḥ kṛta-puṇya-puñjāḥ

SYNONYMS

ittham—in this way; *satām*—of persons who prefer the impersonal feature of the Lord; *brahma*—of the impersonal effulgence; *sukha*—by the happiness; *anubhūtyā*—who is realized; *dāsyam*—the mode of servitude; *gatānām*—of those who have accepted; *para-daivatena*—who is the supreme worshipable

Deity; *māyā-āśritānām*—for ordinary persons under the clutches of external energy; *nara-dārakeṇa*—with He who is like a boy of this material world; *sārdham*—in friendship; *vijahruḥ*—played; *kṛta-puṇya-puñjāḥ*—those who have accumulated volumes of pious activities.

TRANSLATION

" 'Those who are engaged in self-realization, appreciating the Brahman effulgence of the Lord, and those engaged in devotional service, accepting the Supreme Personality of Godhead as master, as well as those who are under the clutches of māyā, thinking the Lord an ordinary person, cannot understand that certain exalted personalities—after accumulating volumes of pious activities—are now playing with the Lord in friendship as cowherd boys.' "

PURPORT

This is a statement made by Śukadeva Gosvāmī (*Bhāg.* 10.12.11), who appreciated the good fortune of the cowherd boys who played with Kṛṣṇa and ate with Him on the banks of the Yamunā.

TEXT 76

প্রভু কহে,—"এহো উত্তম, আগে কহ আর।"
রায় কহে, "বাৎসল্য-প্রেম– সর্বসাধ্যসার ॥"৭৬॥

prabhu kahe,—"eho uttama, āge kaha āra"
rāya kahe, "vātsalya-prema—sarva-sādhya-sāra"

SYNONYMS

prabhu kahe—the Lord said; *eho uttama*—it is very good; *āge*—still further; *kaha*—speak; *āra*—more; *rāya kahe*—Rāya replied; *vātsalya-prema*—loving service to the Lord in the stage of paternal love; *sarva-sādhya-sāra*—the highest perfectional stage.

TRANSLATION

The Lord said, "This statement is very good, but please proceed even further." Rāmānanda Rāya then replied, "Loving service to the Lord in the parental relationship is the highest perfectional stage."

PURPORT

The stage of loving service to the Lord in paternal affection is an advanced stage of love in fraternity. In the fraternal relationship there is a sense of equality, but when that sense of equality is advanced in affection, one attains the platform of parental love. In this connection, the following verse is cited from *Śrīmad-Bhāgavatam* (10.8.46), wherein Śukadeva Gosvāmī voices his appreciation of Nanda Mahārāja's and mother Yaśodā's intense love for Kṛṣṇa.

TEXT 77

নন্দঃ কিমকরোদ্‌ব্রহ্মন্ শ্রেয় এবং মহোদয়ম্ ।
যশোদা বা মহাভাগা পপৌ যস্যাঃ স্তনং হরিঃ ॥৭৭॥

nandaḥ kim akarod brahman
śreya evaṁ mahodayam
yaśodā vā mahā-bhāgā
papau yasyāḥ stanaṁ hariḥ

SYNONYMS

nandaḥ—Nanda Mahārāja; *kim*—what; *akarot*—has performed; *brahman*—O *brāhmaṇa; śreyaḥ*—auspicious activities; *evam*—thus; *mahā-udayam*—rising to such an exalted position as the father of Kṛṣṇa; *yaśodā*—mother Yaśodā; *vā*—or; *mahā-bhāgā*—most fortunate; *papau*—drank; *yasyāḥ*—of whom; *stanam*—by the breasts; *hariḥ*—the Supreme Personality of Godhead.

TRANSLATION

Rāmānanda Rāya continued: " 'O brāhmaṇa, what pious activities did Nanda Mahārāja perform by which he received the Supreme Personality of Godhead Kṛṣṇa as his son, and what pious activities did mother Yaśodā perform that made the Absolute Supreme Personality of Godhead Kṛṣṇa call her mother and suck her breasts?'

TEXT 78

নেমং বিরিঞ্চো ন ভবো ন শ্রীরপ্যঙ্গসংশ্রয়া ।
প্রসাদং লেভিরে গোপী যত্তৎ প্রাপ বিমুক্তিদাৎ ॥ ৭৮ ॥

nemaṁ viriñco na bhavo
na śrīr apy aṅga-saṁśrayā
prasādaṁ lebhire gopī
yat tat prāpa vimuktidāt

SYNONYMS

na—not; *imam*—this (love of Godhead); *viriñcaḥ*—Lord Brahmā; *na*—not; *bhavaḥ*—Lord Śiva; *na*—nor; *śrīḥ*—the goddess of fortune; *api*—even; *aṅga*—on the chest of Viṣṇu; *saṁśrayā*—who is sheltered; *prasādam*—favor; *lebhire*—have obtained; *gopī*—mother Yaśodā; *yat*—which; *tat*—that; *prāpa*—obtained; *vimukti-dāt*—from the person who gives liberation.

TRANSLATION

" 'The favor mother Yaśodā obtained from Śrī Kṛṣṇa, the bestower of liberation, was never obtained even by Lord Brahmā or Lord Śiva, nor even by the goddess of fortune, who always remains on the chest of the Supreme Personality of Godhead Viṣṇu.' "

PURPORT

This is a statement from *Śrīmad-Bhāgavatam* (10.9.20). Kṛṣṇa agreed to be bound by mother Yaśodā after she had given up trying to bind Kṛṣṇa with ropes. This is another appreciation made by Śukadeva Gosvāmī in his narration of the pastimes of Kṛṣṇa before Mahārāja Parīkṣit.

TEXT 79

প্রভু কহে,—"এহো উত্তম, আগে কহ আর।"
রায় কহে, "কান্তাপ্রেম সর্বসাধ্যসার॥" ৭৯॥

prabhu kahe,——"eho uttama, āge kaha āra"
rāya kahe, "kāntā-prema sarva-sādhya-sāra"

SYNONYMS

prabhu kahe—the Lord replied; *eho uttama*—this is very good; *āge*—ahead; *kaha*—speak; *āra*—more; *rāya kahe*—Rāmānanda Rāya replied; *kāntā-prema*—loving service between husband and wife; *sarva-sādhya-sāra*—the highest perfectional stage.

TRANSLATION

The Lord said, "Your statements are certainly getting better and better one after the other, but surpassing all of them is another transcendental mellow, and you can speak of that as the most sublime." Rāmānanda Rāya then replied, "Conjugal attachment for Kṛṣṇa is the topmost position in love of Godhead.

PURPORT

In general, love of Godhead is devoid of the intimacy of ownership. In the case of love in servitude, there is a want of confidence. There is a want of increased affection in the fraternal relationship, but when this affection increases in the paternal relationship, there is nonetheless a want of complete freedom. However, when one becomes a conjugal lover of Kṛṣṇa, everything lacking in the other relationships is completely manifest. Love of Godhead lacks nothing in the conjugal stage. The summary of this verse is that paternal love of Godhead is certainly higher than fraternal love and that conjugal love is higher yet. It was when Śrī Caitanya Mahāprabhu requested Rāmānanda Rāya to go further that he came to the point of the conjugal relationship, which is the highest perfectional stage of transcendental love.

TEXT 80

নায়ং শ্রিয়োঽঙ্গ উ নিতান্তরতেঃ প্রসাদঃ
স্বর্যোষিতাং নলিনগন্ধরুচাং কুতোঽন্যাঃ ।
রাসোৎসবেঽস্য ভুজদণ্ডগৃহীতকণ্ঠ-
লব্ধাশিষাং য উদগাদ্ব্রজসুন্দরীণাম্ ॥ ৮০ ॥

nāyaṁ śriyo 'ṅga u nitānta-rateḥ prasādaḥ
svar-yoṣitāṁ nalina-gandha-rucāṁ kuto 'nyāḥ
rāsotsave 'sya bhuja-daṇḍa-gṛhīta-kaṇṭha-
labdhāśiṣāṁ ya udagād-vraja-sundarīṇām

SYNONYMS

na—not; *ayam*—this; *śriyaḥ*—of the goddess of fortune; *aṅge*—on the chest; *u*—alas; *nitānta-rateḥ*—who is very intimately related; *prasādaḥ*—the favor; *svaḥ*—of the heavenly planets; *yoṣitām*—of women; *nalina*—of the lotus flower; *gandha*—having the aroma; *rucām*—and bodily luster; *kutaḥ*—much less; *anyāḥ*—others; *rāsa-utsave*—in the festival of the *rāsa* dance; *asya*—of Lord Śrī Kṛṣṇa; *bhuja-daṇḍa*—by the arms; *gṛhīta*—embraced; *kaṇṭha*—their necks; *labdha-āśiṣām*—who achieved such a blessing; *yaḥ*—which; *udagāt*—became manifest; *vraja-sundarīṇām*—of the beautiful *gopīs,* the transcendental girls of Vrajabhūmi.

TRANSLATION

" 'When Lord Śrī Kṛṣṇa was dancing with the gopīs in the rāsa-līlā, the gopīs were embraced by the arms of the Lord. This transcendental favor was never bestowed upon the goddess of fortune or the other consorts in the spiritual world. Indeed, never was such a thing even imagined by the most beautiful girls in the heavenly planets whose bodily luster and aroma resemble the lotus flower. And what to speak of worldly women who are very beautiful according to the material estimation?'

PURPORT

This verse (*Bhāg.* 10.47.60) was spoken by Uddhava when he visited Śrī Vṛndāvana to deliver a message from Kṛṣṇa to the *gopīs*. Uddhava remained in Vṛndāvana to observe the movements of the *gopīs* there. When he saw the ecstatic love for Kṛṣṇa in separation manifested by the *gopīs,* he appreciated their supreme love and therefore expressed his feelings in this verse. He admitted that the fortune of the *gopīs* could not be compared even to the fortune of the goddess of fortune, to say nothing of the beautiful girls in the heavenly planets.

TEXT 81

তাসামাবিরভূচ্ছৌরিঃ স্ময়মানমুখাম্বুজঃ ।
পীতাম্বরধরঃ স্রগ্বী সাক্ষান্মন্মথমন্মথঃ ॥ ৮১ ॥

tāsām āvirabhūc chauriḥ
smayamāna-mukhāmbujaḥ
pītāmbara-dharaḥ sragvī
sākṣān manmatha-manmathaḥ

SYNONYMS

tāsām—among them; *āvirabhūt*—appeared; *śauriḥ*—Lord Kṛṣṇa; *smayamāna*—smiling; *mukha-ambujaḥ*—with a face like a lotus flower; *pīta-ambara-dharaḥ*—wearing yellow garments; *sragvī*—garlanded with flowers; *sākṣāt*—directly; *manmatha*—of Cupid; *manmathaḥ*—the bewilderer.

TRANSLATION

" 'Suddenly, due to the gopīs' feelings of separation, Lord Kṛṣṇa appeared among them dressed in yellow garments and wearing a flower garland. His lotus face was smiling, and He was directly attracting the mind of Cupid.'

PURPORT

This verse is from *Śrīmad-Bhāgavatam* (10.32.2). When the *rāsa* dance was going on, Kṛṣṇa suddenly disappeared, and the *gopīs* became so overwhelmed, due to His separation and their intense love for Him, that Kṛṣṇa was obliged to appear again.

TEXT 82

কৃষ্ণ-প্রাপ্তির উপায় বহুবিধ হয় ।
কৃষ্ণপ্রাপ্তি-তারতম্য বহুত আছয় ॥ ৮২ ॥

kṛṣṇa-prāptira upāya bahu-vidha haya
kṛṣṇa-prāpti-tāratamya bahuta āchaya

SYNONYMS

kṛṣṇa-prāptira—of achieving the lotus feet of Kṛṣṇa; *upāya*—means; *bahu-vidha*—various; *haya*—there are; *kṛṣṇa-prāpti*—of achieving the favor of Lord Kṛṣṇa; *tāratamya*—comparisons; *bahuta*—various; *āchaya*—there are.

TRANSLATION

"There are various means and processes by which one may attain the favor of Lord Kṛṣṇa. All those transcendental processes will be studied from the viewpoint of comparative importance.

TEXT 83

কিন্তু যাঁর যেই রস, সেই সর্বোত্তম ।
তটস্থ হঞা বিচারিলে, আছে তর-তম ॥ ৮৩ ॥

kintu yāṅra yei rasa, sei sarvottama
taṭa-stha hañā vicārile, āche tara-tama

SYNONYMS

kintu—nevertheless; *yāṅra*—of some devotees; *yei rasa*—whatever the mellow of exchanges of love; *sei*—that; *sarva-uttama*—the best; *taṭa-stha*—neutral; *hañā*—being; *vicārile*—if considering; *āche*—there is; *tara-tama*—lower and higher levels.

TRANSLATION

"It is true that whatever relationship a particular devotee has with the Lord is the best for him; still, when we study all the different methods from a neutral position, we can understand that there are higher and lower degrees of love.

PURPORT

In this regard, Śrīla Bhaktisiddhānta Sarasvatī Ṭhākura explains that this verse does not advocate the whimsical invention of some methods of love of Godhead. Such inventions cannot be accepted as topmost. Indeed, such concoctions are not recommended in these verses. Śrīla Rūpa Gosvāmī has said in the *Bhakti-rasāmṛta-sindhu* (1.2.101):

śruti-smṛti-purāṇādi-
pañcarātra-vidhiṁ vinā
aikāntikī harer bhaktir
utpātāyaiva kalpate

He clearly mentions in this verse that one must refer to the Vedic literatures and other supplementary literatures and follow the conclusion of the *Vedas.* An invented devotional attitude simply creates disturbances in the transcendental realm. If a person overly addicted to family life takes to *Śrīmad-Bhāgavatam* or Kṛṣṇa consciousness to earn a livelihood, his activity is certainly offensive. One should not become a caste *guru* and sell *mantras* for the benefit of mundane customers, nor should one make disciples for a livelihood. All these activities are offensive. One should not make a livelihood by forming a professional band to carry out congregational chanting, nor should one perform devotional service when one is attached to mundane society, friendship and love. Nor should one be dependent on so-called social etiquette. All of this is mental speculation. None of these things can be compared to unalloyed devotional service. No one can compare unalloyed devotional service, Kṛṣṇa consciousness, to mundane activities. There are many unauthorized parties pretending to belong to the Śrī Caitanya cult, and some are known as: *āula, bāula, karttābhajā, neḍā, daraveśa, sāṅi, sakhībhekī, smārta, jāta-gosāñi, ativāḍi, cūḍādhārī* and *gaurāṅga-nāgarī.*

Moreover, there are those who take the caste *gosvāmīs'* opinion of such parties as bona fide, comparing their opinions to those of the six Gosvāmīs headed by Śrī Rūpa and Śrī Sanātana. This is simply another cheating process. There are also nondevotees who compose unauthorized songs, who establish different temples for money, who worship the Deity as priests for salaries, who accept caste brahmanism as all in all and who do not know the value of a pure Vaiṣṇava. Actually the caste *brāhmaṇas* of the *smārta* community are opposed to the principles of the *Sātvata-pañcarātra.* Furthermore, there are many Māyāvādīs and those overly addicted to material sense enjoyment. None of these can be compared to a person who is purely engaged in preaching Kṛṣṇa consciousness. Every Kṛṣṇa conscious person is constantly endeavoring to utilize different transcendental devices in the service of the Lord. Such a devotee renounces all material enjoyment and completely dedicates himself to the service of his spiritual master and Lord Śrī Caitanya Mahāprabhu. He may be a perfect celibate, a restrained householder, a regulated *vānaprastha,* or a *tridaṇḍi-sannyāsī* in the renounced order. It doesn't matter. The pseudo-transcendentalists and the pure devotees cannot be compared, nor can one argue that a person can invent his own way of worship.

The purport in presenting this verse necessitates explaining the comparative positions of the transcendental mellows known as *śānta, dāsya, sakhya, vātsalya* and *mādhurya.* All these *rasas,* or mellows, are situated on the transcendental platform. Pure devotees take shelter of one of them and thus progress in spiritual life. Actually one can take shelter of such spiritual mellows only when one is completely uncontaminated by material attachment. When one is completely free from material attachment, the feelings of the transcendental mellows are awakened in the heart of the devotee. That is *svarūpa-siddhi,* the perfection of one's eternal relationship with the Supreme Lord. *Svarūpa-siddhi,* the eternal relationship with the Supreme Lord, may be situated in one of the transcendental mellows. Each and every one of them is as perfect as the others. However, by comparative study an unbiased person can realize that the mellow of servitorship is better than the mellow of neutrality. The mellow of fraternity is better than the mellow of servitorship. Similarly, the mellow of paternity is better than that of fraternity. Above all the mellows is the mellow of conjugal love. However, these are all spiritually situated on the same platform because all these relationships of perfection in love are based on a central point—Kṛṣṇa.

These mellows cannot be compared to the feelings one derives from demigod worship. Kṛṣṇa is one, but the demigods are different. They are material. Love for Kṛṣṇa cannot be compared to material love for different demigods. Because Māyāvādīs are on the material platform, they recommend the worship of Śiva or Durgā and say that worship of Kālī and Kṛṣṇa are the same. However, on the spiritual platform there is no demigod worship. The only worshipable object is Kṛṣṇa. Therefore although there is no difference between a devotee in *śānta-rasa* or *dāsya-rasa, vātsalya-rasa* or *mādhurya-rasa,* one can still make a comparative study of the intensity of love in these different transcendental positions. For example, it may be said that *dāsya-rasa* is better than *śānta-rasa,* yet transcendental love of God is there in both of them. Similarly, we can judge that love of Godhead in fraternity is better than love of Godhead in neutrality and servitorship. Similarly, love of Godhead in paternal affection is better than love in fraternity. And, as stated before, love of God in the conjugal *rasa* is superior to that in the paternal *rasa.*

The analysis of different types of love of Godhead has been made by expert *ācāryas* who know all about devotional service on the transcendental platform. Unfortunately, inexperienced and unauthorized persons in the mundane world, not understanding the transcendental position of pure love, try to find some material fault in the transcendental process. This is simply impudence on the part of spiritually inexperienced people. Such faultfinding is symptomatic of unfortunate mundane wranglers.

TEXT 84

যথোত্তরমসৌ স্বাদবিশেষোল্লাসময্যপি ।
রতির্বাসনয়া স্বাদ্বী ভাসতে কাপি কস্যচিৎ ॥ ৮৪ ॥

yathottaram asau svāda-
viśeṣollāsa-mayy api
ratir vāsanayā svādvī
bhāsate kāpi kasyacit

SYNONYMS

yathā uttaram—one after another; *asau*—that; *svāda-viśeṣa*—of particular tastes; *ullāsa*—pleasing; *mayī*—empowered with; *api*—although; *ratiḥ*—love; *vāsanayā*—by desire; *svādvī*—sweet; *bhāsate*—appears; *kā api*—someone; *kasyacit*—one of them.

TRANSLATION

" 'Increasing love is experienced in various tastes, one above another. But that love which has the highest taste in the gradual succession of desires manifests itself in the form of conjugal love.'

PURPORT

This verse is from Śrīla Rūpa Gosvāmī's *Bhakti-rasāmṛta-sindhu* (2.5.38), and it also appears in the *Ādi-līlā*, Chapter Four, verse forty-five.

TEXT 85

পূর্ব-পূর্ব-রসের গুণ — পরে পরে হয় ।
দুই-তিন গণনে পঞ্চ পর্যন্ত বাড়য় ॥ ৮৫ ॥

pūrva-pūrva-rasera guṇa——pare pare haya
dui-tina gaṇane pañca paryanta bāḍaya

SYNONYMS

pūrva-pūrva—of each previous; *rasera*—of the mellow; *guṇa*—the qualities; *pare pare*—in each subsequent; *haya*—there are; *dui-tina*—two and then three; *gaṇane*—in counting; *pañca*—five; *paryanta*—up to; *bāḍaya*—increases.

TRANSLATION

"There is a gradual order of improvement in transcendental mellows from the initial ones to the later ones. In each subsequent mellow the qualities of the previous mellows are manifest, counting from two, then three and up to the point of five complete qualities.

TEXT 86

গুণাধিক্যে স্বাদাধিক্য বাড়ে প্রতি-রসে ।
শান্ত-দাস্য-সখ্য-বাৎসল্যের গুণ মধুরেতে বৈসে॥৮৬॥

guṇādhikye svādādhikya bāḍe prati-rase
śānta-dāsya-sakhya-vātsalyera guṇa madhurete vaise

SYNONYMS

guṇa-ādhikye—by the increase of transcendental qualities; *svāda-ādhikya*—increase of taste; *bāḍe*—increases; *prati-rase*—in each mellow; *śānta*—of neutrality; *dāsya*—of servitude; *sakhya*—of fraternity; *vātsalyera*—and of paternal affection; *guṇa*—the qualities; *madhurete*—in the conjugal mellow; *vaise*—appear.

TRANSLATION

"As the qualities increase, so the taste also increases in each and every mellow. Therefore the qualities found in śānta-rasa, dāsya-rasa, sakhya-rasa and vātsalya-rasa are all manifest in conjugal love [mādhurya-rasa].

TEXT 87

আকাশাদির গুণ যেন পর-পর ভূতে ।
দুই-তিন ক্রমে বাড়ে পঞ্চ পৃথিবীতে ॥ ৮৭ ॥

ākāśādira guṇa yena para-para bhūte
dui-tina krame bāḍe pañca pṛthivīte

SYNONYMS

ākāśa-ādira—of the sky, air, and so on; *guṇa*—the qualities; *yena*—just as; *para-para*—one after another; *bhūte*—in the material elements; *dui-tina*—two and then three; *krame*—by gradations; *bāḍe*—increase; *pañca*—all five; *pṛthivīte*—in earth.

TRANSLATION

"The qualities in the material elements—sky, air, fire, water and earth—increase one after another by a gradual process of one, two and three, and at the last stage, in the element earth, all five qualities are completely visible.

TEXT 88

পরিপূর্ণ-কৃষ্ণপ্রাপ্তি এই 'প্রেমা' হৈতে ।
এই প্রেমার বশ কৃষ্ণ -কহে ভাগবতে ॥ ৮৮ ॥

paripūrṇa-kṛṣṇa-prāpti ei 'premā' haite
ei premāra vaśa kṛṣṇa——kahe bhāgavate

SYNONYMS

paripūrṇa—completely full; *kṛṣṇa-prāpti*—achievement of the lotus feet of Lord Kṛṣṇa; *ei*—this; *premā*—love of Godhead; *haite*—from; *ei premāra*—of this type of love of Godhead; *vaśa*—under the control; *kṛṣṇa*—Lord Kṛṣṇa; *kahe*—it is said; *bhāgavate*—in *Śrīmad-Bhāgavatam.*

TRANSLATION

"Complete attainment of the lotus feet of Lord Kṛṣṇa is made possible by love of Godhead, specifically mādhurya-rasa or conjugal love. Lord Kṛṣṇa is indeed captivated by this standard of love. This is also stated in Śrīmad-Bhāgavatam.

PURPORT

To explain the topmost quality of conjugal love, Śrīla Kṛṣṇadāsa Kavirāja Gosvāmī gives the example of the material elements—sky, air, fire, water and earth. In the sky (space) there is the quality of sound. Similarly, in air there are the qualities of sound and touch. In fire, there are three qualities—sound, touch and form. In water there are four qualities—sound, touch, form and taste. Finally, in earth there are all five qualities—sound, touch, form, taste and also smell. Now, one can see that the quality of the sky is in all—namely in air, fire, water and earth. In earth we can find all the qualities of material nature. The same can be applied to the *rasa* known as *mādhurya-rasa,* or conjugal love. In conjugal love there are the qualities of neutrality, servitorship, fraternity and paternity as well as conjugal love itself. The conclusion is that through conjugal love, the Lord is completely satisfied.

Conjugal love (*mādhurya-rasa*) is also known as *śṛṅgāra-rasa.* It is the conclusion of *Śrīmad-Bhāgavatam* that in the complete combination of loving service to the Lord—namely in conjugal love—the Supreme Lord fully agrees to be under the control of the devotee. The highest form of conjugal love is represented by Śrīmatī Rādhārāṇī; therefore in the pastimes of Rādhā and Kṛṣṇa we can see that Kṛṣṇa is always subjugated by Śrīmatī Rādhārāṇī's influence.

TEXT 89

ময়ি ভক্তির্হি ভূতানামমৃতত্বায় কল্পতে ।
দিষ্ট্যা যদাসীন্মৎস্নেহো ভবতীনাং মদাপনঃ ॥ ৮৯ ॥

mayi bhaktir hi bhūtānām
amṛtatvāya kalpate
diṣṭyā yad āsīn mat-sneho
bhavatīnāṁ mad-āpanaḥ

SYNONYMS

mayi—unto Me; *bhaktiḥ*—devotional service; *hi*—certainly; *bhūtānām*—of all living entities; *amṛtatvāya*—for becoming eternal; *kalpate*—is meant; *diṣṭyā*—fortunately; *yat*—what; *āsīt*—there is; *mat-snehaḥ*—affection for Me; *bhavatīnām*—of all of you; *mat-āpanaḥ*—the means of getting My favor.

TRANSLATION

"Lord Kṛṣṇa told the gopīs: 'The means of attaining My favor is loving service unto Me, and fortunately you are all thus engaged. Those living beings who render service unto Me are eligible to be transferred to the spiritual world and attain eternal life with knowledge and bliss.'

PURPORT

The fulfillment of human life is summarized in this verse from *Śrīmad-Bhāgavatam* (10.82.45). There are two important words in this verse: *bhakti* (devotional service) and *amṛtatva* (eternal life). The aim of human life is to attain the natural position of eternal life. This eternal life can be achieved only by devotional service.

TEXT 90

কৃষ্ণের প্রতিজ্ঞা দৃঢ় সর্বকালে আছে ।
যে যৈছে ভজে, কৃষ্ণ তারে ভজে তৈছে ॥ ৯০ ॥

kṛṣṇera pratijñā dṛḍha sarva-kāle āche
ye yaiche bhaje, kṛṣṇa tāre bhaje taiche

SYNONYMS

kṛṣṇera—of Lord Kṛṣṇa; *pratijñā*—the promise; *dṛḍha*—firm; *sarva-kāle*—in all times; *āche*—there is; *ye*—anyone; *yaiche*—just as; *bhaje*—renders service; *kṛṣṇa*—Lord Kṛṣṇa; *tāre*—him; *bhaje*—reciprocates with; *taiche*—so for all time.

TRANSLATION

"Lord Kṛṣṇa has made a firm promise for all time. If one renders service unto Him, Kṛṣṇa correspondingly gives him an equal amount of success in devotional service to the Lord.

PURPORT

It is a completely mistaken idea that one can worship Kṛṣṇa in any form or in any way and still attain the ultimate result by receiving the favor of the Lord. This is a decision made by gross materialistic men. Generally such men say that you can manufacture your own way of worshiping the Supreme Lord and that any type of worship is sufficient to approach the Supreme Personality of Godhead. Certainly there are different means for attaining different results in fruitive activity, speculative knowledge, mystic *yoga,* and austerity. Crude men therefore say that if one adopts any of these methods, one achieves the Supreme Personality of Godhead's favor. They claim that it doesn't matter what kind of method one adopts. A general example is given. If one wishes to arrive at a certain place, there are many roads leading there, and one can go to that place by any one of these roads. Similarly, these gross materialists say that there are different ways to attain the favor of the Supreme Personality of Godhead. They claim that one can conceive of the Supreme Personality of Godhead as goddess Durgā, goddess Kālī, Lord Śiva, demigod Gaṇeśa, Lord Rāmacandra, Kṛṣṇa, impersonal Brahman or whatever, and one can chant the Lord's name in any way and in any form and ultimately become one. Such materialists claim that the result is the same. They also say that a man may have different names, but he will answer if called by any one of them. Therefore they claim that there is no need to chant the Hare Kṛṣṇa *mantra.* If one chants the name of Kālī, Durgā, Śiva, Gaṇeśa or anyone else, the result will be the same. Such claims made by mental speculators are no doubt very pleasing to mental speculators, but those who are actually in knowledge do not admit such conclusions, which are against the authority of the *śāstras.* A bona fide *ācārya* will certainly not accept such a conclusion. As Kṛṣṇa clearly states in *Bhagavad-gītā:*

yānti deva-vratā devān
pitṝn yānti pitṛ-vratāḥ
bhūtāni yānti bhūtejyā
yānti mad-yājino 'pi mām

"Those who worship the demigods will take birth among the demigods; those who worship ghosts and spirits will take birth among such beings; those who worship ancestors go to the ancestors; and those who worship Me will live with Me." (Bg. 9.25)

Only the devotees of the Lord can be admitted to His kingdom—not the demigod worshipers, *karmīs, yogīs,* or anyone else. A person who desires elevation to the heavenly planets worships various demigods, and material nature may be pleased to offer such devotees their desired positions. Consequently material nature gives one one's own nature by which he increases affection for different types of demigods. However, *Bhagavad-gītā* says that demigod worship is meant for men who have lost all their intelligence.

kāmais tais tair hṛta-jñānāḥ
prapadyante 'nya-devatāḥ
taṁ taṁ niyamam āsthāya
prakṛtyā niyatāḥ svayā

"Those whose minds are distorted by material desires surrender unto demigods and follow the particular rules and regulations of worship according to their own natures." (Bg. 7.20)

Although one may be elevated to the heavenly planets, the results of such benediction are limited.

antavat tu phalaṁ teṣāṁ
tad bhavaty alpa-medhasām
devān deva-yajo yānti
mad-bhaktā yānti mām api

"Men of small intelligence worship the demigods, and their fruits are limited and temporary. Those who worship the demigods go to the planets of the demigods, but My devotees ultimately reach My supreme planet." (Bg. 7.23)

Being elevated to the heavenly planets or other material planets does not mean attaining an eternal life of knowledge and bliss. At the end of the material world, all attainments of material elevation will also end. Again, according to Kṛṣṇa in *Bhagavad-gītā,* only those who engage in His loving devotional service will be admitted to the spiritual world and return to Godhead, not others.

bhaktyā mām abhijānāti
yāvān yaś cāsmi tattvataḥ
tato māṁ tattvato jñātvā
viśate tad-anantaram

"One can understand the Supreme Personality as He is only by devotional service. And when one is in full consciousness of the Supreme Lord by such devotion, he can enter into the kingdom of God." (Bg. 18.55)

Impersonalists cannot understand the Supreme Personality of Godhead; therefore it is not possible for them to enter into the spiritual kingdom of God and return home, back to Godhead. Actually one attains different results by different means. It is not that all achievements are one and the same. Those interested in the four principles of *dharma, artha, kāma* and *mokṣa* cannot be compared to those interested in the unalloyed devotional service of the Lord. *Śrīmad-Bhāgavatam* therefore says:

dharmaḥ projjhita-kaitavo 'tra paramo nirmatsarāṇāṁ satāṁ
vedyaṁ vāstavam atra vastu śivadaṁ tāpa-trayonmūlanam
śrīmad-bhāgavate mahā-muni-kṛte kiṁ vā parair īśvaraḥ
sadyo hṛdy avarudhyate 'tra kṛtibhiḥ śuśrūṣubhis tat-kṣaṇāt

"Completely rejecting all religious activities which are materially motivated, this *Bhāgavata Purāṇa* propounds the highest truth, which is understandable by those devotees who are pure in heart. The highest truth is reality distinguished from illusion for the welfare of all. Such truth uproots the threefold miseries. This beautiful

Bhāgavatam, compiled by the great sage Śrī Vyāsadeva, is sufficient in itself for God realization. As soon as one attentively and submissively hears the message of *Bhāgavatam,* he becomes attached to the Supreme Lord." (*Bhāg.* 1.1.2)

Those who aspire after liberation attempt to merge into the impersonal Brahman. To this end they execute ritualistic religious ceremonies, but *Śrīmad-Bhāgavatam* considers this a cheating process. Indeed, such people can never dream of returning home, back to Godhead. There is a gulf of difference between the goal of *dharma, artha, kāma* and *mokṣa* and the goal of devotional service.

The goddess Durgā is the superintending deity of this material world, which is made of material elements. The demigods are simply different directors engaged in operating the departments of material activities, and they are under the influence of the same material energy. Kṛṣṇa's internal potencies, however, have nothing to do with the creation of this cosmic material world. The spiritual world and all spiritual activities are under the direction of the internal spiritual energy, and such activities are performed by *yogamāyā,* the spiritual energy. *Yogamāyā* is the spiritual or internal energy of the Supreme Personality of Godhead. Those who are interested in being promoted to the spiritual world and engaging in the service of the Lord attain spiritual perfection under the control of *yogamāyā.* Those who are interested in material promotion engage in ritualistic religious ceremonies and economic development to develop sense gratification. They ultimately attempt to merge into the impersonal existence of the Lord. Such people generally become impersonalists. They are interested in worshiping Lord Śiva or goddess Durgā, but their return is one hundred percent materialistic.

Following the example of the *gopīs,* the devotees sometimes worship the goddess Kātyāyanī, but they understand that Kātyāyanī is an incarnation of *yogamāyā.* The *gopīs* worshiped Kātyāyanī, *yogamāyā,* to attain Kṛṣṇa for their husband. On the other hand, it is stated in the *Sapta-śatī* scripture that a *kṣatriya* king named Suratha and a rich *vaiśya* named Samādhi worshiped material nature in the form of goddess Durgā to attain material perfection. If one tries to mingle the worship of *yogamāyā* with *mahāmāyā,* considering them one and the same, he does not really show very high intelligence. The idea that everything is one is a kind of foolishness indulged in by those with less brain substance. Fools and rascals say that the worship of *yogamāyā* and *mahāmāyā* is the same. This conclusion is simply the result of mental speculation, and it has no practical effect. In the material world, sometimes one produces a title to an utterly worthless thing, and in Bengal this is known as giving a blind child a name like Padmalocana, which means "lotus eyed." One may foolishly call a blind child Padmalocana, but such an appellation does not bear any meaning.

In the spiritual world the Absolute Lord is always identical with His name, fame, form, qualities and pastimes. Such identity is impossible in the material world, where the name of a person is different from the person himself. The Supreme Lord has many holy names like Paramātmā, Brahman and the creator, but one who worships the Lord as the creator cannot understand the relationship between a devotee and the Lord in the five types of transcendental mellows, nor can he understand the conception of Kṛṣṇa. One cannot understand the six transcendental opulences of the Lord simply by understanding the Supreme Personality of Godhead as impersonal Brahman.

Impersonal realization of the Absolute Truth is certainly transcendental, but this does not mean that one can understand the *sac-cid-ānanda* form of the Lord. Similarly, Paramātmā realization is also an incomplete understanding of the Absolute Truth. The plenary expansion of the Absolute Truth within everyone's heart is the Paramātmā feature of the Lord. A devotee of the Personality of Godhead Nārāyaṇa cannot actually understand the transcendental attractive features of Kṛṣṇa. On the other hand, the devotee of Kṛṣṇa who is attached to the sublime attractive feature of the Lord does not consider Nārāyaṇa very important. When the *gopīs* sometimes saw Kṛṣṇa in the form of Nārāyaṇa, they were not very attracted to Him. The *gopīs* never addressed Kṛṣṇa as Rukmiṇī-ramaṇa. Kṛṣṇa's devotees in Vṛndāvana address Him as Rādhāramaṇa, Nandanandana and Yaśodā-nandana, but not as Vasudeva-nandana or Devakī-nandana. Although according to the material conception, Nārāyaṇa, Rukmiṇī-ramaṇa and Kṛṣṇa are one and the same, in the spiritual world one cannot use the name of Kṛṣṇa in the place of Rukmiṇī-ramaṇa or Nārāyaṇa. If one does so out of a poor fund of knowledge, his mellow with the Lord becomes spiritually faulty and is called *rasābhāsa,* an overlapping of transcendental mellows. The advanced devotee who has actually realized the transcendental features of the Lord will not commit the mistake of creating a *rasābhāsa* situation by using one name for another. Because of the influence of Kali-yuga, there is much *rasābhāsa* in the name of extravagance and liberal-mindedness. Such fanaticism is not very much appreciated by pure devotees.

TEXT 91

যে যথা মাং প্রপদ্যন্তে তাংস্তথৈব ভজাম্যহম্ ।
মম বর্ত্মানুবর্ত্তন্তে মনুষ্যাঃ পার্থ সর্বশঃ ॥ ৯১ ॥

ye yathā māṁ prapadyante
tāṁs tathaiva bhajāmy aham
mama vartmānuvartante
manuṣyāḥ pārtha sarvaśaḥ

SYNONYMS

ye—they; *yathā*—as; *mām*—unto Me; *prapadyante*—surrender; *tān*—unto them; *tathā eva*—in the same proportion; *bhajāmi*—bestow My favor; *aham*—I; *mama*—My; *vartma*—way; *anuvartante*—follow; *manuṣyāḥ*—men; *pārtha*—My dear Arjuna; *sarvaśaḥ*—in all respects.

TRANSLATION

"According to Lord Kṛṣṇa in Bhagavad-gītā [4.11], 'All of them—as they surrender unto Me—I reward accordingly. Everyone follows My path in all respects, O son of Pṛthā.'

TEXT 92

এই 'প্রেমে'র অনুরূপ না পারে ভজিতে ।
অতএব 'ঋণী' হয়—কহে ভাগবতে ॥ ৯২ ॥

ei 'preme'ra anurūpa nā pāre bhajite
ataeva 'ṛṇī' haya——kahe bhāgavate

SYNONYMS

ei—this; *premera*—of love of God; *anurūpa*—exactly to the proportion; *nā*—not; *pāre*—is able; *bhajite*—to reciprocate; *ataeva*—therefore; *ṛṇī*—debtor; *haya*—becomes; *kahe*—is stated; *bhāgavate*—in the *Śrīmad-Bhāgavatam.*

TRANSLATION

"In Śrīmad-Bhāgavatam [10.32.22] it is said that Lord Kṛṣṇa cannot proportionately reciprocate devotional service in the mādhurya-rasa; therefore He always remains a debtor to such devotees.

TEXT 93

ন পারয়েঽহং নিরবদ্যসংযুজাং
স্বসাধুকৃত্যং বিবুধায়ুষাপি বঃ ।
যা মাভজন্ দুর্জয়-গেহশৃঙ্খলাঃ
সংবৃশ্চ্য তদ্বঃ প্রতিযাতু সাধুনা ॥ ৯৩ ॥

na pāraye 'haṁ niravadya-saṁyujāṁ
sva-sādhu-kṛtyaṁ vibudhāyuṣāpi vaḥ
yā mābhajan durjaya-geha-śṛṅkhalāḥ
saṁvṛścya tad vaḥ pratiyātu sādhunā

SYNONYMS

na—not; *pāraye*—am able; *aham*—I; *niravadya*—without duplicity; *saṁyujām*—meeting; *sva-sādhu-kṛtyam*—your own honest activities; *vibudha-āyuṣā api*—even with a duration of life like that of the demigods; *vaḥ*—you; *yā*—who; *mā*—Me; *abhajan*—have worshiped; *durjaya*—difficult to surmount; *geha*—of household life; *śṛṅkhalāḥ*—the chains; *saṁvṛścya*—cutting off; *tat*—that; *vaḥ*—your; *pratiyātu*—let there be a return; *sādhunā*—by pious activities.

TRANSLATION

"When the gopīs were overwhelmed with dissatisfaction due to Lord Kṛṣṇa's absence from the rāsa-līlā, Kṛṣṇa returned to them and told them, 'My dear gopīs, our meeting is certainly free from all material contamination. I must admit that in many lives it would be impossible for Me to repay My debt to you because you have cut off the bondage of family life just to search for Me. Consequently I am unable to repay you. Therefore please be satisfied with your honest activities in this regard.'

TEXT 94

যদ্যপি কৃষ্ণ-সৌন্দর্য—মাধুর্যের ধুর্য ।
ব্রজদেবীর সঙ্গে তাঁর বাড়য়ে মাধুর্য ॥ ৯৪ ॥

yadyapi kṛṣṇa-saundarya——mādhuryera dhurya
vraja-devīra saṅge tāṅra bāḍaye mādhurya

SYNONYMS

yadyapi—although; *kṛṣṇa-saundarya*—the beauty of Lord Kṛṣṇa; *mādhuryera*—of sweetness; *dhurya*—the supermost; *vraja-devīra*—the *gopīs*; *saṅge*—in company with; *tāṅra*—His; *bāḍaye*—increases; *mādhurya*—the sweetness.

TRANSLATION

"Although Kṛṣṇa's unparalleled beauty is the topmost sweetness of love of Godhead, His sweetness increases unlimitedly when He is in the company of the gopīs. Consequently Kṛṣṇa's exchange of love with the gopīs is the topmost perfection of love of Godhead.

PURPORT

Kṛṣṇa and His devotees become perfectly intimate in conjugal love of Godhead. In other mellows, the Lord and the devotees do not enjoy transcendental bliss as perfectly. The next verse from *Śrīmad-Bhāgavatam* (10.33.6) will illustrate this verse.

TEXT 95

তত্রাতিশুশুভে তাভির্ভগবান্ দেবকীসুতঃ ।
মধ্যে মণীনাং হৈমানাং মহামারকতো যথা ॥ ৯৫ ॥

tatrātiśuśubhe tābhir
bhagavān devakī-sutaḥ
madhye maṇīnāṁ haimānāṁ
mahā-mārakato yathā

SYNONYMS

tatra—there; *ati-śuśubhe*—was very beautiful; *tābhiḥ*—by them; *bhagavān*—the Supreme Personality of Godhead; *devakī-sutaḥ*—son of Devakī; *madhye*—in the midst; *maṇīnām*—of valuable jewels; *haimānām*—lined with gold; *mahā-mārakataḥ*—the jewel of the name; *yathā*—as.

TRANSLATION

" 'Although the son of Devakī, the Supreme Personality of Godhead, is also the reservoir of all kinds of beauty, when He is among the gopīs He nonetheless becomes more beautiful, for He resembles a mārakata jewel surrounded by gold and other jewels.' "

TEXT 96

প্রভু কহে, এই –‘সাধ্যাবধি’ সুনিশ্চয় ।
কৃপা করি’ কহ, যদি আগে কিছু হয় ॥ ৯৬ ॥

prabhu kahe, ei——'sādhyāvadhi' suniścaya
kṛpā kari' kaha, yadi āge kichu haya

SYNONYMS

prabhu kahe—Lord Śrī Caitanya Mahāprabhu replied; *ei*—this; *sādhya-avadhi*—the highest limit of perfection; *su-niścaya*—certainly; *kṛpā kari'*—being merciful to Me; *kaha*—please speak; *yadi*—if; *āge*—further; *kichu haya*—there is something.

TRANSLATION

Lord Caitanya Mahāprabhu replied, "This is certainly the limit of perfection, but please be merciful to Me and speak more if there is more."

TEXT 97

রায় কহে,—ইহার আগে পুছে হেন জনে ।
এতদিন নাহি জানি, আছয়ে ভুবনে ॥ ৯৭ ॥

rāya kahe,——ihāra āge puche hena jane
eta-dina nāhi jāni, āchaye bhuvane

SYNONYMS

rāya kahe—Rāmānanda Rāya replied; *ihāra āge*—beyond this point; *puche*—inquires; *hena*—such; *jane*—a person; *eta-dina*—until this day; *nāhi jāni*—I did not know; *āchaye*—there is; *bhuvane*—within this material world.

TRANSLATION

Rāya Rāmānanda replied, "Until this day I did not know anyone within this material world who could inquire beyond this perfectional stage of devotional service.

TEXT 98

ইঁহার মধ্যে রাধার প্রেম—'সাধ্যশিরোমণি' ।
যাঁহার মহিমা সর্বশাস্ত্রেতে বাখানি ॥ ৯৮ ॥

iṅhāra madhye rādhāra prema——'sādhya-śiromaṇi'
yāṅhāra mahimā sarva-śāstrete vākhāni

SYNONYMS

iṅhāra madhye—among the loving affairs of the *gopīs*; *rādhāra prema*—the love of Godhead of Śrīmatī Rādhārāṇī; *sādhya-śiromaṇi*—the topmost perfection; *yāṅhāra*—of which; *mahimā*—the glorification; *sarva-śāstrete*—in every scripture; *vākhāni*—description.

TRANSLATION

"Among the loving affairs of the gopīs," Rāmānanda Rāya continued, "the love of Śrīmatī Rādhārāṇī for Śrī Kṛṣṇa is topmost. Indeed, the glories of Śrīmatī Rādhārāṇī are highly estimated in all revealed scriptures.

TEXT 99

যথা রাধা প্রিয়া বিষ্ণোস্তস্যাঃ কুণ্ডং প্রিয়ং তথা ।
সর্বগোপীষু সৈবৈকা বিষ্ণোরত্যন্তবল্লভা ॥ ৯৯ ॥

yathā rādhā priyā viṣṇos
tasyāḥ kuṇḍaṁ priyaṁ tathā
sarva-gopīṣu saivaikā
viṣṇor atyanta-vallabhā

SYNONYMS

yathā—just as; *rādhā*—Śrīmatī Rādhārāṇī; *priyā*—very dear; *viṣṇoḥ*—to Lord Kṛṣṇa; *tasyāḥ*—Her; *kuṇḍam*—bathing place; *priyam*—very dear; *tathā*—so also; *sarva-gopīṣu*—among all the *gopīs*; *sā*—She; *eva*—certainly; *ekā*—alone; *viṣṇoḥ*—of Lord Kṛṣṇa; *atyanta-vallabhā*—very dear.

TRANSLATION

" 'Just as Śrīmatī Rādhārāṇī is most dear to Śrī Kṛṣṇa, Her bathing place known as Rādhā-kuṇḍa is also dear to Him. Among all the gopīs, Śrīmatī Rādhārāṇī is supermost and very dear to Lord Kṛṣṇa.'

PURPORT

This verse is from the *Padma Purāṇa* and is included in the *Laghu-bhāgavatāmṛta* (2.45), by Śrīla Rūpa Gosvāmī. It also appears in *Ādi-līlā,* Chapter Four, verse 215, and again in *Madhya-līlā,* Chapter Eighteen, verse 8.

TEXT 100

অনয়ারাধিতো নূনং ভগবান্ হরিরীশ্বরঃ ।
যন্নো বিহায় গোবিন্দঃ প্রীতো যামনয়দ্রহঃ ॥ ১০০ ॥

anayārādhito nūnaṁ
bhagavān harir īśvaraḥ
yan no vihāya govindaḥ
prīto yām anayad rahaḥ

SYNONYMS

anayā—by Her; *ārādhitaḥ*—worshiped; *nūnam*—indeed; *bhagavān*—the Supreme Personality of Godhead; *hariḥ*—Kṛṣṇa; *īśvaraḥ*—the Lord; *yat*—from which; *naḥ*—us; *vihāya*—rejecting; *govindaḥ*—Lord Śrī Kṛṣṇa; *prītaḥ*—satisfied; *yām*—whom; *anayat*—brought; *rahaḥ*—a secluded place.

TRANSLATION

"When the gopīs began to talk among themselves, they said, 'Dear friends, the gopī who has been taken away by Kṛṣṇa to a secluded place must have worshiped the Lord more than anyone else.' "

PURPORT

The name Rādhā is derived from this verse (*Bhāg.* 10.30.28), from the word *anayārādhitaḥ,* meaning "by Her the Lord is worshiped." Sometimes the critics of

Śrīmad-Bhāgavatam find it difficult to find Rādhārāṇī's holy name, but the secret is disclosed here in the word *ārādhitaḥ,* from which the word *Rādhā* has come. Of course, the name of Rādhārāṇī is directly mentioned in other *Purāṇas*. This *gopī's* worship of Kṛṣṇa is topmost, and therefore Her name is Rādhā, or the topmost worshiper.

TEXT 101

প্রভু কহে,—আগে কহ, শুনিতে পাই সুখে ।
অপূর্বামৃত-নদী বহে তোমার মুখে ॥ ১০১ ॥

prabhu kahe,——āge kaha, śunite pāi sukhe
apūrvāmṛta-nadī vahe tomāra mukhe

SYNONYMS

prabhu kahe—the Lord said; *āge*—ahead; *kaha*—please speak; *śunite*—to hear; *pāi*—I get; *sukhe*—happiness; *apūrva-amṛta*—of unprecedented nectar; *nadī*—a river; *vahe*—flows; *tomāra mukhe*—from your mouth.

TRANSLATION

Lord Śrī Caitanya Mahāprabhu said, "Please speak on. I am very happy to hear you because a river of unprecedented nectar is flowing from your mouth.

TEXT 102

চুরি করি' রাধাকে নিল গোপীগণের ডরে ।
অন্যাপেক্ষা হৈলে প্রেমের গাঢ়তা না স্ফুরে ॥ ১০২ ॥

curi kari' rādhāke nila gopī-gaṇera ḍare
anyāpekṣā haile premera gāḍhatā nā sphure

SYNONYMS

curi kari'—stealing; *rādhāke*—Śrīmatī Rādhārāṇī; *nila*—took away; *gopī-gaṇera*—of the *gopīs*; *ḍare*—out of fear; *anya-apekṣā*—dependence on others; *haile*—if there is; *premera*—of love; *gāḍhatā*—the intensity; *nā*—not; *sphure*—manifests.

TRANSLATION

"During the rāsa dance Śrī Kṛṣṇa did not exchange loving affairs with Śrīmatī Rādhārāṇī due to the presence of the other gopīs. Because of the

dependence of the others, the intensity of love between Rādhā and Kṛṣṇa was not manifest. Therefore He stole Her away.

PURPORT

Out of fear of the other *gopīs,* Lord Śrī Kṛṣṇa took Śrīmatī Rādhārāṇī to a secluded place. In this regard, the verse *kaṁsārir api* (the following verse 106) will be quoted from the *Gīta-govinda* of Jayadeva Gosvāmī.

TEXT 103

রাধা লাগি' গোপীরে যদি সাক্ষাৎ করে ত্যাগ ।
তবে জানি,– রাধায় কৃষ্ণের গাঢ়-অনুরাগ ॥ ১০৩ ॥

rādhā lāgi' gopīre yadi sākṣāt kare tyāga
tabe jāni,——rādhāya kṛṣṇera gāḍha-anurāga

SYNONYMS

rādhā lāgi'—for the sake of Śrīmatī Rādhārāṇī; *gopīre*—the *gopīs; yadi*—if; *sākṣāt*—directly; *kare*—does; *tyāga*—rejection; *tabe*—then; *jāni*—we can understand; *rādhāya*—in Śrīmatī Rādhārāṇī; *kṛṣṇera*—of Lord Kṛṣṇa; *gāḍha*—intense; *anurāga*—affection.

TRANSLATION

"If Lord Kṛṣṇa rejected the company of the other gopīs for Śrīmatī Rādhārāṇī, we can understand that Lord Śrī Kṛṣṇa has intense affection for Her."

TEXT 104

রায় কহে,—তবে শুন প্রেমের মহিমা ।
ত্রিজগতে রাধা-প্রেমের নাহিক উপমা ॥ ১০৪ ॥

rāya kahe,——tabe śuna premera mahimā
tri-jagate rādhā-premera nāhika upamā

SYNONYMS

rāya kahe—Rāmānanda Rāya replied; *tabe*—then; *śuna*—please hear; *premera*—of that love; *mahimā*—the glories; *tri-jagate*—within the three worlds; *rādhā-premera*—of the loving affairs of Śrīmatī Rādhārāṇī; *nāhika*—there is not; *upamā*—comparison.

TRANSLATION

Rāmānanda Rāya continued, "Please therefore hear from me about the glories of Śrīmatī Rādhārāṇī's loving affairs. They are beyond compare within these three worlds.

TEXT 105

গোপীগণের রাস-নৃত্য-মণ্ডলী ছাড়িয়া।
রাধা চাহি' বনে ফিরে বিলাপ করিয়া॥ ১০৫॥

gopī-gaṇera rāsa-nṛtya-maṇḍalī chāḍiyā
rādhā cāhi' vane phire vilāpa kariyā

SYNONYMS

gopī-gaṇera—of the *gopīs*; *rāsa-nṛtya*—of *rāsa* dancing; *maṇḍalī*—the circle; *chāḍiyā*—rejecting; *rādhā*—Śrīmatī Rādhārāṇī; *cāhi'*—desiring; *vane*—in the forest; *phire*—wanders; *vilāpa*—lamentation; *kariyā*—doing.

TRANSLATION

"Finding Herself treated equally with all the other gopīs, Śrīmatī Rādhārāṇī displayed Her tricky behavior and left the circle of the rāsa dance. Missing Śrīmatī Rādhārāṇī's presence, Kṛṣṇa became very unhappy and began to lament and wander throughout the forest to search Her out.

TEXT 106

কংসারিরপি সংসারবাসনাবদ্ধশৃঙ্খলাম্।
রাধামাধায় হৃদয়ে তত্যাজ ব্রজসুন্দরীঃ॥ ১০৬॥

kaṁsārir api saṁsāra-
vāsanā-baddha-śṛṅkhalām
rādhām ādhāya hṛdaye
tatyāja vraja-sundarīḥ

SYNONYMS

kaṁsāriḥ—the enemy of Kaṁsa; *api*—moreover; *saṁsāra-vāsanā*—desirous of the essence of enjoyment (*rāsa-līlā*); *baddha-śṛṅkhalām*—being perfectly attracted to such activities; *rādhām*—Śrīmatī Rādhārāṇī; *ādhāya*—taking; *hṛdaye*—within the heart; *tatyāja*—left aside; *vraja-sundarīḥ*—the other beautiful *gopīs*.

TRANSLATION

" 'Lord Kṛṣṇa, the enemy of Kaṁsa, took Śrīmatī Rādhārāṇī within His heart, for He desired to dance with Her. Thus He left the area of the rāsa dance and the company of all the other beautiful damsels of Vraja.'

TEXT 107

ইতস্ততস্তামনুসৃত্য রাধিকা-
মনঙ্গবাণব্রণখিন্নমানসঃ ।
কৃতানুতাপঃ স কলিন্দনন্দিনী
তটান্তকুঞ্জে বিষসাদ মাধবঃ ॥ ১০৭ ॥

itas-tatas tām anusṛtya rādhikām
anaṅga-vāṇa-vraṇa-khinna-mānasaḥ
kṛtānutāpaḥ sa kalinda-nandinī
taṭānta-kuñje viṣasāda mādhavaḥ

SYNONYMS

itaḥ-tataḥ—hither and thither; *tām*—Her; *anusṛtya*—searching out; *rādhikām*—Śrīmatī Rādhārāṇī; *anaṅga*—of Cupid; *vāṇa-vraṇa*—by a wound from the arrow; *khinna-mānasaḥ*—whose heart is injured; *kṛta-anutāpaḥ*—repentant for misbehavior; *saḥ*—He (Lord Kṛṣṇa); *kalinda-nandinī*—of the River Yamunā; *taṭa-anta*—on the edge of the bank; *kuñje*—in the bushes; *viṣasāda*—lamented; *mādhavaḥ*—Lord Kṛṣṇa.

TRANSLATION

" 'Being afflicted by the arrow of Cupid and unhappily regretting His mistreating Rādhārāṇī, Mādhava, Lord Kṛṣṇa, began to search for Śrīmatī Rādhārāṇī along the banks of the Yamunā River. When He failed to find Her, He entered the bushes of Vṛndāvana and began to lament.'

PURPORT

These two verses are from the *Gīta-govinda* (3.1,2), written by Jayadeva Gosvāmī.

TEXT 108

এই দুই-শ্লোকের অর্থ বিচারিলে জানি ।
বিচারিতে উঠে যেন অমৃতের খনি ॥ ১০৮ ॥

ei dui-ślokera artha vicārile jāni
vicārite uṭhe yena amṛtera khani

SYNONYMS

ei—these; *dui*—two; *ślokera*—of the verses; *artha*—the meanings; *vicārile*—if considering; *jāni*—I can understand; *vicārite*—while considering; *uṭhe*—arises; *yena*—like; *amṛtera*—of nectar; *khani*—a mine.

TRANSLATION

"Simply by considering these two verses one can understand what nectar there is in such dealings. It is exactly like freeing a mine of nectar.

TEXT 109

শতকোটি গোপী-সঙ্গে রাস-বিলাস ।
তার মধ্যে এক-মূর্ত্যে রহে রাধা-পাশ ॥ ১০৯ ॥

śata-koṭi gopī-saṅge rāsa-vilāsa
tāra madhye eka-mūrtye rahe rādhā-pāśa

SYNONYMS

śata-koṭi—hundreds of thousands; *gopī-saṅge*—with the *gopīs*; *rāsa-vilāsa*—dancing in the *rāsa* dance; *tāra madhye*—among them; *eka-mūrtye*—by one of His transcendental forms; *rahe*—remains; *rādhā-pāśa*—by the side of Śrīmatī Rādhārāṇī.

TRANSLATION

"Although Kṛṣṇa was in the midst of hundreds of thousands of gopīs during the rāsa dance, He still kept Himself in one of His transcendental forms by the side of Śrīmatī Rādhārāṇī.

TEXT 110

সাধারণ-প্রেমে দেখি সর্বত্র 'সমতা' ।
রাধার কুটিল-প্রেমে হইল 'বামতা' ॥ ১১০ ॥

sādhāraṇa-preme dekhi sarvatra 'samatā'
rādhāra kuṭila-preme ha-ila 'vāmatā'

SYNONYMS

sādhāraṇa-preme—in general love of Godhead; *dekhi*—we see; *sarvatra*—everywhere; *samatā*—equality; *rādhāra*—of Śrīmatī Rādhārāṇī; *kuṭila-preme*—in the crooked love of Godhead; *ha-ila*—there was; *vāmatā*—opposition.

TRANSLATION

"Lord Kṛṣṇa is equal to everyone in His general dealings, but due to the conflicting ecstatic love of Śrīmatī Rādhārāṇī, there were opposing elements.

TEXT 111

অহেরিব গতিঃ প্রেম্ণঃ স্বভাবকুটিলা ভবেৎ ।
অতো হেতোরহেতোশ্চ যূনোর্মান উদঞ্চতি ॥ ১১১ ॥

aher iva gatiḥ premṇaḥ
svabhāva-kuṭilā bhavet
ato hetor ahetoś ca
yūnor māna udañcati

SYNONYMS

aheḥ—of the snake; *iva*—like; *gatiḥ*—the movement; *premṇaḥ*—of the loving affairs; *sva-bhāva*—by nature; *kuṭilā*—crooked; *bhavet*—is; *ataḥ*—therefore; *hetoḥ*—from some cause; *ahetoḥ*—from the absence of a cause; *ca*—and; *yūnoḥ*—of the young couple; *mānaḥ*—anger; *udañcati*—appears.

TRANSLATION

" 'The progress of loving affairs between young couples is like the movement of a snake. On account of this, two types of anger arise between young couples—anger with cause and anger without cause.'

PURPORT

During the *rāsa* dance, one form of Kṛṣṇa was between every two *gopīs.* However, by the side of Śrīmatī Rādhārāṇī there was only one Kṛṣṇa. Although this was the case, Śrīmatī Rādhārāṇī still manifested disagreement with Kṛṣṇa. This verse is from the *Ujjvala-nīlamaṇi* (*Śṛṅgāra-bheda-kathana* 102), written by Śrīla Rūpa Gosvāmī.

TEXT 112

ক্রোধ করি' রাস ছাড়ি' গেলা মান করি' ।
তাঁরে না দেখিয়া ব্যাকুল হৈল শ্রীহরি ॥ ১১২ ॥

krodha kari' rāsa chāḍi' gelā māna kari'
tāṅre nā dekhiyā vyākula haila śrī-hari

SYNONYMS

krodha kari'—becoming angry; *rāsa chāḍi'*—leaving the *rāsa* dance; *gelā*—went; *māna kari'*—being angry; *tāṅre*—Śrīmatī Rādhārāṇī; *nā dekhiyā*—not seeing; *vyākula*—very much anxious; *haila*—became; *śrī-hari*—Lord Kṛṣṇa.

TRANSLATION

"When Rādhārāṇī, out of anger and resentment, left the rāsa dance, Lord Śrī Kṛṣṇa, not seeing Her, became very anxious.

TEXT 113

সম্যক্‌সার বাসনা কৃষ্ণের রাসলীলা।
রাসলীলা-বাসনাতে রাধিকা শৃঙ্খলা ॥ ১১৩ ॥

samyak-sāra vāsanā kṛṣṇera rāsa-līlā
rāsa-līlā-vāsanāte rādhikā śṛṅkhalā

SYNONYMS

samyak-sāra—the complete and essential; *vāsanā*—desire; *kṛṣṇera*—of Lord Kṛṣṇa; *rāsa-līlā*—the dancing in the *rāsa-līlā*; *rāsa-līlā-vāsanāte*—in the desire to dance the *rāsa* dance; *rādhikā*—Śrīmatī Rādhārāṇī; *śṛṅkhalā*—the medium of bondage.

TRANSLATION

"Lord Kṛṣṇa's desire in the rāsa-līlā circle is perfectly complete, but Śrīmatī Rādhārāṇī is the binding link in that desire.

TEXT 114

তাঁহা বিনু রাসলীলা নাহি ভায় চিত্তে।
মণ্ডলী ছাড়িয়া গেলা রাধা অন্বেষিতে ॥ ১১৪ ॥

tāṅhā vinu rāsa-līlā nāhi bhāya citte
maṇḍalī chāḍiyā gelā rādhā anveṣite

SYNONYMS

tāṅhā vinu—without Her; *rāsa-līlā*—the *rāsa* dance; *nāhi*—not; *bhāya*—illuminates; *citte*—within the heart; *maṇḍalī chāḍiyā*—leaving the circle of the *rāsa* dance; *gelā*—went; *rādhā*—Śrīmatī Rādhārāṇī; *anveṣite*—to search for.

TRANSLATION

"The rāsa dance does not shine in the heart of Kṛṣṇa without Śrīmatī Rādhārāṇī. Therefore, He also gave up the circle of the rāsa dance and went out to search for Her.

TEXT 115

ইতস্ততঃ ভ্রমি' কাহাঁ রাধা না পাঞা ।
বিষাদ করেন কামবাণে খিন্ন হঞা ॥ ১১৫ ॥

itas-tataḥ bhrami' kāhāṅ rādhā nā pāñā
viṣāda karena kāma-vāṇe khinna hañā

SYNONYMS

itaḥ-tataḥ—here and there; *bhrami'*—wandering; *kāhāṅ*—anywhere; *rādhā*—Śrīmatī Rādhārāṇī; *nā*—not; *pāñā*—finding; *viṣāda*—lamentation; *karena*—does; *kāma-vāṇe*—by the arrow of Cupid; *khinna*—hurt; *hañā*—becoming.

TRANSLATION

"When Kṛṣṇa went out to search for Śrīmatī Rādhārāṇī, He wandered here and there. However, not finding Her, He became afflicted by the arrow of Cupid and began to lament.

TEXT 116

শতকোটি-গোপীতে নহে কাম-নির্বাপণ ।
তাহাতেই অনুমানি শ্রীরাধিকার গুণ ॥ ১১৬ ॥

śata-koṭi-gopīte nahe kāma-nirvāpaṇa
tāhātei anumāni śrī-rādhikāra guṇa

SYNONYMS

śata-koṭi—hundreds and thousands; *gopīte*—in the midst of *gopīs*; *nahe*—there is not; *kāma-nirvāpaṇa*—satisfaction of lust; *tāhātei*—by that way; *anumāni*—we can imagine; *śrī-rādhikāra guṇa*—the transcendental quality of Śrīmatī Rādhārāṇī.

TRANSLATION

"Since Kṛṣṇa's lusty desires were not satisfied even in the midst of hundreds of thousands of gopīs and He was thus searching after Śrīmatī Rādhārāṇī, we can easily imagine how transcendentally qualified She is."

TEXT 117

প্রভু কহে—যে লাগি' আইলাম তোমা-স্থানে ।
সেই সব তত্ত্ববস্তু হৈল মোর জ্ঞানে ॥ ১১৭ ॥

prabhu kahe——ye lāgi' āilāma tomā-sthāne
sei saba tattva-vastu haila mora jñāne

SYNONYMS

prabhu kahe—the Lord said; *ye lāgi'*—for the matter of which; *āilāma*—I have come; *tomā-sthāne*—to your place; *sei saba*—all those; *tattva-vastu*—objects of truth; *haila*—were; *mora*—My; *jñāne*—in knowledge.

TRANSLATION

After hearing this, Lord Caitanya Mahāprabhu said to Rāmānanda Rāya, "That for which I have come to your residence has now become an object of truth in My knowledge.

TEXT 118

এবে সে জানিলুঁ সাধ্য-সাধন-নির্ণয় ।
আগে আর আছে কিছু, শুনিতে মন হয় ॥ ১১৮ ॥

ebe se jāniluṅ sādhya-sādhana-nirṇaya
āge āra āche kichu, śunite mana haya

SYNONYMS

ebe—now; *se*—that; *jāniluṅ*—I have understood; *sādhya*—of the ultimate goal; *sādhana*—and of the process; *nirṇaya*—the ascertainment; *āge*—ahead; *āra*—more; *āche*—there is; *kichu*—something; *śunite*—to hear; *mana*—the mind; *haya*—it is.

TRANSLATION

"Now I have come to understand the sublime goal of life and the process of achieving it. Nevertheless, I think that there is something more ahead, and My mind is desiring to have it.

TEXT 119

'কৃষ্ণের স্বরূপ' কহ 'রাধার স্বরূপ' ।
'রস' কোন্ তত্ত্ব, 'প্রেম'—কোন্ তত্ত্বরূপ ॥ ১১৯ ॥

'kṛṣṇera svarūpa' kaha 'rādhāra svarūpa'
'rasa' kon tattva, 'prema'—kon tattva-rūpa

SYNONYMS

kṛṣṇera—of Lord Kṛṣṇa; *svarūpa*—the transcendental features; *kaha*—speak; *rādhāra*—of Śrīmatī Rādhārāṇī; *svarūpa*—the transcendental features; *rasa*—mellows; *kon*—what; *tattva*—that truth; *prema*—love of Godhead; *kon*—what; *tattva-rūpa*—actual form.

TRANSLATION

"Kindly explain the transcendental features of Kṛṣṇa and Śrīmatī Rādhārāṇī. Also explain the truth of transcendental mellow and the transcendental form of love of Godhead.

TEXT 120

কৃপা করি' এই তত্ত্ব কহ ত' আমারে ।
তোমা-বিনা কেহ ইহা নিরূপিতে নারে ॥ ১২০ ॥

kṛpā kari' ei tattva kaha ta' āmāre
tomā-vinā keha ihā nirūpite nāre

SYNONYMS

kṛpā kari'—showing your mercy; *ei tattva*—all these truths; *kaha*—explain; *ta'*—certainly; *āmāre*—unto Me; *tomā-vinā*—except for you; *keha*—someone; *ihā*—this; *nirūpite*—to ascertain; *nāre*—not able.

TRANSLATION

"Kindly explain all these truths to Me. But for yourself, no one can ascertain them."

TEXT 121

রায় কহে,—ইহা আমি কিছুই না জানি ।
তুমি যেই কহাও, সেই কহি আমি বাণী ॥ ১২১ ॥

rāya kahe,—ihā āmi kichui nā jāni
tumi yei kahāo, sei kahi āmi vāṇī

SYNONYMS

rāya kahe—Rāmānanda Rāya said; *ihā*—this; *āmi*—I; *kichui*—something; *nā*—not; *jāni*—know; *tumi*—You; *yei*—whatever; *kahāo*—make me say; *sei*—those; *kahi*—speak; *āmi*—I; *vāṇī*—words.

TRANSLATION

Śrī Rāmānanda Rāya replied, "I do not know anything about this. I simply vibrate the sound You make me speak.

TEXT 122

তোমার শিক্ষায় পড়ি যেন শুক-পাঠ ।
সাক্ষাৎ ঈশ্বর তুমি, কে বুঝে তোমার নাট ॥ ১২২ ॥

tomāra śikṣāya paḍi yena śuka-pāṭha
sākṣāt īśvara tumi, ke bujhe tomāra nāṭa

SYNONYMS

tomāra śikṣāya—by Your instruction; *paḍi*—I read; *yena*—like; *śuka-pāṭha*—the reading of a parrot; *sākṣāt*—directly; *īśvara*—the Supreme Personality of Godhead; *tumi*—You; *ke*—who; *bujhe*—can understand; *tomāra*—Your; *nāṭa*—dramatic performance.

TRANSLATION

"I simply repeat like a parrot whatever instructions You have given me. You are the Supreme Personality of Godhead Himself. Who can understand Your dramatic performances?

TEXT 123

হৃদয়ে প্রেরণ কর, জিহ্বায় কহাও বাণী ।
কি কহিয়ে ভাল-মন্দ, কিছুই না জানি ॥ ১২৩ ॥

hṛdaye preraṇa kara, jihvāya kahāo vāṇī
ki kahiye bhāla-manda, kichui nā jāni

SYNONYMS

hṛdaye—within the heart; *preraṇa*—direction; *kara*—You give; *jihvāya*—on the tongue; *kahāo*—You make me speak; *vāṇī*—words; *ki*—what; *kahiye*—I am speaking; *bhāla-manda*—good or bad; *kichui*—something; *nā*—not; *jāni*—I know.

TRANSLATION

"You inspire me within the heart and make me speak with the tongue. I do not know whether I am speaking well or badly."

TEXT 124

প্রভু কহে,—মায়াবাদী আমি ত' সন্ন্যাসী ।
ভক্তিতত্ত্ব নাহি জানি, মায়াবাদে ভাসি ॥ ১২৪ ॥

prabhu kahe,——māyāvādī āmi ta' sannyāsī
bhakti-tattva nāhi jāni, māyāvāde bhāsi

SYNONYMS

prabhu kahe—the Lord said; *māyāvādī*—a follower of the Māyāvāda philosophy; *āmi*—I; *ta'*—certainly; *sannyāsī*—one in the renounced order of life; *bhakti-tattva*—the truths of transcendental loving service; *nāhi*—not; *jāni*—I know; *māyāvāde*—in the philosophy of impersonalism; *bhāsi*—I float.

TRANSLATION

Lord Caitanya Mahāprabhu said, "I am a Māyāvādī in the renounced order of life, and I do not even know what transcendental loving service to the Lord is. I simply float in the ocean of Māyāvāda philosophy.

TEXT 125

সার্বভৌম-সঙ্গে মোর মন নির্মল হইল ।
'কৃষ্ণভক্তি-তত্ত্ব কহ', তাঁহারে পুছিল ॥ ১২৫ ॥

sārvabhauma-saṅge mora mana nirmala ha-ila
'kṛṣṇa-bhakti-tattva kaha,' tāṅhāre puchila

SYNONYMS

sārvabhauma-saṅge—in the company of Sārvabhauma Bhaṭṭācārya; *mora*—My; *mana*—mind; *nirmala*—clarified; *ha-ila*—became; *kṛṣṇa-bhakti-tattva*—the truths of transcendental loving service to Kṛṣṇa; *kaha*—please explain; *tāṅhāre*—to him; *puchila*—I inquired.

TRANSLATION

"Due to the association of Sārvabhauma Bhaṭṭācārya, My mind has been enlightened. Therefore I have asked Sārvabhauma Bhaṭṭācārya about the truths of transcendental loving service to Kṛṣṇa.

TEXT 126

তেঁহো কহে—আমি নাহি জানি কৃষ্ণকথা ।
সবে রামানন্দ জানে, তেঁহো নাহি এথা ॥ ১২৬ ॥

teṅho kahe——āmi nāhi jāni kṛṣṇa-kathā
sabe rāmānanda jāne, teṅho nāhi ethā

SYNONYMS

teṅho kahe—he replied; *āmi*—I; *nāhi*—not; *jāni*—know; *kṛṣṇa-kathā*—topics of Lord Kṛṣṇa; *sabe*—all; *rāmānanda*—Rāmānanda Rāya; *jāne*—knows; *teṅho*—he; *nāhi*—not; *ethā*—here.

TRANSLATION

"Sārvabhauma Bhaṭṭācārya told me, 'I do not actually know about the topics of Lord Kṛṣṇa. They are all known only to Rāmānanda Rāya, but he is not present here.' "

TEXT 127

তোমার ঠাঞি আইলাঙ তোমার মহিমা শুনিয়া।
তুমি মোরে স্তুতি কর 'সন্ন্যাসী' জানিয়া॥ ১২৭॥

tomāra ṭhāñi āilāṅa tomāra mahimā śuniyā
tumi more stuti kara 'sannyāsī' jāniyā

SYNONYMS

tomāra-ṭhāñi—to your presence; *āilāṅa*—I have come; *tomāra*—your; *mahimā*—glories; *śuniyā*—hearing; *tumi*—you; *more*—Me; *stuti*—praising; *kara*—do; *sannyāsī*—a person in the renounced order of life; *jāniyā*—knowing as.

TRANSLATION

Lord Śrī Caitanya Mahāprabhu continued: "After hearing about your glories, I have come to your place. However, you are offering Me words of praise out of respect for a sannyāsī, one in the renounced order of life.

PURPORT

Śrīla Bhaktisiddhānta Sarasvatī Ṭhākura explains that a mundane person, being enriched by mundane opulences, must always know that the transcendental opulences of the advanced devotees are far more important than the materialistic opulences of a person like himself. A materialistic person with material opulences should not be very proud or puffed up before a transcendental devotee. If one approaches a transcendental devotee on the strength of his material heritage, opulence, education and beauty and does not offer respect to the advanced devotee of the Lord, the Vaiṣṇava devotee may offer formal respects to such a materially puffed-up person, but he may not deliver transcendental knowledge to him. Indeed, the devotee sees him as a non-*brāhmaṇa* or *śūdra*. Such a puffed-up person cannot understand the science of Kṛṣṇa. A proud person is deceived in transcendental life and despite attaining a human form will again glide into hellish conditions. By His personal example, Śrī Caitanya Mahāprabhu explains how one should be submissive and humble before a Vaiṣṇava, even though one may be situated on a high platform. Such is the teaching of Śrī Caitanya Mahāprabhu as the *ācārya* of the world, the supreme spiritual master and teacher.

TEXT 128

কিবা বিপ্র, কিবা ন্যাসী, শূদ্র কেনে নয় ।
যেই কৃষ্ণতত্ত্ববেত্তা, সেই 'গুরু' হয় ॥ ১২৮ ॥

kibā vipra, kibā nyāsī, śūdra kene naya
yei kṛṣṇa-tattva-vettā, sei 'guru' haya

SYNONYMS

kibā—whether; *vipra*—a *brāhmaṇa*; *kibā*—whether; *nyāsī*—a *sannyāsī*; *śūdra*—a *śūdra*; *kene*—why; *naya*—not; *yei*—anyone who; *kṛṣṇa-tattva-vettā*—a knower of the science of Kṛṣṇa; *sei*—that person; *guru*—the spiritual master; *haya*—is.

TRANSLATION

"Whether one is a brāhmaṇa, a sannyāsī or a śūdra—regardless of what he is—he can become a spiritual master if he knows the science of Kṛṣṇa."

PURPORT

This verse is very important to the Kṛṣṇa consciousness movement. In his *Amṛta-pravāha-bhāṣya*, Śrīla Bhaktivinoda Ṭhākura explains that one should not think that because Śrī Caitanya Mahāprabhu was born a *brāhmaṇa* and was situated in the topmost spiritual order as a *sannyāsī*, it was improper for Him to receive instructions from Śrīla Rāmānanda Rāya, who belonged to the *śūdra* caste. To clarify this matter, Śrī Caitanya Mahāprabhu informed Rāmānanda Rāya that knowledge of Kṛṣṇa consciousness is more important than caste. In the system of *varṇāśrama-dharma* there are various duties for the *brāhmaṇas, kṣatriyas* and *śūdras*. Actually the *brāhmaṇa* is supposed to be the spiritual master of all other *varṇas* or sects, but as far as Kṛṣṇa consciousness is concerned, everyone is capable of becoming a spiritual master because knowledge in Kṛṣṇa consciousness is on the platform of the spirit soul. To spread Kṛṣṇa consciousness, one need only be cognizant of the science of the spirit soul. It does not matter whether one is a *brāhmaṇa, kṣatriya, vaiśya, śūdra, sannyāsī, gṛhastha* or whatever. If one simply understands this science, he can become a spiritual master.

It is stated in the *Hari-bhakti-vilāsa* that one should not accept initiation from a person who is not in the brahminical order if there is a fit person in the brahminical order present. This instruction is meant for those who are overly dependent on the mundane social order and is suitable for those who want to remain in mundane life. If one understands the truth of Kṛṣṇa consciousness and seriously desires to attain transcendental knowledge for the perfection of life, he can accept a spiritual master from any social status, provided the spiritual master is fully conversant with the science of Kṛṣṇa. Śrīla Bhaktisiddhānta Sarasvatī Ṭhākura also states that although one is situated as a *brāhmaṇa, kṣatriya, vaiśya, śūdra, brahmacārī, vānaprastha, gṛhastha* or *sannyāsī,* if he is conversant in the science of Kṛṣṇa he can become a spiritual master as *vartma-pradarśaka-guru, dīkṣā-guru* or *śikṣā-guru.* One who first gives information about spiritual life is called the *vartma-pradarśaka-guru* or spiritual master. The spiritual master who initiates according to the regulations of the *śāstras* is called *dīkṣā-guru,* and the spiritual master who gives instructions for elevation is called *śikṣā-guru.* Factually the qualifications of a spiritual master depend on his knowledge of the science of Kṛṣṇa. It does not matter whether he is a *brāhmaṇa, kṣatriya, sannyāsī* or *śūdra.* This injunction given by Śrī Caitanya Mahāprabhu is not at all against the injunctions of the *śāstras.* In the *Padma Purāṇa* it is said:

na śūdrāḥ bhagavad-bhaktās
te 'pi bhāgavatottamāḥ
sarva-varṇeṣu te śūdrā
ye na bhaktā janārdane

One who is actually advanced in spiritual knowledge of Kṛṣṇa is never a *śūdra,* even though he may have been born in a *śūdra* family. However, if a *vipra* or a *brāhmaṇa* is very expert in the six brahminical activities (*paṭhana, pāṭhana, yajana, yājana, dāna, pratigraha*) and is also well versed in the Vedic hymns, he cannot become a spiritual master unless he is a Vaiṣṇava. But if one is born in the family of *caṇḍālas* yet is well versed in Kṛṣṇa consciousness, he can become a *guru.* These are the śāstric injunctions, and strictly following these injunctions, Śrī Caitanya Mahāprabhu, as a *gṛhastha* named Śrī Viśvambhara, was initiated by a *sannyāsī-guru* named Īśvara Purī. Similarly, Śrī Nityānanda Prabhu was initiated by Mādhavendra Purī, a *sannyāsī.* According to others, however, He was initiated by Lakṣmīpati Tīrtha. Advaita Ācārya, although a *gṛhastha,* was initiated by Mādhavendra Purī, and Śrī Rasikānanda, although born in a *brāhmaṇa* family, was initiated by Śrī Śyāmānanda Prabhu, who was not born in a caste *brāhmaṇa* family. There are many instances in which a born *brāhmaṇa* took initiation from a person who was not born in a *brāhmaṇa* family. The brahminical symptoms are explained in *Śrīmad-Bhāgavatam* (7.11.35), wherein it is stated:

yasya yal-lakṣaṇaṁ proktaṁ
puṁso varṇābhivyañjakam
yad anyatrāpi dṛśyeta
tat tenaiva vinirdiśet

If a person is born in a *śūdra* family but has all the qualities of a spiritual master, he should be accepted not only as a *brāhmaṇa* but as a qualified spiritual master also. This is also the instruction of Śrī Caitanya Mahāprabhu. Śrīla Bhaktisiddhānta Ṭhākura therefore introduced the sacred thread ceremony for all Vaiṣṇavas according to the rules and regulations.

Sometimes a Vaiṣṇava who is a *bhajanānandī* does not take the *sāvitra-saṁskāra* (sacred thread initiation), but this does not mean that this system should be used for preaching work. There are two kinds of Vaiṣṇavas—*bhajanānandī* and *goṣṭhyānandī.* A *bhajanānandī* is not interested in preaching work, but a *goṣṭhyānandī* is interested in spreading Kṛṣṇa consciousness to benefit the people and increase the number of Vaiṣṇavas. A Vaiṣṇava is understood to be above the position of a *brāhmaṇa.* As a preacher, he should be recognized as a *brāhmaṇa;* otherwise there may be a misunderstanding of his position as a Vaiṣṇava. However, a Vaiṣṇava *brāhmaṇa* is not selected on the basis of his birth but according to his qualities. Unfortunately, those who are unintelligent do not know the difference between a *brāhmaṇa* and a Vaiṣṇava. They are under the impression that unless one is a *brāhmaṇa* he cannot be a spiritual master. For this reason only, Śrī Caitanya Mahāprabhu makes the statement in this verse:

kibā vipra, kibā nyāsī, śūdra kene naya
yei kṛṣṇa-tattva-vettā, sei 'guru' haya

If one becomes a *guru,* he is automatically a *brāhmaṇa.* Sometimes a caste *guru* says that *ye kṛṣṇa-tattva-vettā, sei guru haya* means that one who is not a *brāhmaṇa* may become a *śikṣā-guru* or a *vartma-pradarśaka-guru* but not an initiator *guru.* According to such caste *gurus,* birth and family ties are considered foremost. However, the hereditary consideration is not acceptable to Vaiṣṇavas. The word *guru* is equally applicable to the *vartma-pradarśaka-guru, śikṣā-guru* and *dīkṣā-guru.* Unless we accept the principle enunciated by Śrī Caitanya Mahāprabhu, this Kṛṣṇa consciousness movement cannot spread all over the world. According to Śrī Caitanya Mahāprabhu's intentions: *pṛthivīte āche yata nagarādi-grāma sarvatra pracāra haibe mora nāma.* Śrī Caitanya Mahāprabhu's cult must be preached all over the world. This does not mean that people should take to His teachings and remain *śūdras* or *caṇḍālas.* As soon as one is trained as a pure Vaiṣṇava, he must be accepted as a bona fide *brāhmaṇa.* This is the essence of Śrī Caitanya Mahāprabhu's instructions in this verse.

TEXT 129

'সন্ন্যাসী' বলিয়া মোরে না করিহ বঞ্চন।
কৃষ্ণ-রাধা-তত্ত্ব কহি' পূর্ণ কর মন ॥ ১২৯ ॥

'sannyāsī' baliyā more nā kariha vañcana
kṛṣṇa-rādhā-tattva kahi' pūrṇa kara mana

SYNONYMS

sannyāsī—a person in the renounced order of life; *baliyā*—taking as; *more*—Me; *nā kariha*—do not do; *vañcana*—cheating; *kṛṣṇa-rādhā-tattva*—the truth about Rādhā-Kṛṣṇa; *kahi'*—describing; *pūrṇa*—complete; *kara*—make; *mana*—my mind.

TRANSLATION

Śrī Caitanya Mahāprabhu continued, "Please do not try to cheat me, thinking of Me as a learned sannyāsī. Please satisfy My mind by just describing the truth of Rādhā and Kṛṣṇa."

TEXTS 130-131

যদ্যপি রায় - প্রেমী, মহাভাগবতে।
তাঁর মন কৃষ্ণমায়া নারে আচ্ছাদিতে ॥ ১৩০ ॥
তথাপি প্রভুর ইচ্ছা—পরম প্রবল।
জানিলেহ রায়ের মন হৈল টলমল ॥ ১৩১ ॥

yadyapi rāya——premī, mahā-bhāgavate
tāṅra mana kṛṣṇa-māyā nāre ācchādite

tathāpi prabhura icchā——parama prabala
jānileha rāyera mana haila ṭalamala

SYNONYMS

yadyapi—although; *rāya*—Rāmānanda Rāya; *premī*—a great lover of Kṛṣṇa; *mahā-bhāgavate*—a topmost devotee; *tāṅra*—his; *mana*—mind; *kṛṣṇa-māyā*—the illusory energy of Kṛṣṇa; *nāre*—not able; *ācchādite*—to cover; *tathāpi*—still; *prabhura icchā*—the Lord's desire; *parama prabala*—very intense; *jānileha*—even though it was known; *rāyera mana*—the mind of Rāmānanda Rāya; *haila*—there was; *ṭalamala*—agitation.

TRANSLATION

Śrī Rāmānanda Rāya was a great devotee of the Lord and a lover of God, and although his mind could not be covered by Kṛṣṇa's illusory energy, and although he could understand the mind of the Lord, which was very strong and intense, Rāmānanda's mind became a little agitated.

PURPORT

The perfect devotee always acts according to the desires of the Supreme Personality of Godhead. However, a materialistic man is carried away by the waves of the material energy. Śrīla Bhaktivinoda Ṭhākura has said, *māyāra vaśe, yāccha bhese, khāccha hābuḍubu, bhāi.*

A person under the grip of the material energy is carried away by the waves of that illusory energy. In other words, a person in the material world is a servant of *māyā*. However, a person in the spiritual energy is a servant of the Supreme Personality of Godhead. Although Rāmānanda Rāya knew that nothing was unknown to Śrī Caitanya Mahāprabhu, he nonetheless began to speak further on the subject because the Lord desired it.

TEXT 132

রায় কহে—"আমি—নট, তুমি—সূত্রধার।
যেই মত নাচাও, তৈছে চাহি নাচিবার ॥ ১৩২ ॥

rāya kahe——"āmi——naṭa, tumi——sūtra-dhāra
yei mata nācāo, taiche cāhi nācibāra

SYNONYMS

rāya kahe—Rāmānanda Rāya replied; *āmi*—I; *naṭa*—dancer; *tumi*—You; *sūtra-dhāra*—the puller of the strings; *yei*—whatever; *mata*—way; *nācāo*—You make me dance; *taiche*—in that way; *cāhi*—I want; *nācibāra*—to dance.

TRANSLATION

Śrī Rāmānanda Rāya said, "I am just a dancing puppet, and You pull the strings. Whichever way You make me dance, I will dance.

TEXT 133

মোর জিহ্বা—বীণাযন্ত্র, তুমি—বীণা-ধারী।
তোমার মনে যেই উঠে, তাহাই উচ্চারি ॥ ১৩৩ ॥

mora jihvā——vīṇā-yantra, tumi——vīṇā-dhārī
tomāra mane yei uṭhe, tāhāi uccāri

SYNONYMS

mora jihvā—my tongue; *vīṇā-yantra*—a stringed instrument; *tumi*—You; *vīṇā-dhārī*—the player of the stringed instrument; *tomāra mane*—in Your mind; *yei uṭhe*—whatever arises; *tāhāi*—that; *uccāri*—I vibrate.

TRANSLATION

"My dear Lord, my tongue is just like a stringed instrument, and You are its player. Therefore I simply vibrate whatever arises in Your mind."

TEXT 134

পরম ঈশ্বর কৃষ্ণ—স্বয়ং ভগবান্ ।
সর্ব-অবতারী, সর্বকারণ-প্রধান ॥ ১৩৪ ॥

parama īśvara kṛṣṇa——svayaṁ bhagavān
sarva-avatārī, sarva-kāraṇa-pradhāna

SYNONYMS

parama—supreme; *īśvara*—controller; *kṛṣṇa*—Lord Kṛṣṇa; *svayam*—personally; *bhagavān*—the Supreme Personality of Godhead; *sarva-avatārī*—the source of all incarnations; *sarva-kāraṇa-pradhāna*—the supreme cause of all causes.

TRANSLATION

Rāmānanda Rāya then began to speak on kṛṣṇa-tattva. "He is the Supreme Personality of Godhead," he said. "He is personally the original Godhead, the source of all incarnations and the cause of all causes.

TEXT 135

অনন্ত বৈকুণ্ঠ, আর অনন্ত অবতার ।
অনন্ত ব্রহ্মাণ্ড ইহাঁ,— সবার আধার ॥ ১৩৫ ॥

ananta vaikuṇṭha, āra ananta avatāra
ananta brahmāṇḍa ihāṅ,——sabāra ādhāra

SYNONYMS

ananta vaikuṇṭha—innumerable Vaikuṇṭha planets; *āra*—and; *ananta avatāra*—innumerable incarnations; *ananta brahmāṇḍa*—innumerable universes; *ihāṅ*—in this material world; *sabāra*—of all of them; *ādhāra*—the resting place.

TRANSLATION

"There are innumerable Vaikuṇṭha planets as well as innumerable incarnations. In the material world also there are innumerable universes, and Kṛṣṇa is the supreme resting place for all of them.

TEXT 136

সচ্চিদানন্দ-তনু, ব্রজেন্দ্রনন্দন ।
সর্বৈশ্বর্য-সর্বশক্তি-সর্বরস-পূর্ণ ॥ ১৩৬ ॥

sac-cid-ānanda-tanu, vrajendra-nandana
sarvaiśvarya-sarvaśakti-sarvarasa-pūrṇa

SYNONYMS

sat-cit-ānanda-tanu—Kṛṣṇa's body is transcendental, full of knowledge, bliss and eternity; *vrajendra-nandana*—the son of Mahārāja Nanda; *sarva-aiśvarya*—all opulences; *sarva-śakti*—all potencies; *sarva-rasa-pūrṇa*—the reservoir of all transcendental mellows.

TRANSLATION

"The transcendental body of Śrī Kṛṣṇa is eternal and full of bliss and knowledge. He is the son of Nanda Mahārāja. He is full of all opulences and potencies, as well as all spiritual mellows.

TEXT 137

ঈশ্বরঃ পরমঃ কৃষ্ণঃ সচ্চিদানন্দবিগ্রহঃ ।
অনাদিরাদির্গোবিন্দঃ সর্বকারণকারণম্ ॥ ১৩৭ ॥

īśvaraḥ paramaḥ kṛṣṇaḥ
sac-cid-ānanda-vigrahaḥ
anādir ādir govindaḥ
sarva-kāraṇa-kāraṇam

SYNONYMS

īśvaraḥ—the controller; *paramaḥ*—supreme; *kṛṣṇaḥ*—Lord Kṛṣṇa; *sat*—eternal existence; *cit*—absolute knowledge; *ānanda*—absolute bliss; *vigrahaḥ*—whose form; *anādiḥ*—without beginning; *ādiḥ*—the origin of everything; *govindaḥ*—a name of Lord Kṛṣṇa; *sarva*—all; *kāraṇa*—of causes; *kāraṇam*—He is the original cause.

TRANSLATION

" 'Kṛṣṇa, who is known as Govinda, is the supreme controller. He has an eternal, blissful, spiritual body. He is the origin of all. He has no other origin, for He is the prime cause of all causes.

PURPORT

This verse is from the *Brahma-saṁhitā* (5.1) and also appears in *Ādi-līlā,* Chapter Two, verse 107.

TEXT 138

বৃন্দাবনে 'অপ্রাকৃত নবীন মদন'।
কামগায়ত্রী.কামবীজে যাঁর উপাসন ॥ ১৩৮ ॥

vṛndāvane 'aprākṛta navīna madana'
kāma-gāyatrī kāma-bīje yāṅra upāsana

SYNONYMS

vṛndāvane—in Vṛndāvana; *aprākṛta*—spiritual; *navīna*—new; *madana*—Cupid; *kāma-gāyatrī*—hymns of desire; *kāma-bīje*—by the spiritual seed of desire called *klīṁ*; *yāṅra*—of whom; *upāsana*—the worship.

TRANSLATION

"In the spiritual realm of Vṛndāvana, Kṛṣṇa is the spiritual ever-fresh Cupid. He is worshiped by the chanting of the kāma-gāyatrī-mantra with the spiritual seed klīṁ.

PURPORT

This Vṛndāvana is described in the *Brahma-saṁhitā* (5.56) in this way:

śriyaḥ kāntāḥ kāntaḥ parama-puruṣaḥ kalpa-taravo
drumā bhūmiś cintāmaṇi-gaṇa-mayī toyam amṛtam
kathā gānaṁ nāṭyaṁ gamanam api vaṁśī priya-sakhī
cid-ānandaṁ jyotiḥ param api tad āsvādyam api ca

sa yatra kṣīrābdhiḥ sravati surabhībhyaś ca sumahān
nimeṣārdhākhyo vā vrajati na hi yatrāpi samayaḥ
bhaje śveta-dvīpaṁ tam aham iha golokam iti yaṁ
vidantas te santaḥ kṣiti-virala-cārāḥ katipaye

The spiritual realm of Vṛndāvana is always spiritual. The goddess of fortune and the *gopīs* are always present there. They are beloved by Kṛṣṇa, and all of them are equally spiritual like Kṛṣṇa. In Vṛndāvana, Kṛṣṇa is the Supreme Person and is the husband of all the *gopīs* and the goddess of fortune. The trees in Vṛndāvana are wish-fulfilling trees. The land is made of touchstone, and the water is nectar. Words are musical vibrations, and all movements are dancing. The flute is the Lord's constant companion. The planet Goloka Vṛndāvana is self-luminous like the sun and is full of spiritual bliss. The perfection of life lies in tasting that spiritual existence; therefore everyone should cultivate its knowledge. In Vṛndāvana, spiritual cows are always supplying spiritual milk. Not a single moment is wasted there—in other words, there is no past, present or future. Not a single particle of time is wasted. Within this material universe, the devotees worship that transcendental abode as Goloka Vṛndāvana. Lord Brahmā himself said, "Let me worship that spiritual land where Kṛṣṇa is present." This transcendental Vṛndāvana is not appreciated by those who are not devotees or self-realized souls because this Vṛndāvana-dhāma is all spiritual. The pastimes of the Lord there are also spiritual. None are material. According to the prayer of Śrīla Narottama dāsa Ṭhākura (*Prārthanā* 1):

āra kabe nitāi-cāṅdera karuṇā haibe
saṁsāra-vāsanā mora kabe tuccha ha'be.

"When will Lord Nityānanda have mercy upon me so that I can realize the uselessness of material pleasure?"

viṣaya-chāḍiyā kabe śuddha ha'be mana
kabe hāma heraba śrī-vṛndāvana

"When will my mind be cleansed of all material dirt so that I will be able to feel the presence of spiritual Vṛndāvana?"

rūpa-raghunātha-pade haibe ākuti
kabe hāma bujhaba se yugala-pirīti

"When will I be attracted to the instructions of the Gosvāmīs so that I will be able to understand what is Rādhā and Kṛṣṇa and what is Vṛndāvana?"

These verses indicate that one first has to be purified of all material desires and all attraction for fruitive activity and speculative knowledge if one wishes to understand Vṛndāvana.

In reference to the words *aprākṛta navīna madana, "aprākṛta"* refers to that which is the very opposite of the material conception. The Māyāvādīs consider this to be zero or impersonal, but that is not the case. Everything in the material world is dull, but in the spiritual world everything is alive. The desire for enjoyment is present both in Kṛṣṇa and in His parts and parcels, the living entities. In the spiritual world, such desires are also spiritual. No one should mistakenly consider such desires to be material. In the material world, if one is sexually inclined and enjoys sex life, he enjoys something temporary. His enjoyment vanishes after a few minutes. However, in the spiritual world the same enjoyment may be there, but it never vanishes. It is continually enjoyed. In the spiritual world such sex desire appears to the enjoyer to be more and more relishable with each new feature. In the material world, however, sex enjoyment becomes distasteful after a few minutes only, and it is never permanent. Because Kṛṣṇa appears very much sexually inclined, He is called the new Cupid in the spiritual world. There is no material inebriety in such desire, however.

Gāyantaṁ trāyate yasmāt gāyatrī tvaṁ tataḥ smṛtā: if one chants the *gāyatrī-mantra,* he is gradually delivered from the material clutches. That which delivers one from material entanglement is called *gāyatrī.* An explanation of the *gāyatrī-mantra* can be found in *Madhya-līlā,* Chapter Twenty-one, text 125:

kāma-gāyatrī-mantra-rūpa, haya kṛṣṇera svarūpa,
sārdha-cabiśa akṣara tāra haya
se akṣara 'candra' haya, kṛṣṇe kari' udaya,
trijagat kailā kāma-maya

This *mantra* is just like a Vedic hymn, but it is the Supreme Personality of Godhead Himself. There is no difference between the *kāma-gāyatrī* and Kṛṣṇa. Both are composed of twenty-four and a half transcendental letters. The *mantra* depicted in letters is also Kṛṣṇa, and the *mantra* rises just like the moon. Due to this, there is a perverted reflection of desire in human society and among all kinds of living entities. In the *mantra: klīṁ kāma-devāya vidmahe puṣpa-bāṇāya dhīmahi tan no 'naṅgaḥ pracodayāt,* Kṛṣṇa is called Kāma-deva or Madana-mohana, the Deity who establishes our relationship with Kṛṣṇa. Govinda, or *puṣpa-bāṇa,* who carries an arrow made of flowers, is the Personality of Godhead who accepts our devotional service. *Anaṅga,* or Gopijana-vallabha, satisfies all the *gopīs* and is the ultimate goal of life. This *kāma-gāyatrī* (*klīṁ kāma-devāya vidmahe puṣpa-bāṇāya dhīmahi tan no 'naṅgaḥ pracodayāt*) simply does not belong to this material world. When one is advanced in spiritual understanding, he can worship the Supreme Personality of Godhead with his spiritually purified senses and fulfill the desires of the Lord.

man-manā bhava mad-bhakto
mad-yājī māṁ namaskuru
mām evaiṣyasi satyaṁ te
pratijāne priyo 'si me

"Always think of Me and become My devotee. Worship Me and offer your homage unto Me. Thus you will come to Me without fail. I promise you this because you are My very dear friend." (Bg. 18.65)

In *Brahma-saṁhitā* it is stated (5.27-28):

atha veṇu-ninādasya
trayī-mūrti-mayī gatiḥ
sphurantī praviveśāśu
mukhābjāni svayambhuvaḥ

gāyatrīṁ gāyatas tasmād
adhigatya saroja-jaḥ
saṁskṛtaś cādi-guruṇā
dvijatām agamat tataḥ

trayyā prabuddho 'tha vidhir
vijñāta-tattva-sāgaraḥ
tuṣṭāva veda-sāreṇa
stotreṇānena keśavam

"Then Gāyatrī, mother of the *Vedas,* having been manifested by the divine sound of Śrī Kṛṣṇa's flute, entered the lotus mouth of Brahmā, the self-born, through his eight earholes. The lotus-born Brahmā received the *gāyatrī-mantra,* which had sprung from the song of Śrī Kṛṣṇa's flute. Thus he attained twice-born status, having been initiated by the supreme primal preceptor, Godhead Himself. Enlightened by the recollection of that *gāyatrī,* which embodies the three *Vedas,* Brahmā became acquainted with the expanse of the ocean of truth. Then he worshiped Śrī Kṛṣṇa, the essence of all the *Vedas,* with a hymn."

The vibration of Kṛṣṇa's flute is the origin of the Vedic hymns. Lord Brahmā, who is seated on a lotus flower, heard the sound vibration of Kṛṣṇa's flute and was thereby initiated by the *gāyatrī-mantra.*

TEXT 139

পুরুষ, যোষিৎ, কিবা স্থাবর-জঙ্গম।
সর্ব-চিত্তাকর্ষক, সাক্ষাৎ মন্মথ-মদন ॥ ১৩৯ ॥

puruṣa, yoṣit, kibā sthāvara-jaṅgama
sarva-cittākarṣaka, sākṣāt manmatha-madana

SYNONYMS

puruṣa—a male; *yoṣit*—a female; *kibā*—all; *sthāvara-jaṅgama*—living entities who cannot move and living entities who can move; *sarva*—of everyone; *citta-*

ākarṣaka—the attractor of the minds; *sākṣāt*—directly; *manmatha-madana*—captivator of Cupid himself.

TRANSLATION

"The very name Kṛṣṇa means that He attracts even Cupid. He is therefore attractive to everyone—male and female, moving and inert living entities. Indeed, Kṛṣṇa is known as the all-attractive one.

PURPORT

Just as there are many orbs in the material world called stars or planets, in the spiritual world there are many spiritual planets called Vaikuṇṭhalokas. The spiritual universe, however, is situated far, far away from the cluster of material universes. Material scientists cannot even estimate the number of planets and stars within this universe. They are also incapable of traveling to other stars by spaceships. According to *Bhagavad-gītā,* there is also a spiritual world:

paras tasmāt tu bhāvo 'nyo
'vyakto 'vyaktāt sanātanaḥ
yaḥ sa sarveṣu bhūteṣu
naśyatsu na vinaśyati

"Yet there is another nature, which is eternal and is transcendental to this manifested and unmanifested matter. It is supreme and is never annihilated. When all in this world is annihilated, that part remains as it is." (Bg. 8.20)

Thus there is another nature, which is superior to material nature. The word *bhāva* or *svabhāva* refers to nature. The spiritual nature is eternal, and even when all the material universes are destroyed, the planets in the spiritual world abide. They remain exactly as the spirit soul remains even after the annihilation of the material body. That spiritual world is called *aprākṛta,* or the anti-material world. In this transcendental spiritual world or universe, the highest planetary system is known as Goloka Vṛndāvana. That is the abode of Lord Kṛṣṇa Himself, who is also all-spiritual. Kṛṣṇa is known there as Aprākṛta-madana. The name Madana refers to Cupid, but Kṛṣṇa is the spiritual Madana. His body is not material like the body of Cupid in this material universe. Kṛṣṇa's body is all-spiritual—*sac-cid-ānanda-vigraha.* Therefore He is called Aprākṛta-madana. He is also known as Manmatha-madana, which means that He is attractive even to Cupid. Sometimes Kṛṣṇa's activities and attractive features are misinterpreted by gross materialists who accuse Him of being immoral because He danced with the *gopīs,* but such an accusation results from not knowing that Kṛṣṇa is beyond this material world. His body is *sac-cid-ānanda-vigraha,* completely spiritual. There is no material contamination in His body, and one should not consider His body a lump of flesh and bones. The Māyāvādī philosophers conceive of Kṛṣṇa's body as material, and this is an abominable, gross, materialistic conception. Just as Kṛṣṇa is completely spiritual, the *gopīs* are also spiritual, and this is confirmed in *Brahma-saṁhitā* (5.37):

ānanda-cin-maya-rasa-pratibhāvitābhis
tābhir ya eva nija-rūpatayā kalābhiḥ
goloka eva nivasaty akhilātma-bhūto
govindam ādi-puruṣaṁ tam ahaṁ bhajāmi

"I worship Govinda, the primeval Lord. He resides in His own realm, Goloka, with Rādhā, who resembles His own spiritual figure and who embodies the ecstatic potency [*hlādinī*]. Their companions are Her confidantes, who embody extensions of Her bodily form and who are imbued and permeated with ever-blissful spiritual *rasa*."

The *gopīs* are also of the same spiritual quality (*nija-rūpatayā*) because they are expansions of Kṛṣṇa's pleasure potency. Neither Kṛṣṇa nor the *gopīs* have anything to do with lumps of matter or the material conception. In the material world, the living entity is encaged within a material body, and due to ignorance he thinks that he is the body. Lusty desire, enjoyment between male and female, is all material. One cannot compare the lusty desires of a materialistic man to the lusty desires of Kṛṣṇa. Unless one is advanced in spiritual science, he cannot understand the lusty desires between Kṛṣṇa and the *gopīs*. In *Caitanya-caritāmṛta* the lusty desire of the *gopīs* is compared to gold. The lusty desires of a materialistic man, on the other hand, are compared to iron. At no stage can iron and gold be compared. The living entities—moving and nonmoving—are part and parcel of Kṛṣṇa; therefore they originally have the same kind of lusty desire. However, when this lusty desire is expressed through matter, it is abominable. When a living entity is spiritually advanced and liberated from material bondage, he can understand Kṛṣṇa in truth. As stated in *Bhagavad-gītā:*

janma karma ca me divyam
evaṁ yo vetti tattvataḥ
tyaktvā dehaṁ punar janma
naiti mām eti so 'rjuna

"One who knows the transcendental nature of My appearance and activities does not, upon leaving the body, take his birth again in this material world, but attains My eternal abode, O Arjuna." (Bg. 4.9)

When one can understand the body of Kṛṣṇa as well as the Lord's lusty desires, one is immediately liberated. A conditioned soul encaged within the material body cannot understand Kṛṣṇa. As stated in *Bhagavad-gītā:*

manuṣyāṇāṁ sahasreṣu
kaścid yatati siddhaye
yatatām api siddhānāṁ
kaścin māṁ vetti tattvataḥ

"Out of many thousands among men, one may endeavor for perfection, and of those who have achieved perfection, hardly one knows Me in truth." (Bg. 7.3)

The word *siddhaye* indicates liberation. Only after being liberated from material conditioning can one understand Kṛṣṇa. When one can understand Kṛṣṇa as He is (*tattvataḥ*), one actually lives in the spiritual world, although apparently living within the material body. This technical science can be understood when one is actually spiritually advanced.

In his *Bhakti-rasāmṛta-sindhu* (1.2.187), Śrīla Rūpa Gosvāmī says:

īhā yasya harer dāsye
karmaṇā manasā girā
nikhilāsv apy avasthāsu
jīvan-muktaḥ sa ucyate

When a person in this material world desires only to serve Kṛṣṇa with love and devotion, he is liberated, even though functioning within this material world. As *Bhagavad-gītā* confirms:

māṁ ca yo 'vyabhicāreṇa
bhakti-yogena sevate
sa guṇān samatītyaitān
brahma-bhūyāya kalpate

"One who engages in full devotional service, who does not fall down in any circumstance, at once transcends the modes of material nature and thus comes to the level of Brahman." (Bg. 14.26)

Simply by engaging in the loving service of the Lord one can attain liberation. As stated in *Bhagavad-gītā* (18.54): *brahma-bhūtaḥ prasannātmā na śocati na kāṅkṣati.* A person who is highly advanced in spiritual knowledge and who has attained the *brahma-bhūta* stage neither laments nor hankers for anything material. That is the stage of spiritual realization.

Śrīla Bhaktivinoda Ṭhākura considered the *brahma-bhūta* stage in two divisions—*svarūpa-gata* and *vastu-gata.* When one has understood Kṛṣṇa in truth but is still maintaining some material connection, he is known to be situated in his *svarūpa,* his original consciousness. When that original consciousness is completely spiritual, it is called Kṛṣṇa consciousness. One who lives in such consciousness is actually living in Vṛndāvana. He may live anywhere; material location doesn't matter. When by the grace of Kṛṣṇa one thus advances, he becomes completely uncontaminated by the material body and mind and at that time factually lives in Vṛndāvana. That stage is called *vastu-gata.*

One should execute his spiritual activities in the *svarūpa-gata* stage of consciousness. He should also chant the *cinmayī gāyatrī,* the spiritual *mantras: oṁ namo bhagavate vāsudevāya,* or *klīṁ kṛṣṇāya govindāya gopījana-vallabhāya svāhā. Klīṁ kāmadevāya vidmahe puṣpa-bāṇāya dhīmahi tan no 'naṅgaḥ pracodayāt.* These are the *kāma-gāyatrī* or *kāma-bīja mantras.* One should be initiated by a bona fide spiritual master and worship Kṛṣṇa with these transcendental *mantras* known as *kāma-gāyatrī* or *kāma-bīja.*

As explained by Kṛṣṇadāsa Kavirāja Gosvāmī:

vṛndāvane 'aprākṛta navīna madana'
kāma-gāyatrī kāma-bīje yāṅra upāsana

puruṣa, yoṣit, kibā sthāvara-jaṅgama
sarva-cittākarṣaka, sākṣāt manmatha-madana
(Cc. Madhya 8.138-139)

A person who is properly purified and initiated by the spiritual master worships the Supreme Personality of Godhead, Kṛṣṇa, by this *mantra.* He chants the *kāma-gāyatrī* with the *kāma-bīja.* As *Bhagavad-gītā* confirms, one should engage in transcendental worship in order to be fit for being attracted by Kṛṣṇa, the all-attractive.

man-manā bhava mad-bhakto
mad-yājī māṁ namaskuru
mām evaiṣyasi satyaṁ te
pratijāne priyo 'si me

"Always think of Me and become My devotee. Worship Me and offer your homage unto Me. Thus you will come to Me without fail. I promise you this because you are My very dear friend." (Bg. 18.65)

Since every living entity is part and parcel of Kṛṣṇa, Kṛṣṇa is naturally attractive. Due to material covering, one's attraction for Kṛṣṇa is checked. One is not usually attracted by Kṛṣṇa in the material world, but as soon as one is liberated from material conditioning, he is naturally attracted. Therefore it is said in this verse, *sarva-cittākarṣaka.* Everyone is naturally attracted by Kṛṣṇa. This attraction is within everyone's heart, and when the heart is cleansed, attraction is manifest (*ceto-darpaṇa-mārjanaṁ bhava-mahā-dāvāgni-nirvāpaṇam*).

TEXT 140

তাসামাবিরভূচ্ছৌরিঃ স্ময়মানমুখাম্বুজঃ ।
পীতাম্বরধরঃ স্রগ্বী সাক্ষান্মন্মথ-মন্মথঃ ॥ ১৪০ ॥

tāsām āvirabhūc chauriḥ
smayamāna-mukhāmbujaḥ

pītāmbara-dharaḥ sragvī
sākṣān manmatha-manmathaḥ

SYNONYMS

tāsām—among them; *āvirabhūt*—appeared; *śauriḥ*—Lord Kṛṣṇa; *smayamāna*—smiling; *mukha-ambujaḥ*—lotus face; *pīta-ambara-dharaḥ*—dressed with yellow garments; *sragvī*—decorated with a flower garland; *sākṣāt*—directly; *manmatha*—of Cupid; *manmathaḥ*—Cupid.

TRANSLATION

" 'When Kṛṣṇa left the rāsa-līlā dance, the gopīs became very morose, and when they were grieving, Kṛṣṇa reappeared dressed in yellow garments. Wearing a flower garland and smiling, He was attractive even to Cupid. In this way Kṛṣṇa appeared among the gopīs.'

PURPORT

This verse is from *Śrīmad-Bhāgavatam* (10.32.2).

TEXT 141

নানা-ভক্তের রসামৃত নানাবিধ হয় ।
সেই সব রসামৃতের 'বিষয়' 'আশ্রয়' ॥ ১৪১ ॥

nānā-bhaktera rasāmṛta nānā-vidha haya
sei saba rasāmṛtera 'viṣaya' 'āśraya'

SYNONYMS

nānā-bhaktera—of various types of devotees; *rasa-amṛta*—the nectar of devotion or transcendental mellows; *nānā-vidha*—different varieties; *haya*—there are; *sei saba*—all these; *rasa-amṛtera*—of the nectar of devotion; *viṣaya*—subject; *āśraya*—object.

TRANSLATION

"Each and every devotee has a certain type of transcendental mellow in relation to Kṛṣṇa. However, in all transcendental relationships the devotee is the worshiper [āśraya], and Kṛṣṇa is the object of worship [viṣaya].

TEXT 142

অখিলরসামৃতমূর্তিঃ
প্রসৃমর-রুচিরুদ্ধ-তারকা-পালিঃ ।

কলিত-শ্যামা-ললিতো
রাধাপ্রেয়ান্ বিধুর্জয়তি ॥ ১৪২ ॥

akhila-rasāmṛta-mūrtiḥ
prasṛmara-ruci-ruddha-tārakā-pāliḥ
kalita-śyāmā-lalito
rādhā-preyān vidhur jayati

SYNONYMS

akhila-rasa-amṛta-mūrtiḥ—the reservoir of all pleasure, in which exist the mellows, namely *śānta, dāsya, sakhya, vātsalya* and *mādhurya; prasṛmara*—spreading forth; *ruci*—by His bodily luster; *ruddha*—who has subjugated; *tārakā*—the *gopī* named Tārakā; *pāliḥ*—the *gopī* named Pāli; *kalita*—who has absorbed; *śyāmā*—the *gopī* named Śyāmā; *lalitaḥ*—and the *gopī* named Lalitā; *rādhā-preyān*—dearmost to Srīmatī Rādhārāṇī; *vidhuḥ*—Kṛṣṇa, the Supreme Personality of Godhead; *jayati*—all glories to.

TRANSLATION

" 'Let Kṛṣṇa, the Supreme Personality of Godhead, be glorified! By virtue of His expanding attractive features, He subjugated the gopīs named Tārakā and Pāli and absorbed Śyāmā and Lalitā. He is the most attractive lover of Śrīmatī Rādhārāṇī and is the reservoir of pleasure for all devotional mellows.'

PURPORT

Everyone has a particular transcendental mellow by which he loves and serves Kṛṣṇa. Kṛṣṇa is the most attractive feature for every kind of devotee. He is therefore called *akhila-rasāmṛta-mūrti,* the transcendental form of attraction for all kinds of devotees, whether the devotee be in the *śānta-rasa, dāsya-rasa, sakhya-rasa, mādhurya-rasa* or *vātsalya-rasa.*

This is the opening verse of *Bhakti-rasāmṛta-sindhu* by Śrīla Rūpa Gosvāmī.

TEXT 143

শৃঙ্গার-রসরাজময়-মূর্তিধর ।
অতএব আত্মপর্যন্ত-সর্ব-চিত্ত-হর ॥ ১৪৩ ॥

śṛṅgāra-rasarāja-maya-mūrti-dhara
ataeva ātma-paryanta-sarvacitta-hara

SYNONYMS

śṛṅgāra-rasa-rāja-maya—consisting of the mellow of conjugal love, which is the king of mellows; *mūrti-dhara*—Kṛṣṇa, the personified reservoir of all pleasure;

ataeva—therefore; *ātma-paryanta*—even up to His own self; *sarva*—all; *citta*—of hearts; *hara*—the attractor.

TRANSLATION

"Kṛṣṇa is all-attractive for all devotional mellows because He is the personification of the conjugal mellow. Kṛṣṇa is attractive not only to all the devotees, but to Himself as well.

TEXT 144

বিশ্বেষামনুরঞ্জনেন জনয়ন্নানন্দমিন্দীবর-
শ্রেণীশ্যামলকোমলৈরুপনয়ন্নঙ্গৈরনঙ্গোৎসবম্ ।
স্বচ্ছন্দং ব্রজসুন্দরীভিরভিতঃ প্রত্যঙ্গমালিঙ্গিতঃ
শৃঙ্গারঃ সখি মূর্তিমানিব মধৌ মুগ্ধো হরিঃ ক্রীড়তি ॥১৪৪॥

viśveṣām anurañjanena janayann ānandam indīvara-
śreṇī-śyāmala-komalair upanayann aṅgair anaṅgotsavam
svacchandaṁ vraja-sundarībhir abhitaḥ pratyaṅgam āliṅgitaḥ
śṛṅgāraḥ sakhi mūrtimān iva madhau mugdho hariḥ krīḍati

SYNONYMS

viśveṣām—of all the *gopīs; anurañjanena*—by the act of pleasing; *janayan*—producing; *ānandam*—the bliss; *indīvara-śreṇī*—like a row of blue lotuses; *śyāmala*—bluish black; *komalaiḥ*—and soft; *upanayan*—bringing; *aṅgaiḥ*—with His limbs; *anaṅga-utsavam*—a festival for Cupid; *svacchandam*—without restriction; *vraja-sundarībhiḥ*—by the young women of Vraja; *abhitaḥ*—on both sides; *prati-aṅgam*—each limb; *āliṅgitaḥ*—embraced; *śṛṅgāraḥ*—amorous love; *sakhi*—O friend; *mūrtimān*—embodied; *iva*—like; *madhau*—in the springtime; *mugdhaḥ*—perplexed; *hariḥ*—Lord Hari; *krīḍati*—plays.

TRANSLATION

" 'My dear friends, just see how Śrī Kṛṣṇa is enjoying the season of spring! With the gopīs embracing each of His limbs, He is like amorous love personified. With His transcendental pastimes, He enlivens all the gopīs and the entire creation. With His soft bluish black arms and legs, which resemble blue lotus flowers, He has created a festival for Cupid.'

PURPORT

This is a verse from the *Gīta-govinda* (1.11). See also *Caitanya-caritāmṛta, Ādi-līlā,* Chapter Four, text 224.

TEXT 145

লক্ষ্মীকান্তাদি অবতারের হরে মন।
লক্ষ্মী-আদি নারীগণের করে আকর্ষণ ॥ ১৪৫ ॥

lakṣmī-kāntādi avatārera hare mana
lakṣmī-ādi nārī-gaṇera kare ākarṣaṇa

SYNONYMS

lakṣmī-kānta-ādi—of the husband of the goddess of fortune (Nārāyaṇa); *avatārera*—of the incarnation; *hare*—He enchants; *mana*—the mind; *lakṣmī*—the goddess of fortune; *ādi*—headed by; *nārī-gaṇera*—of all women; *kare*—does; *ākarṣaṇa*—attraction.

TRANSLATION

"He also attracts Nārāyaṇa, the incarnation of Saṅkarṣaṇa and the husband of the goddess of fortune. He attracts not only Nārāyaṇa, but all women, headed by the goddess of fortune, the consort of Nārāyaṇa.

TEXT 146

দ্বিজাত্মজা মে যুবয়োদিদৃক্ষুণা, ময়োপনীতা ভুবি ধর্মগুপ্তয়ে।
কলাবতীর্ণাববনের্ভরাসুরান্,হত্বেহ ভূয়স্ত্বরয়েতমন্তি মে ॥১৪৬

dvijātmajā me yuvayor didṛkṣuṇā
mayopanītā bhuvi dharma-guptaye
kalāvatīrṇāv avaner bharāsurān
hatveha bhūyas tvarayetam anti me

SYNONYMS

dvija-ātma-jāḥ—the sons of the *brāhmaṇa; me*—by Me; *yuvayoḥ*—of both of you; *didṛkṣuṇā*—desiring the sight; *mayā*—by Me; *upanītāḥ*—brought; *bhuvi*—in the world; *dharma-guptaye*—for the protection of religious principles; *kalā*—with all potencies; *avatīrṇau*—who descended; *avaneḥ*—of the world; *bharā-asurān*—the heavy load of demons; *hatvā*—having killed; *iha*—here in the spiritual world; *bhūyaḥ*—again; *tvarayā*—very soon; *itam*—please come back; *anti*—near; *me*—Me.

TRANSLATION

"Addressing Kṛṣṇa and Arjuna, Lord Mahā-Viṣṇu [the Mahāpuruṣa] said, 'I wanted to see both of you, and therefore I have brought the sons of the brāhmaṇa here. Both of you have appeared in the material world to reestablish

religious principles, and you have both appeared here with all your potencies. After killing all the demons, please quickly return to the spiritual world.'

PURPORT

This is a quotation from *Śrīmad-Bhāgavatam* (10.89.58) concerning Kṛṣṇa's endeavor to take Arjuna beyond the material universe when Arjuna was searching for the sons of a *brāhmaṇa.*

Lord Mahā-Viṣṇu, who is situated beyond this material world, was also attracted by the bodily features of Kṛṣṇa. Mahā-Viṣṇu had actually stolen the sons of the *brāhmaṇa* in Dvārakā so that Kṛṣṇa and Arjuna would come visit Him. This verse is quoted to show that Kṛṣṇa is so attractive that He attracts Mahā-Viṣṇu.

TEXT 147

কস্যানুভাবোঽস্য ন দেব বিদ্মহে
তবাঙ্ঘ্রিরেণুস্পরশাধিকারঃ।
যদ্বাঞ্ছয়া শ্রীর্ললনাচরত্তপো
বিহায় কামান্ সুচিরং ধৃতব্রতা ॥ ১৪৭ ॥

kasyānubhāvo 'sya na deva vidmahe
tavāṅghri-reṇu-sparaśādhikāraḥ
yad-vāñchayā śrīr lalanācarat tapo
vihāya kāmān suciraṁ dhṛta-vratā

SYNONYMS

kasya—of what; *anubhāvaḥ*—a result; *asya*—of the serpent (Kāliya); *na*—not; *deva*—my Lord; *vidmahe*—we know; *tava-aṅghri*—of Your lotus feet; *reṇu*—of the dust; *sparaśa*—for touching; *adhikāraḥ*—qualification; *yat*—which; *vāñchayā*—by desiring; *śrīḥ*—the goddess of fortune; *lalanā*—the topmost woman; *acarat*—performed; *tapaḥ*—austerity; *vihāya*—giving up; *kāmān*—all desires; *suciram*—for a long time; *dhṛta*—a law upheld; *vratā*—as a vow.

TRANSLATION

" 'O Lord, we do not know how the serpent Kāliya attained such an opportunity to be touched by the dust of Your lotus feet. For this end, the goddess of fortune performed austerities for centuries, giving up all other desires and taking austere vows. Indeed, we do not know how this serpent Kāliya got such an opportunity.'

PURPORT

This verse from *Śrīmad-Bhāgavatam* (10.16.36) was spoken by the wives of the Kāliya demon.

TEXT 148

আপন-মাধুর্যে হরে আপনার মন।
আপনা আপনি চাহে করিতে আলিঙ্গন ॥ ১৪৮ ॥

āpana-mādhurye hare āpanāra mana
āpanā āpani cāhe karite āliṅgana

SYNONYMS

āpana—own; *mādhurye*—by sweetness; *hare*—steals; *āpanāra*—His own; *mana*—mind; *āpanā*—Himself; *āpani*—He; *cāhe*—wants; *karite*—to do; *āliṅgana*—embracing.

TRANSLATION

"Lord Kṛṣṇa's sweetness is so attractive that it steals away His own mind. Thus He even wants to embrace Himself.

TEXT 149

অপরিকলিতপূর্বঃ কশ্চমৎকারকারী
স্ফুরতি মম গরীয়ানেষ মাধুর্যপূরঃ।
অয়মহমপি হন্ত প্রেক্ষ্য যং লুব্ধচেতাঃ
সরভসমুপভোক্তুং কাময়ে রাধিকেব ॥ ১৪৯ ॥

aparikalita-pūrvaḥ kaś camatkāra-kārī
sphurati mama garīyān eṣa mādhurya-pūraḥ
ayam aham api hanta prekṣya yaṁ lubdha-cetāḥ
sarabhasam upabhoktuṁ kāmaye rādhikeva

SYNONYMS

aparikalita-pūrvaḥ—not previously experienced; *kaḥ*—who; *camatkāra-kārī*—causing wonder; *sphurati*—manifests; *mama*—My; *garīyān*—more great; *eṣaḥ*—this; *mādhurya-pūraḥ*—abundance of sweetness; *ayam*—this; *aham*—I; *api*—even; *hanta*—alas; *prekṣya*—seeing; *yam*—which; *lubdha-cetāḥ*—My mind being bewildered; *sa-rabhasam*—impetuously; *upabhoktum*—to enjoy; *kāmaye*—desire; *rādhikā iva*—like Śrīmatī Rādhārāṇī.

TRANSLATION

"'Upon seeing His own reflection in a bejeweled pillar of His Dvārakā palace, Kṛṣṇa desired to embrace it, saying, "Alas, I have never seen such a

person before. Who is He? Just by seeing Him I have become eager to embrace Him, exactly like Śrīmatī Rādhārāṇī.'' ' ''

PURPORT

This is a verse from Śrīla Rūpa Gosvāmī's *Lalita-mādhava* (8.34).

TEXT 150

এই ত' সংক্ষেপে কহিল কৃষ্ণের স্বরূপ ।
এবে সংক্ষেপে কহি শুন রাধা-তত্ত্বরূপ ॥ ১৫০ ॥

ei ta' saṅkṣepe kahila kṛṣṇera svarūpa
ebe saṅkṣepe kahi śuna rādhā-tattva-rūpa

SYNONYMS

ei ta'—thus; *saṅkṣepe*—in brief; *kahila*—I have said; *kṛṣṇera*—of Lord Kṛṣṇa; *svarūpa*—the original form; *ebe*—now; *saṅkṣepe*—in summary; *kahi*—I shall speak; *śuna*—please hear; *rādhā*—of Śrīmatī Rādhārāṇī; *tattva-rūpa*—the actual position.

TRANSLATION

Śrī Rāmānanda Rāya then said, "I have thus briefly explained the original form of the Supreme Personality of Godhead. Now let me describe the position of Śrīmatī Rādhārāṇī.

TEXT 151

কৃষ্ণের অনন্ত-শক্তি, তাতে তিন – প্রধান ।
'চিচ্ছক্তি', 'মায়াশক্তি', 'জীবশক্তি'-নাম ॥ ১৫১ ॥

kṛṣṇera ananta-śakti, tāte tina——pradhāna
'cic-chakti', 'māyā-śakti', 'jīva-śakti'-nāma

SYNONYMS

kṛṣṇera—of Lord Kṛṣṇa; *ananta-śakti*—unlimited potencies; *tāte*—in that; *tina*—three; *pradhāna*—chief; *cit-śakti*—spiritual potency; *māyā-śakti*—material potency; *jīva-śakti*—marginal potency, or living entities; *nāma*—named.

TRANSLATION

"Kṛṣṇa has unlimited potencies, which can be divided into three main parts. These are the spiritual potency, the material potency and the marginal potency, which is known as the living entities.

TEXT 152

‘অন্তরঙ্গা’, ‘বহিরঙ্গা’, ‘তটস্থা’ কহি যারে ।
অন্তরঙ্গা ‘স্বরূপ-শক্তি’—সবার উপরে ॥ ১৫২ ॥

'antaraṅgā', 'bahiraṅgā', 'taṭasthā' kahi yāre
antaraṅgā 'svarūpa-śakti'——sabāra upare

SYNONYMS

antaraṅgā—internal; *bahiraṅgā*—external; *taṭa-sthā*—marginal; *kahi*—we say; *yāre*—to whom; *antaraṅgā*—the internal potency; *svarūpa-śakti*—the personal energy; *sabāra upare*—above all.

TRANSLATION

"In other words, these are all potencies of God—internal, external and marginal. However, the internal potency is the Lord's personal energy and stands over the other two.

TEXT 153

বিষ্ণুশক্তিঃ পরা প্রোক্তা ক্ষেত্রজ্ঞাখ্যা তথাপরা ।
অবিদ্যা-কর্মসংজ্ঞান্যা তৃতীয়া শক্তিরিষ্যতে ॥ ১৫৩ ॥

viṣṇu-śaktiḥ parā proktā
kṣetrajñākhyā tathā parā
avidyā-karma-saṁjñānyā
tṛtīyā śaktir iṣyate

SYNONYMS

viṣṇu-śaktiḥ—the potency of Lord Viṣṇu; *parā*—spiritual; *proktā*—it is said; *kṣetrajña-ākhyā*—the potency known as *kṣetrajña;* *tathā*—as well as; *parā*—spiritual; *avidyā*—ignorance; *karma*—fruitive activities; *saṁjña*—known as; *anyā*—other; *tṛtīyā*—third; *śaktiḥ*—potency; *iṣyate*—known thus.

TRANSLATION

" 'The original potency of Lord Viṣṇu is superior or spiritual. The living entity actually belongs to that superior energy, but there is another energy, called the material energy, and this third energy is full of ignorance.'

PURPORT

This is a quotation from the *Viṣṇu Purāṇa* (6.7.61).

TEXT 154

সচ্চিদানন্দময় কৃষ্ণের স্বরূপ ।
অতএব স্বরূপ-শক্তি হয় তিন রূপ ॥ ১৫৪ ॥

sac-cid-ānanda-maya kṛṣṇera svarūpa
ataeva svarūpa-śakti haya tina rūpa

SYNONYMS

sat-cit-ānanda-maya—eternal bliss and knowledge; *kṛṣṇera*—of Lord Kṛṣṇa; *svarūpa*—the real transcendental form; *ataeva*—therefore; *svarūpa-śakti*—His spiritual personal potency; *haya*—is; *tina rūpa*—three forms.

TRANSLATION

"Originally Lord Kṛṣṇa is sac-cid-ānanda-vigraha, the transcendental form of eternity, bliss and knowledge; therefore His personal potency, the internal potency, has three different forms.

TEXT 155

আনন্দাংশে 'হ্লাদিনী', সদংশে 'সন্ধিনী ।
চিদংশে 'সম্বিৎ', যারে জ্ঞান করি' মানি ॥ ১৫৫ ॥

ānandāṁśe 'hlādinī', sad-aṁśe 'sandhinī'
cid-aṁśe 'samvit', yāre jñāna kari' māni

SYNONYMS

ānanda-aṁśe—in bliss; *hlādinī*—the pleasure-giving potency; *sat-aṁśe*—in eternity; *sandhinī*—the creative potency; *cit-aṁśe*—in knowledge; *samvit*—*samvit;* *yāre*—which; *jñāna*—knowledge; *kari'*—taking as; *māni*—I accept.

TRANSLATION

"Hlādinī is His aspect of bliss; sandhinī, of eternal existence; and samvit, of cognizance, which is also accepted as knowledge.

TEXT 156

হ্লাদিনী সন্ধিনী সম্বিৎ ত্বয্যেকা সর্বসংশ্রয়ে ।
হ্লাদতাপকরী মিশ্রা ত্বয়ি নো গুণবর্জিতে ॥ ১৫৬ ॥

hlādinī sandhinī samvit
tvayy ekā sarva-saṁśraye

hlāda-tāpa-karī miśrā
tvayi no guṇa-varjite

SYNONYMS

hlādinī—that which generates pleasure; *sandhinī*—the potency of existence; *samvit*—the potency of knowledge; *tvayi*—unto You; *ekā*—principal internal potency; *sarva-saṁśraye*—You are the reservoir of all potencies; *hlāda*—pleasure; *tāpa-karī*—generator of pains; *miśrā*—mixed; *tvayi*—unto You; *no*—never; *guṇa-varjite*—You, transcendence, the Supreme Personality of Godhead.

TRANSLATION

" 'My dear Lord, You are the transcendental reservoir of all transcendental qualities. Your pleasure potency, existence potency and knowledge potency are actually all one spiritual internal potency. The conditioned soul, although actually spiritual, experiences sometimes pleasure, sometimes pain and sometimes a mixture of pain and pleasure. This is due to his being touched by matter. However, because You are above all material qualities, these are not found in You. Your superior spiritual potency is completely transcendental, and for You there is no such thing as relative pleasure, pleasure mixed with pain, or pain itself.'

PURPORT

This is a quotation from the *Viṣṇu Purāṇa* (1.12.69).

TEXT 157

কৃষ্ণকে আহ্লাদে, তা'তে নাম—'হ্লাদিনী' ।
সেই শক্তি-দ্বারে সুখ আস্বাদে আপনি ॥ ১৫৭ ॥

kṛṣṇake āhlāde, tā'te nāma——'hlādinī'
sei śakti-dvāre sukha āsvāde āpani

SYNONYMS

kṛṣṇake—unto Kṛṣṇa; *āhlāde*—gives pleasure; *tā'te*—therefore; *nāma*—the name; *hlādinī*—pleasure-giving potency; *sei śakti*—that potency; *dvāre*—by means of; *sukha*—happiness; *āsvāde*—tastes; *āpani*—Lord Kṛṣṇa personally.

TRANSLATION

"The potency called hlādinī gives Kṛṣṇa transcendental pleasure. Through this pleasure potency, Kṛṣṇa personally tastes all spiritual pleasure.

TEXT 158

সুখরূপ কৃষ্ণ করে সুখ আস্বাদন ।
ভক্তগণে সুখ দিতে 'হ্লাদিনী'—কারণ ॥ ১৫৮ ॥

sukha-rūpa kṛṣṇa kare sukha āsvādana
bhakta-gaṇe sukha dite 'hlādinī'——kāraṇa

SYNONYMS

sukha-rūpa—embodiment of pleasure; *kṛṣṇa*—Lord Kṛṣṇa; *kare*—does; *sukha*—happiness; *āsvādana*—tasting; *bhakta-gaṇe*—unto the devotee; *sukha*—happiness; *dite*—to give; *hlādinī*—the pleasure potency; *kāraṇa*—the cause.

TRANSLATION

"Lord Kṛṣṇa tastes all kinds of transcendental happiness, although He Himself is happiness personified. The pleasure relished by His pure devotee is also manifest by His pleasure potency.

TEXT 159

হ্লাদিনীর সার অংশ, তার 'প্রেম' নাম ।
আনন্দচিন্ময়রস প্রেমের আখ্যান ॥ ১৫৯ ॥

hlādinīra sāra aṁśa, tāra 'prema' nāma
ānanda-cinmaya-rasa premera ākhyāna

SYNONYMS

hlādinīra—of this pleasure potency; *sāra*—the essential; *aṁśa*—part; *tāra*—its; *prema*—love of God; *nāma*—name; *ānanda*—full of pleasure; *cit-maya-rasa*—the platform of spiritual mellows; *premera*—of love of Godhead; *ākhyāna*—the explanation.

TRANSLATION

"The most essential part of this pleasure potency is love of Godhead [prema]. Consequently, the explanation of love of Godhead is also a transcendental mellow full of pleasure.

TEXT 160

প্রেমের পরম-সার 'মহাভাব' জানি ।
সেই মহাভাবরূপা রাধা-ঠাকুরাণী ॥ ১৬০ ॥

premera parama-sāra 'mahābhāva' jāni
sei mahābhāva-rūpā rādhā-ṭhākurāṇī

SYNONYMS

premera—of love of Godhead; *parama-sāra*—the essential part; *mahā-bhāva*—the transcendental ecstasy of the name *mahābhāva; jāni*—we know; *sei*—that; *mahā-bhāva-rūpā*—the personification of the *mahābhāva* transcendental ecstasy; *rādhā-ṭhākurāṇī*—Śrīmatī Rādhārāṇī.

TRANSLATION

"The essential part of love of Godhead is called mahābhāva, transcendental ecstasy, and that ecstasy is represented by Śrīmatī Rādhārāṇī.

TEXT 161

তয়োরপ্যুভয়োর্মধ্যে রাধিকা সর্বথাধিকা।
মহাভাবস্বরূপেয়ং গুণৈরতিবরীয়সী ॥ ১৬১ ॥

tayor apy ubhayor madhye
rādhikā sarvathādhikā
mahābhāva-svarūpeyaṁ
guṇair ativarīyasī

SYNONYMS

tayoḥ—of them; *api*—even; *ubhayoḥ*—of both (Candrāvalī and Rādhārāṇī); *madhye*—in the middle; *rādhikā*—Śrīmatī Rādhārāṇī; *sarvathā*—in every way; *adhikā*—greater; *mahā-bhāva-svarūpa*—the form of *mahābhāva; iyam*—this one; *guṇaiḥ*—with good qualities; *ativarīyasī*—the best of all.

TRANSLATION

" 'Among the gopīs of Vṛndāvana, Śrīmatī Rādhārāṇī and another gopī are considered chief. However, when we compare the gopīs, it appears that Śrīmatī Rādhārāṇī is most important because Her real feature expresses the highest ecstasy of love. The ecstasy of love experienced by the other gopīs cannot be compared to that of Śrīmatī Rādhārāṇī.'

PURPORT

This is a quotation from Śrīla Rūpa Gosvāmī's *Ujjvala-nīlamaṇi* (4.3).

TEXT 162

প্রেমের 'স্বরূপ-দেহ'—প্রেম-বিভাবিত ।
কৃষ্ণের প্রেয়সী-শ্রেষ্ঠা জগতে বিদিত ॥ ১৬২ ॥

premera 'svarūpa-deha'—prema-vibhāvita
kṛṣṇera preyasī-śreṣṭhā jagate vidita

SYNONYMS

premera—love of Godhead; *svarūpa-deha*—actual body; *prema*—by love of Godhead; *vibhāvita*—influence; *kṛṣṇera*—of Lord Kṛṣṇa; *preyasī*—of the dear friends; *śreṣṭhā*—topmost; *jagate*—throughout the whole world; *vidita*—known.

TRANSLATION

"The body of Śrīmatī Rādhārāṇī is the veritable transformation of love of Godhead; She is the dearmost friend of Kṛṣṇa, and this is known throughout the world.

TEXT 163

আনন্দচিন্ময়রস-প্রতিভাবিতাভি-
স্তাভির্য এব নিজরূপতয়া কলাভিঃ ।
গোলোক এব নিবসত্যখিলাত্মভূতো
গোবিন্দমাদিপুরুষং তমহং ভজামি ॥ ১৬৩ ॥

ānanda-cinmaya-rasa-pratibhāvitābhis
tābhir ya eva nija-rūpatayā kalābhiḥ
goloka eva nivasty akhilātma-bhūto
govindam ādi-puruṣaṁ tam ahaṁ bhajāmi

SYNONYMS

ānanda—bliss; *cit*—knowledge; *maya*—consisting of; *rasa*—mellows; *prati*—every second; *bhāvitābhiḥ*—who are engrossed with; *tābhiḥ*—with those; *yaḥ*—who; *eva*—certainly; *nija-rūpatayā*—with His own form; *kalābhiḥ*—who are parts of portions of His pleasure potency; *goloke*—in Goloka Vṛndāvana; *eva*—certainly; *nivasti*—resides; *akhila-ātma*—as the soul of all; *bhūtaḥ*—who exists; *govindam*—Lord Govinda; *ādi-puruṣam*—the original personality; *tam*—Him; *aham*—I; *bhajāmi*—worship.

TRANSLATION

" 'I worship Govinda, the primeval Lord, who resides in His own realm, Goloka, with Rādhā, who resembles His own spiritual figure and who embodies the ecstatic potency [hlādinī]. Their companions are Her confidantes, who embody extensions of Her bodily form and who are imbued and permeated with ever-blissful spiritual rasa.'

PURPORT

This is a quotation from *Brahma-saṁhitā* (5.37).

TEXT 164

সেই মহাভাব হয় 'চিন্তামণি-সার' ।
কৃষ্ণ-বাঞ্ছা পূর্ণ করে এই কার্য তাঁর ॥ ১৬৪ ॥

sei mahābhāva haya 'cintāmaṇi-sāra'
kṛṣṇa-vāñchā pūrṇa kare ei kārya tāṅra

SYNONYMS

sei—that; *mahā-bhāva*—supreme ecstasy; *haya*—is; *cintāmaṇi-sāra*—the essence of spiritual life; *kṛṣṇa-vāñchā*—all the desires of Lord Kṛṣṇa; *pūrṇa kare*—fulfills; *ei*—this; *kārya*—business; *tāṅra*—Her.

TRANSLATION

"That supreme ecstasy of Śrīmatī Rādhārāṇī is the essence of spiritual life. Her only business is to fulfill all the desires of Kṛṣṇa.

TEXT 165

'মহাভাব-চিন্তামণি' রাধার স্বরূপ ।
ললিতাদি সখী—তাঁর কায়ব্যূহরূপ ॥ ১৬৫ ॥

'mahābhāva-cintāmaṇi' rādhāra svarūpa
lalitādi sakhī——tāṅra kāya-vyūha-rūpa

SYNONYMS

mahā-bhāva—of the topmost spiritual ecstasy; *cintā-maṇi*—the touchstone; *rādhāra svarūpa*—the transcendental form of Śrīmatī Rādhārāṇī; *lalitā-ādi sakhī*—the *gopī* associates of Śrīmatī Rādhārāṇī; *tāṅra kāya-vyūha-rūpa*—expansions of Her spiritual body.

TRANSLATION

"Śrīmatī Rādhārāṇī is the topmost spiritual gem, and the other gopīs—Lalitā, Viśākhā and so on—are expansions of Her spiritual body.

TEXT 166

রাধা-প্রতি কৃষ্ণ-স্নেহ—সুগন্ধি উদ্বর্তন ।
তা'তে অতি সুগন্ধি দেহ—উজ্জ্বল-বরণ ॥ ১৬৬ ॥

rādhā-prati kṛṣṇa-sneha——sugandhi udvartana
tā'te ati sugandhi deha——ujjvala-varaṇa

SYNONYMS

rādhā-prati—toward Śrīmatī Rādhārāṇī; *kṛṣṇa-sneha*—the affection of Lord Kṛṣṇa; *su-gandhi udvartana*—perfumed massage; *tā'te*—in that; *ati*—very; *su-gandhi*—perfumed; *deha*—the body; *ujjvala*—brilliant; *varaṇa*—luster.

TRANSLATION

"Śrīmatī Rādhārāṇī's transcendental body is brilliant in luster and full of all transcendental flavors. Lord Kṛṣṇa's affection for Her is like a perfumed massage.

PURPORT

Sugandhi udvartana refers to a paste made of several perfumes and flavored oils. This paste is massaged all over the body, and in this way the body's dirt and perspiration are removed. Śrīmatī Rādhārāṇī's body is automatically perfumed, but when Her body is massaged with the scented paste of Lord Kṛṣṇa's affection, Her entire body is doubly perfumed and made brilliant and lustrous. This is the beginning of Kṛṣṇadāsa Kavirāja Gosvāmī's description of Śrīmatī Rādhārāṇī's transcendental body. This description is based on the book known as *Premāmbhoja-maranda* compiled by Śrī Raghunātha dāsa Gosvāmī. Śrīla Kavirāja Gosvāmī's descriptions in verses 165-181 are based on this book. A translation of the original Sanskrit as described by Śrīla Bhaktivinoda Ṭhākura reads as follows:

"The love of the *gopīs* for Kṛṣṇa is full of transcendental ecstasy. It appears to be a brilliant jewel, and enlightened by such a transcendental jewel, Rādhārāṇī's body is further perfumed and decorated with *kuṅkuma*. In the morning Her body is bathed in the nectar of compassion, in the afternoon in the nectar of youth, and in the evening in the nectar of luster itself. In this way the bathing is performed, and Her body becomes as brilliant as the *cintāmaṇi* jewel. Her dress is composed of various kinds of silken garments, which may be compared to Her natural shyness.

Her beauty is more and more enhanced, being decorated with *kuṅkuma,* which is compared to beauty itself, and with blackish musk, which is compared to conjugal love. Thus Her body is decorated with different colors. The *kuṅkuma* is red, and the musk is black. Her ornaments embody the natural symptoms of ecstasy—trembling, tears, jubilation, stunning, perspiration, faltering of the voice, bodily redness, madness and dullness. In this way the entire body is bedecked with these nine different jewels. Over and above this, the beauty of Her body is enhanced by Her transcendental qualities, which hang as a flower garland on Her body. The ecstasy of love for Kṛṣṇa is known as *dhīrā* and *adhīrā,* sober and restless. Such ecstasy constitutes the covering of Śrīmatī Rādhārāṇī's body, and it is adorned by camphor. Her transcendental anger toward Kṛṣṇa is embodied as the arrangement of the hair on Her head, and the *tilaka* of Her great fortune shines on Her beautiful forehead. The earrings of Śrīmatī Rādhārāṇī are the holy names of Kṛṣṇa, as well as the hearing of His name and fame. Her lips are always reddish due to the betel nut of ecstatic affection for Kṛṣṇa. The black ointment around Her eyes is Her tricky behavior with Kṛṣṇa brought about by love. Her joking with Kṛṣṇa and gentle smiling is the camphor with which She is perfumed. She sleeps in Her room with the aroma of pride, and when She lies down in Her bed, the transcendental variety of Her loving ecstasies is like a jeweled locket in the midst of Her necklace of separation. Her transcendental breasts are covered by Her sari in the form of affection and anger toward Kṛṣṇa. She has a stringed instrument known as a *kacchapī-vīṇā,* which is the fame and fortune that actually dries up the faces and breasts of the other *gopīs.* She always keeps Her hands on the shoulder of Her *gopī* friend, who is compared to Her youthful beauty, and although She is highly qualified with so many spiritual assets, She is nonetheless affected by the Cupid known as Kṛṣṇa. Thus She is defeated. Śrīla Raghunātha dāsa Gosvāmī offers his respectful obeisances to Śrīmatī Rādhārāṇī, taking a straw in his mouth. Indeed, he prays, 'O Gāndharvikā, Śrīmatī Rādhārāṇī, just as Lord Kṛṣṇa never rejects a surrendered soul, please don't reject me.'" This is a summary translation of the *Premāmbhoja-maranda* which Kavirāja Gosvāmī quotes.

TEXT 167

কারুণ্যামৃত-ধারায় স্নান প্রথম ।
তারুণ্যামৃত-ধারায় স্নান মধ্যম ॥ ১৬৭ ॥

kāruṇyāmṛta-dhārāya snāna prathama
tāruṇyāmṛta-dhārāya snāna madhyama

SYNONYMS

kāruṇya-amṛta—of the nectar of mercy; *dhārāya*—in the shower; *snāna*—bath; *prathama*—first; *tāruṇya-amṛta*—of the nectar of youth; *dhārāya*—in the shower; *snāna*—bath; *madhyama*—in the middle.

TRANSLATION

"Śrīmatī Rādhārāṇī takes Her first bath in the shower of the nectar of compassion, and She takes Her second bath in the nectar of youth.

PURPORT

Śrīmatī Rādhārāṇī first smears Her body with the paste of affection for Kṛṣṇa. She then takes Her bath in the water of mercy. After passing the *paugāṇḍa* age (from five to ten years), Śrīmatī Rādhārāṇī first appears as mercy. The second bath, taken at noon, is taken in the water of *tāruṇyāmṛta,* or the nectar of youth. This is the actual expression of Her new youthfulness.

TEXT 168

লাবণ্যামৃত-ধারায় তদুপরি স্নান।
নিজ-লজ্জা-শ্যাম-পট্টসাটি-পরিধান ॥ ১৬৮ ॥

lāvaṇyāmṛta-dhārāya tad-upari snāna
nija-lajjā-śyāma-paṭṭasāṭi-paridhāna

SYNONYMS

lāvaṇya-amṛta-dhārāya—in the shower of the nectar of bodily luster; *tat-upari*—over and above that; *snāna*—the bath; *nija*—own; *lajjā*—shyness; *śyāma*—blackish; *paṭṭa*—silk; *sāṭi*—garments; *paridhāna*—wearing.

TRANSLATION

"After Her midday bath, Rādhārāṇī takes another bath in the nectar of bodily luster, and She puts on the garment of shyness, which is exactly like a black silk sari.

PURPORT

Over and above the other baths, the bath taken in the afternoon is taken in the nectar of full beauty. This nectar represents the personal qualities of beauty and luster. Thus there are three baths in different kinds of water. Rādhārāṇī then puts on two dresses—a lower and upper dress. The upper dress is Her attachment for Kṛṣṇa, and the lower dress is Her shyness. That lower portion is compared to a blackish silk garment or a bluish sari, and Her upper garment is pinkish. That pink garment is Her affection and attraction for Kṛṣṇa.

TEXT 169

কৃষ্ণ-অনুরাগ দ্বিতীয় অরুণ-বসন।
প্রণয়-মান-কঞ্চুলিকায় বক্ষ আচ্ছাদন ॥ ১৬৯ ॥

kṛṣṇa-anurāga dvitīya aruṇa-vasana
praṇaya-māna-kañculikāya vakṣa ācchādana

SYNONYMS

kṛṣṇa-anurāga—attraction for Kṛṣṇa; *dvitīya*—second; *aruṇa-vasana*—pinkish garment; *praṇaya*—of love; *māna*—and anger; *kañculikāya*—by a short blouse; *vakṣa*—breasts; *ācchādana*—covering.

TRANSLATION

"Śrīmatī Rādhārāṇī's affection for Kṛṣṇa is the upper garment, which is pinkish in color. She then covers Her breasts with another garment, comprised of affection and anger toward Kṛṣṇa.

TEXT 170

সৌন্দর্য -কুঙ্কুম, সখী-প্রণয় চন্দন ।
স্মিতকান্তি -কর্পূর, তিনে—অঙ্গে বিলেপন ॥ ১৭০ ॥

saundarya——kuṅkuma, sakhī-praṇaya——candana
smita-kānti——karpūra, tine——aṅge vilepana

SYNONYMS

saundarya—Her personal beauty; *kuṅkuma*—a red powder known as *kuṅkuma; sakhī-praṇaya*—Her love for Her associates; *candana*—the sandalwood pulp; *smita-kānti*—the sweetness of Her smile; *karpūra*—camphor; *tine*—by these three things; *aṅge*—on the body; *vilepana*—smearing.

TRANSLATION

"Śrīmatī Rādhārāṇī's personal beauty is compared to the reddish powder known as kuṅkuma. Her affection for Her associates is compared to sandalwood pulp, and the sweetness of Her smile is compared to camphor. All these, combined together, are smeared over Her body.

TEXT 171

কৃষ্ণের-উজ্জ্বল রস—মৃগমদ-ভর ।
সেই মৃগমদে বিচিত্রিত কলেবর ॥ ১৭১ ॥

kṛṣṇera ujjvala-rasa——mṛgamada-bhara
sei mṛgamade vicitrita kalevara

SYNONYMS

kṛṣṇera—of Lord Kṛṣṇa; *ujjvala-rasa*—the conjugal mellow; *mṛga-mada*—of musk; *bhara*—an abundance; *sei*—that; *mṛga-made*—made by the aroma of the musk; *vicitrita*—decorated; *kalevara*—Her whole body.

TRANSLATION

"Conjugal love for Kṛṣṇa is just like an abundance of musk. By that musk, Her whole body is decorated.

TEXT 172

প্রচ্ছন্ন-মান বাম্য—ধম্মিল্ল-বিন্যাস ।
'ধীরাধীরাত্মক' গুণ—অঙ্গে পটবাস ॥ ১৭২ ॥

pracchanna-māna vāmya——dhammilla-vinyāsa
'dhīrādhīrātmaka' guṇa——aṅge paṭa-vāsa

SYNONYMS

pracchanna—covered; *māna*—anger; *vāmya*—craftiness; *dhammilla*—of the bunches of hair; *vinyāsa*—arrangement; *dhīrā-adhīrā-ātmaka*—consisting of anger sometimes expressed and sometimes suppressed due to jealousy; *guṇa*—the quality; *aṅge*—on the body; *paṭa-vāsa*—silk covering.

TRANSLATION

"Covered anger and craftiness constitute the arrangement of Her hair. The quality of anger due to jealousy is just like the silk covering Her body.

TEXT 173

রাগ-তাম্বূলরাগে অধর উজ্জ্বল ।
প্রেমকৌটিল্য—নেত্রযুগলে কজ্জল ॥ ১৭৩ ॥

rāga-tāmbūla-rāge adhara ujjvala
prema-kauṭilya——netra-yugale kajjala

SYNONYMS

rāga—of love; *tāmbūla*—of the betel nut; *rāge*—by the reddish color; *adhara*—lies; *ujjvala*—brilliant; *prema-kauṭilya*—the double dealings in loving affairs; *netra-yugale*—on the two eyes; *kajjala*—the ointment.

TRANSLATION

"Her attachment for Kṛṣṇa is the reddish color of betel nuts on Her brilliant lips. Her double-dealings in loving affairs are just like the black ointment around Her eyes.

TEXT 174

'সূদ্দীপ্ত-সাত্ত্বিক' ভাব, হর্ষাদি 'সঞ্চারী'।
এই সব ভাব-ভূষণ সব-অঙ্গে ভরি' ॥ ১৭৪ ॥

'sūddīpta-sāttvika' bhāva, harṣādi 'sañcārī'
ei saba bhāva-bhūṣaṇa saba-aṅge bhari'

SYNONYMS

su-uddīpta-sāttvika—blazing of goodness; *bhāva*—the ecstasies; *harṣa-ādi*—like jubilation; *sañcārī*—the continuously existing ecstasies; *ei saba*—all these; *bhāva*—ecstasies; *bhūṣaṇa*—ornaments; *saba*—all; *aṅge*—body; *bhari'*—filling.

TRANSLATION

"The decorated ornaments on Her body are the blazing ecstasies of goodness, and these constantly existing ecstasies are headed by jubilation. All these ecstasies are like ornaments all over Her body.

TEXT 175

'কিলকিঞ্চিতাদি'-ভাব-বিংশতি-ভূষিত।
গুণশ্রেণী-পুষ্পমালা সর্বাঙ্গে পূরিত ॥ ১৭৫ ॥

'kila-kiñcitādi'-bhāva-viṁśati-bhūṣita
guṇa-śreṇī-puṣpamālā sarvāṅge pūrita

SYNONYMS

kila-kiñcita-ādi—headed by *kila-kiñcita*; *bhāva*—with the ecstasies; *viṁśati*—twenty; *bhūṣita*—decorated; *guṇa-śreṇī*—of Her attractive qualities; *puṣpa-mālā*—as a garland of flowers; *sarva-aṅge*—all over the body; *pūrita*—filled.

TRANSLATION

"These bodily ornaments constitute twenty kinds of ecstatic symptoms, beginning with kila-kiñcita. Her transcendental qualities are the flower garland hanging in fullness over Her body.

PURPORT

The twenty different moods headed by *kila-kiñcita* are described as follows. First, in connection with the body, there are *bhāva* (ecstasy), *hāva* (gestures) and *helā* (negligence); in relation to the self there are *śobhā* (beauty), *kānti* (luster), *dīpti* (brilliance), *mādhurya* (sweetness), *pragalbhatā* (impudence), *audārya* (magnanimity) and *dhairya* (patience); and in relation to nature, there are *līlā* (pastimes), *vilāsa* (enjoyment), *vicchitti* (breaking off) and *vibhrama* (puzzlement). There are no English equivalents for the words *kila-kiñcita, moṭṭāyita* and *kuṭṭamita.*

A flower garland constitutes the qualities of Śrīmatī Rādhārāṇī and is divided into mental, verbal and bodily parts. Her attitude of forgiveness and mercy is all mental. Her talks, which are very pleasing to the ear, are verbal. The physical qualities—age, beauty, luster and grace—are bodily qualities.

TEXT 176

সৌভাগ্য-তিলক চারু-ললাটে উজ্জ্বল ।
প্রেম-বৈচিত্ত্য—রত্ন, হৃদয়—তরল ॥ ১৭৬ ॥

saubhāgya-tilaka cāru-lalāṭe ujjvala
prema-vaicittya——ratna, hṛdaya——tarala

SYNONYMS

saubhāgya-tilaka—the *tilaka* of good fortune; *cāru*—beautiful; *lalāṭe*—on the forehead; *ujjvala*—brilliant; *prema*—of love of Godhead; *vaicittya*—diversity; *ratna*—the jewel; *hṛdaya*—the heart; *tarala*—the locket.

TRANSLATION

"The tilaka of fortune is on Her beautiful broad forehead. Her various loving affairs are a gem, and Her heart is the locket.

TEXT 177

মধ্য-বয়স, সখী-স্কন্ধে কর-ন্যাস ।
কৃষ্ণলীলা-মনোবৃত্তি-সখী আশপাশ ॥ ১৭৭ ॥

madhya-vayasa, sakhī-skandhe kara-nyāsa
kṛṣṇalīlā-manovṛtti-sakhī āśa-pāśa

SYNONYMS

madhya-vayasa—middle age; *sakhī*—of a friend; *skandhe*—on the shoulder; *kara*—hand; *nyāsa*—keeping; *kṛṣṇa*—of Lord Kṛṣṇa; *līlā*—the pastimes; *manaḥ*—of the mind; *vṛtti*—activities; *sakhī*—*gopīs*; *āśa-pāśa*—here and there.

TRANSLATION

"Śrīmatī Rādhārāṇī's gopī friends are Her mental activities, which are concentrated on the pastimes of Śrī Kṛṣṇa. She keeps Her hand on the shoulder of a friend, who represents youth.

PURPORT

Rādhārāṇī's eight companions (*aṣṭa-sakhī*) are different varieties of pleasure connected with the pastimes of Kṛṣṇa. Following those pastimes of Śrī Kṛṣṇa are other activities, which are represented by the assistants of the *gopīs*.

TEXT 178

নিজাঙ্গ-সৌরভালয়ে গর্ব-পর্যঙ্ক ।
তা'তে বসি' আছে, সদা চিন্তে কৃষ্ণসঙ্গ ॥ ১৭৮ ॥

nijāṅga-saurabhālaye garva-paryaṅka
tā'te vasi' āche, sadā cinte kṛṣṇa-saṅga

SYNONYMS

nija-aṅga—Her personal body; *saurabha-ālaye*—in the abode of aroma; *garva*—pride; *paryaṅka*—bedstead; *tā'te*—on that; *vasi'*—lying; *āche*—there is; *sadā*—always; *cinte*—thinks; *kṛṣṇa-saṅga*—the association of Kṛṣṇa.

TRANSLATION

"Śrīmatī Rādhārāṇī's bedstead is pride itself, and it is situated in the abode of Her bodily aroma. She is always seated there thinking of Kṛṣṇa's association.

TEXT 179

কৃষ্ণ-নাম-গুণ-যশ—অবতংস কাণে ।
কৃষ্ণ-নাম-গুণ-যশ-প্রবাহ-বচনে ॥ ১৭৯ ॥

kṛṣṇa-nāma-guṇa-yaśa——avataṁsa kāṇe
kṛṣṇa-nāma-guṇa-yaśa-pravāha-vacane

SYNONYMS

kṛṣṇa—of Lord Kṛṣṇa; *nāma*—the holy name; *guṇa*—the qualities; *yaśa*—the fame; *avataṁsa*—ornaments; *kāṇe*—on the ear; *kṛṣṇa*—of Lord Kṛṣṇa; *nāma*—of the holy name; *guṇa*—of the qualities; *yaśa*—of the fame; *pravāha*—waves; *vacane*—in Her talking.

TRANSLATION

"Śrīmatī Rādhārāṇī's earrings represent the name, fame and qualities of Lord Kṛṣṇa. The glories of Lord Kṛṣṇa's name, fame and qualities are always inundating Her speech.

TEXT 180

কৃষ্ণকে করায় শ্যামরস-মধু পান।
নিরন্তর পূর্ণ করে কৃষ্ণের সর্বকাম ॥ ১৮০ ॥

kṛṣṇake karāya śyāma-rasa-madhu pāna
nirantara pūrṇa kare kṛṣṇera sarva-kāma

SYNONYMS

kṛṣṇake—unto Kṛṣṇa; *karāya*—She induces; *śyāma-rasa*—of the mellow of conjugal love; *madhu*—the honey; *pāna*—drinking; *nirantara*—constantly; *pūrṇa*—complete; *kare*—makes; *kṛṣṇera*—of Lord Kṛṣṇa; *sarva-kāma*—all kinds of lusty desires.

TRANSLATION

"Śrīmatī Rādhārāṇī induces Kṛṣṇa to drink the honey of the conjugal relationship. She is therefore engaged in satisfying all the lusty desires of Kṛṣṇa.

TEXT 181

কৃষ্ণের বিশুদ্ধপ্রেম-রত্নের আকর।
অনুপম-গুণগণ-পূর্ণ কলেবর ॥ ১৮১ ॥

kṛṣṇera viśuddha-prema-ratnera ākara
anupama-guṇagaṇa-pūrṇa kalevara

SYNONYMS

kṛṣṇera—of Lord Kṛṣṇa; *viśuddha-prema*—of pure transcendental love; *ratnera*—of the valuable jewel; *ākara*—a mine; *anupama*—unparalleled; *guṇagaṇa*—of groups of qualities; *pūrṇa*—full; *kalevara*—transcendental body.

TRANSLATION

"Śrīmatī Rādhārāṇī is exactly like a mine filled with valuable jewels of love for Kṛṣṇa. Her transcendental body is complete with unparalleled spiritual qualities.

TEXT 182

কা কৃষ্ণস্য প্রণয়জনিভূঃ শ্রীমতী রাধিকৈকা
কাস্য প্রেয়স্যনুপমগুণা রাধিকৈকা ন চান্যা ।
জৈহ্ম্যং কেশে দৃশি তরলতা নিষ্ঠুরত্বং কুচেঽস্যা
বাঞ্ছাপূর্ত্যৈ প্রভবতি হরে রাধিকৈকা ন চান্যা ॥১৮২ ॥

kā kṛṣṇasya praṇaya-janibhūḥ śrīmatī rādhikaikā
kāsya preyasy anupama-guṇā rādhikaikā na cānyā
jaihmyaṁ keśe dṛśi taralatā niṣṭhuratvaṁ kuce 'syā
vāñchā-pūrtyai prabhavati hare rādhikaikā na cānyā

SYNONYMS

kā—who; *kṛṣṇasya*—of Lord Kṛṣṇa; *praṇaya-janibhūḥ*—the birthplace of love of Kṛṣṇa; *śrīmatī*—all-beautiful; *rādhikā*—Śrīmatī Rādhārāṇī; *ekā*—alone; *kā*—who; *asya*—His; *preyasī*—most dear friend; *anupama-guṇā*—having unparalleled qualities; *rādhikā*—Śrīmatī Rādhārāṇī; *ekā*—alone; *na*—not; *ca*—also; *anyā*—anyone else; *jaihmyam*—crookedness; *keśe*—in the hair; *dṛśi*—in the eyes; *taralatā*—unsteadiness; *niṣṭhuratvam*—firmness; *kuce*—in the breasts; *asyāḥ*—Her; *vāñchā*—of the desires; *pūrtyai*—to fulfill; *prabhavati*—manifests; *hareḥ*—of Lord Kṛṣṇa; *rādhikā*—Śrīmatī Rādhārāṇī; *ekā*—alone; *na*—not; *ca anyā*—anyone else.

TRANSLATION

" 'If one asks about the origin of love of Kṛṣṇa, the answer is that the origin is in Śrīmatī Rādhārāṇī alone. Who is the most dear friend of Kṛṣṇa? The answer again is Śrīmatī Rādhārāṇī alone. No one else. Śrīmatī Rādhārāṇī's hair is very curly, Her two eyes are always moving to and fro, and Her breasts are firm. Since all transcendental qualities are manifest in Śrīmatī Rādhārāṇī, She alone is able to fulfill all the desires of Kṛṣṇa. No one else.'

PURPORT

This is a quotation from *Śrī Govinda-līlāmṛta* (11.122) by Kṛṣṇadāsa Kavirāja Gosvāmī. It is a verse in the form of questions and answers describing the glories of Śrīmatī Rādhārāṇī.

TEXTS 183-184

যাঁর সৌভাগ্য-গুণ বাঞ্ছে সত্যভামা ।
যাঁর ঠাঞি কলাবিলাস শিখে ব্রজ-রামা ॥ ১৮৩ ॥
যাঁর সৌন্দর্যাদি-গুণ বাঞ্ছে লক্ষ্মী-পার্বতী ।
যাঁর পতিব্রতা-ধর্ম বাঞ্ছে অরুন্ধতী ॥ ১৮৪ ॥

yāṅra saubhāgya-guṇa vāñche satyabhāmā
yāṅra ṭhāñi kalā-vilāsa śikhe vraja-rāmā

yāṅra saundaryādi-guṇa vāñche lakṣmī-pārvatī
yāṅra pativratā-dharma vāñche arundhatī

SYNONYMS

yāṅra—whose; *saubhāgya*—of fortune; *guṇa*—quality; *vāñche*—desires; *satyabhāmā*—Satyabhāmā, one of the queens of Kṛṣṇa; *yāṅra ṭhāñi*—from whom; *kalā-vilāsa*—the sixty-four arts; *śikhe*—learn; *vraja-rāmā*—all the *gopīs* in Vṛndāvana; *yāṅra*—whose; *saundarya-ādi*—such as beauty; *guṇa*—qualities; *vāñche*—desires; *lakṣmī*—the goddess of fortune; *pārvatī*—the wife of Lord Śiva; *yāṅra*—whose; *pati-vratā*—of chastity; *dharma*—principle; *vāñche*—desires; *arundhatī*—the wife of Vasiṣṭha Muni.

TRANSLATION

"Even Satyabhāmā, one of the queens of Śrī Kṛṣṇa, desires the fortunate position and excellent qualities of Śrīmatī Rādhārāṇī. All the gopīs learn the art of dressing from Śrīmatī Rādhārāṇī, and even the goddess of fortune, Lakṣmī, and the wife of Lord Śiva, Pārvatī, desire Her beauty and qualities. Indeed, Arundhatī, the celebrated chaste wife of Vasiṣṭha, also wants to imitate the chastity and religious principles of Śrīmatī Rādhārāṇī.

TEXT 185

যাঁর সদ্গুণ-গণনে কৃষ্ণ না পায় পার ।
তাঁর গুণ গণিবে কেমনে জীব ছার ॥ ১৮৫ ॥

yāṅra sadguṇa-gaṇane kṛṣṇa nā pāya pāra
tāṅra guṇa gaṇibe kemane jīva chāra

SYNONYMS

yāṅra—whose; *sat-guṇa*—good qualities; *gaṇane*—in counting; *kṛṣṇa*—Lord Kṛṣṇa; *nā*—not; *pāya*—obtains; *pāra*—the limit; *tāṅra*—Her; *guṇa*—qualities;

gaṇibe—can count; *kemane*—how; *jīva*—a living entity; *chāra*—most insignificant.

TRANSLATION

"Even Lord Kṛṣṇa Himself cannot reach the limit of the transcendental qualities of Śrīmatī Rādhārāṇī. How, then, can an insignificant living entity count them?"

TEXT 186

প্রভু কহে,—জানিলুঁ কৃষ্ণ-রাধা-প্রেম-তত্ত্ব।
শুনিতে চাহিয়ে দুঁহার বিলাস-মহত্ত্ব ॥ ১৮৬ ॥

prabhu kahe,——jāniluṅ kṛṣṇa-rādhā-prema-tattva
śunite cāhiye duṅhāra vilāsa-mahattva

SYNONYMS

prabhu kahe—Lord Śrī Caitanya replied; *jāniluṅ*—now I have understood; *kṛṣṇa*—of Lord Kṛṣṇa; *rādhā*—of Śrīmatī Rādhārāṇī; *prema*—of the loving affairs; *tattva*—the truth; *śunite*—to hear; *cāhiye*—I desire; *duṅhāra*—of both of Them; *vilāsa-mahattva*—the greatness of the enjoyment.

TRANSLATION

Lord Śrī Caitanya Mahāprabhu replied, "Now I have come to understand the truth of the loving affairs between Rādhā and Kṛṣṇa. Nonetheless, I still want to hear how both of Them gloriously enjoy such love."

TEXT 187

রায় কহে,—কৃষ্ণ হয় 'ধীর-ললিত'।
নিরন্তর কামক্রীড়া—যাঁহার চরিত ॥ ১৮৭ ॥

rāya kahe,——kṛṣṇa haya 'dhīra-lalita'
nirantara kāma-krīḍā——yāṅhāra carita

SYNONYMS

rāya kahe—Rāya replied; *kṛṣṇa*—Lord Kṛṣṇa; *haya*—is; *dhīra-lalita*—a person who can keep his girl friend always in subjugation by different qualities; *nirantara*—constantly; *kāma-krīḍā*—pastimes of sexual enjoyment; *yāṅhāra*—of whom; *carita*—the character.

TRANSLATION

Rāya Rāmānanda replied, "Lord Kṛṣṇa is dhīra-lalita, for He can always keep His girl friends in a subjugated state. Thus His only business is in enjoying sense gratification.

PURPORT

We should always remember that Kṛṣṇa's sense gratification is never to be compared to the sense gratification of the material world. As we have already explained, Kṛṣṇa's sense gratification is just like gold. The perverted reflection of that sense gratification found in the material world is just like iron. The purport is that Kṛṣṇa is not impersonal. He has all the desires that are manifest in the perverted reflection within this material world. However, the qualities are different—one is spiritual, and the other is material. Just as there is a difference between life and death, there is a difference between spiritual sense gratification and material sense gratification.

TEXT 188

বিদগ্ধো নবতারুণ্যঃ পরিহাস-বিশারদঃ ।
নিশ্চিন্তো ধীরললিতঃ স্যাৎ প্রায়ঃ প্রেয়সীবশঃ ॥১৮৮॥

vidagdho nava-tāruṇyaḥ
parihāsa-viśāradaḥ
niścinto dhīra-lalitaḥ
syāt prāyaḥ preyasī-vaśaḥ

SYNONYMS

vidagdhaḥ—clever; *nava-tāruṇyaḥ*—always freshly youthful; *parihāsa*—in joking; *viśāradaḥ*—expert; *niścintaḥ*—without anxiety; *dhīra-lalitaḥ*—a hero in loving affairs; *syāt*—is; *prāyaḥ*—almost always; *preyasī-vaśaḥ*—one who keeps His girl friends subjugated.

TRANSLATION

"A person who is very cunning and always youthful, expert in joking and without anxiety, and who can keep his girl friends always subjugated, is called dhīra-lalita.

PURPORT

This verse is from *Bhakti-rasāmṛta-sindhu* (2.1.230).

TEXT 189

রাত্রি-দিন কুঞ্জে ক্রীড়া করে রাধা-সঙ্গে ।
কৈশোর বয়স সফল কৈল ক্রীড়া-রঙ্গে ॥ ১৮৯ ॥

rātri-dina kuñje krīḍā kare rādhā-saṅge
kaiśora vayasa saphala kaila krīḍā-raṅge

SYNONYMS

rātri-dina—day and night; *kuñje*—in the gardens or bushes of Vṛndāvana; *krīḍā*—pastimes; *kare*—performs; *rādhā-saṅge*—with Rādhārāṇī; *kaiśora*—the pre-youthful; *vayasa*—age; *sa-phala*—fruitful; *kaila*—made; *krīḍā-raṅge*—taking pleasure in different pastimes.

TRANSLATION

"Day and night Lord Śrī Kṛṣṇa enjoys the company of Śrīmatī Rādhārāṇī in the bushes of Vṛndāvana. Thus His pre-youthful age was fulfilled through His affairs with Śrīmatī Rādhārāṇī.

TEXT 190

বাচা সূচিতশর্বরীরতিকলা-প্রাগল্‌ভ্যয়া রাধিকাং
ব্রীড়াকুঞ্চিত-লোচনাং বিরচয়ন্নগ্রে সখীনামসৌ ।
তদ্বক্ষোরুহচিত্রকেলিমকরীপাণ্ডিত্যপারং গতঃ
কৈশোরং সফলীকরোতি কলয়ন্ কুঞ্জে বিহারং হরিঃ ॥১৯০॥

vācā sūcita-śarvarī-rati-kalā-prāgalbhyayā rādhikāṁ
vrīḍā-kuñcita-locanāṁ viracayann agre sakhīnām asau
tad-vakṣoruha-citra-keli-makarī-pāṇḍitya-pāraṁ gataḥ
kaiśoraṁ saphalī-karoti kalayan kuñje vihāraṁ hariḥ

SYNONYMS

vācā—by speech; *sūcita*—revealing; *śarvarī*—of the night; *rati*—in amorous pastimes; *kalā*—of the portion; *prāgalbhyayā*—the importance; *rādhikām*—Śrīmatī Rādhārāṇī; *vrīḍā*—from shame; *kuñcita-locanām*—having Her eyes closed; *viracayan*—making; *agre*—before; *sakhīnām*—Her friends; *asau*—that one; *tat*—of Her; *vakṣaḥ-ruha*—on the breasts; *citra-keli*—with variegated pastimes; *makarī*—in drawing dolphins; *pāṇḍitya*—of cleverness; *pāram*—the limit; *gataḥ*—who reached; *kaiśoram*—adolescence; *sa-phalī-karoti*—makes successful; *kalayan*—performing; *kuñje*—in the bushes; *vihāram*—pastimes; *hariḥ*—the Supreme Personality of Godhead.

TRANSLATION

" 'Thus Lord Śrī Kṛṣṇa spoke of the sexual activities of the previous night. In this way He made Śrīmatī Rādhārāṇī close Her eyes out of shyness. Taking this

opportunity, Śrī Kṛṣṇa painted various types of dolphins on Her breasts. Thus He became a very expert artist for all the gopīs. During such pastimes, the Lord enjoyed the fulfillment of His youth.' "

PURPORT

This quotation is also found in *Bhakti-rasāmṛta-sindhu* (2.1.231).

TEXT 191

প্রভু কহে,- এহো হয়, আগে কহ আর।
রায় কহে,- ইহা বই বুদ্ধি-গতি নাহি আর ॥ ১৯১ ॥

prabhu kahe,——eho haya, āge kaha āra
rāya kahe,——ihā va-i buddhi-gati nāhi āra

SYNONYMS

prabhu kahe—Lord Caitanya Mahāprabhu said; *eho haya*—this is all right; *āge kaha āra*—please go forward and say more; *rāya kahe*—Rāmānanda Rāya replied; *ihā va-i*—except this; *buddhi-gati*—movement of my intelligence; *nāhi*—there is not; *āra*—any more.

TRANSLATION

Śrī Caitanya Mahāprabhu said, "This is all right, but please continue." At that time Rāya Rāmānanda replied, "I don't think my intelligence goes beyond this."

TEXT 192

যেবা 'প্রেমবিলাস-বিবর্ত' এক হয়।
তাহা শুনি' তোমার সুখ হয়, কি না হয় ॥ ১৯২ ॥

yebā 'prema-vilāsa-vivarta' eka haya
tāhā śuni' tomāra sukha haya, ki nā haya

SYNONYMS

yebā—whatever; *prema-vilāsa-vivarta*—the resultant bewilderment or revolution in the ecstasy of loving affairs; *eka haya*—there is one topic; *tāhā*—that; *śuni'*—hearing; *tomāra*—Your; *sukha*—happiness; *haya*—is; *ki*—or; *nā*—not; *haya*—is.

TRANSLATION

Rāya Rāmānanda then informed Śrī Caitanya Mahāprabhu that there was another topic, known as prema-vilāsa-vivarta. "You may hear of this from

me," Rāmānanda Rāya said. "However, I do not know whether You will be happy with it or not."

PURPORT

These statements are set forth for our understanding, according to Śrīla Bhaktivinoda Ṭhākura in his *Amṛta-pravāha-bhāṣya.* In essence, Śrī Caitanya Mahāprabhu told Rāmānanda Rāya, "My dear Rāmānanda, the explanation you have given about the goal of life and the pastimes of Śrīmatī Rādhārāṇī and Kṛṣṇa is certainly the truth. Although this is factual, you can continue telling Me more if there is anything more to say." In reply, Rāmānanda Rāya said, "I do not think I have anything to say beyond this, but there is a topic known as *prema-vilāsa-vivarta,* which I may explain to You. I do not know whether it will bring You happiness or not."

TEXT 193

এত বলি' আপন-কৃত গীত এক গাহিল ।
প্রেমে প্রভু স্বহস্তে তাঁর মুখ আচ্ছাদিল ॥ ১৯৩ ॥

eta bali' āpana-kṛta gīta eka gāhila
preme prabhu sva-haste tāṅra mukha ācchādila

SYNONYMS

eta bali'—saying this; *āpana-kṛta*—composed by himself; *gīta*—song; *eka*—one; *gāhila*—sang; *preme*—in love of Godhead; *prabhu*—Śrī Caitanya Mahāprabhu; *sva-haste*—by His own hand; *tāṅra*—his (Rāmānanda Rāya's); *mukha*—mouth; *ācchādila*—covered.

TRANSLATION

Saying this, Rāmānanda Rāya began to sing a song he had composed, but Śrī Caitanya Mahāprabhu, out of ecstasy of love of Godhead, immediately covered Rāmānanda's mouth with His own hand.

PURPORT

The topics that are about to be discussed between Lord Śrī Caitanya Mahāprabhu and Rāmānanda Rāya cannot be understood by a materialistic poet, nor by intelligence or material perception. Śrīla Bhaktisiddhānta Sarasvatī Ṭhākura states that the spiritual mellow can be realized only when one is situated on the transcendental platform beyond the material stage of goodness. That platform is called *viśuddha-sattva* (*sattvaṁ viśuddhaṁ vasudeva-śabditam*). Realization of the *viśuddha-sattva* is beyond the pale of the material world and is not perceived by bodily senses or mental speculation. Our identification with the gross body and subtle mind is different from spiritual understanding. Since the intelligence and mind are material, the loving affairs of Śrī Rādhā and Kṛṣṇa are beyond their perception. (*sarvopādhi-vinirmuktaṁ tat-paratvena nirmalam*): when we are free from all material designations and our senses are completely purified by the *bhakti* process, we can understand the sense activities of the Absolute Truth (*hṛṣīkeṇa hṛṣīkeśa-sevanaṁ bhaktir ucyate*).

The spiritual senses are beyond the material senses. A materialist can think only of the negation of material variety; he cannot understand spiritual variety. He thinks that spiritual variety simply contradicts material variety and is a negation or void, but such conceptions cannot even reach the precincts of spiritual realization. The wonderful activities of the gross body and subtle mind are always imperfect. They are below the degree of spiritual understanding and are ephemeral. The spiritual mellow is eternally wonderful and is described as *pūrṇa, śuddha, nitya-mukta*—that is completely purified and eternally liberated from all material conceptions. When we are unable to fulfill our material desires, there is certainly sorrow and confusion. This may be described as *vivarta.* However, in spiritual life there is no sorrow, inebriety or imperfection. Śrīla Rāmānanda Rāya was expert in realizing the spiritual activities of Śrīmatī Rādhārāṇī and Kṛṣṇa, and Rāmānanda's spiritual experience was placed before Śrī Caitanya Mahāprabhu as he inquired whether the Lord approved his realization of spiritual truth.

There are three books prominent in this connection. One was written by Bhakta dāsa Bāula and is called *Vivarta-vilāsa.* Another was compiled by Jagadānanda and is called *Prema-vivarta.* Śrī Rāmānanda Rāya's book is called *Prema-vilāsa-vivarta.* The *Vivarta-vilāsa* by Bhakta dāsa Bāula is completely different from the other two books. Sometimes a university student or professor tries to study these transcendental literatures and attempts to put forth a critical analysis from the mundane view, with an end to receiving degrees like a Ph. D. Such realization is certainly different from that of Rāmānanda Rāya. If one actually wants to take a Ph. D. degree from Śrī Caitanya Mahāprabhu and be approved by Rāmānanda Rāya, he must first become free from all material designations (*sarvopādhi-vinirmuktaṁ tat-paratvena nirmalam*). A person who identifies with his material body cannot understand these talks between Śrī Rāmānanda Rāya and Śrī Caitanya Mahāprabhu. Man-made religious scriptures and transcendental philosophical talks are quite different. Indeed, there is a gulf of difference between the two. This subject matter has been very diligently described by Śrīman Madhvācārya. Since material philosophers are situated in the material *prema* of *vilāsa-vivarta,* they are unable to realize the spiritual *prema-vilāsa-vivarta.* They cannot accommodate an elephant upon a dish. Similarly, mundane speculators cannot capture the spiritual elephant within their limited conception. It is just like a frog's trying to measure the Atlantic Ocean by imagining it so many times larger than his well. Materialistic philosophers and *sahajiyās* cannot understand the talks between Rāmānanda

Rāya and Śrī Caitanya Mahāprabhu concerning the pastimes of Śrī Rādhā and Kṛṣṇa. The only tendency of the impersonalists or the *prākṛta-sahajiyās* is to face the platform of impersonalism. They cannot understand the spiritual. Consequently, when Rāmānanda Rāya attempted to sing his own verses, Śrī Caitanya Mahāprabhu stopped him by covering his mouth with His own hand.

TEXT 194

পহিলেহি রাগ নয়নভঙ্গে ভেল ।
অনুদিন বাঢ়ল, অবধি না গেল ॥
না সো রমণ, না হাম রমণী ।
দুঁহু-মন মনোভব পেষল জানি' ॥
এ সখি, সে-সব প্রেমকাহিনী ।
কানুঠামে কহবি বিছুরল জানি' ॥
না খোঁজলুঁ দূতী, না খোঁজলুঁ আন্ ।
দুঁহুকেরি মিলনে মধ্য ত পাঁচবাণ ॥
অব্ সোহি বিরাগ, তুঁহু ভেলি দূতী ।
সু-পুরুখ-প্রেমকি ঐছন রীতি ॥ ১৯৪ ॥

pahilehi rāga nayana-bhaṅge bhela
anudina bāḍhala, avadhi nā gela

nā so ramaṇa, nā hāma ramaṇī
duṅhu-mana manobhava peṣala jāni'

e sakhi, se-saba prema-kāhinī
kānu-ṭhāme kahabi vichurala jāni'

nā khoṅjaluṅ dūtī, nā khoṅjaluṅ ān
duṅhukeri milane madhya ta pāṅca-bāṇa

ab sohi virāga, tuṅhu bheli dūtī
su-purukha-premaki aichana rīti

SYNONYMS

pahilehi—in the beginning; *rāga*—attraction; *nayana-bhaṅge*—by activities of the eyes; *bhela*—there was; *anu-dina*—gradually, day after day; *bāḍhala*—increased; *avadhi*—limit; *nā*—not; *gela*—reached; *nā*—not; *so*—He; *ramaṇa*—the enjoyer; *nā*—not; *hāma*—I; *ramaṇī*—the enjoyed; *duṅhu-mana*—both the minds; *manaḥ-bhava*—the mental situation; *peṣala*—pressed together; *jāni'*—knowing; *e*—this; *sakhi*—My dear friend; *se-saba*—all those; *prema-kāhinī*—affairs of love; *kānu-ṭhāme*—before Kṛṣṇa; *kahabi*—you will say; *vichurala*—He has forgotten; *jāni'*—knowing; *nā*—not; *khoṅjaluṅ*—searched out; *dūtī*—a messenger; *nā*—not; *khoṅjaluṅ*—searched out; *ān*—anyone else; *duṅhukeri*—of both of Us; *milane*—by the meeting; *madhya*—in the middle; *ta*—indeed; *pāñca-bāṇa*—five arrows of Cupid; *ab*—now; *sohi*—that; *virāga*—separation; *tuṅhu*—you; *bheli*—became; *dūtī*—the messenger; *su-purukha*—of a beautiful person; *premaki*—of loving affairs; *aichana*—such; *rīti*—the consequence.

TRANSLATION

" 'Alas, before We met there was an initial attachment between Us brought about by an exchange of glances. In this way attachment evolved. That attachment has gradually begun to grow, and there is no limit to it. Now, that attachment has become a natural sequence between Ourselves. It is not that it is due to Kṛṣṇa, the enjoyer, nor is it due to Me, for I am the enjoyed. It is not like that. This attachment was made possible by mutual meeting. This mutual exchange of attraction is known as manobhava, or Cupid. Kṛṣṇa's mind and My mind have merged together. Now, during this time of separation, it is very difficult to explain these loving affairs. My dear friend, Kṛṣṇa might have forgotten all these things. However, you can understand and bring this message to Him, but during Our first meeting there was no messenger between Us, nor did I request anyone to see Him. Indeed, Cupid's five arrows were Our via media. Now, during this separation, that attraction has increased to another ecstatic state. My dear friend, please act as a messenger on My behalf because if one is in love with a beautiful person, this is the consequence.'

PURPORT

These verses were originally composed and sung by Rāmānanda Rāya himself. Śrīla Bhaktivinoda Ṭhākura suggests that during the time of enjoyment, the attachment might be compared to Cupid himself. However, during the period of separation, Cupid becomes a messenger of highly elevated love. This is called *prema-vilāsa-vivarta.* When there is a separation, enjoyment itself acts like a messenger, and that messenger was addressed by Śrīmatī Rādhārāṇī as a friend. The essence of this transaction is simple: loving affairs are as relishable during separation as during enjoyment. When Śrīmatī Rādhārāṇī was fully absorbed in love of Kṛṣṇa, She mistook a black *tamāla* tree for Kṛṣṇa and embraced it. Such a mistake is called *prema-vivarta-vilāsa.*

TEXT 195

রাধায়া ভবতশ্চ চিত্তজতুনী স্বেদৈর্বিলাপ্য ক্রমাদ্
যুঞ্জন্নদ্রি-নিকুঞ্জ-কুঞ্জরপতে নির্ধূত-ভেদভ্রমম্ ।
চিত্রায় স্বয়মন্বরঞ্জয়দিহ ব্রহ্মাণ্ডহর্ম্যোদরে
ভূয়োভির্নব-রাগ-হিঙ্গুলভরৈঃ শৃঙ্গার-কারুঃ কৃতী ॥১৯৫

rādhāyā bhavataś ca citta-jatunī svedair vilāpya kramād
yuñjann adri-nikuñja-kuñjara-pate nirdhūta-bheda-bhramam
citrāya svayam anvarañjayad iha brahmāṇḍa-harmyodare
bhūyobhir nava-rāga-hiṅgula-bharaiḥ śṛṅgāra-kāruḥ kṛtī

SYNONYMS

rādhāyāḥ—of Śrīmatī Rādhārāṇī; *bhavataḥ ca*—and of You; *citta-jatunī*—the two minds like shellac; *svedaiḥ*—by perspiration; *vilāpya*—melting; *kramāt*—gradually; *yuñjan*—making; *adri*—of Govardhana Hill; *nikuñja*—in a solitary place for enjoyment; *kuñjara-pate*—O king of the elephants; *nirdhūta*—completely taken away; *bheda-bhramam*—the misunderstanding of differentiation; *citrāya*—for increasing the wonder; *svayam*—personally; *anvarañjayat*—colored; *iha*—in this world; *brahmāṇḍa*—of the universe; *harmya-udare*—within the palace; *bhūyobhiḥ*—by varieties of means; *nava-rāga*—of new attraction; *hiṅgula-bharaiḥ*—by the vermilion; *śṛṅgāra*—of love affairs; *kāruḥ*—the craftsman; *kṛtī*—very expert.

TRANSLATION

" 'O my Lord, You live in the forest of Govardhana Hill, and, like the king of elephants, You are expert in the art of conjugal love. O master of the universe, Your heart and Śrīmatī Rādhārāṇī's heart are just like shellac and are now melted in Your spiritual perspiration. Therefore one can no longer distinguish between You and Śrīmatī Rādhārāṇī. Now You have mixed Your newly invoked affection, which is like vermilion, with Your melted hearts, and for the benefit of the whole world You have painted both Your hearts red within this great palace of the universe.' "

PURPORT

This verse quoted by Rāmānanda Rāya is included in Śrīla Rūpa Gosvāmī's *Ujjvala-nīlamaṇi* (14.155).

TEXT 196

প্রভু কহে,—'সাধ্যবস্তুর অবধি' এই হয় ।
তোমার প্রসাদে ইহা জানিলুঁ নিশ্চয় ॥ ১৯৬ ॥

prabhu kahe, —'sādhya-vastura avadhi' ei haya
tomāra prasāde ihā jāniluṅ niścaya

SYNONYMS

prabhu kahe—Śrī Caitanya Mahāprabhu confirmed; *sādhya-vastura*—of the object of life; *avadhi'*—the limit; *ei*—this; *haya*—is; *tomāra*—of you; *prasāde*—by the mercy; *ihā*—this; *jāniluṅ*—I have understood; *niścaya*—conclusively.

TRANSLATION

Śrī Caitanya Mahāprabhu confirmed these verses recited by Śrī Rāmānanda Rāya, saying, "This is the limit of the goal of human life. Only by your mercy have I come to understand it conclusively.

TEXT 197

'সাধ্যবস্তু' 'সাধন' বিনু কেহ নাহি পায়।
কৃপা করি' কহ, রায়, পাবার উপায়॥ ॥ ১৯৭ ॥

'sādhya-vastu' 'sādhana' vinu keha nāhi pāya
kṛpā kari' kaha, rāya, pābāra upāya

SYNONYMS

sādhya-vastu—the goal of life; *sādhana vinu*—without practicing the process; *keha nāhi pāya*—no one achieves; *kṛpā kari'*—very mercifully; *kaha*—please explain; *rāya*—My dear Rāmānanda Rāya; *pābāra upāya*—the means of achieving.

TRANSLATION

"The goal of life cannot be achieved unless one practices the process. Now, being merciful upon Me, please explain that means by which this goal can be attained."

TEXT 198

রায় কহে,—যেই কহাও, সেই কহি বাণী।
কি কহিয়ে ভাল-মন্দ, কিছুই না জানি॥ ১৯৮ ॥

rāya kahe, —yei kahāo, sei kahi vāṇī
ki kahiye bhāla-manda, kichui nā jāni

SYNONYMS

rāya kahe—Rāmānanda Rāya replied; *yei*—whatever; *kahāo*—You make me speak; *sei*—that; *kahi*—I speak; *vāṇī*—message; *ki*—what; *kahiye*—I am speaking; *bhāla-manda*—good or bad; *kichui nā jāni*—I do not know anything.

TRANSLATION

Śrī Rāmānanda Rāya replied, "I do not know what I am saying, but You have made me speak what I have spoken, be it good or bad. I am simply repeating that message.

TEXT 199

ত্রিভুবন-মধ্যে ঐছে হয় কোন্ ধীর ।
যে তোমার মায়া-নাটে হইবেক স্থির ॥ ১৯৯ ॥

tribhuvana-madhye aiche haya kon dhīra
ye tomāra māyā-nāṭe ha-ibeka sthira

SYNONYMS

tri-bhuvana-madhye—within the three worlds; *aiche*—so much; *haya*—there is; *kon*—who; *dhīra*—patient; *ye*—who; *tomāra*—Your; *māyā-nāṭe*—in the manipulation of different energies; *ha-ibeka*—will be; *sthira*—steady.

TRANSLATION

"Within these three worlds who is so undisturbed that he can remain steady as You manipulate Your different energies?

TEXT 200

মোর মুখে বক্তা তুমি, তুমি হও শ্রোতা ।
অত্যন্ত রহস্য, শুন, সাধনের কথা ॥ ২০০ ॥

mora mukhe vaktā tumi, tumi hao śrotā
atyanta rahasya, śuna, sādhanera kathā

SYNONYMS

mora mukhe—in my mouth; *vaktā*—speaker; *tumi*—You are; *tumi*—You; *hao*—are; *śrotā*—the hearer; *atyanta rahasya*—extremely mysterious; *śuna*—now please hear; *sādhanera kathā*—the discussion of the process.

TRANSLATION

"Actually You are speaking through my mouth, and at the same time You are listening. This is very mysterious. Anyway, kindly hear the explanation by which the goal can be attained.

PURPORT

Śrīla Sanātana Gosvāmī has advised us to hear about Kṛṣṇa from a Vaiṣṇava. He has explicitly forbidden us to hear from an *avaiṣṇava.*

avaiṣṇava-mukhodgīrṇaṁ
pūtaṁ hari-kathāmṛtam
śravaṇaṁ naiva kartavyaṁ
sarpocchiṣṭaṁ yathā payaḥ

Thus quoting from *Padma Purāṇa,* Śrīla Sanātana Gosvāmī warns that one should not hear anything about Kṛṣṇa from an *avaiṣṇava,* however great a mundane scholar he may be. Milk touched by the lips of a serpent has poisonous effects; similarly, talks about Kṛṣṇa given by an *avaiṣṇava* are also poisonous. However, because a Vaiṣṇava is surrendered to the Supreme Personality of Godhead, his talks are spiritually potent. In *Bhagavad-gītā* the Supreme Lord says,

teṣāṁ satata-yuktānāṁ
bhajatāṁ prīti-pūrvakam
dadāmi buddhi-yogaṁ taṁ
yena mām upayānti te

"To those who are constantly devoted and worship Me with love, I give the understanding by which they can come to Me." (Bg. 10.10) When a pure Vaiṣṇava speaks, he speaks perfectly. How is this? His speech is managed by Kṛṣṇa Himself from within the heart. Śrīla Rāmānanda Rāya accepts this benediction from Śrī Caitanya Mahāprabhu; therefore he admits that whatever he was speaking was not derived from his own intelligence. Rather, everything was coming from Śrī Caitanya Mahāprabhu. According to *Bhagavad-gītā:*

sarvasya cāhaṁ hṛdi sanniviṣṭo
mattaḥ smṛtir jñānam apohanaṁ ca
vedaiś ca sarvair aham eva vedyo
vedānta-kṛd veda-vid eva cāham

"I am seated in everyone's heart, and from Me come remembrance, knowledge and forgetfulness. By all the *Vedas* I am to be known; indeed I am the compiler of *Vedānta,* and I am the knower of the *Vedas.*" (Bg. 15.15)

All intelligence emanates from the Supreme Personality of Godhead, the Supersoul within the heart of everyone. Nondevotees want to ask the Supreme Lord for sense gratification; therefore nondevotees come under the influence of *māyā,* the illusory energy. A devotee, however, is directed by the Supreme Personality of

Godhead and comes under the influence of *yogamāyā.* Consequently there is a gulf of difference between statements made by a devotee and those made by a nondevotee.

TEXT 201

রাধাকৃষ্ণের লীলা এই অতি গূঢ়তর।
দাস্য-বাৎসল্যাদি-ভাবে না হয় গোচর ॥ ২০১ ॥

rādhā-kṛṣṇera līlā ei ati gūḍhatara
dāsya-vātsalyādi-bhāve nā haya gocara

SYNONYMS

rādhā-kṛṣṇera līlā—the pastimes of Rādhā and Kṛṣṇa; *ei*—this is; *ati*—very much; *gūḍhatara*—more confidential; *dāsya*—of servitude; *vātsalya-ādi*—and of paternal love, etc.; *bhāve*—in the moods; *nā haya*—is not; *gocara*—appreciated.

TRANSLATION

"The pastimes of Rādhā and Kṛṣṇa are very confidential. They cannot be understood through the mellows of servitude, fraternity or paternal affection.

TEXT 202

সবে এক সখীগণের ইহাঁ অধিকার।
সখী হৈতে হয় এই লীলার বিস্তার ॥ ২০২ ॥

sabe eka sakhī-gaṇera ihāṅ adhikāra
sakhī haite haya ei līlāra vistāra

SYNONYMS

sabe—only; *eka*—one; *sakhī-gaṇera*—of the *gopīs*; *ihāṅ*—in this; *adhikāra*—qualification; *sakhī*—the *gopīs*; *haite*—from; *haya*—is; *ei līlāra*—of these pastimes; *vistāra*—the expansion.

TRANSLATION

"Actually, only the gopīs have the right to appreciate these transcendental pastimes, and only from them can these pastimes be expanded.

TEXT 203

সখী বিনা এই লীলা পুষ্ট নাহি হয়।
সখী লীলা বিস্তারিয়া, সখী আস্বাদয় ॥ ২০৩ ॥

sakhī vinā ei līlā puṣṭa nāhi haya
sakhī līlā vistāriyā, sakhī āsvādaya

SYNONYMS

sakhī vinā—without the *gopīs*; *ei līlā*—these pastimes; *puṣṭa*—nourished; *nāhi haya*—are never; *sakhī*—the *gopīs*; *līlā*—the pastimes; *vistāriyā*—expanding; *sakhī*—the *gopīs; āsvādaya*—taste this mellow.

TRANSLATION

"Without the gopīs, these pastimes between Rādhā and Kṛṣṇa cannot be nourished. Only by their cooperation are such pastimes broadcast. It is their business to taste the mellows.

TEXTS 204-205

সখী বিনা এই লীলায় অন্যের নাহি গতি।
সখীভাবে যে তাঁরে করে অনুগতি॥ ২০৪॥
রাধাকৃষ্ণ-কুঞ্জসেবা-সাধ্য সেই পায়।
সেই সাধ্য পাইতে আর নাহিক উপায়॥ ২০৫॥

sakhī vinā ei līlāya anyera nāhi gati
sakhī-bhāve ye tāṅre kare anugati

rādhā-kṛṣṇa-kuñjasevā-sādhya sei pāya
sei sādhya pāite āra nāhika upāya

SYNONYMS

sakhī vinā—without the *gopīs*; *ei līlāya*—in these pastimes; *anyera*—of others; *nāhi*—there is not; *gati*—entrance; *sakhī-bhāve*—in the mood of the *gopīs*; *ye*—anyone who; *tāṅre*—Lord Kṛṣṇa; *kare*—does; *anugati*—following; *rādhā-kṛṣṇa*—of Rādhā and Kṛṣṇa; *kuñja-sevā*—of service in the *kuñjas,* or gardens, of Vṛndāvana; *sādhya*—the goal; *sei pāya*—he gets; *sei*—that; *sādhya*—achievement; *pāite*—to receive; *āra*—other; *nāhika*—there is not; *upāya*—means.

TRANSLATION

"Without the help of the gopīs, one cannot enter into these pastimes. Only he who worships the Lord in the ecstasy of the gopīs, following in their footsteps, can engage in the service of Śrī Śrī Rādhā-Kṛṣṇa in the bushes of Vṛndāvana. Only then can one understand the conjugal love between Rādhā and Kṛṣṇa. There is no other procedure for understanding.

PURPORT

The means for returning home, for going back to Godhead, is devotional service, but everyone has a different taste in the Lord's service. One may be inclined to serve the Lord in servitude (*dāsya-rasa*), fraternity (*sakhya-rasa*), or paternal love (*vātsalya-rasa*), but all these cannot enable one to enter into the service of the Lord in conjugal love. To attain such service, one has to follow in the footsteps of the *gopīs* in the ecstasy of *sakhī-bhāva*. Then only can one understand the transcendental mellow of conjugal love.

In the *Ujjvala-nīlamaṇi*, Śrīla Rūpa Gosvāmī advises:

prema-līlā-vihārāṇāṁ
samyag vistārikā sakhī
viśrambha-ratna-peṭī ca

One who expands the conjugal love of Kṛṣṇa and His enjoyment among the *gopīs* is called a *sakhī*. Such a person is a confidential *gopī* in the conjugal affairs. Such assistants are like jewels in the form of Kṛṣṇa's confidence. The actual business of the *sakhīs* is described thus in *Ujjvala-nīlamaṇi*:

mithaḥ prema-guṇotkīrtis
tayor āsakti-kāritā
abhisāro dvayor eva
sakhyāḥ kṛṣṇe samarpaṇam

narmāśvāsana-nepathyaṁ
hṛdayodghāṭa-pāṭavam
chidra-saṁvṛtir etasyāḥ
paty-ādeḥ parivañcanā

śikṣā saṅgamanaṁ kāle
sevanaṁ vyajanādibhiḥ
tayor dvayor upālambhaḥ
sandeśa-preṣaṇaṁ tathā

nāyikā-prāṇa-saṁrakṣā
prayatnādyāḥ sakhī-kriyāḥ

In the conjugal pastimes of Kṛṣṇa, Kṛṣṇa is the hero (*nāyaka*), and Rādhikā is the heroine (*nāyikā*). The first business of the *gopīs* is to chant the glories of both the hero and the heroine. Their second business is to create gradually a situation in which the hero may be attracted to the heroine and vice versa. Their third business is to induce both of Them to approach one another. Their fourth business is to surrender unto Kṛṣṇa, the fifth is to create a jovial atmosphere, the sixth to give Them assurance to enjoy Their pastimes, the seventh to dress and decorate both hero and heroine, the eighth to show expertise in expressing Their desires, the ninth to conceal the faults of the heroine, the tenth to cheat their respective husbands and relatives, the eleventh to educate, the twelfth to enable both hero and heroine to meet at the proper time, the thirteenth to fan both hero and heroine, the fourteenth to sometimes reproach the hero and heroine, the fifteenth to set conversations in motion, and the sixteenth to protect the heroine by various means.

Some material *sahajiyās* who cannot actually understand the pastimes of Rādhā and Kṛṣṇa manufacture their own life-styles without referring to authority. Such *sahajiyās* are called *sakhī-bhekī,* and sometimes they are called *gaura-nāgarī.* They believe that the material body, which is fit to be eaten by jackals and dogs, is enjoyable for Kṛṣṇa. Consequently they artificially decorate the material body to attract Kṛṣṇa, thinking themselves *sakhīs.* However, Kṛṣṇa is never attracted by the artificial grooming of the material body. As far as Śrīmatī Rādhārāṇī and Her *gopīs* are concerned, their bodies, homes, dresses, ornaments, endeavors and activities are all spiritual. All of these are meant to satisfy the spiritual senses of Kṛṣṇa. Indeed, they are so pleasing and endearing to Kṛṣṇa that He is subjugated by the influence of Śrīmatī Rādhārāṇī and Her friends. They have nothing to do with anything mundane within the fourteen planetary systems of the universe. Although Kṛṣṇa is attractive to everyone, He is nonetheless attracted by the *gopīs* and Śrīmatī Rādhārāṇī.

One should not be misled by mental concoctions, supposing his material body to be perfect and deeming oneself a *sakhī.* This is something like *ahaṅgrahopāsanā,* that is, a Māyāvādī's worship of his own body as the Supreme. Śrīla Jīva Gosvāmī has cautioned mundaners to abstain from such conceptions. He also warns that thinking oneself one of the associates of the Supreme without following in the footsteps of the *gopīs* is as offensive as thinking oneself the Supreme. Such thinking is an *aparādha.* One has to practice living in Vṛndāvana by hearing about the talks of the *gopīs* with Kṛṣṇa. However, one should not consider himself a *gopī,* for this is offensive.

TEXT 206

বিভুরপি সুখরূপঃ স্বপ্রকাশোঽপি ভাবঃ
ক্ষণমপি ন হি রাধাকৃষ্ণয়োর্যা ঋতে স্বাঃ ।
প্রবহতি রসপুষ্টিং চিদ্বিভূতীরিবেশঃ
শ্রয়তি ন পদমাসাং কঃ সখীনাং রসজ্ঞঃ ॥ ২০৬ ॥

vibhur api sukha-rūpaḥ sva-prakāśo 'pi bhāvaḥ
kṣaṇam api na hi rādhā-kṛṣṇayor yā ṛte svāḥ
pravahati rasa-puṣṭiṁ cid-vibhūtīr iveśaḥ
śrayati na padam āsāṁ kaḥ sakhīnāṁ rasa-jñaḥ

SYNONYMS

vibhuḥ—all-powerful; *api*—although; *sukha-rūpaḥ*—happiness personified; *sva-prakāśaḥ*—self-effulgent; *api*—although; *bhāvaḥ*—the completely spiritual activities; *kṣaṇam api*—even for a moment; *na*—never; *hi*—certainly; *rādhā-kṛṣṇayoḥ*—of Śrī Rādhā and Kṛṣṇa; *yāḥ*—whom; *ṛte*—without; *svāḥ*—His own entourage (the *gopīs*); *pravahati*—leads to; *rasa-puṣṭim*—completion of the highest humor; *cit-vibhūtīḥ*—spiritual potencies; *iva*—like; *īśaḥ*—the Supreme Personality of Godhead; *śrayati*—takes shelter of; *na*—not; *padam*—the position; *āsām*—of them; *kaḥ*—who; *sakhīnām*—of the personal associates; *rasa-jñaḥ*—one who is conversant with the science of mellows.

TRANSLATION

" 'The pastimes of Śrī Rādhā and Kṛṣṇa are self-effulgent. They are happiness personified, unlimited and all-powerful. Even so, the spiritual humors of such pastimes are never complete without the gopīs, the Lord's personal friends. The Supreme Personality of Godhead is never complete without His spiritual potencies; therefore unless one takes shelter of the gopīs, one cannot enter into the company of Rādhā and Kṛṣṇa. Who can be interested in Their spiritual pastimes without taking their shelter?'

PURPORT

This is a quotation from *Govinda-līlāmṛta* (10.17).

TEXT 207

সখীর স্বভাব এক অকথ্য-কথন ।
কৃষ্ণ-সহ নিজলীলায় নাহি সখীর মন ॥ ২০৭ ॥

sakhīra svabhāva eka akathya-kathana
kṛṣṇa-saha nija-līlāya nāhi sakhīra mana

SYNONYMS

sakhīra—of the *gopīs*; *sva-bhāva*—natural inclination; *eka*—one; *akathya*—inexplicable; *kathana*—narration; *kṛṣṇa-saha*—with Kṛṣṇa; *nija-līlāya*—in His personal pastimes; *nāhi*—not; *sakhīra*—of the *gopīs*; *mana*—the mind.

TRANSLATION

"There is an inexplicable fact about the natural inclinations of the gopīs. The gopīs never want to enjoy themselves with Kṛṣṇa personally.

TEXT 208

কৃষ্ণ সহ রাধিকার লীলা যে করায়।
নিজ-সুখ হৈতে তাতে কোটি সুখ পায়॥ ২০৮॥

kṛṣṇa saha rādhikāra līlā ye karāya
nija-sukha haite tāte koṭi sukha pāya

SYNONYMS

kṛṣṇa saha—with Kṛṣṇa; *rādhikāra*—of Śrīmatī Rādhārāṇī; *līlā*—the pastimes; *ye*—which; *karāya*—they bring about; *nija-sukha*—personal happiness; *haite*—than; *tāte*—in that; *koṭi*—ten million times; *sukha*—the happiness; *pāya*—they derive.

TRANSLATION

"The happiness of the gopīs increases ten million times when they serve to engage Śrī Śrī Rādhā and Kṛṣṇa in Their transcendental pastimes.

TEXT 209

রাধার স্বরূপ—কৃষ্ণপ্রেম-কল্পলতা।
সখীগণ হয় তার পল্লব-পুষ্প-পাতা॥ ২০৯॥

rādhāra svarūpa——kṛṣṇa-prema-kalpalatā
sakhī-gaṇa haya tāra pallava-puṣpa-pātā

SYNONYMS

rādhāra svarūpa—the spiritual nature of Śrīmatī Rādhārāṇī; *kṛṣṇa-prema*—of love of Kṛṣṇa; *kalpa-latā*—a creeper; *sakhī-gaṇa*—the *gopīs*; *haya*—are; *tāra*—of that creeper; *pallava*—the twigs; *puṣpa*—flowers; *pātā*—and leaves.

TRANSLATION

"By nature, Śrīmatī Rādhārāṇī is just like a creeper of love of Godhead, and the gopīs are the twigs, flowers and leaves of that creeper.

TEXT 210

কৃষ্ণলীলামৃত যদি লতাকে সিঞ্চয় ।
নিজ-সুখ হৈতে পল্লবাদ্যের কোটি-সুখ হয় ॥ ২১০ ॥

kṛṣṇa-līlāmṛta yadi latāke siñcaya
nija-sukha haite pallavādyera koṭi-sukha haya

SYNONYMS

kṛṣṇa-līlāmṛta—the nectar of Kṛṣṇa's pastimes; *yadi*—if; *latāke*—the creeper; *siñcaya*—sprinkles; *nija-sukha haite*—than personal happiness; *pallava-ādyera*—of the twigs, flowers and leaves; *koṭi*—ten million times; *sukha*—the happiness; *haya*—there is.

TRANSLATION

"When the nectar of Kṛṣṇa's pastimes is sprinkled on that creeper, the happiness derived by the twigs, flowers and leaves is ten million times greater than that derived by the creeper itself.

PURPORT

In his *Amṛta-pravāha-bhāṣya,* Śrīla Bhaktivinoda Ṭhākura states: "Śrīmatī Rādhārāṇī is the creeper of love of Godhead, and the *gopīs* are exactly like twigs, flowers and leaves. When water is sprinkled on the creeper, the twigs, flowers and leaves indirectly receive all the benefits of the creeper itself. However, water sprinkled directly on the twigs, leaves and flowers is not as effective as water sprinkled on the creeper's root. The *gopīs* are not as pleased when they directly mix with Kṛṣṇa as when they serve to unite Śrīmatī Rādhārāṇī with Kṛṣṇa. Their transcendental pleasure lies in uniting Them."

TEXT 211

সখ্যঃ শ্রীরাধিকায়া ব্রজকুমুদবিধোর্হ্লাদিনী-নামশক্তেঃ
সারাংশ-প্রেমবল্ল্যাঃ কিসলয়দলপুষ্পাদিতুল্যাঃ স্বতুল্যাঃ।
সিক্তায়াং কৃষ্ণলীলামৃতরসনিচয়ৈরুল্লসন্ত্যামমুষ্যাং
জাতোল্লাসাঃ স্বসেকাচ্ছতগুণমধিকং সন্তি যত্তন্ন চিত্রম্ ॥২১১॥

sakhyaḥ śrī-rādhikāyā vraja-kumuda-vidhor hlādinī-nāma-śakteḥ
sārāṁśa-prema-vallyāḥ kisalaya-dala-puṣpādi-tulyāḥ sva-tulyāḥ
siktāyāṁ kṛṣṇa-līlāmṛta-rasa-nicayair ullasantyām amuṣyāṁ
jātollāsāḥ sva-sekāc chata-guṇam adhikaṁ santi yat tan na citram

SYNONYMS

sakhyaḥ—friends like Lalitā and Viśākhā; *śrī-rādhikāyāḥ*—of Śrīmatī Rādhārāṇī; *vraja-kumuda*—of the lotuslike inhabitants of Vrajabhūmi; *vidhoḥ*—of the moon (Kṛṣṇa); *hlādinī*—pleasure-giving; *nāma*—of the name; *śakteḥ*—of the potency; *sāra-aṁśa*—the active principle; *prema-vallyāḥ*—of the creeper of love of Godhead; *kisalaya*—newly grown; *dala*—leaves; *puṣpa*—flowers; *ādi*—and so on; *tulyāḥ*—equal to; *sva-tulyāḥ*—equal to Herself; *siktāyām*—when sprinkled; *kṛṣṇa-līlā*—of the pastimes of Kṛṣṇa; *amṛta*—of the nectar; *rasa-nicayaiḥ*—by drops of the juice; *ullasantyām*—shining; *amuṣyām*—of Her, Śrīmatī Rādhārāṇī; *jāta-ullāsāḥ*—having awakened pleasure; *sva-sekāt*—than her own sprinkling; *śata-guṇam*—a hundred times; *adhikam*—more; *santi*—are; *yat*—which; *tat*—that; *na*—not; *citram*—wonderful.

TRANSLATION

" 'All the gopīs, the personal friends of Śrīmatī Rādhārāṇī, are equal to Her. Kṛṣṇa is pleasing to the inhabitants of Vrajabhūmi, just as the moon is pleasing to the lotus flower. His pleasure-giving potency is known as āhlādinī, of which the active principle is Śrīmatī Rādhārāṇī. She is compared to a creeper with newly grown flowers and leaves. When the nectar of Kṛṣṇa's pastimes is sprinkled on Śrīmatī Rādhārāṇī, all Her friends, the gopīs, immediately appreciate the pleasure a hundred times more than if they were sprinkled themselves. Actually this is not at all wonderful.'

PURPORT

This verse is also from *Govinda-līlāmṛta* (10.16).

TEXT 212

যদ্যপি সখীর কৃষ্ণ-সঙ্গমে নাহি মন ।
তথাপি রাধিকা যত্নে করান সঙ্গম ॥ ২১২ ॥

yadyapi sakhīra kṛṣṇa-saṅgame nāhi mana
tathāpi rādhikā yatne karāna saṅgama

SYNONYMS

yadyapi—although; *sakhīra*—of the *gopīs*; *kṛṣṇa-saṅgame*—directly enjoying with Kṛṣṇa; *nāhi*—not; *mana*—the mind; *tathāpi*—still; *rādhikā*—Śrīmatī Rādhārāṇī; *yatne*—with great endeavor; *karāna*—causes; *saṅgama*—association with Kṛṣṇa.

TRANSLATION

"Although the gopīs, Śrīmatī Rādhārāṇī's friends, do not desire to enjoy themselves directly with Kṛṣṇa, Śrīmatī Rādhārāṇī makes a great endeavor to induce Kṛṣṇa to enjoy Himself with the gopīs.

TEXT 213

নানা-চ্ছলে কৃষ্ণে প্রেরি' সঙ্গম করায় ।
আত্মকৃষ্ণ-সঙ্গ হৈতে কোটি-সুখ পায় ॥ ২১৩ ॥

nānā-cchale kṛṣṇe preri' saṅgama karāya
ātma-kṛṣṇa-saṅga haite koṭi-sukha pāya

SYNONYMS

nānā-chale—under different pleas; *kṛṣṇe*—unto Kṛṣṇa; *preri'*—sending; *saṅgama*—direct association; *karāya*—induces; *ātma-kṛṣṇa-saṅga*—personal association with Kṛṣṇa; *haite*—than; *koṭi-sukha*—ten million times more happiness; *pāya*—She gets.

TRANSLATION

"Presenting various pleas for the gopīs, Śrīmatī Rādhārāṇī sometimes sends the gopīs to Kṛṣṇa just to enable them to associate with Him directly. At such times, She enjoys a happiness ten million times greater than that enjoyed by direct association.

TEXT 214

অন্যোন্যে বিশুদ্ধ প্রেমে করে রস পুষ্ট ।
তাঁ-সবার প্রেম দেখি' কৃষ্ণ হয় তুষ্ট ॥ ২১৪ ॥

anyonye viśuddha preme kare rasa puṣṭa
tāṅ-sabāra prema dekhi' kṛṣṇa haya tuṣṭa

SYNONYMS

anyonye—by one another; *viśuddha*—transcendental; *preme*—in love of Godhead; *kare*—makes; *rasa*—the mellow; *puṣṭa*—nourished; *tāṅ-sabāra*—of all of them; *prema*—the love of Godhead; *dekhi'*—seeing; *kṛṣṇa*—Lord Kṛṣṇa; *haya*—becomes; *tuṣṭa*—satisfied.

TRANSLATION

"The transcendental mellow is nourished by that mutual behavior in transcendental love of Godhead. When Lord Kṛṣṇa sees how the gopīs have developed pure love for Him, He becomes very satisfied.

PURPORT

Śrīmatī Rādhārāṇī and the *gopīs* are not interested in their personal happiness derived from association with Kṛṣṇa. Rather, they become happy by seeing one another associate with Kṛṣṇa. In this way their dealings are further nourished by love of Godhead, and seeing this, Kṛṣṇa is very pleased.

TEXT 215

সহজ গোপীর প্রেম,—নহে প্রাকৃত কাম।
কামক্রীড়া-সাম্যে তার কহি 'কাম'-নাম ॥ ২১৫

sahaja gopīra prema,——nahe prākṛta kāma
kāma-krīḍā-sāmye tāra kahi 'kāma'-nāma

SYNONYMS

sahaja—natural; *gopīra*—of the *gopīs*; *prema*—love of Godhead; *nahe*—is not; *prākṛta*—material; *kāma*—lust; *kāma-krīḍā*—lusty affairs; *sāmye*—in appearing equal to; *tāra*—of such activities; *kahi*—I speak; *kāma-nāma*—the name "lust."

TRANSLATION

"It is to be noted that the natural characteristic of the gopīs is to love the Supreme Lord. Their lusty desire is not to be compared to material lust. Nonetheless, because their desire sometimes appears to resemble material lust, their transcendental love for Kṛṣṇa is sometimes described as lust.

PURPORT

Bhaktisiddhānta Sarasvatī Ṭhākura says that material lust should never be attributed to Kṛṣṇa, who is full of transcendental knowledge. Material lust cannot be engaged in the service of the Lord, for it is applicable to materialists, not to Kṛṣṇa. Only *prema,* or love of Godhead, is applicable for the satisfaction of Kṛṣṇa. *Prema* is full service rendered unto the Lord. The lusty affairs of the *gopīs* actually constitute the topmost love of Godhead because the *gopīs* never act for their own personal satisfaction. They are simply pleased by engaging other *gopīs* in the service of the Lord. The *gopīs* derive more transcendental pleasure from indirectly engaging other *gopīs* in the service of Kṛṣṇa than from engaging in His service themselves. That is the difference between material lust and love of Godhead. Lust applies to the material world, and love of Godhead applies only to Kṛṣṇa.

TEXT 216

প্রেমৈব গোপরামাণাং কাম ইত্যগমৎ প্রথাম্।
ইত্যুদ্ধবাদয়োঽপ্যেতং বাঞ্ছন্তি ভগবৎপ্রিয়াঃ ॥ ২১৬ ॥

premaiva gopa-rāmāṇāṁ
kāma ity agamat prathām
ity uddhavādayo 'py etaṁ
vāñchanti bhagavat-priyāḥ

SYNONYMS

premā—love of Godhead; *eva*—certainly; *gopa-rāmāṇām*—of all the *gopīs*; *kāmaḥ*—lust; *iti*—thus; *agamat*—became current; *prathām*—the process; *iti*—thus; *uddhava-ādayaḥ*—all devotees, headed by Uddhava; *api*—certainly; *etam*—this type of behavior; *vāñchanti*—desire; *bhagavat-priyāḥ*—those who are very, very dear to the Supreme Personality of Godhead.

TRANSLATION

"The dealings of the gopīs with Kṛṣṇa are on the platform of pure love of Godhead. However, they are sometimes considered to be lusty. But because such dealings are completely spiritual, all the dearmost devotees of the Lord like Uddhava and others also desire to participate in them.

PURPORT

This is a quotation from *Bhakti-rasāmṛta-sindhu* (1.2.285).

TEXT 217

নিজেন্দ্রিয়সুখহেতু কামের তাৎপর্য।
কৃষ্ণসুখ-তাৎপর্য গোপীভাব-বর্য ॥ ২১৭ ॥

nijendriya-sukha-hetu kāmera tātparya
kṛṣṇa-sukha-tātparya gopī-bhāva-varya

SYNONYMS

nija-indriya—of one's own senses; *sukha*—of the happiness; *hetu*—for the reason; *kāmera*—of lusty desire; *tātparya*—intention; *kṛṣṇa*—of Kṛṣṇa; *sukha*—the happiness; *tātparya*—intention; *gopī-bhāva-varya*—the foremost mood of the *gopīs*.

TRANSLATION

"Lusty desires are experienced when one is concerned with his own personal sense gratification. The mood of the gopīs is not like that. Their only desire is to satisfy the senses of Kṛṣṇa.

TEXT 218

নিজেন্দ্রিয়সুখবাঞ্ছা নাহি গোপিকার।
কৃষ্ণে সুখ দিতে করে সঙ্গম-বিহার ॥ ২১৮ ॥

nijendriya-sukha-vāñchā nāhi gopikāra
kṛṣṇe sukha dite kare saṅgama-vihāra

SYNONYMS

nija-indriya-sukha—for personal sense gratification; *vāñchā*—the desire; *nāhi*—there is not; *gopikāra*—of the *gopīs*; *kṛṣṇe*—unto Kṛṣṇa; *sukha*—happiness; *dite*—to give; *kare*—do; *saṅgama-vihāra*—mingling and enjoying with Kṛṣṇa.

TRANSLATION

"Among the gopīs, there is not a pinch of desire for sense gratification. Their only desire is to give pleasure to Kṛṣṇa, and in this way they mingle with Him and enjoy Him.

TEXT 219

যত্তে সুজাতচরণাম্বুরুহং স্তনেষু
ভীতাঃ শনৈঃ প্রিয় দধীমহি কর্কশেষু।
তেনাটবীমটসি তদ্ব্যথতে ন কিংস্বিৎ
কূর্পাদিভির্ভ্রমতি ধীর্ভবদায়ুষাং নঃ ॥ ২১৯ ॥

yat te sujāta-caraṇāmburuhaṁ staneṣu
bhītāḥ śanaiḥ priya dadhīmahi karkaśeṣu
tenāṭavīm aṭasi tad vyathate na kiṁ svit
kūrpādibhir bhramati dhīr bhavad-āyuṣāṁ naḥ

SYNONYMS

yat—because; *te*—Your; *sujāta*—delicate; *caraṇa-ambu-ruham*—lotus feet; *staneṣu*—on the breasts; *bhītāḥ*—being afraid of; *śanaiḥ*—very carefully; *priya*—O dear one; *dadhīmahi*—we place; *karkaśeṣu*—very rough and hard; *tena*—by such lotus feet; *aṭavīm*—the forest; *aṭasi*—You wander; *tat vyathate*—that gives us pain; *na*—not; *kim svit*—whether; *kūrpa-ādibhiḥ*—by the small particles of stone; *bhramati*—bewilders; *dhīḥ*—intelligence; *bhavat-āyuṣām*—of persons who consider You as the duration of life; *naḥ*—of us.

TRANSLATION

"All the gopīs said, 'Dear Kṛṣṇa, we carefully hold Your delicate lotus feet upon our hard breasts. When You walk in the forest, Your soft lotus feet are pricked by small bits of stone. We fear that this is paining You. You are our life and soul, and our minds are very disturbed when Your lotus feet are pained.'

PURPORT

This is a quotation from *Śrīmad-Bhāgavatam* (10.31.19).

TEXT 220

সেই গোপীভাবামৃতে যাঁর লোভ হয় ।
বেদধর্মলোক ত্যজি' সে কৃষ্ণে ভজয় ॥ ২২০ ॥

sei gopī-bhāvāmṛte yāṅra lobha haya
veda-dharma-loka tyaji' se kṛṣṇe bhayaja

SYNONYMS

sei—that; *gopī*—of the *gopīs*; *bhāva-amṛte*—in the nectar of the ecstasy; *yāṅra*—whose; *lobha*—attachment; *haya*—is; *veda-dharma*—religious principles of the *Vedas*; *loka*—popular opinion; *tyaji'*—giving up; *se*—he; *kṛṣṇe*—unto Kṛṣṇa; *bhajaya*—renders loving service.

TRANSLATION

"One who is attracted by that ecstatic love of the gopīs does not care about the regulative principles of Vedic life or popular opinion. Rather, he completely surrenders unto Kṛṣṇa and renders service unto Him.

TEXT 221

রাগানুগ-মার্গে তাঁরে ভজে যেই জন ।
সেইজন পায় ব্রজে ব্রজেন্দ্রনন্দন ॥ ২২১ ॥

rāgānuga-mārge tāṅre bhaje yei jana
sei-jana pāya vraje vrajendra-nandana

SYNONYMS

rāga-anuga—of spontaneous attachment; *mārge*—on the path; *tāṅre*—Kṛṣṇa; *bhaje*—worships; *yei*—who; *jana*—a person; *sei-jana*—that person; *pāya*—gets; *vraje*—in Vṛndāvana; *vrajendra-nandana*—the son of Mahārāja Nanda.

TRANSLATION

"If one worships the Lord on the path of spontaneous love and goes to Vṛndāvana, he receives the shelter of Vrajendra-nandana, the son of Nanda Mahārāja.

PURPORT

In all, there are sixty-four items listed for the rendering of service unto Kṛṣṇa, and these are the the regulative principles enjoined in the *śāstras* and given by the spiritual master. One has to serve Kṛṣṇa according to these regulative principles, but if one develops spontaneous love for Kṛṣṇa as exhibited in the activities of those who live in Vrajabhūmi, one attains the platform of *rāgānugā-bhakti.* One who has developed this spontaneous love is eligible for elevation to the platform enjoyed by the inhabitants of Vrajabhūmi. In Vrajabhūmi, there are no regulative principles set forth for Kṛṣṇa's service. Rather, everything is carried out in spontaneous, natural love for Kṛṣṇa. There is no question of following the principles of the Vedic system. Such principles are followed within this material world, and as long as one is on the material platform, he has to execute them. However, spontaneous love of Kṛṣṇa is transcendental. It may seem that the regulative principles are being violated, but the devotee is on the transcendental platform. Such service is called *guṇātīta,* or *nirguṇa,* for it is not contaminated by the three modes of material nature.

TEXT 222

ব্রজলোকের কোন ভাব লঞা যেই ভজে ।
ভাবযোগ্য দেহ পাঞা কৃষ্ণ পায় ব্রজে ॥ ২২২ ॥

vraja-lokera kona bhāva lañā yei bhaje
bhāva-yogya deha pāñā kṛṣṇa pāya vraje

SYNONYMS

vraja-lokera—of the planet known as Goloka Vṛndāvana; *kona*—some; *bhāva*—mood; *lañā*—accepting; *yei*—anyone who; *bhaje*—executes devotional service; *bhāva-yogya*—suitable for that spiritual attraction; *deha*—a body; *pāñā*—getting; *kṛṣṇa*—Lord Kṛṣṇa; *pāya*—gets; *vraje*—in Vṛndāvana.

TRANSLATION

"In his liberated stage the devotee is attracted by one of the five humors in the transcendental loving service of the Lord. As he continues to serve the Lord in that transcendental mood, he attains a spiritual body to serve Kṛṣṇa in Goloka Vṛndāvana.

TEXT 223

তাহাতে দৃষ্টান্ত—উপনিষদ্ শ্রুতিগণ ।
রাগমার্গে ভজি' পাইল ব্রজেন্দ্রনন্দন ॥ ২২৩ ॥

tāhāte dṛṣṭānta——upaniṣad śruti-gaṇa
rāga-mārge bhaji' pāila vrajendra-nandana

SYNONYMS

tāhāte—in this matter; *dṛṣṭānta*—the example; *upaniṣad śruti-gaṇa*—the great sages known as the personified *Upaniṣads* or *śrutis*; *rāga-mārge*—on the path of spontaneous love; *bhaji'*—worshiping; *pāila*—obtained; *vrajendra-nandana*—the lotus feet of Lord Kṛṣṇa.

TRANSLATION

"Those saintly persons who presented the Upaniṣads are vivid examples of this. By worshiping the Lord on the path of spontaneous love, they attained the lotus feet of Vrajendra-nandana, the son of Nanda Mahārāja.

PURPORT

In the Goloka Vṛndāvana planet, Kṛṣṇa's servants are headed by Raktaka and Patraka. Kṛṣṇa's friends are headed by Śrīdāmā, Subala and others. There are also elderly *gopīs* and the cowherd men headed by Nanda Mahārāja, mother Yaśodā and others. All of these personalities are eternally engaged in the loving service of the Lord in accordance with their specific attachments for Kṛṣṇa. One who wants to return home to serve the Lord directly is attracted to Kṛṣṇa as a servant, friend, father or mother. By continuously serving Kṛṣṇa during this life in a particular ecstasy, one gives up the material body and attains a suitable spiritual body to serve Kṛṣṇa in terms of a particular attachment. One may serve as a servant, friend, father or mother. In the same way, if one wants to serve Kṛṣṇa in conjugal love, he can also attain a body under the guidance of the *gopīs*. The most vivid example in this connection is those saintly personalities known as *śrutis,* who presented the *Upaniṣads*. These *śrutis* understand that without serving Kṛṣṇa and following in the footsteps of the *gopīs,* there is no possibility of entering the kingdom of God. Therefore they engage in spontaneous loving service unto Kṛṣṇa and follow in the footsteps of the *gopīs*.

TEXT 224

নিভৃতমরুন্মনোঽক্ষদৃঢ়যোগযুজো হৃদি য-
ন্মুনয় উপাসতে তদরয়োঽপি যযুঃ স্মরণাৎ ।

স্ত্রিয় উরগেন্দ্রভোগভুজদণ্ডবিষক্ত-ধিয়ো
বয়মপি তে সমাঃ সমদৃশোঽঙ্ঘ্রিসরোজসুধাঃ ॥ ২২৪ ॥

nibhṛta-marun-mano 'kṣa-dṛḍha-yoga-yujo hṛdi yan
munaya upāsate tad arayo 'pi yayuḥ smaraṇāt
striya uragendra-bhoga-bhuja-daṇḍa-viṣakta-dhiyo
vayam api te samāḥ samadṛśo 'ṅghri-saroja-sudhāḥ

SYNONYMS

nibhṛta—controlled; *marut*—the life air; *manaḥ*—the mind; *akṣa*—senses; *dṛḍha*—strong; *yoga*—in the mystic *yoga* process; *yujaḥ*—who are engaged; *hṛdi*—within the heart; *yat*—who; *munayaḥ*—the great sages; *upāsate*—worship; *tat*—that; *arayaḥ*—the enemies; *api*—also; *yayuḥ*—obtain; *smaraṇāt*—from remembering; *striyaḥ*—the *gopīs*; *uragendra*—of serpents; *bhoga*—like the bodies; *bhuja*—the arms; *daṇḍa*—like rods; *viṣakta*—fastened to; *dhiyaḥ*—whose minds; *vayam api*—we also; *te*—Your; *samāḥ*—equal to them; *samadṛśaḥ*—having the same ecstatic emotions; *aṅghri-saroja*—of the lotus feet; *sudhāḥ*—the nectar.

TRANSLATION

" 'By practicing the mystic yoga system and controlling their breath, the great sages conquered the mind and senses. Thus engaging in mystic yoga, they saw the Supersoul within their hearts and ultimately entered into the impersonal Brahman. However, even the enemies of the Supreme Personality of Godhead attain that position simply by thinking of the Supreme Lord. The damsels of Vraja, the gopīs, simply wanted to embrace Kṛṣṇa and hold His arms, which are like serpents. Being attracted by the beauty of Kṛṣṇa, they ultimately acquired a taste for the nectar of the Lord's lotus feet. We can also taste the nectar of Kṛṣṇa's lotus feet by following in the footsteps of the gopīs.'

PURPORT

This is a quotation from *Śrīmad-Bhāgavatam* (10.87.23) spoken by the *śrutis,* the personified *Vedas.*

TEXT 225

'সমদৃশঃ'-শব্দে কহে 'সেই ভাবে অনুগতি'।
'সমাঃ'-শব্দে কহে শ্রুতির গোপীদেহ-প্রাপ্তি ॥২২৫॥

'samadṛśaḥ'-śabde kahe 'sei bhāve anugati'
'samāḥ'-śabde kahe śrutira gopī-deha-prāpti

SYNONYMS

sama-dṛśaḥ—*samadṛśaḥ*; *śabde*—by this word; *kahe*—it says; *sei*—that; *bhāve*—in the emotion; *anugati*—following; *samāḥ*—*samāḥ*; *śabde*—by this word; *kahe*—it says; *śrutira*—of the persons known as the *śrutis*; *gopī-deha*—the bodies of the *gopīs*; *prāpti*—attainment.

TRANSLATION

The word 'samadṛśaḥ,' mentioned in the fourth line of the previous verse, means 'following the mood of the gopīs.' The word 'samāḥ' means 'attaining a body like those of the gopīs.'

TEXT 226

‘অঙ্ঘ্রিপদ্মসুধা’য় কহে ‘কৃষ্ণসঙ্গানন্দ’।
বিধিমার্গে না পাইয়ে ব্রজে কৃষ্ণচন্দ্র ॥ ২২৬ ॥

'aṅghri-padma-sudhā'ya kahe 'kṛṣṇa-saṅgānanda'
vidhi-mārge nā pāiye vraje kṛṣṇa-candra

SYNONYMS

aṅghri-padma-sudhāya—by the nectar derived from the lotus feet of Kṛṣṇa; *kahe*—it says; *kṛṣṇa-saṅgānanda*—transcendental bliss by the association of Kṛṣṇa; *vidhi-mārge*—on the path of regulative principles; *nā pāiye*—one does not get; *vraje*—in Goloka Vṛndāvana; *kṛṣṇa-candra*—Lord Kṛṣṇa.

TRANSLATION

"The word 'aṅghri-padma-sudhā' means 'associating intimately with Kṛṣṇa.' One can attain such perfection only by spontaneous love of God. One cannot obtain Kṛṣṇa in Goloka Vṛndāvana simply by serving the Lord according to regulative principles.

TEXT 227

নায়ং সুখাপো ভগবান্ দেহিনাং গোপিকাসুতঃ।
জ্ঞানিনাঞ্চাত্মভূতানাং যথা ভক্তিমতামিহ ॥ ২২৭ ॥

nāyaṁ sukhāpo bhagavān
dehināṁ gopikā-sutaḥ
jñāninąṁ cātma-bhūtānāṁ
yathā bhaktimatām iha

SYNONYMS

na—not; *ayam*—this Lord Śrī Kṛṣṇa; *sukha-āpaḥ*—easily available; *bhagavān*—the Supreme Personality of Godhead; *dehinām*—for materialistic persons who have accepted the body as the self; *gopikā-sutaḥ*—the son of mother Yaśodā; *jñāninām*—for persons addicted to mental speculation; *ca*—and; *ātma-bhūtānām*—for persons performing severe austerities and penances; *yathā*—as; *bhakti-matām*—for persons engaged in spontaneous devotional service; *iha*—in this world.

TRANSLATION

" 'The Supreme Personality of Godhead, Kṛṣṇa, the son of mother Yaśodā, is accessible to those devotees engaged in spontaneous loving service, but He is not as easily accessible to mental speculators, to those striving for self-realization by severe austerities and penances, or to those who consider the body the same as the self.'

PURPORT

This verse from *Śrīmad-Bhāgavatam* (10.9.21) is spoken by Śrīla Śukadeva Gosvāmī. It concerns the statement about Kṛṣṇa's being subjugated by the *gopīs* and thus glorifying them.

TEXT 228

অতএব গোপীভাব করি অঙ্গীকার ।
রাত্রি-দিন চিন্তে রাধাকৃষ্ণের বিহার ॥ ২২৮ ॥

ataeva gopī-bhāva kari aṅgīkāra
rātri-dina cinte rādhā-kṛṣṇera vihāra

SYNONYMS

ataeva—therefore; *gopī-bhāva*—the loving mood of the *gopīs*; *kari*—making; *aṅgīkāra*—acceptance; *rātri-dina*—day and night; *cinte*—one thinks; *rādhā-kṛṣṇera*—of Rādhā and Kṛṣṇa; *vihāra*—the pastimes.

TRANSLATION

"Therefore one should accept the mood of the gopīs in their service. In such a transcendental mood, one should always think of the pastimes of Śrī Rādhā and Kṛṣṇa.

TEXT 229

সিদ্ধদেহে চিন্তি' করে তাহাঁঞি সেবন ।
সখীভাবে পায় রাধাকৃষ্ণের চরণ ॥ ২২৯ ॥

siddha-dehe cinti' kare tāhāṅñi sevana
sakhī-bhāve pāya rādhā-kṛṣṇera caraṇa

SYNONYMS

siddha-dehe—in the perfected stage; *cinti'*—by remembering; *kare*—does; *tāhāṅñi*—in the spiritual world; *sevana*—service; *sakhī-bhāve*—in mood of the *gopīs*; *pāya*—gets; *rādhā-kṛṣṇera*—of Rādhā and Kṛṣṇa; *caraṇa*—the lotus feet.

TRANSLATION

"After thinking of Rādhā and Kṛṣṇa and Their pastimes for a long time and after getting completely free from material contamination, one is transferred to the spiritual world. There the devotee attains an opportunity to serve Rādhā and Kṛṣṇa as one of the gopīs.

PURPORT

Śrīla Bhaktisiddhānta Sarasvatī Ṭhākura comments that the word *siddha-deha,* "perfected spiritual body," refers to a body beyond the material gross body composed of five elements and the subtle astral body composed of mind, intelligence and false ego. In other words, one attains a completely spiritual body fit to render service to the transcendental couple Rādhā and Kṛṣṇa: *sarvopādhi-vinirmuktaṁ tat-paratvena nirmalam.*

When one is situated in his spiritual body, which is beyond this gross and subtle material body, he is fit to serve Rādhā and Kṛṣṇa. That body is called *siddha-deha.* The living entity attains a particular type of gross body in accordance with his past activities and mental condition. In this life the mental condition changes in different ways, and the same living entity gets another body in the next life according to his desires. The mind, intelligence and false ego are always engaged in an attempt to dominate material nature. According to that subtle astral body, one attains a gross body to enjoy the objects of one's desires. According to the activities of the present body, one prepares another subtle body. And according to the subtle body, one attains another gross body. This is the process of material existence. However, when one is spiritually situated and does not desire a gross or subtle body, he attains his original spiritual body. As confirmed by *Bhagavad-gītā* (4.9): *tyaktvā dehaṁ punar janma naiti mām eti so 'rjuna.*

One is elevated to the spiritual world by the spiritual body and is situated either in Goloka Vṛndāvana or in another Vaikuṇṭha planet. In the spiritual body there are no longer material desires, and one is fully satisfied by rendering service to the Supreme Personality of Godhead, Rādhā and Kṛṣṇa. This is the platform of *bhakti* (*hṛṣīkeṇa hṛṣīkeśa-sevanaṁ bhaktir ucyate*). When the spiritual body, mind and senses are completely purified, one can render service to the Supreme Personality of Godhead and His consort. In Vaikuṇṭha, the consort is Lakṣmī, and in Goloka

Vṛndāvana the consort if Śrīmatī Rādhārāṇī. In the spiritual body, free from material contamination, one can serve Rādhā-Kṛṣṇa and Lakṣmī-Nārāyaṇa. When one is thus spiritually situated, he no longer thinks of his own personal sense gratification. This spiritual body is called *siddha-deha,* the body by which one can render transcendental service unto Rādhā and Kṛṣṇa. The process is that of engaging the transcendental senses in loving devotional service. This verse specifically mentions, *sakhī-bhāve pāya rādhā-kṛṣṇera caraṇa:* only transcendentally elevated persons in the mood of the *gopīs* can engage in the service of the lotus feet of Rādhā and Kṛṣṇa.

TEXT 230

গোপী-আনুগত্য বিনা ঐশ্বর্যজ্ঞানে ।
ভজিলেহ নাহি পায় ব্রজেন্দ্রনন্দনে ॥ ২৩০ ॥

gopī-ānugatya vinā aiśvarya-jñāne
bhajileha nāhi pāya vrajendra-nandane

SYNONYMS

gopī-ānugatya—subservience to the *gopīs*; *vinā*—without; *aiśvarya-jñāne*—in the knowledge of opulence; *bhajileha*—if serving the Supreme Lord; *nāhi*—not; *pāya*—gets; *vrajendra-nandane*—the son of Mahārāja Nanda, Kṛṣṇa.

TRANSLATION

"Unless one follows in the footsteps of the gopīs, he cannot attain the service of the lotus feet of Kṛṣṇa, the son of Nanda Mahārāja. If one is overcome by knowledge of the Lord's opulence, he cannot attain the Lord's lotus feet, even though he is engaged in devotional service.

PURPORT

One can worship Lakṣmī-Nārāyaṇa by the process of *vidhi-mārga,* worshiping the Lord with regulative principles according to the instructions of the *śāstra* and the spiritual master. However, the Supreme Personality of Godhead, Rādhā-Kṛṣṇa, cannot be directly worshiped by this process. The dealings between Rādhā and Kṛṣṇa and the *gopīs* are devoid of the opulences of Lakṣmī-Nārāyaṇa. The process of *vidhi-mārga,* following the regulative principles, is utilized in the worship of Lakṣmī-Nārāyaṇa, whereas the process of spontaneous service—following in the footsteps of the *gopīs,* who are the denizens of Vṛndāvana—is transcendentally more advanced and is the process whereby Rādhā and Kṛṣṇa are worshiped. One cannot attain this elevated position while worshiping the Lord in His opulence. Those attracted by the conjugal love between Rādhā and Kṛṣṇa must follow in the footsteps of the *gopīs*. Only then is it possible to enter into the Lord's service in Goloka Vṛndāvana and directly associate with Rādhā and Kṛṣṇa.

TEXT 231

তাহাতে দৃষ্টান্ত—লক্ষ্মী করিল ভজন।
তথাপি না পাইল ব্রজে ব্রজেন্দ্রনন্দন ॥ ২৩১ ॥

tāhāte dṛṣṭānta——lakṣmī karila bhajana
tathāpi nā pāila vraje vrajendra-nandana

SYNONYMS

tāhāte—in that; *dṛṣṭānta*—the evidence; *lakṣmī*—the goddess of fortune; *karila*—did; *bhajana*—worship; *tathāpi*—still; *nā*—not; *pāila*—got; *vraje*—in Vṛndāvana; *vrajendra-nandana*—the son of Mahārāja Nanda, Kṛṣṇa.

TRANSLATION

"The unspoken example in this connection is the goddess of fortune, who worshiped Lord Kṛṣṇa in order to attain His pastimes in Vṛndāvana. However, due to her opulent life-style, she could not attain the service of Kṛṣṇa in Vṛndāvana.

TEXT 232

নায়ং শ্রিয়োঽঙ্গ উ নিতান্তরতেঃ প্রসাদঃ
স্বর্যোষিতাং নলিনগন্ধরুচাং কুতোঽন্যাঃ।
রাসোৎসবেঽস্য ভুজদণ্ডগৃহীতকণ্ঠ-
লব্ধাশিষাং য উদগাদ্‌ব্রজসুন্দরীণাম্ ॥ ২৩২ ॥

nāyaṁ śriyo 'ṅga u nitānta-rateḥ prasādaḥ
svar-yoṣitāṁ nalina-gandha-rucāṁ kuto 'nyāḥ
rāsotsave 'sya bhuja-daṇḍa-gṛhīta-kaṇṭha-
labdhāśiṣāṁ ya udagād vraja-sundarīṇām

SYNONYMS

na—not; *ayam*—this; *śriyaḥ*—of the goddess of fortune; *aṅge*—on the chest; *u*—alas; *nitānta-rateḥ*—who is very intimately related; *prasādaḥ*—the favor; *svaḥ*—of the heavenly planets; *yoṣitām*—of women; *nalina*—of the lotus flower; *gandha*—having the flavor; *rucām*—and bodily luster; *kutaḥ*—much less; *anyāḥ*—others; *rāsa-utsave*—in the festival of the *rāsa* dance; *asya*—of Lord Śrī

Kṛṣṇa; *bhuja-daṇḍa*—by the arms; *gṛhīta*—embraced; *kaṇṭha*—their necks; *labdha-āśiṣām*—who achieved such a blessing; *yaḥ*—which; *udagāt*—became manifest; *vraja-sundarīṇām*—of the beautiful *gopīs,* the transcendental girls of Vrajabhūmi.

TRANSLATION

" 'When Lord Śrī Kṛṣṇa was dancing with the gopīs in the rāsa-līlā, the gopīs were embraced around the neck by the Lord's arms. This transcendental favor was never enjoyed by the goddess of fortune or other consorts in the spiritual world. Nor was such a thing ever imagined by the most beautiful girls from the heavenly planets, whose bodily luster and flavor exactly resemble a lotus flower. And what to speak of worldly women, who are very beautiful according to the material estimation?' "

PURPORT

This is a quotation from *Śrīmad-Bhāgavatam* (10.47.60).

TEXT 233

এত শুনি' প্রভু তাঁরে কৈল আলিঙ্গন।
দুই জনে গলাগলি করেন ক্রন্দন ॥ ২৩৩ ॥

eta śuni' prabhu tāṅre kaila āliṅgana
dui jane galāgali karena krandana

SYNONYMS

eta śuni'—hearing so much; *prabhu*—Lord Śrī Caitanya Mahāprabhu; *tāṅre*—unto Rāmānanda Rāya; *kaila*—did; *āliṅgana*—embracing; *dui jane*—both of them; *galāgali*—embracing shoulder to shoulder; *karena*—did; *krandana*—crying.

TRANSLATION

After hearing this, Lord Śrī Caitanya Mahāprabhu embraced Rāmānanda Rāya, and both of them, clasping one another's shoulders, began to cry.

TEXT 234

এইমত প্রেমাবেশে রাত্রি গোঙাইলা।
প্রাতঃকালে নিজ-নিজ-কার্যে দুঁহে গেলা ॥ ২৩৪ ॥

ei-mata premāveśe rātri goṅāilā
prātaḥ-kāle nija-nija-kārye duṅhe gelā

SYNONYMS

ei-mata—in this way; *prema-āveśe*—in ecstatic love of Godhead; *rātri*—the night; *goṅāilā*—passed; *prātaḥ-kāle*—in the morning; *nija-nija-kārye*—in their own respective duties; *duṅhe*—both of them; *gelā*—departed.

TRANSLATION

The entire night was passed in this way, in ecstatic love of Godhead. In the morning they both departed to tend to their respective duties.

TEXT 235

বিদায়-সময়ে প্রভুর চরণে ধরিয়া ।
রামানন্দ রায় কহে বিনতি করিয়া ॥ ২৩৫ ॥

vidāya-samaye prabhura caraṇe dhariyā
rāmānanda rāya kahe vinati kariyā

SYNONYMS

vidāya-samaye—at the point of departure; *prabhura caraṇe*—the lotus feet of Lord Śrī Caitanya Mahāprabhu; *dhariyā*—capturing; *rāmānanda rāya*—Rāmānanda Rāya; *kahe*—says; *vinati kariyā*—with great humility.

TRANSLATION

Before departing from Śrī Caitanya Mahāprabhu, Rāmānanda Rāya fell to the ground and caught hold of the Lord's lotus feet. He then spoke submissively as follows.

TEXT 236

'মোরে কৃপা করিতে তোমার ইহাঁ আগমন ।
দিন দশ রহি' শোধ মোর দুষ্ট মন ॥ ২৩৬ ॥

'more kṛpā karite tomāra ihāṅ āgamana
dina daśa rahi' śodha mora duṣṭa mana

SYNONYMS

more—unto me; *kṛpā*—mercy; *karite*—to do; *tomāra*—Your; *ihāṅ*—here; *āgamana*—coming; *dina daśa rahi'*—remaining at least ten days; *śodha*—purify; *mora*—my; *duṣṭa mana*—polluted mind.

TRANSLATION

Śrī Rāmānanda Rāya said, "You have come here just to show me Your causeless mercy. Therefore stay here for at least ten days and purify my polluted mind.

TEXT 237

তোমা বিনা অন্য নাহি জীব উদ্ধারিতে ।
তোমা বিনা অন্য নাহি কৃষ্ণপ্রেম দিতে ॥' ২৩৭ ॥

tomā vinā anya nāhi jīva uddhārite
tomā vinā anya nāhi kṛṣṇa-prema dite'

SYNONYMS

tomā vinā—without You; *anya*—anyone else; *nāhi*—there is not; *jīva*—the living entity; *uddhārite*—to liberate; *tomā vinā*—without You; *anya*—anyone else; *nāhi*—there is not; *kṛṣṇa-prema dite*—to bestow love of Kṛṣṇa.

TRANSLATION

"But for You, there is no one who can deliver all the living entities, for You alone can deliver love of Kṛṣṇa."

TEXT 238

প্রভু কহে,—আইলাঙ শুনি' তোমার গুণ ।
কৃষ্ণকথা শুনি, শুদ্ধ করাইতে মন ॥ ২৩৮ ॥

prabhu kahe,——āilāṅa śuni' tomāra guṇa
kṛṣṇa-kathā śuni, śuddha karāite mana

SYNONYMS

prabhu kahe—the Lord said; *āilāṅa*—I have come; *śuni'*—hearing; *tomāra*—your; *guṇa*—qualities; *kṛṣṇa-kathā*—these topics about Kṛṣṇa; *śuni*—I hear; *śuddha karāite*—just to make pure; *mana*—the mind.

TRANSLATION

The Lord replied, "Having heard about your good qualities, I have come here. I have come to hear about Kṛṣṇa from you and thus purify My mind.

TEXT 239

যৈছে শুনিলুঁ, তৈছে দেখিলুঁ তোমার মহিমা ।
রাধাকৃষ্ণ-প্রেমরস-জ্ঞানের তুমি সীমা ॥ ২৩৯ ॥

yaiche śuniluṅ, taiche dekhiluṅ tomāra mahimā
rādhā-kṛṣṇa-premarasa-jñānera tumi sīmā

SYNONYMS

yaiche—as much; *śuniluṅ*—as I have heard; *taiche*—that much; *dekhiluṅ*—I have seen; *tomāra mahimā*—your glories; *rādhā-kṛṣṇa-prema-rasa-jñānera*—of transcendental knowledge about the loving affairs of Rādhā and Kṛṣṇa; *tumi*—you; *sīmā*—the ultimate goal.

TRANSLATION

"Just as I have heard from you, I have also actually seen your glories. As far as Rādhā and Kṛṣṇa's pastimes in a loving mood are concerned, you are the limit of knowledge."

PURPORT

Śrī Caitanya Mahāprabhu found Rāmānanda Rāya to be the best authority in transcendental knowledge of the loving affairs between Rādhā and Kṛṣṇa. In this verse the Lord actually states that Rāmānanda Rāya was the limit of this knowledge.

TEXT 240

দশ দিনের কা-কথা যাবৎ আমি জীব' ।
তাবৎ তোমার সঙ্গ ছাড়িতে নারিব ॥ ২৪০ ॥

daśa dinera kā-kathā yāvat āmi jība'
tāvat tomāra saṅga chāḍite nāriba

SYNONYMS

daśa dinera—of ten days; *kā-kathā*—what to speak; *yāvat*—as long as; *āmi*—I; *jība*—shall live; *tāvat*—that long; *tomāra*—of you; *saṅga*—the association; *chāḍite*—to give up; *nāriba*—I shall not be able.

TRANSLATION

Śrī Caitanya Mahāprabhu continued, "To say nothing of ten days, as long as I live I shall find it impossible to give up your company.

TEXT 241

নীলাচলে তুমি-আমি থাকিব এক-সঙ্গে ।
সুখে গোঙাইব কাল কৃষ্ণকথা-রঙ্গে ॥ ২৪১ ॥

nīlācale tumi-āmi thākiba eka-saṅge
sukhe goṅāiba kāla kṛṣṇa-kathā-raṅge

SYNONYMS

nīlācale—in Jagannātha Purī; *tumi*—you; *āmi*—I; *thākiba*—shall stay; *eka-saṅge*—together; *sukhe*—in happiness; *goṅāiba*—will pass; *kāla*—time; *kṛṣṇa-kathā-raṅge*—in the joy of talking about Kṛṣṇa.

TRANSLATION

"Both you and I shall remain together at Jagannātha Purī. We shall pass our time together in joy, talking about Kṛṣṇa and His pastimes."

TEXT 242

এত বলি' দুঁহে নিজ-নিজ কার্যে গেলা ।
সন্ধ্যাকালে রায় পুনঃ আসিয়া মিলিলা ॥ ২৪২ ॥

eta bali' duṅhe nija-nija kārye gelā
sandhyā-kāle rāya punaḥ āsiyā mililā

SYNONYMS

eta bali'—saying this; *duṅhe*—both of them; *nija-nija*—their own respective; *kārye*—in the duties; *gelā*—departed; *sandhyā-kāle*—in the evening; *rāya*—Rāmānanda Rāya; *punaḥ*—again; *āsiyā*—coming there; *mililā*—met.

TRANSLATION

In this way they both departed to perform their respective duties. Then, in the evening, Rāmānanda Rāya returned to see Lord Caitanya Mahāprabhu.

TEXT 243

অন্যোন্যে মিলি' দুঁহে নিভৃতে বসিয়া ।
প্রশ্নোত্তর-গোষ্ঠী কহে আনন্দিত হঞা ॥ ২৪৩ ॥

anyonye mili' duṅhe nibhṛte vasiyā
praśnottara-goṣṭhī kahe ānandita hañā

SYNONYMS

anyonye—one another; *mili'*—meeting; *duṅhe*—both of them; *nibhṛte*—in a secluded place; *vasiyā*—sitting; *praśna-uttara*—of questions and answers; *goṣṭhī*—a discussion; *kahe*—spoke; *ānandita*—jubilant; *hañā*—becoming.

TRANSLATION

Thus they met time and time again, both sitting in a secluded place and jubilantly discussing the pastimes of Kṛṣṇa by the question and answer process.

TEXT 244

প্রভু পুছে, রামানন্দ করেন উত্তর ।
এই মত সেই রাত্রে কথা পরস্পর ॥ ২৪৪ ॥

prabhu puche, rāmānanda karena uttara
ei mata sei rātre kathā paraspara

SYNONYMS

prabhu puche—the Lord inquires; *rāmānanda*—Rāya Rāmānanda; *karena*—gives; *uttara*—answers; *ei mata*—in this way; *sei rātre*—on that night; *kathā*—discussion; *paraspara*—mutual.

TRANSLATION

Śrī Caitanya Mahāprabhu asked the questions, and Śrī Rāmānanda Rāya gave the answers. In this way they were engaged in discussion throughout the night.

TEXT 245

প্রভু কহে,—"কোন্ বিদ্যা বিদ্যা-মধ্যে সার ?"
রায় কহে,—"কৃষ্ণভক্তি বিনা বিদ্যা নাহি আর ॥"২৪৫॥

prabhu kahe,——"kon vidyā vidyā-madhye sāra?"
rāya kahe,——"kṛṣṇa-bhakti vinā vidyā nāhi āra"

SYNONYMS

prabhu kahe—the Lord inquired; *kon*—what; *vidyā*—knowledge; *vidyā-madhye*—in the midst of knowledge; *sāra*—the most important; *rāya kahe*—Rāmānanda Rāya answered; *kṛṣṇa-bhakti*—devotional service to Kṛṣṇa; *vinā*—except; *vidyā*—education; *nāhi*—there is not; *āra*—any other.

TRANSLATION

On one occasion, the Lord inquired, "Of all types of education, which is the most important?" Rāmānanda Rāya replied, "There is no education that is important other than the transcendental devotional service of Kṛṣṇa."

PURPORT

Texts 245 to 257 are all questions and answers between Śrī Caitanya Mahāprabhu and Rāmānanda Rāya. In these exchanges there is an attempt to show the difference between material and spiritual existence. Education in Kṛṣṇa consciousness is always transcendental and is the best of all forms of education. Material education aims at increasing the activities of material sense gratification. Beyond material sense gratification is another negative form of knowledge called *brahma-vidyā,* or transcendental knowledge. However, beyond that *brahma-vidyā,* or knowledge of the impersonal Brahman, is knowledge of devotional service to the Supreme Lord, Viṣṇu. This knowledge is higher. And higher still is devotional service to Lord Kṛṣṇa, which is the topmost form of education. According to *Śrīmad-Bhāgavatam* (4.29.49):

tat karma hari-toṣaṁ yat
sā vidyā tan-matir yayā

"Work meant for pleasing the Supreme Lord is best, and education that enhances one's Kṛṣṇa consciousness is the best."

Also, according to *Śrīmad-Bhāgavatam* (7.5.23-24):

śravaṇaṁ kīrtanaṁ viṣṇoḥ
smaraṇaṁ pāda-sevanam
arcanaṁ vandanaṁ dāsyam
sakhyam ātma-nivedanam

iti puṁsārpitā viṣṇau
bhaktiś cen nava-lakṣaṇā
kriyeta bhagavaty addhā
tan manye 'dhītam uttamam

This is a statement given by Prahlāda Mahārāja in answer to a question raised by his father. Prahlāda Mahārāja said, "To hear or chant about Lord Viṣṇu, to remember Him, to serve His lotus feet, to worship Him, to offer prayers to Him, to become His servant and His friend, to sacrifice everything for His service—all these are varieties of devotional service. One who is engaged in such activities is understood to be educated to the topmost perfection."

TEXT 246

'কীর্তিগণ-মধ্যে জীবের কোন্ বড় কীর্তি ?'
'কৃষ্ণভক্ত বলিয়া যাঁহার হয় খ্যাতি ॥' ২৪৬ ॥

'kīrti-gaṇa-madhye jīvera kon baḍa kīrti?'
'kṛṣṇa-bhakta baliyā yāṅhāra haya khyāti'

SYNONYMS

kīrti-gaṇa-madhye—among glorious activities; *jīvera*—of the living entity; *kon*—which; *baḍa*—greatest; *kīrti*—glory; *kṛṣṇa-bhakta*—a devotee of Lord Kṛṣṇa; *baliyā*—as; *yāṅhāra*—of whom; *haya*—there is; *khyāti*—the reputation.

TRANSLATION

Śrī Caitanya Mahāprabhu then asked Rāmānanda Rāya, "Out of all glorious activities, which is the most glorious?" Rāmānanda Rāya replied, "That person who is reputed to be a devotee of Lord Kṛṣṇa's enjoys the utmost fame and glory."

PURPORT

The greatest reputation a living being can have is to be a devotee of Kṛṣṇa's and to act in Kṛṣṇa consciousness. In the material world everyone is trying to be famous by accumulating a large bank balance or material opulence. There is a steady competition among *karmīs* attempting to advance in a wealthy society. The whole world is turning in accordance with that competitive mood. However, this kind of name and fame is temporary, for it lasts only as long as the temporary material body exists. One may become famous as a *brahma-jñānī,* an impersonalist scholar, or one may become a materially opulent person. In either case, such reputations are inferior to the reputation of Kṛṣṇa's devotee. In the *Garuḍa Purāṇa* it is said:

kalau bhāgavataṁ nāma
durlabhaṁ naiva labhyate
brahma-rudra-padotkṛṣṭaṁ
guruṇā kathitaṁ mama

"In this age of Kali, the fame of one who is known as a great devotee is very rare. However, such a position is superior to that of the great demigods like Brahmā and Mahādeva. This is the opinion of all spiritual masters."

In the *Itihāsa-samuccaya,* Nārada tells Puṇḍarīka:

janmāntara-sahasreṣu
yasya syād buddhir īdṛśī
dāso 'haṁ vāsudevasya
sarvāl lokān samuddharet

"After many, many births, when a person realizes that he is the eternal servant of Vāsudeva, he can deliver all the worlds."

In the *Ādi Purāṇa,* in a conversation between Kṛṣṇa and Arjuna, it is said:

bhaktānām anugacchanti
muktayaḥ śrutibhiḥ saha

"The most exalted position of liberation is given by Vedic knowledge. Everyone follows in the footsteps of the devotee."

Similarly, in the *Bṛhan-nāradīya Purāṇa,* it is further stated:

adyāpi ca muni-śreṣṭhā
brahmādyā api devatāḥ

"Until now, even the great demigods like Brahmā and Lord Śiva did not know the influence of a devotee."

Similarly, in the *Garuḍa Purāṇa* it is stated:

brāhmaṇānāṁ sahasrebhyaḥ satra-yājī viśiṣyate
satra-yājī-sahasrebhyaḥ sarva-vedānta-pāragaḥ
sarva-vedānta-vit-koṭyā viṣṇu-bhakto viśiṣyate
vaiṣṇavānāṁ sahasrebhya ekānty eko viśiṣyate

"It is said that out of thousands of *brāhmaṇas,* one is qualified to perform sacrifices, and out of many thousands of such qualified *brāhmaṇas* expert in sacrificial offerings, one learned *brāhmaṇa* may have passed beyond all Vedic knowledge. He is considered the best among all these *brāhmaṇas.* And yet, out of thousands of such *brāhmaṇas* who have surpassed Vedic knowledge, one person may be a *viṣṇu-bhakta,* and he is most famous. Out of many thousands of such Vaiṣṇavas, one who is completely fixed in the service of Lord Kṛṣṇa is most famous. Indeed, a person who is completely devoted to the service of the Lord certainly returns home, back to Godhead."

There is also a statement in the *Śrīmad-Bhāgavatam* (3.13.4), stating:

śrutasya puṁsāṁ sucira-śramasya
nanv añjasā sūribhir īḍito 'rthaḥ

tat-tad-guṇānuśravaṇaṁ mukunda-
pādāravindaṁ hṛdayeṣu yeṣām

"After much hard labor, a person highly learned in Vedic literature is certainly very famous. However, one who is always hearing and chanting the glories of the lotus feet of Mukunda within his heart is certainly superior."

In the *Nārāyaṇa-vyūha-stava,* it is said:

nāhaṁ brahmāpi bhūyāsaṁ
tvad-bhakti-rahito hare
tvayi bhaktas tu kīṭo 'pi
bhūyāsaṁ janma-janmasu

"I do not aspire to take birth as a Brahmā if that Brahmā is not a devotee of the Lord. I shall be satisfied simply to take birth as an insect if I am given a chance to remain in the house of a devotee."

There are many similar verses in *Śrīmad-Bhāgavatam,* especially 3.25.38, 4.24.29, 4.31.22, 7.9.24, and 10.14.30.

It was Lord Śiva who said: "I do not know the truth about Kṛṣṇa, but a devotee of Lord Kṛṣṇa's knows all the truth. Out of all the devotees of Lord Kṛṣṇa, Prahlāda is the greatest."

Above Prahlāda, the Pāṇḍavas are supposedly more advanced. Above the Pāṇḍavas are the members of the Yadu dynasty, who are even more advanced. In the Yadu dynasty, Uddhava is the furthest advanced, and above Uddhava are the damsels of Vraja-dhāma, the *gopīs* themselves.

In the *Bṛhad-vāmana Purāṇa,* Bhṛgu is told by Lord Brahmā:

ṣaṣṭi-varṣa-sahasrāṇi
mayā taptaṁ tapaḥ purā
nanda-gopa-vraja-strīṇāṁ
pāda-reṇūpalabdhaye

"I underwent meditation and austerities for 60,000 years just to understand the dust of the lotus feet of the *gopīs.* Still, I could not understand them. To say nothing of me, even Lord Śiva, Lord Śeṣa and the goddess of fortune Lakṣmī could not understand them."

In the *Ādi Purāṇa* the Supreme Personality of Godhead Himself says:

na tathā me priyatamo
brahmā rudraś ca pārthiva
na ca lakṣmīr na cātmā ca
yathā gopī-jano mama

"Lord Brahmā, Lord Śiva, the goddess of fortune and even My own Self are not as dear to Me as the *gopīs*." Of all the *gopīs* Śrīmatī Rādhārāṇī is the topmost. Rūpa Gosvāmī and Sanātana Gosvāmī are the most exalted servitors of Śrīmatī Rādhārāṇī and Lord Śrī Caitanya Mahāprabhu. Those who adhere to their service are known as *rūpānuga* devotees. *Caitanya-candrāmṛta* (127) gives the following statement about Śrīla Rūpa Gosvāmī:

āstāṁ vairāgya-koṭir bhavatu śama-dama-kṣānti-maitry-ādi-koṭis
tattvānudhyāna-koṭir bhavatu vā vaiṣṇavī bhakti-koṭiḥ
koṭy-aṁśo 'py asya na syāt tad api guṇa-gaṇo yaḥ svataḥ-siddha āste
śrīmac-caitanyacandra-priya-caraṇa-nakha-jyotir āmoda-bhājām

The qualities of one engaged in the service of Lord Śrī Caitanya Mahāprabhu—such as reputation, austerities, penances and knowledge—are not to be compared to the good qualities of others. Such is the perfection of a devotee always engaged in the service of Śrī Caitanya Mahāprabhu.

TEXT 247

'সম্পত্তির মধ্যে জীবের কোন্ সম্পত্তি গণি ?'
'রাধাকৃষ্ণে প্রেম যাঁর, সেই বড় ধনী ॥' ২৪৭ ॥

'sampattira madhye jīvera kon sampatti gaṇi?'
'rādhā-kṛṣṇe prema yāṅra, sei baḍa dhanī'

SYNONYMS

sampattira—riches; *madhye*—among; *jīvera*—of the living entities; *kon*—what; *sampatti*—the wealth; *gaṇi*—we accept; *rādhā-kṛṣṇe*—to Śrīmatī Rādhārāṇī and Kṛṣṇa; *prema*—loving service; *yāṅra*—whose; *sei*—he; *baḍa*—very great; *dhanī*—capitalist.

TRANSLATION

Śrī Caitanya Mahāprabhu asked, "Of the many capitalists who possess great riches, who is the topmost?" Rāmānanda Rāya replied, "He who is richest in love for Rādhā and Kṛṣṇa is the greatest capitalist."

PURPORT

Everyone in this material world is attempting to acquire riches to satisfy the senses. Actually no one cares for anything other than acquiring material possessions and maintaining them. The wealthy are generally accepted as the most important personalities in this material world, but when we compare a material man of wealth to one wealthy in devotional service to Rādhā and Kṛṣṇa, the latter is found to be the greatest capitalist. According to *Śrīmad-Bhāgavatam* (10.39.2):

kim alabhyaṁ bhagavati
prasanne śrī-niketane
tathāpi tat-parā rājan
na hi vāñchanti kiñcana

"What is difficult for the devotees of Lord Kṛṣṇa, who is the shelter of the goddess of fortune? Although such devotees can obtain anything, O King, they do not desire anything."

TEXT 248

'দুঃখ-মধ্যে কোন দুঃখ হয় গুরুতর ?'
'কৃষ্ণভক্ত-বিরহ বিনা দুঃখ নাহি দেখি পর ॥'২৪৮ ॥

'duḥkha-madhye kona duḥkha haya gurutara?'
'kṛṣṇa-bhakta-viraha vinā duḥkha nāhi dekhi para'

SYNONYMS

duḥkha-madhye—among the miserable conditions of life; *kona*—what; *duḥkha*—misery; *haya*—is; *gurutara*—more painful; *kṛṣṇa-bhakta-viraha*—separation from the devotee of Lord Kṛṣṇa; *vinā*—besides; *duḥkha*—unhappiness; *nāhi*—there is not; *dekhi*—I see; *para*—other.

TRANSLATION

Śrī Caitanya Mahāprabhu asked, "Of all kinds of distress, what is the most painful?" Śrī Rāmānanda Rāya replied, "Apart from separation from the devotee of Kṛṣṇa, I know of no unbearable unhappiness."

PURPORT

Concerning this, *Śrīmad-Bhāgavatam* states:

mām anārādhya duḥkhārtaḥ
kuṭumbāsakta-mānasaḥ
sat-saṅga-rahito martyo
vṛddha-sevā-paricyutaḥ

"A person who does not worship Me, who is unduly attached to family and who does not stick to devotional service must be considered a most unhappy person.

Similarly, one who does not associate with Vaiṣṇavas, or who does not render service to his superior, is also a most unhappy person."

There is also a statement given in the *Bṛhad-bhāgavatāmṛta* (1.5.44):

sva-jīvanādhikaṁ prārthyaṁ
śrī-viṣṇu-jana-saṅgataḥ
vicchedena kṣaṇaṁ cātra
na sukhāṁśaṁ labhāmahe

"Out of all kinds of desirable things experienced in the life of a living entity, association with the devotees of the Lord is the greatest. When we are separated from a devotee even for a moment, we cannot enjoy happiness."

TEXT 249

'মুক্ত-মধ্যে কোন্ জীব মুক্ত করি' মানি ?'
'কৃষ্ণপ্রেম যাঁর, সেই মুক্ত-শিরোমণি ॥' ২৪৯ ॥

'mukta-madhye kon jīva mukta kari' māni?'
'kṛṣṇa-prema yāṅra, sei mukta-śiromaṇi'

SYNONYMS

mukta-madhye—among the liberated; *kon*—what; *jīva*—living entity; *mukta*—liberated; *kari'*—considering as; *māni*—we accept; *kṛṣṇa-prema*—one who loves Kṛṣṇa; *yāṅra*—of whom; *sei*—such a person; *mukta-śiromaṇi*—the topmost of all liberated souls.

TRANSLATION

Śrī Caitanya Mahāprabhu then inquired, "Out of all liberated persons, who should be accepted as the greatest? Rāmānanda Rāya replied, "He who has love for Kṛṣṇa has attained the topmost liberation."

PURPORT

In *Śrīmad-Bhāgavatam* (6.14.5), it is said:

muktānām api siddhānāṁ
nārāyaṇa-parāyaṇaḥ
sudurlabhaḥ praśāntātmā
koṭiṣv api mahāmune

"O great sage, of the many millions of liberated persons and of the millions who have attained perfection, he who is a devotee of Lord Nārāyaṇa is very, very rare. Indeed, he is the most perfect and peaceful person."

TEXT 250

'গান-মধ্যে কোন গান—জীবের নিজ ধর্ম ?'
'রাধাকৃষ্ণের প্রেমকেলি'—যেই গীতের মর্ম ॥২৫০॥

'gāna-madhye kona gāna—jīvera nija dharma?'
'rādhā-kṛṣṇera prema-keli'—yei gītera marma

SYNONYMS

gāna-madhye—among songs; *kona gāna*—which song; *jīvera*—of the living entity; *nija*—his own; *dharma*—religion; *rādhā-kṛṣṇera prema-keli*—the loving affairs of Rādhā and Kṛṣṇa; *yei*—which; *gītera*—of the song; *marma*—purport.

TRANSLATION

Śrī Caitanya Mahāprabhu next asked Rāmānanda Rāya, "Among many songs, which song is to be considered the actual religion of the living entity?" Rāmānanda Rāya replied, "That song describing the loving affairs of Śrī Rādhā and Kṛṣṇa is superior to all other songs."

PURPORT

As stated in *Śrīmad-Bhāgavatam* (10.33.37):

anugrahāya bhūtānāṁ
mānuṣaṁ deham āsthitaḥ
bhajate tādṛśīḥ krīḍā
yāḥ śrutvā tat-paro bhavet

"Lord Kṛṣṇa descends apparently as a human being, and He exhibits His transcendental pastimes in Vṛndāvana so that the conditioned soul may be attracted to hearing His transcendental activities." Nondevotees are strictly prohibited from participating in songs celebrating the loving affairs of Rādhā and Kṛṣṇa. Unless one is a devotee, it is very dangerous to hear the songs about the pastimes of Rādhā and Kṛṣṇa that were written by Jayadeva Gosvāmī, Caṇḍīdāsa and other exalted devotees. Lord Śiva drank an ocean of poison, but one should not imitate this. One must first become a pure devotee of Lord Kṛṣṇa. Only then can one enjoy hearing the songs of Jayadeva and relish transcendental bliss. If one simply imitates the activities of Lord Śiva and drinks poison, one will certainly meet with death.

Talks between Lord Śrī Caitanya Mahāprabhu and Rāmānanda Rāya were meant for advanced devotees only. Those who are on the mundane platform and who study these talks in order to put forward some thesis for a Ph. D. will not be able to understand them. Instead, these conversations will have a poisonous effect.

TEXT 251

'শ্রেয়ো-মধ্যে কোন শ্রেয়ঃ জীবের হয় সার ?'
'কৃষ্ণভক্ত-সঙ্গ বিনা শ্রেয়ঃ নাহি আর ॥' ২৫১ ॥

'śreyo-madhye kona śreyaḥ jīvera haya sāra?'
'kṛṣṇa-bhakta-saṅga vinā śreyaḥ nāhi āra'

SYNONYMS

śreyaḥ-madhye—among beneficial activities; *kona*—which; *śreyaḥ*—beneficial function; *jīvera*—of the living entity; *haya*—is; *sāra*—the essence; *kṛṣṇa-bhakta-saṅga*—for associating with the devotees of Lord Kṛṣṇa; *vinā*—except; *śreyaḥ*—beneficial activity; *nāhi*—there is not; *āra*—another.

TRANSLATION

"Out of all auspicious and beneficial activities, which is best for the living entity?" Rāmānanda Rāya replied, "The only auspicious activity is association with the devotees of Kṛṣṇa."

PURPORT

According to *Śrīmad-Bhāgavatam* (11.2.30):

ata ātyantikaṁ kṣemaṁ
pṛcchāmo bhavato 'naghāḥ
saṁsāre 'smin kṣaṇārdho 'pi
sat-saṅgaḥ śevadhir nṛṇām

"We are asking the most perfect welfare activity from you. I think that in this material world, association with devotees—even if it be for a moment—is the greatest treasure house for mankind."

TEXT 252

'কাঁহার স্মরণ জীব করিবে অনুক্ষণ ?'
'কৃষ্ণ'-নাম-গুণ-লীলা—প্রধান স্মরণ ॥' ২৫২ ॥

'kāṅhāra smaraṇa jīva karibe anukṣaṇa?'
'kṛṣṇa-nāma-guṇa-līlā——pradhāna smaraṇa'

SYNONYMS

kāṅhāra—of whom; *smaraṇa*—remembering; *jīva*—the living entity; *karibe*—should do; *anukṣaṇa*—constantly; *kṛṣṇa-nāma*—the holy name of Lord Kṛṣṇa; *guṇa-līlā*—His qualities and pastimes; *pradhāna smaraṇa*—most important remembrance.

TRANSLATION

Śrī Caitanya Mahāprabhu asked, "What should all living entities constantly remember?" Rāmānanda Rāya replied, "The chief object of remembrance is always the holy name of the Lord, His qualities and pastimes."

PURPORT

Śrīmad-Bhāgavatam states (2.2.36):

tasmāt sarvātmanā rājan
hariḥ sarvatra sarvadā
śrotavyaḥ kīrtitavyaś ca
smartavyo bhagavān nṛṇām

Śukadeva Gosvāmī concludes: "The business of the living entity is to always remember the Supreme Personality of Godhead in every circumstance. The Lord should be heard about, glorified and remembered by all human beings."

TEXT 253

'ধ্যেয়-মধ্যে জীবের কর্তব্য কোন্ ধ্যান ?'
'রাধাকৃষ্ণপদাম্বুজ-ধ্যান—প্রধান ॥' ২৫৩ ॥

'dhyeya-madhye jīvera kartavya kon dhyāna?'
'rādhā-kṛṣṇa-padāmbuja-dhyāna——pradhāna'

SYNONYMS

dhyeya-madhye—out of all types of meditation; *jīvera*—of the living entity; *kartavya*—the duty; *kon*—what; *dhyāna*—meditation; *rādhā-kṛṣṇa-pada-ambuja*—on the lotus feet of Rādhā and Kṛṣṇa; *dhyāna*—meditation; *pradhāna*—is the chief.

TRANSLATION

Śrī Caitanya Mahāprabhu further inquired, "Out of many types of meditation, which is required for all living entities?" Śrīla Rāmānanda Rāya replied, "The chief duty of every living entity is to meditate upon the lotus feet of Rādhā and Kṛṣṇa."

PURPORT

Śrīmad-Bhāgavatam states (1.2.14):

tasmād ekena manasā
bhagavān sātvatāṁ patiḥ
śrotavyaḥ kīrtitavyaś ca
dhyeyaḥ pūjyaś ca nityadā

Sūta Gosvāmī replied to the sages headed by Śaunaka: "Everyone should very attentively listen to the pastimes of the Supreme Personality of Godhead. One should glorify His activities and meditate upon Him regularly."

TEXT 254

'সর্ব ত্যজি' জীবের কর্তব্য কাহাঁ বাস ?'
ব্রজভূমি বৃন্দাবন যাহাঁ লীলারাস ॥' ২৫৪ ॥

'sarva tyaji' jīvera kartavya kāhāṅ vāsa?'
vraja-bhūmi vṛndāvana yāhāṅ līlā-rāsa'

SYNONYMS

sarva—everything; *tyaji'*—giving up; *jīvera*—of the living entity; *kartavya*—to be done; *kāhāṅ*—where; *vāsa*—residence; *vraja-bhūmi*—the land known as Vrajabhūmi; *vṛndāvana*—the holy place named Vṛndāvana; *yāhāṅ*—where; *līlā-rāsa*—Lord Kṛṣṇa performed His *rāsa* dance.

TRANSLATION

Śrī Caitanya Mahāprabhu asked, "Where should the living entity live, abandoning all other places?" Rāmānanda Rāya replied, "The holy place known as Vṛndāvana or Vrajabhūmi, where the Lord performed His rāsa dance."

PURPORT

According to *Śrīmad-Bhāgavatam* (10.47.61):

āsām aho caraṇa-reṇu-juṣām ahaṁ
syāṁ vṛndāvane kim api gulma-latauṣadhīnām
yā dustyajaṁ svajanam ārya-pathaṁ ca hitvā
bhejur mukunda-padavīṁ śrutibhir vimṛgyām

"Let me become one of the herbs and plants of Vṛndāvana that the *gopīs* trample, giving up all connections with family and friends and deciding to worship the lotus feet of Mukunda. Those lotus feet are sought by all great saintly persons expert in the study of Vedic literature."

TEXT 255

'শ্রবণমধ্যে জীবের কোন্ শ্রেষ্ঠ শ্রবণ ?'
'রাধাকৃষ্ণ-প্রেমকেলি কর্ণ-রসায়ন ॥' ২৫৫ ॥

'śravaṇa-madhye jīvera kon śreṣṭha śravaṇa?'
'rādhā-kṛṣṇa-prema-keli karṇa-rasāyana'

SYNONYMS

śravaṇa-madhye—out of all topics for hearing; *jīvera*—of the living entity; *kon*—what; *śreṣṭha*—most important; *śravaṇa*—topic of hearing; *rādhā-kṛṣṇa-prema-keli*—the loving affairs between Rādhā and Kṛṣṇa; *karṇa-rasa-ayana*—most pleasing to the ear.

TRANSLATION

Śrī Caitanya Mahāprabhu asked, "Out of all topics people listen to, which is best for all living entities?" Rāmānanda Rāya replied, "Hearing about the loving affairs between Rādhā and Kṛṣṇa is most pleasing to the ear."

PURPORT

According to *Śrīmad-Bhāgavatam* (10.33.40):

vikrīḍitaṁ vraja-vadhūbhir idaṁ ca viṣṇoḥ
śraddhānvito 'nuśṛṇuyād atha varṇayed yaḥ
bhaktiṁ parāṁ bhagavati pratilabhya kāmaṁ
hṛd-rogam āśv apahinoty acireṇa dhīraḥ

"He who faithfully hears about the dealings between Lord Kṛṣṇa and the *gopīs* in the *rāsa* dance and he who describes these activities attain to the perfectional stage of devotional service and simultaneously lose material, lusty desires."

When one is liberated and hears of Lord Kṛṣṇa's and Rādhā's loving affairs, he is not inclined to have lusty desires. One mundane rogue once said that when the Vaiṣṇavas chant the name "Rādhā, Rādhā," he simply remembers a barber's wife named Rādhā. This is a practical example. Unless one is liberated, he should not try to hear about the loving affairs between Rādhā and Kṛṣṇa. If one is not liberated and listens to a relation of the *rāsa* dance, he may remember his mundane activities and illicit connections with some woman whose name may also be Rādhā. In the conditioned stage one should not even try to remember such things. By practicing the regulative principles, one should rise to the platform of spontaneous attraction for Kṛṣṇa. Then and only then should one hear about the *rādhā-kṛṣṇa-līlā.* Although these affairs may be very pleasing both to conditioned and to liberated souls, the conditioned soul should not try to hear them. The talks between Rāmānanda Rāya and Śrī Caitanya Mahāprabhu are conducted on the platform of liberation.

TEXT 256

'উপাস্যের মধ্যে কোন্ উপাস্য প্রধান ?'
'শ্রেষ্ঠ উপাস্য—যুগল 'রাধাকৃষ্ণ' নাম ॥' ২৫৬ ॥

'upāsyera madhye kon upāsya pradhāna?'
'śreṣṭha upāsya——yugala 'rādhā-kṛṣṇa' nāma'

SYNONYMS

upāsyera—objects of worship; *madhye*—among; *kon*—which; *upāsya*—worshipable object; *pradhāna*—the chief; *śreṣṭha*—the chief; *upāsya*—worshipable object; *yugala*—the couple; *rādhā-kṛṣṇa nāma*—the holy name of Rādhā-Kṛṣṇa, or Hare Kṛṣṇa.

TRANSLATION

Śrī Caitanya Mahāprabhu asked, "Among all worshipable objects, which is the chief?" Rāmānanda Rāya replied, "The chief worshipable object is the holy name of Rādhā and Kṛṣṇa, the Hare Kṛṣṇa mantra."

PURPORT

According to *Śrīmad-Bhāgavatam* (6.3.22):

etāvān eva loke 'smin
puṁsāṁ dharmaḥ paraḥ smṛtaḥ
bhakti-yogo bhagavati
tan-nāma-grahaṇādibhiḥ

"In this material world the living entity's only business is to accept the path of *bhakti-yoga* and chant the holy name of the Lord."

TEXT 257

'মুক্তি, ভুক্তি বাঞ্ছে যেই, কাহাঁ দুঁহার গতি ?'
'স্থাবরদেহ, দেবদেহ যৈছে অবস্থিতি ॥' ২৫৭ ॥

'mukti, bhukti vāñche yei, kāhāṅ duṅhāra gati?'
'sthāvara-deha, deva-deha yaiche avasthiti'

SYNONYMS

mukti—liberation; *bhukti*—sense enjoyment; *vāñche*—desires; *yei*—one who; *kāhāṅ*—where; *duṅhāra*—of both of them; *gati*—the destination; *sthāvara-deha*—the body of a tree; *deva-deha*—the body of a demigod; *yaiche*—just as; *avasthiti*—situated.

TRANSLATION

"And what is the destination of those who desire liberation and those who desire sense gratification?" Śrī Caitanya Mahāprabhu asked. Rāmānanda Rāya replied, "Those who attempt to merge into the existence of the Supreme Lord will have to accept a body like that of a tree. And those who are overly inclined toward sense gratification will attain the bodies of demigods."

PURPORT

Those who desire liberation by merging into the existence of God do not desire sense gratification within the material world. On the other hand, they have no information about serving the lotus feet of the Lord. Consequently, they are doomed to stand like trees for many thousands of years. Although trees are living entities, they are nonmoving. The liberated soul who attempts to merge into the existence of the Lord is no better than the trees. Trees also stand in the Lord's existence because material energy and the Lord's energy are the same. Similarly, the Brahman effulgence is also the energy of the Supreme Lord. It is the same whether one remains in the Brahman effulgence or in the material energy because in either there is no spiritual activity. Better situated are those who desire sense gratification and promotion to the heavenly planets. Such people want to enjoy themselves like denizens of heaven in gardens of paradise. They at least retain their individuality in order to enjoy life, but the impersonalists, who try to lose their individuality, also love both material and spiritual pleasure. The stone is immovable and has neither material nor spiritual activity. As far as the hard-working *karmīs* are concerned, *Śrīmad-Bhāgavatam* states (11.10.23):

iṣṭveha devatā yajñaiḥ
svar-lokaṁ yāti yājñikaḥ
bhuñjīta devavat tatra
bhogān divyān nijārjitān

"After performing various sacrificial rituals for elevation to the heavenly planets, the *karmīs* go there and enjoy themselves with the demigods to the extent that they have obtained the results of pious activities."

As stated in *Bhagavad-gītā* (9.20-21):

trai-vidyā māṁ soma-pāḥ pūta-pāpā
yajñair iṣṭvā svar-gatiṁ prārthayante
te puṇyam āsādya surendra-lokam
aśnanti divyān divi deva-bhogān

te taṁ bhuktvā svarga-lokaṁ viśālaṁ
kṣīṇe puṇye martya-lokaṁ viśanti
evaṁ trayī-dharmam anuprapannā
gatāgataṁ kāma-kāmā labhante

"Those who study the *Vedas* and drink *soma* juice, seeking the heavenly planets, worship Me indirectly. They take birth on the planet of Indra, where they enjoy godly delights. When they have thus enjoyed heavenly sense pleasure, they return to this mortal planet again. Thus, through the Vedic principles, they achieve only flickering happiness."

Therefore after finishing the results of pious activities, the *karmīs* again return to this planet in the form of rain, and they begin their life as grass and plants in the evolutionary process.

TEXT 258

অরসজ্ঞ কাক চূষে জ্ঞান-নিম্বফলে ।
রসজ্ঞ কোকিল খায় প্রেমাম্র-মুকুলে ॥ ২৫৮ ॥

arasa-jña kāka cūṣe jñāna-nimba-phale
rasa-jña kokila khāya premāmra-mukule

SYNONYMS

arasa-jña—without mellows; *kāka*—the crows; *cūṣe*—suck; *jñāna*—of knowledge; *nimba-phale*—on the bitter *nimba* fruit; *rasa-jña*—who are humorous; *kokila*—the cuckoos; *khāya*—eat; *prema-āmra-mukule*—the buds of the mango of love of Godhead.

TRANSLATION

Rāmānanda Rāya continued, "Those who are devoid of all mellows are like the crows that suck the juice from the bitter fruits of the nimba tree of knowledge, whereas those who enjoy mellows are like the cuckoos who eat the buds of the mango tree of love of Godhead."

PURPORT

The speculative process of empiric philosophy is as bitter as the fruit of the *nimba* tree. The tasting of this fruit is the business of crows. In other words, the philosophical process of realizing the Absolute Truth is a process taken up by crowlike men. The cuckoos have very sweet voices with which to chant the holy name of the Lord and taste the sweet fruit of the mango tree. Such devotees relish sweet mellows with the Lord.

TEXT 259

অভাগিয়া জ্ঞানী আস্বাদয়ে শুষ্ক জ্ঞান ।
কৃষ্ণ-প্রেমামৃত পান করে ভাগ্যবান্ ॥ ২৫৯ ॥

abhāgiyā jñānī āsvādaye śuṣka jñāna
kṛṣṇa-premāmṛta pāna kare bhāgyavān

SYNONYMS

abhāgiyā—unfortunate; *jñānī*—the philosophical speculators; *āsvādaye*—taste; *śuṣka*—dry; *jñāna*—empiric knowledge; *kṛṣṇa-prema-amṛta*—the nectar of love of Kṛṣṇa; *pāna*—drinking; *kare*—do; *bhāgyavān*—the fortunate.

TRANSLATION

Rāmānanda Rāya concluded, "The unfortunate empiric philosophers taste the dry process of philosophical knowledge, whereas the devotees regularly drink the nectar of love of Kṛṣṇa. Therefore they are most fortunate of all."

TEXT 260

এইমত দুই জন কৃষ্ণকথা-রসে ।
নৃত্য-গীত-রোদনে হৈল রাত্রি-শেষে ॥ ২৬০ ॥

ei-mata dui jana kṛṣṇa-kathā-rase
nṛtya-gīta-rodane haila rātri-śeṣe

SYNONYMS

ei-mata—in this way; *dui jana*—both of them (Lord Caitanya and Rāmānanda Rāya); *kṛṣṇa-kathā-rase*—in the mellows of discussing topics about Kṛṣṇa; *nṛtya-gīta*—in dancing and chanting; *rodane*—in crying; *haila*—there was; *rātri-śeṣe*—the end of the night.

TRANSLATION

In this way both Caitanya Mahāprabhu and Rāmānanda Rāya passed the full night relishing the mellow of kṛṣṇa-kathā, topics about Kṛṣṇa. While they were chanting, dancing and crying, the night ended.

TEXT 261

দোঁহে নিজ-নিজ-কার্যে চলিলা বিহানে ।
সন্ধ্যাকালে রায় আসি' মিলিলা আর দিনে ॥২৬১॥

doṅhe nija-nija-kārye calilā vihāne
sandhyā-kāle rāya āsi' mililā āra dine

SYNONYMS

doṅhe—both of them; *nija-nija-kārye*—in their respective duties; *calilā*—departed; *vihāne*—in the morning; *sandhyā-kāle*—in the evening; *rāya*—Rāmānanda Rāya; *āsi'*—coming again; *mililā*—met; *āra*—next; *dine*—on the day.

TRANSLATION

The next morning they both departed to perform their respective duties, but in the evening Rāmānanda Rāya returned to meet the Lord again.

TEXT 262

ইষ্ট-গোষ্ঠী কৃষ্ণকথা কহি' কতক্ষণ ।
প্রভুপদ ধরি' রায় করে নিবেদন ॥ ২৬২ ॥

iṣṭa-goṣṭhī kṛṣṇa-kathā kahi' kata-kṣaṇa
prabhu-pada dhari' rāya kare nivedana

SYNONYMS

iṣṭa-goṣṭhī—spiritual discussion; *kṛṣṇa-kathā*—topics of Kṛṣṇa; *kahi'*—talking; *kata-kṣaṇa*—for some time; *prabhu-pada*—the lotus feet of the Lord; *dhari'*—catching; *rāya*—Rāmānanda Rāya; *kare*—makes; *nivedana*—submission.

TRANSLATION

That next evening, after discussing the topic of Kṛṣṇa for some time, Rāmānanda Rāya caught hold of the lotus feet of the Lord and spoke as follows.

TEXT 263

'কৃষ্ণতত্ত্ব', 'রাধাতত্ত্ব', 'প্রেমতত্ত্বসার' ।
'রসতত্ত্ব' 'লীলাতত্ত্ব' বিবিধ প্রকার ॥ ২৬৩ ॥

'kṛṣṇa-tattva', 'rādhā-tattva', 'prema-tattva-sāra'
'rasa-tattva' 'līlā-tattva' vividha prakāra

SYNONYMS

kṛṣṇa-tattva—the truth about Kṛṣṇa; *rādhā-tattva*—the truth about Rādhā; *prema-tattva-sāra*—the essence of Their loving affairs; *rasa-tattva*—the truth about transcendental mellow; *līlā-tattva*—the truth about the pastimes of the Lord; *vividha prakāra*—of different varieties.

TRANSLATION

"There is transcendental variety in talks about Kṛṣṇa and Rādhārāṇī and Their transcendental loving affairs, humors and pastimes."

TEXT 264

এত তত্ত্ব মোর চিত্তে কৈলে প্রকাশন ।
ব্রহ্মাকে বেদ যেন পড়াইল নারায়ণ ॥২৬৪ ॥

eta tattva mora citte kaile prakāśana
brahmāke veda yena paḍāila nārāyaṇa

SYNONYMS

eta tattva—all these varieties of truth; *mora citte*—in my heart; *kaile*—you did; *prakāśana*—manifesting; *brahmāke*—unto Lord Brahmā; *veda*—the Vedic knowledge; *yena*—as; *paḍāila*—taught; *nārāyaṇa*—the Supreme Lord.

TRANSLATION

Rāmānanda Rāya then admitted, "You have manifested many transcendental truths in my heart. This is exactly the way Nārāyaṇa educated Lord Brahmā."

PURPORT

The heart of Brahmā was enlightened by the Supreme Personality of Godhead. This is Vedic information given in the *Śvetāśvatara Upaniṣad* (6.18):

yo brahmāṇaṁ vidadhāti pūrvaṁ
yo vai vedāṁś ca prahiṇoti tasmai
taṁ ha devam ātma-buddhi-prakāśaṁ
mumukṣur vai śaraṇam ahaṁ prapadye

"Because I desire liberation, let me surrender unto the Supreme Personality of Godhead, who first enlightened Lord Brahmā in Vedic knowledge through Lord Brahmā's heart. The Lord is the original source of all enlightenment and spiritual advancement." In this connection there are other references given in *Śrīmad-Bhāgavatam* 2.9.30-35, 11.14.3, 12.4.40 and 12.13.19.

TEXT 265

অন্তর্যামী ঈশ্বরের এই রীতি হয়ে ।
বাহিরে না কহে, বস্তু প্রকাশে হৃদয়ে ॥ ২৬৫ ॥

antaryāmī īśvarera ei rīti haye
bāhire nā kahe, vastu prakāśe hṛdaye

SYNONYMS

antaryāmī—the Supersoul; *īśvarera*—of the Personality of Godhead; *ei*—this; *rīti*—the system; *haye*—is; *bāhire*—externally; *nā kahe*—does not speak; *vastu*—the facts; *prakāśe*—manifests; *hṛdaye*—within the heart.

TRANSLATION

Rāmānanda Rāya continued, "The Supersoul within everyone's heart speaks not externally but from within. He instructs the devotees in all respects, and that is His way of instruction."

PURPORT

Here Śrī Rāmānanda Rāya admits that Śrī Caitanya Mahāprabhu is the Supersoul. It is the Supersoul that inspires the devotee; therefore He is the original source of the *gāyatrī mantra.* In the *gāyatrī* it is stated: *oṁ bhūr bhuvaḥ svaḥ tat savitur vareṇyaṁ bhargo devasya dhīmahi dhiyo yo naḥ pracodayāt. Savitṛ* is the original source of all intelligence. That *savitṛ* is Lord Caitanya Mahāprabhu. This is confirmed in *Śrīmad-Bhāgavatam* (2.4.22):

pracoditā yena purā sarasvatī
vitanvatājasya satīṁ smṛtiṁ hṛdi
sva-lakṣaṇā prādurabhūt kilāsyataḥ
sa me ṛṣīṇām ṛṣabhaḥ prasīdatām

"May the Lord, who in the beginning of the creation amplified the potent knowledge of Brahmā from within his heart and inspired him with full knowledge of creation and His own self, and who appeared to be generated from the mouth of Brahmā, be pleased with me." This was spoken by Śukadeva Gosvāmī when he invoked the blessing of the Supreme Personality of Godhead before delivering *Śrīmad-Bhāgavatam* to Mahārāja Parīkṣit.

TEXT 266

জন্মাদ্যস্য যতোঽন্বয়াদিতরতশ্চার্থেষ্বভিজ্ঞঃ স্বরাট্
তেনে ব্রহ্ম হৃদা য আদিকবয়ে মুহ্যন্তি যৎ সূরয়ঃ ।
তেজোবারিমৃদাং যথা বিনিময়ো যত্র ত্রিসর্গোঽমৃষা
ধাম্না স্বেন সদা নিরস্তকুহকং সত্যং পরং ধীমহি ॥২৬৬॥

janmādy asya yato 'nvayād itarataś cārtheṣv abhijñaḥ svarāṭ
tene brahma hṛdā ya ādi-kavaye muhyanti yat sūrayaḥ
tejo-vāri-mṛdāṁ yathā vinimayo yatra tri-sargo 'mṛṣā
dhāmnā svena sadā nirasta-kuhakaṁ satyaṁ paraṁ dhīmahi

SYNONYMS

janma-ādi—creation, maintenance and dissolution; *asya*—of this (the universe); *yataḥ*—from whom; *anvayāt*—directly from the spiritual connection; *itarataḥ*—indirectly from the lack of material contact; *ca*—also; *artheṣu*—in all affairs; *abhijñaḥ*—perfectly cognizant; *sva-rāṭ*—independent; *tene*—imparted; *brahma*—the Absolute Truth; *hṛdā*—through the heart; *yaḥ*—who; *ādi-kavaye*—unto Lord Brahmā; *muhyanti*—are bewildered; *yat*—in whom; *sūrayaḥ*—great personalities like Lord Brahmā and other demigods or great *brāhmaṇas*; *tejaḥ-vāri-mṛdām*—of fire, water and earth; *yathā*—as; *vinimayaḥ*—the exchange; *yatra*—in whom; *tri-sargaḥ*—the material creation of three modes; *amṛṣā*—factual; *dhāmnā*—with the abode; *svena*—His own personal; *sadā*—always; *nirasta-kuhakam*—devoid of all illusion; *satyam*—the truth; *param*—absolute; *dhīmahi*—let us meditate upon.

TRANSLATION

" 'I offer my obeisances unto Lord Śrī Kṛṣṇa, son of Vasudeva, who is the supreme all-pervading Personality of Godhead. I meditate upon Him, the

transcendent reality, who is the primeval cause of all causes, from whom all manifested universes arise, in whom they dwell and by whom they are destroyed. I meditate upon that eternally effulgent Lord who is directly and indirectly conscious of all manifestations and yet is beyond them. It is He only who first imparted Vedic knowledge unto the heart of Brahmā, the first created being. Through Him this world, like a mirage, appears real even to great sages and demigods. Because of Him, the material universes, created by the three modes of nature, appear to be factual, although they are unreal. I meditate therefore upon Him, the Absolute Truth, who is eternally existent in His transcendental abode, and who is forever free of illusion.' "

PURPORT

This is the opening invocation of *Śrīmad-Bhāgavatam* (1.1.1).

TEXT 267

এক সংশয় মোর আছয়ে হৃদয়ে ।
কৃপা করি' কহ মোরে তাহার নিশ্চয়ে ॥ ২৬৭ ॥

eka saṁśaya mora āchaye hṛdaye
kṛpā kari' kaha more tāhāra niścaye

SYNONYMS

eka saṁśaya—one doubt; *mora*—my; *āchaye*—there is; *hṛdaye*—in the heart; *kṛpā kari'*—being merciful; *kaha*—please say; *more*—unto me; *tāhāra*—of that; *niścaye*—the ascertainment.

TRANSLATION

Rāmānanda Rāya then said that he had but one doubt within his heart, and he petitioned the Lord, "Please be merciful upon me and just remove my doubt."

TEXT 268

পহিলে দেখিলুঁ তোমার সন্ন্যাসি-স্বরূপ ।
এবে তোমা দেখি মুঞি শ্যাম-গোপরূপ ॥ ২৬৮ ॥

pahile dekhiluṅ tomāra sannyāsi-svarūpa
ebe tomā dekhi muñi śyāma-gopa-rūpa

SYNONYMS

pahile—in the beginning; *dekhiluṅ*—I saw; *tomāra*—Your; *sannyāsi-svarūpa*—form as a person in the renounced order; *ebe*—now; *tomā*—You; *dekhi*—see; *muñi*—I; *śyāma-gopa-rūpa*—form as Śyāmasundara, the cowherd boy.

TRANSLATION

Rāmānanda Rāya then told Lord Śrī Caitanya Mahāprabhu: "At first I saw You appear like a sannyāsī, but now I am seeing You as Śyāmasundara, the cowherd boy.

TEXT 269

তোমার সম্মুখে দেখি কাঞ্চন-পঞ্চালিকা।
তাঁর গৌরকান্ত্যে তোমার সর্ব অঙ্গ ঢাকা॥ ২৬৯ ॥

tomāra sammukhe dekhi kāñcana-pañcālikā
tāṅra gaura-kāntye tomāra sarva aṅga ḍhākā

SYNONYMS

tomāra—of You; *sammukhe*—in front; *dekhi*—I see; *kāñcana-pañcālikā*—a doll made of gold; *tāṅra*—of it; *gaura-kāntye*—by a white complexion; *tomāra*—Your; *sarva*—all; *aṅga*—body; *ḍhākā*—covering.

TRANSLATION

"I now see You appearing like a golden doll, and Your entire body appears covered by a golden luster.

PURPORT

Śyāmasundara is blackish, but here Rāmānanda Rāya says that he saw Śrī Caitanya Mahāprabhu appear golden. The lustrous body of Śrī Caitanya Mahāprabhu was covered by the bodily complexion of Śrīmatī Rādhārāṇī.

TEXT 270

তাহাতে প্রকট দেখোঁ স-বংশী বদন।
নানা ভাবে চঞ্চল তাহে কমল-নয়ন ॥ ২৭০ ॥

tāhāte prakaṭa dekhoṅ sa-vaṁśī vadana
nānā bhāve cañcala tāhe kamala-nayana

SYNONYMS

tāhāte—in that; *prakaṭa*—manifested; *dekhoṅ*—I see; *sa-vaṁśī*—with the flute; *vadana*—the face; *nānā bhāve*—in various modes; *cañcala*—restless; *tāhe*—in that; *kamala-nayana*—the lotus eyes.

TRANSLATION

"I see that You are holding a flute to Your mouth, and Your lotus eyes are moving very restlessly due to various ecstasies.

TEXT 271

এইমত তোমা দেখি' হয় চমৎকার ।
অকপটে কহ, প্রভু, কারণ ইহার ॥ ২৭১ ॥

ei-mata tomā dekhi' haya camatkāra
akapaṭe kaha, prabhu, kāraṇa ihāra

SYNONYMS

ei-mata—in this way; *tomā*—You; *dekhi'*—seeing; *haya*—there is; *camatkāra*—wonder; *akapaṭe*—without duplicity; *kaha*—please tell; *prabhu*—my Lord; *kāraṇa*—the cause; *ihāra*—of this.

TRANSLATION

"I actually see You in this way, and this is very wonderful. My Lord, please tell me without duplicity what is causing this."

TEXT 272

প্রভু কহে,—কৃষ্ণে তোমার গাঢ়প্রেম হয় ।
প্রেমার স্বভাব এই জানিহ নিশ্চয় ॥ ২৭২ ॥

prabhu kahe,——kṛṣṇe tomāra gāḍha-prema haya
premāra svabhāva ei jāniha niścaya

SYNONYMS

prabhu kahe—the Lord replied; *kṛṣṇe*—unto Kṛṣṇa; *tomāra*—your; *gāḍha-prema*—deep love; *haya*—there is; *premāra*—of such transcendental love; *sva-bhāva*—the nature; *ei*—this; *jāniha*—please know; *niścaya*—certainly.

TRANSLATION

Lord Śrī Caitanya Mahāprabhu replied, "You have a deep love for Kṛṣṇa, and one who has such deep ecstatic love for the Lord naturally sees things in such a way. Please take this from Me to be certain.

TEXT 273

মহাভাগবত দেখে স্থাবর-জঙ্গম ।
তাহাঁ তাহাঁ হয় তাঁর শ্রীকৃষ্ণ-স্ফুরণ ॥ ২৭৩ ॥

mahā-bhāgavata dekhe sthāvara-jaṅgama
tāhāṅ tāhāṅ haya tāṅra śrī-kṛṣṇa-sphuraṇa

SYNONYMS

mahā-bhāgavata—a first-class advanced devotee; *dekhe*—sees; *sthāvara-jaṅgama*—the movable and inert; *tāhāṅ tāhāṅ*—here and there; *haya*—is; *tāṅra*—his; *śrī-kṛṣṇa-sphuraṇa*—manifestation of Lord Kṛṣṇa.

TRANSLATION

"A devotee advanced on the spiritual platform sees everything movable and inert as the Supreme Lord. For him, everything he sees here and there is but the manifestation of Lord Kṛṣṇa.

TEXT 274

স্থাবর-জঙ্গম দেখে, না দেখে তার মূর্তি ।
সর্বত্র হয় নিজ ইষ্টদেব-স্ফূর্তি ॥ ২৭৪ ॥

sthāvara-jaṅgama dekhe, nā dekhe tāra mūrti
sarvatra haya nija iṣṭa-deva-sphūrti

SYNONYMS

sthāvara-jaṅgama—movable and inert; *dekhe*—he sees; *nā*—not; *dekhe*—sees; *tāra*—its; *mūrti*—form; *sarvatra*—everywhere; *haya*—there is; *nija*—his own; *iṣṭa-deva*—worshipable Lord; *sphūrti*—manifestation.

TRANSLATION

"The mahā-bhāgavata, the advanced devotee, certainly sees everything mobile and immobile, but he does not exactly see their forms. Rather, everywhere he immediately sees manifest the form of the Supreme Lord."

PURPORT

Due to his deep ecstatic love for Kṛṣṇa, the *mahā-bhāgavata* sees Kṛṣṇa everywhere and nothing else. This is confirmed in *Brahma-saṁhitā* (5.38): *premāñjana-cchurita-bhakti-vilocanena santaḥ sadaiva hṛdayeṣu vilokayanti.*

As soon as a devotee sees something—be it movable or inert—he immediately remembers Kṛṣṇa. An advanced devotee is advanced in knowledge. This knowledge is very natural to a devotee, for he has already read in *Bhagavad-gītā* how to awaken Kṛṣṇa consciousness. According to *Bhagavad-gītā:*

raso 'ham apsu kaunteya
prabhāsmi śaśi-sūryayoḥ
praṇavaḥ sarva-vedeṣu
śabdaḥ khe pauruṣaṁ nṛṣu

"O son of Kuntī [Arjuna], I am the taste of water, the light of the sun and the moon, the syllable *om* in the Vedic *mantras*; I am the sound in ether and ability in man." (Bg. 7.8)

Thus when a devotee drinks water or any other liquid, he immediately remembers Kṛṣṇa. For a devotee there is no difficulty in awakening Kṛṣṇa consciousness twenty-four hours a day. It is therefore said:

sthāvara jaṅgama dekhe nā dekhe tāra mūrti
sarvatra haya nija iṣṭa-deva-sphūrti

A saintly person, an advanced devotee, sees Kṛṣṇa twenty-four hours a day and nothing else. As far as movable and inert things are concerned, a devotee sees them all as transformations of Kṛṣṇa's energy. As stated in *Bhagavad-gītā*:

bhūmir āpo 'nalo vāyuḥ
khaṁ mano buddhir eva ca
ahaṅkāra itīyaṁ me
bhinnā prakṛtir aṣṭadhā

"Earth, water, fire, air, ether, mind, intelligence and false ego—all together these eight comprise My separated material energies." (Bg. 7.4)

Actually nothing is separate from Kṛṣṇa. When a devotee sees a tree, he knows that the tree is a combination of two energies—material and spiritual. The inferior energy, which is material, forms the body of the tree; however, within the tree is the living entity, the spiritual spark, which is part and parcel of Kṛṣṇa. This is the superior energy of Kṛṣṇa within this world. Whatever living thing we see is simply a combination of these two energies. When an advanced devotee thinks of these energies, he immediately understands that they are manifestations of the Supreme Lord. As soon as we see the sun rise in the morning, we arise and set about doing our morning duties. Similarly, as soon as a devotee sees the energy of the Lord, he immediately remembers Lord Śrī Kṛṣṇa. This is explained in this verse:

sarvatra haya nija iṣṭa-deva-sphūrti

A devotee who has purified his existence through devotional service sees only Kṛṣṇa in every step of life. This is also explained in the next verse, which is a quotation from *Śrīmad-Bhāgavatam* (11.2.45).

TEXT 275

সর্বভূতেষু যঃ পশ্যেদ্ভগবদ্ভাবমাত্মনঃ ।
ভূতানি ভগবত্যাত্মন্যেষ ভাগবতোত্তমঃ ॥ ২৭৫ ॥

sarva-bhūteṣu yaḥ paśyed
bhagavad-bhāvam ātmanaḥ
bhūtāni bhagavaty ātmany
eṣa bhāgavatottamaḥ

SYNONYMS

sarva-bhūteṣu—in all objects (in matter, spirit, and combinations of matter and spirit); *yaḥ*—anyone who; *paśyet*—sees; *bhagavat-bhāvam*—the ability to be engaged in the service of the Lord; *ātmanaḥ*—of the supreme spirit soul or the transcendence beyond the material conception of life; *bhūtāni*—all beings; *bhagavati*—in the Supreme Personality of Godhead; *ātmani*—the basic principle of all existence; *eṣaḥ*—this; *bhāgavata-uttamaḥ*—a person advanced in devotional service.

TRANSLATION

Śrī Caitanya Mahāprabhu continued, " 'A person advanced in devotional service sees within everything the soul of souls, the Supreme Personality of Godhead, Śrī Kṛṣṇa. Consequently he always sees the form of the Supreme Personality of Godhead as the cause of all causes and understands that all things are situated in Him.'

TEXT 276

বনলতাস্তরব আত্মনি বিষ্ণুং ব্যঞ্জয়ন্ত্য ইব পুষ্পফলাঢ্যাঃ ।
প্রণতভারবিটপা মধুধারাঃ প্রেমহৃষ্টতনবো ববৃষুঃ স্ম ॥২৭৬॥

vana-latās tarava ātmani viṣṇuṁ
vyañjayantya iva puṣpa-phalāḍhyāḥ
praṇata-bhāra-viṭapā madhu-dhārāḥ
prema-hṛṣṭa-tanavo vavṛṣuḥ sma

SYNONYMS

vana-latāḥ—the herbs and plants; *taravaḥ*—the trees; *ātmani*—in the Supreme Soul; *viṣṇum*—the Supreme Personality of Godhead; *vyañjayantyaḥ*—manifesting; *iva*—like; *puṣpa-phala-āḍhyāḥ*—filled with luxuriant fruits and flowers; *praṇata-bhāra*—bowed down because of loads; *viṭapāḥ*—the trees; *madhu-dhārāḥ*—showers; *prema-hṛṣṭa*—inspired by love of Godhead; *tanavaḥ*—whose bodies; *vavṛṣuḥ*—constantly rained; *sma*—certainly.

TRANSLATION

" 'The plants, creepers and trees were full of fruits and flowers due to ecstatic love of Kṛṣṇa. Indeed, being so full, they were bowing down. They were inspired by such deep love for Kṛṣṇa that they were constantly pouring showers of honey. In this way the gopīs saw all the forest of Vṛndāvana.' "

PURPORT

This verse (*Bhāg.* 10.35.9) is one of the songs the *gopīs* sang during Kṛṣṇa's absence. In Kṛṣṇa's absence the *gopīs* were always absorbed in thought of Him. Similarly, the *bhāgavata,* the advanced devotee, sees everything as potentially serving the Lord. Śrīla Rūpa Gosvāmī recommends:

prāpañcikatayā buddhyā
hari-sambandhi-vastunaḥ
mumukṣubhiḥ parityāgo
vairāgyaṁ phalgu kathyate
(*Bhakti-rasāmṛta-sindhu,* 1.2.126)

The advanced devotee does not see anything that is not connected with Kṛṣṇa. Unlike the Māyāvādī philosophers, a devotee does not see the material world as false. Rather, he sees everything in the material world connected to Kṛṣṇa. A devotee knows how to utilize such things in the service of the Lord, and this is characteristic of the *mahā-bhāgavata.* The *gopīs* saw the plants, creepers and forest trees loaded with fruits and flowers and ready to serve Kṛṣṇa. In this way they immediately remembered their worshipable Lord Śrī Kṛṣṇa. They did not simply see plants, creepers and trees the way a mundaner sees them.

TEXT 277

রাধাকৃষ্ণে তোমার মহাপ্রেম হয়।
যাহাঁ তাহাঁ রাধাকৃষ্ণ তোমারে স্ফুরয় ॥ ২৭৭ ॥

rādhā-kṛṣṇe tomāra mahā-prema haya
yāhāṅ tāhāṅ rādhā-kṛṣṇa tomāre sphuraya

SYNONYMS

rādhā-kṛṣṇe—unto Rādhā and Kṛṣṇa; *tomāra*—your; *mahā-prema*—great love; *haya*—there is; *yāhāṅ tāhāṅ*—anywhere and everywhere; *rādhā-kṛṣṇa*—Lord Kṛṣṇa and Śrīmatī Rādhārāṇī; *tomāre*—unto you; *sphuraya*—appear.

TRANSLATION

Lord Caitanya Mahāprabhu continued, "My dear Rāya, you are an advanced devotee and are always filled with ecstatic love for Rādhā and Kṛṣṇa. Therefore whatever you see—anywhere and everywhere—simply awakens your Kṛṣṇa consciousness."

TEXT 278

রায় কহে,—প্রভু তুমি ছাড় ভারিভুরি ।
মোর আগে নিজরূপ না করিহ চুরি ॥ ২৭৮ ॥

rāya kahe,——prabhu tumi chāḍa bhāri-bhūri
mora āge nija-rūpa nā kariha curi

SYNONYMS

rāya kahe—Rāmānanda Rāya replied; *prabhu*—my Lord; *tumi*—You; *chāḍa*—give up; *bhāri-bhūri*—these grave talks; *mora*—of me; *āge*—in front; *nija-rūpa*—Your real form; *nā*—not; *kariha*—do; *curi*—stealing.

TRANSLATION

Rāmānanda Rāya replied, "My dear Lord, please give up all these serious talks. Please do not conceal Your real form from me."

TEXT 279

রাধিকার ভাবকান্তি করি' অঙ্গীকার ।
নিজরস আস্বাদিতে করিয়াছ অবতার ॥ ২৭৯ ॥

rādhikāra bhāva-kānti kari' aṅgīkāra
nija-rasa āsvādite kariyācha avatāra

SYNONYMS

rādhikāra—of Śrīmatī Rādhārāṇī; *bhāva-kānti*—ecstatic love and luster; *kari'*—making; *aṅgīkāra*—acceptance; *nija-rasa*—Your own transcendental mellow; *āsvādite*—to taste; *kariyācha*—You have made; *avatāra*—incarnation.

TRANSLATION

Rāmānanda Rāya continued, "My dear Lord, I can understand that You have assumed the ecstasy and bodily complexion of Śrīmatī Rādhārāṇī. By accepting this, You are tasting Your own personal transcendental humor and have therefore appeared as Śrī Caitanya Mahāprabhu.

TEXT 280

নিজগূঢ়কার্য তোমার—প্রেম আস্বাদন ।
আনুষঙ্গে প্রেমময় কৈলে ত্রিভুবন ॥ ২৮০ ॥

nija-gūḍha-kārya tomāra——prema āsvādana
ānuṣaṅge prema-maya kaile tribhuvana

SYNONYMS

nija-gūḍha-kārya—own confidential business; *tomāra*—Your; *prema*—transcendental love; *āsvādana*—tasting; *ānuṣaṅge*—simultaneously; *prema-maya*—transformed into love of God; *kaile*—You have made; *tri-bhuvana*—all the world.

TRANSLATION

"My dear Lord, You have descended in this incarnation of Lord Caitanya for Your own personal reasons. You have come to taste Your own spiritual bliss, and at the same time You are transforming the whole world by spreading the ecstasy of love of Godhead.

TEXT 281

আপনে আইলে মোরে করিতে উদ্ধার ।
এবে কপট কর,—তোমার কোন ব্যবহার ॥ ২৮১ ॥

āpane āile more karite uddhāra
ebe kapaṭa kara,——tomāra kona vyavahāra

SYNONYMS

āpane—personally; *āile*—You have come; *more*—unto me; *karite*—to make; *uddhāra*—deliverance; *ebe*—now; *kapaṭa*—duplicity; *kara*—You do; *tomāra*—Your; *kona*—what; *vyavahāra*—behavior.

TRANSLATION

"My dear Lord, by Your causeless mercy You have appeared before me to grant me liberation. Now You are playing in a duplicitous way. What is the reason for this behavior?"

TEXT 282

তবে হাসি' তাঁরে প্রভু দেখাইল স্বরূপ ।
'রসরাজ', 'মহাভাব'—দুই এক রূপ ॥ ২৮২ ॥

tabe hāsi' tāṅre prabhu dekhāila svarūpa
'rasa-rāja', 'mahābhāva'——dui eka rūpa

SYNONYMS

tabe—therefore; *hāsi'*—smiling; *tāṅre*—unto him (Rāmānanda Rāya); *prabhu*—the Lord; *dekhāila*—showed; *svarūpa*—His personal form; *rasa-rāja*—the king of all transcendental humors; *mahā-bhāva*—the condition of ecstatic love; *dui*—two; *eka*—one; *rūpa*—form.

TRANSLATION

Lord Śrī Kṛṣṇa is the reservoir of all pleasure, and Śrīmatī Rādhārāṇī is the personification of ecstatic love of Godhead. These two forms combined as one in Śrī Caitanya Mahāprabhu. This being the case, Lord Śrī Caitanya Mahāprabhu revealed His real form to Rāmānanda Rāya.

PURPORT

This is described as *rādhā-bhāva-dyuti-suvalitaṁ naumi kṛṣṇa-svarūpam.* Lord Śrī Kṛṣṇa was absorbed in the features of Śrīmatī Rādhārāṇī. This was disclosed to Rāmānanda Rāya when he saw Lord Śrī Caitanya Mahāprabhu. An advanced devotee can understand *śrī-kṛṣṇa-caitanya, rādhā-kṛṣṇa nahe anya.* Śrī Caitanya Mahāprabhu, being a combination of Kṛṣṇa and Rādhā, is nondifferent from Rādhā-Kṛṣṇa combined. This is explained by Svarūpa Dāmodara Gosvāmī:

rādhā kṛṣṇa-praṇaya-vikṛtir hlādinī śaktir asmād
ekātmānāv api bhuvi purā deha-bhedaṁ gatau tau
caitanyākhyaṁ prakaṭam adhunā tad-dvayaṁ caikyam āptaṁ
rādhā-bhāva-dyuti-suvalitaṁ naumi kṛṣṇa-svarūpam
(Cc. *Ādi* 1.5)

Rādha-Kṛṣṇa is one. Rādhā-Kṛṣṇa is Kṛṣṇa and Kṛṣṇa's pleasure potency combined. When Kṛṣṇa exhibits His pleasure potency, He appears to be two—Rādhā and Kṛṣṇa. Otherwise, both Rādhā and Kṛṣṇa are one. This oneness may be perceived by advanced devotees through the grace of Śrī Caitanya Mahāprabhu. This was the case with Rāmānanda Rāya, and such realization is possible for the advanced devotee. One may aspire to attain such a position, but one should not try to imitate the *maha-bhāgavata.*

TEXT 283

দেখি' রামানন্দ হৈলা আনন্দে মূর্চ্ছিতে ।
ধরিতে না পারে দেহ, পড়িলা ভূমিতে ॥ ২৮৩ ॥

dekhi' rāmānanda hailā ānande mūrcchite
dharite nā pāre deha, paḍilā bhūmite

SYNONYMS

dekhi'—seeing this form; *rāmānanda*—Rāmānanda Rāya; *hailā*—there was; *ānande*—in ecstasy; *mūrcchite*—fainting; *dharite*—to hold him; *nā*—not; *pāre*—able; *deha*—the body; *paḍilā*—fell down; *bhūmite*—on the ground.

TRANSLATION

Upon seeing this form, Rāmānanda Rāya almost lost consciousness in transcendental bliss. Unable to remain standing, he fell to the ground.

TEXT 284

প্রভু তাঁরে হস্ত স্পর্শি' করাইলা চেতন ।
সন্ন্যাসীর বেষ দেখি' বিস্মিত হৈল মন ॥ ২৮৪ ॥

prabhu tāṅre hasta sparśi' karāilā cetana
sannyāsīra veṣa dekhi' vismita haila mana

SYNONYMS

prabhu—the Lord; *tāṅre*—unto Rāmānanda Rāya; *hasta*—the hand; *sparśi'*—touching; *karāilā*—made; *cetana*—conscious; *sannyāsīra*—of the *sannyāsī*; *veṣa*—the dress; *dekhi'*—seeing; *vismita*—struck with wonder; *haila*—became; *mana*—the mind.

TRANSLATION

When Rāmānanda Rāya fell to the ground unconscious, Caitanya Mahāprabhu touched his hand, and he immediately regained consciousness. However, when he saw Lord Caitanya in the dress of a sannyāsī, he was struck with wonder.

TEXT 285

আলিঙ্গন করি' প্রভু কৈল আশ্বাসন ।
তোমা বিনা এইরূপ না দেখে অন্যজন ॥ ২৮৫ ॥

āliṅgana kari' prabhu kaila āśvāsana
tomā vinā ei-rūpa nā dekhe anya-jana

SYNONYMS

āliṅgana kari'—embracing him; *prabhu*—the Lord; *kaila*—did; *āśvāsana*—pacifying; *tomā vinā*—but for you; *ei-rūpa*—this form; *nā*—not; *dekhe*—sees; *anya-jana*—anyone else.

TRANSLATION

After embracing Rāmānanda Rāya, the Lord pacified him, informing him, "But for you, no one has ever seen this form."

PURPORT

In *Bhagavad-gītā* it is stated:

nāhaṁ prakāśaḥ sarvasya
yoga-māyā-samāvṛtaḥ
mūḍho 'yaṁ nābhijānāti
loko mām ajam avyayam

"I am never manifest to the foolish and unintelligent. For them I am covered by My eternal creative potency [*yogamāyā*]; and so the deluded world knows Me not, who am unborn and infallible." (Bg. 7.25)

The Lord always reserves the right of not being exposed to everyone. The devotees, however, are always engaged in the service of the Lord, serving with the tongue by chanting the Hare Kṛṣṇa *mantra* and tasting *mahā-prasāda*. Gradually the sincere devotee pleases the Supreme Personality of Godhead, and the Supreme Lord reveals Himself. One cannot see the Supreme Lord by making personal efforts. Rather, when the Lord is pleased by the service of a devotee, He reveals Himself.

TEXT 286

মোর তত্ত্বলীলা-রস তোমার গোচরে ।
অতএব এইরূপ দেখাইলুঁ তোমারে ॥ ২৮৬ ॥

mora tattva-līlā-rasa tomāra gocare
ataeva ei-rūpa dekhāiluṅ tomāre

SYNONYMS

mora—My; *tattva-līlā*—truth and pastimes; *rasa*—and mellows; *tomāra*—of you; *gocare*—within the knowledge; *ataeva*—therefore; *ei-rūpa*—this form; *dekhāiluṅ*—I have shown; *tomāre*—unto you.

TRANSLATION

Śrī Caitanya Mahāprabhu confirmed, "All the truths about My pastimes and mellows are within your knowledge. Therefore I have shown this form to you.

TEXT 287

গৌর অঙ্গ নহে মোর—রাধাঙ্গ-স্পর্শন ।
গোপেন্দ্রসুত বিনা তেঁহো না স্পর্শে অন্যজন ॥২৮৭॥

gaura aṅga nahe mora——rādhāṅga-sparśana
gopendra-suta vinā teṅho nā sparśe anya-jana

SYNONYMS

gaura—white; *aṅga*—body; *nahe*—not; *mora*—My; *rādhā-aṅga*—of the body of Śrīmatī Rādhārāṇī; *sparśana*—the touching; *gopendra-suta*—the son of Nanda Mahārāja; *vinā*—except; *teṅho*—Śrīmatī Rādhārāṇī; *nā*—not; *sparśe*—touches; *anya-jana*—anyone else.

TRANSLATION

"Actually My body does not have a white complexion. It only appears so because it has touched the body of Śrīmatī Rādhārāṇī. However, She does not touch anyone but the son of Nanda Mahārāja.

TEXT 288

তাঁর ভাবে ভাবিত করি' আত্ম-মন ।
তবে নিজ-মাধুর্য করি আস্বাদন ॥ ২৮৮ ॥

tāṅra bhāve bhāvita kari' ātma-mana
tabe nija-mādhurya kari āsvādana

SYNONYMS

tāṅra—of Śrīmatī Rādhārāṇī; *bhāve*—in the ecstasy; *bhāvita*—enlightened; *kari'*—making; *ātma-mana*—body and mind; *tabe*—thereupon; *nija-mādhurya*—My own transcendental humor; *kari*—I do; *āsvādana*—tasting.

TRANSLATION

"I have now converted My body and mind into the ecstasy of Śrīmatī Rādhārāṇī; thus I am tasting My own personal sweetness in that form."

PURPORT

Gaurasundara here informed Śrī Rāmānanda Rāya, "My dear Rāmānanda Rāya, you were actually seeing a separate person with a white-complexioned body. Actually I am not white. Being Śrī Kṛṣṇa, the son of Nanda Mahārāja, I am blackish, but when I come in touch with Śrīmatī Rādhārāṇī I become white complexioned eternally. Śrīmatī Rādhārāṇī does not touch the body of anyone but Kṛṣṇa. I taste My own transcendental features by accepting the complexion of Śrīmatī Rādhārāṇī. Without Rādhārāṇī, one cannot taste the transcendental pleasure of Kṛṣṇa's conjugal love." In this regard, Śrīla Bhaktisiddhānta Sarasvatī Ṭhākura comments on the *prākṛta-sahajiyā-sampradāya,* which considers Kṛṣṇa and Lord Caitanya to possess different bodies. They misinterpret the words *gaura aṅga nahe mora* mentioned herein. From this verse we can understand that Lord Caitanya Mahāprabhu is nondifferent from Kṛṣṇa. Both are the same Supreme Personality of Godhead. In the form of Kṛṣṇa, the Lord enjoys spiritual bliss and remains the shelter of all devotees, *viṣaya-vigraha.* Kṛṣṇa in His Gaurāṅga feature tastes separation from Kṛṣṇa in the ecstasy of Śrīmatī Rādhārāṇī. This ecstatic form is Śrī Kṛṣṇa Caitanya. Śrī Kṛṣṇa is always the transcendental reservoir of all pleasure, and He is technically called *dhīra-lalita.* Rādhārāṇī is the embodiment of spiritual energy, personified as ecstatic love for Kṛṣṇa; therefore only Kṛṣṇa can touch Śrīmatī Rādhārāṇī. The *dhīra-lalita* aspect is not seen in any other form of the Lord, neither in Viṣṇu nor in Nārāyaṇa. Śrīmatī Rādhārāṇī is therefore known as Govinda-nandinī and Govinda-mohinī, for She is the only source of transcendental pleasure for Śrī Kṛṣṇa. Indeed, She is the only person who can enchant His mind.

TEXT 289

তোমার ঠাঞি আমার কিছু গুপ্ত নাহি কর্ম।
লুকাইলে প্রেম-বলে জান সর্বমর্ম ॥ ২৮৯ ॥

tomāra ṭhāñi āmāra kichu gupta nāhi karma
lukāile prema-bale jāna sarva-marma

SYNONYMS

tomāra ṭhāñi—before you; *āmāra*—My; *kichu*—anything; *gupta*—hidden; *nāhi*—is not; *karma*—action; *lukāile*—even if I conceal; *prema-bale*—by the force of your love; *jāna*—you know; *sarva-marma*—everything in detail.

TRANSLATION

Lord Caitanya Mahāprabhu then admitted to His pure devotee, Rāmānanda Rāya, "Now there is no confidential activity unknown to you. Even though I try to conceal My activities, you can understand everything in detail by virtue of your advanced love for Me."

TEXT 290

গুপ্তে রাখিহ, কাহাঁ না করিও প্রকাশ ।
আমার বাতুল-চেষ্টা লোকে উপহাস ॥ ২৯০ ॥

gupte rākhiha, kāhāṅ nā kario prakāśa
āmāra bātula-ceṣṭā loke upahāsa

SYNONYMS

gupte—in secret; *rākhiha*—keep; *kāhāṅ*—anywhere; *nā*—not; *kario*—make; *prakāśa*—exposure; *āmāra*—My; *bātula-ceṣṭā*—activities like a madman; *loke*—among the general people; *upahāsa*—laughter.

TRANSLATION

The Lord then requested Rāmānanda Rāya: "Keep all these talks a secret. Please do not expose them anywhere and everywhere. Since My activities appear to be like those of a madman, people may take them lightly and laugh."

TEXT 291

আমি—এক বাতুল, তুমি—দ্বিতীয় বাতুল ।
অতএব তোমায় আমায় হই সমতুল ॥ ২৯১ ॥

āmi——eka bātula, tumi——dvitīya bātula
ataeva tomāya āmāya ha-i sama-tula

SYNONYMS

āmi—I; *eka*—one; *bātula*—madman; *tumi*—you; *dvitīya*—second; *bātula*—madman; *ataeva*—therefore; *tomāya*—you; *āmāya*—Me; *ha-i*—are; *sama-tula*—on an equal level.

TRANSLATION

Caitanya Mahāprabhu then said, "Indeed, I am a madman, and you are also a madman. Therefore both of us are on the same platform."

PURPORT

All these conversations between Rāmānanda Rāya and Śrī Caitanya Mahāprabhu appear ludicrous to a common man who is not a devotee. The entire world is filled with material conceptions, and people are unable to understand these conversations due to the conditioning of mundane philosophy. Those who are overly attached to mundane activities cannot understand the ecstatic conversations between Rāmānanda Rāya and Caitanya Mahāprabhu. Consequently the Lord requested that Rāmānanda Rāya keep all these conversations secret and not expose them to the general populace. If one is actually advanced in Kṛṣṇa consciousness, he can understand these confidential talks; otherwise they appear crazy. Śrī Caitanya Mahāprabhu therefore informed Rāmānanda Rāya that they both appeared as madmen and were therefore on the same platform. It is confirmed in *Bhagavad-gītā*:

yā niśā sarva-bhūtānāṁ
tasyāṁ jāgarti saṁyamī
yasyāṁ jāgrati bhūtāni
sā niśā paśyato muneḥ

"What is night for all beings is the time of awakening for the self-controlled; and the time of awakening for all beings is night for the introspective sage." (Bg. 2.69)

Sometimes Kṛṣṇa consciousness appears like a type of madness to mundane people, just as the activities of mundaners are considered a form of madness by Kṛṣṇa conscious men.

TEXT 292

এইরূপ দশরাত্রি রামানন্দ-সঙ্গে ।
সুখে গোঙাইলা প্রভু কৃষ্ণকথা-রঙ্গে ॥ ২৯২ ॥

ei-rūpa daśa-rātri rāmānanda-saṅge
sukhe goṅāilā prabhu kṛṣṇa-kathā-raṅge

SYNONYMS

ei-rūpa—in this way; *daśa-rātri*—ten nights; *rāmānanda saṅge*—with Śrī Rāmānanda Rāya; *sukhe*—in great happiness; *goṅāilā*—passed; *prabhu*—Lord Śrī Caitanya Mahāprabhu; *kṛṣṇa-kathā-raṅge*—in transcendental pleasure by discussing talks of Kṛṣṇa.

TRANSLATION

For ten nights Lord Caitanya Mahāprabhu and Rāmānanda Rāya spent a happy time discussing the pastimes of Kṛṣṇa.

TEXT 293

নিগূঢ় ব্রজের রস-লীলার বিচার ।
অনেক কহিল, তার না পাইল পার ॥ ২৯৩ ॥

nigūḍha vrajera rasa-līlāra vicāra
aneka kahila, tāra nā pāila pāra

SYNONYMS

nigūḍha—very confidential; *vrajera*—of Vṛndāvana, or Vrajabhūmi; *rasa-līlāra*—of the pastimes of conjugal love between Kṛṣṇa and the *gopīs*; *vicāra*—consideration; *aneka*—various; *kahila*—spoke; *tāra*—of that; *nā*—not; *pāila*—got; *pāra*—the limit.

TRANSLATION

The conversations between Rāmānanda Rāya and Śrī Caitanya Mahāprabhu contain the most confidential subject matters touching the conjugal love between Rādhā and Kṛṣṇa in Vṛndāvana [Vrajabhūmi]. Although both talked at great length about these pastimes, they could not reach the limit of discussion.

TEXT 294

তামা, কাঁসা, রূপা, সোনা, রত্নচিন্তামণি ।
কেহ যদি কাহাঁ পোতা পায় একখানি ॥ ২৯৪ ॥

tāmā, kāṅsā, rūpā, sonā, ratna-cintāmaṇi
keha yadi kāhāṅ potā pāya eka-khāni

SYNONYMS

tāmā—copper; *kāṅsā*—bell metal; *rūpā*—silver; *sonā*—gold; *ratna-cintāmaṇi*—the best of all metals, touchstone; *keha*—somebody; *yadi*—if; *kāhāṅ*—somewhere; *potā*—buried; *pāya*—finds; *eka-khāni*—in one place.

TRANSLATION

Actually these conversations are like a great mine wherefrom one can extract all kinds of metal—copper, bell metal, silver, gold, base metals and all others. They are like a touchstone buried in one place.

PURPORT

Śrīla Bhaktivinoda Ṭhākura gives the following summary of the conversations between Rāmānanda Rāya and Śrī Caitanya Mahāprabhu. Rāmānanda Rāya replied to five questions of Śrī Caitanya Mahāprabhu, stated in verses 57-67. The first answer is compared to copper, and the fifth answer is most valuable because it deals with unalloyed devotion, the ultimate goal of devotional life, and illuminates the preceding four subordinate answers.

Śrīla Bhaktisiddhānta Sarasvatī Ṭhākura points out that in Vrajabhūmi there is the Yamunā River with its sandy banks. There are *kadamba* trees, cows, Kṛṣṇa's sticks with which He herds cows, and Kṛṣṇa's flute. All of these belong to the *śānta-rasa,* the mellow of neutrality in devotional service. There are also the direct servants of Kṛṣṇa named Citraka, Patraka and Raktaka, and these are the embodiments of service in the mellow of servitude. There are also friends like Śrīdāmā, Sudāmā and others who embody service in fraternity. Nanda Mahārāja and mother Yaśodā are the embodiments of paternal love. Above all of these is Śrīmatī Rādhārāṇī and Her assistants, the *gopīs* Lalitā, Viśākhā and others. In this way all five mellows—*śānta, dāsya, sakhya, vātsalya* and *mādhurya*—exist eternally. They are also compared to metals like copper, bell metal, silver, gold and touchstone. Śrīla Kavirāja Gosvāmī therefore refers to a metal mine eternally existing in Vṛndāvana, Vrajabhūmi.

TEXT 295

ক্রমে উঠাইতে সেহ উত্তম বস্তু পায় ।
ঐছে প্রশ্নোত্তর কৈল প্রভু-রামরায় ॥ ২৯৫ ॥

krame uṭhāite seha uttama vastu pāya
aiche praśnottara kaila prabhu-rāmarāya

SYNONYMS

krame—gradually; *uṭhāite*—to raise; *seha*—that person; *uttama*—best; *vastu*—metal; *pāya*—gets; *aiche*—so also; *praśna-uttara*—the questions and answers; *kaila*—have done; *prabhu*—Śrī Caitanya Mahāprabhu; *rāma-rāya*—and Rāmānanda Rāya.

TRANSLATION

Both Śrī Caitanya Mahāprabhu and Rāmānanda Rāya worked like miners, excavating all kinds of valuable metals, each one better than the other. Their questions and answers are exactly like that.

TEXT 296

আর দিন রায়-পাশে বিদায় মাগিলা ।
বিদায়ের কালে তাঁরে এই আজ্ঞা দিলা ॥ ২৯৬ ॥

āra dina rāya-pāśe vidāya māgilā
vidāyera kāle tāṅre ei ājñā dilā

SYNONYMS

āra dina—the next day; *rāya-pāśe*—before Rāmānanda Rāya; *vidāya māgilā*—begged farewell; *vidāyera kāle*—at the time of departure; *tāṅre*—unto him; *ei*—this; *ājñā*—order; *dilā*—gave.

TRANSLATION

The next day Śrī Caitanya Mahāprabhu begged Rāmānanda Rāya to give Him permission to leave, and at the time of farewell the Lord gave him the following orders.

TEXT 297

বিষয় ছাড়িয়া তুমি যাহ নীলাচলে।
আমি তীর্থ করি' তাঁহা আসিব অল্পকালে ॥ ২৯৭॥

viṣaya chāḍiyā tumi yāha nīlācale
āmi tīrtha kari' tāṅhā āsiba alpa-kāle

SYNONYMS

viṣaya—material engagement; *chāḍiyā*—giving up; *tumi*—you; *yāha*—go; *nīlācale*—to Jagannātha Purī; *āmi*—I; *tīrtha kari'*—finishing My touring and pilgrimage; *tāṅhā*—there; *āsiba*—shall return; *alpa-kāle*—very soon.

TRANSLATION

Śrī Caitanya Mahāprabhu told him, "Give up all material engagements and come to Jagannātha Purī. I will return there very soon after finishing My tour and pilgrimage.

TEXT 298

দুইজনে নীলাচলে রহিব একসঙ্গে।
সুখে গোঙাইব কাল কৃষ্ণকথা-রঙ্গে ॥ ২৯৮ ॥

dui-jane nīlācale rahiba eka-saṅge
sukhe goṅāiba kāla kṛṣṇa-kathā-raṅge

SYNONYMS

dui-jane—both of us; *nīlācale*—at Jagannātha Purī; *rahiba*—shall stay; *eka-saṅge*—together; *sukhe*—in happiness; *goṅāiba*—shall pass; *kāla*—time; *kṛṣṇa-kathā-raṅge*—in the pleasure of discussing topics about Kṛṣṇa.

TRANSLATION

"The two of us shall remain together at Jagannātha Purī and happily pass our time discussing Kṛṣṇa."

TEXT 299

এত বলি' রামানন্দে করি' আলিঙ্গন।
তাঁরে ঘরে পাঠাইয়া করিল শয়ন ॥ ২৯৯ ॥

eta bali' rāmānande kari' āliṅgana
tāṅre ghare pāṭhāiyā karila śayana

SYNONYMS

eta bali'—saying this; *rāmānande*—to Śrī Rāmānanda Rāya; *kari'*—doing; *āliṅgana*—embracing; *tāṅre*—him; *ghare*—to his home; *pāṭhāiyā*—sending; *karila*—did; *śayana*—lying down.

TRANSLATION

Śrī Caitanya Mahāprabhu then embraced Śrī Rāmānanda Rāya, and after sending him back to his home, the Lord took rest.

TEXT 300

প্রাতঃকালে উঠি' প্রভু দেখি' হনুমান্।
তাঁরে নমস্করি' প্রভু দক্ষিণে করিলা প্রয়াণ ॥ ৩০০ ॥

prātaḥ-kāle uṭhi' prabhu dekhi' hanumān
tāṅre namaskari' prabhu dakṣiṇe karilā prayāṇa

SYNONYMS

prātaḥ-kāle—in the morning; *uṭhi'*—rising; *prabhu*—Lord Śrī Caitanya Mahāprabhu; *dekhi'*—visiting; *hanumān*—the village deity Hanumān; *tāṅre*—unto him; *namaskari'*—offering obeisances; *prabhu*—Śrī Caitanya Mahāprabhu; *dakṣiṇe*—to the south; *karilā*—made; *prayāṇa*—departure.

TRANSLATION

After rising from bed the next morning, Śrī Caitanya Mahāprabhu visited the local temple, where there was a deity of Hanumān. After offering him obeisances, the Lord departed for South India.

PURPORT

In almost all the cities and towns of India there are temples of Hanumānjī, the eternal servant of Lord Rāmacandra. There is even a temple of Hanumān near Govindajī temple in Vṛndāvana. Formerly this temple was in front of the Gopālajī temple, but that Deity Gopālajī went to Orissa to remain as Sākṣi-gopāla. Being the eternal servant of Lord Rāmacandra, Hanumānjī has been respectfully worshiped for many hundreds and thousands of years. Here even Lord Śrī Caitanya Mahāprabhu set the example in showing how one should offer respects to Hanumānjī.

TEXT 301

'বিদ্যাপুরে' নানা-মত লোক বৈসে যত ।
প্রভু-দর্শনে 'বৈষ্ণব' হৈল ছাড়ি' নিজমত ॥ ৩০১ ॥

'vidyāpūre' nānā-mata loka vaise yata
prabhu-darśane 'vaiṣṇava' haila chāḍi' nija-mata

SYNONYMS

vidyāpūre—in the town of Vidyānagara; *nānā-mata*—various opinions; *loka*—people; *vaise*—reside; *yata*—all; *prabhu-darśane*—in seeing Śrī Caitanya Mahāprabhu; *vaiṣṇava*—devotees of Lord Viṣṇu; *haila*—became; *chāḍi'*—giving up; *nija-mata*—own opinions.

TRANSLATION

All the residents of Vidyānagara were of different faiths, but after seeing Śrī Caitanya Mahāprabhu, they abandoned their own faiths and became Vaiṣṇavas.

TEXT 302

রামানন্দ হৈলা প্রভুর বিরহে বিহ্বল ।
প্রভুর ধ্যানে রহে বিষয় ছাড়িয়া সকল ॥ ৩০২ ॥

rāmānanda hailā prabhura virahe vihvala
prabhura dhyāne rahe viṣaya chāḍiyā sakala

SYNONYMS

rāmānanda—Śrīla Rāmānanda Rāya; *hailā*—became; *prabhura*—of Lord Śrī Caitanya Mahāprabhu; *virahe*—in separation; *vihvala*—overwhelmed; *prabhura dhyāne*—in meditation on Śrī Caitanya Mahāprabhu; *rahe*—remains; *viṣaya*—worldly business; *chāḍiyā*—giving up; *sakala*—all.

TRANSLATION

When Rāmānanda Rāya began to feel separation from Śrī Caitanya Mahāprabhu, he was overwhelmed. Meditating on the Lord, he gave up all his material business.

TEXT 303

সংক্ষেপে কহিলুঁ রামানন্দের মিলন।
বিস্তারি' বর্ণিতে নারে সহস্র-বদন ॥ ৩০৩ ॥

saṅkṣepe kahiluṅ rāmānandera milana
vistāri' varṇite nāre sahasra-vadana

SYNONYMS

saṅkṣepe—in brief; *kahiluṅ*—I have described; *rāmānandera milana*—meeting with Śrīla Rāmānanda Rāya; *vistāri'*—expanding; *varṇite*—to describe; *nāre*—not able; *sahasra-vadana*—Lord Śeṣa Nāga, who has thousands of hoods.

TRANSLATION

I have briefly described the meeting between Śrī Caitanya Mahāprabhu and Rāmānanda Rāya. No one can actually describe this meeting exhaustively. It is even impossible for Lord Śeṣa Nāga, who has thousands of hoods.

TEXT 304

সহজে চৈতন্যচরিত্র—ঘনদুগ্ধপূর।
রামানন্দ-চরিত্র তাহে খণ্ড প্রচুর ॥ ৩০৪ ॥

sahaje caitanya-caritra——ghana-dugdha-pūra
rāmānanda-caritra tāhe khaṇḍa pracura

SYNONYMS

sahaje—generally; *caitanya-caritra*—the activities of Śrī Caitanya Mahāprabhu; *ghana-dugdha-pūra*—like condensed milk; *rāmānanda-caritra*—the story of Rāmānanda Rāya; *tāhe*—in that; *khaṇḍa*—sugar candy; *pracura*—a large quantity.

TRANSLATION

The activities of Śrī Caitanya Mahāprabhu are like condensed milk, and the activities of Rāmānanda Rāya are like large quantities of sugar candy.

TEXT 305

রাধাকৃষ্ণলীলা—তাতে কর্পূর-মিলন।
ভাগ্যবান্ যেই, সেই করে আস্বাদন ॥ ৩০৫ ॥

rādhā-kṛṣṇa-līlā——tāte karpūra-milana
bhāgyavān yei, sei kare āsvādana

SYNONYMS

rādhā-kṛṣṇa-līlā—the pastimes of Śrī Rādhā and Kṛṣṇa; *tāte*—in that composition; *karpūra*—the camphor; *milana*—mixture; *bhāgyavān*—fortunate; *yei*—one who; *sei*—that person; *kare*—does; *āsvādana*—tasting.

TRANSLATION

Their meeting is exactly like a mixture of condensed milk and sugar candy. When they talk of the pastimes of Rādhā and Kṛṣṇa, camphor is added. If one tastes this combined preparation, he is most fortunate.

TEXT 306

যে ইহা একবার পিয়ে কর্ণদ্বারে।
তার কর্ণ লোভে ইহা ছাড়িতে না পারে ॥ ৩০৬ ॥

ye ihā eka-bāra piye karṇa-dvāre
tāra karṇa lobhe ihā chāḍite nā pāre

SYNONYMS

ye—anyone; *ihā*—this; *eka-bāra*—once; *piye*—drinks; *karṇa-dvāre*—through aural reception; *tāra*—his; *karṇa*—ears; *lobhe*—in greed; *ihā*—this; *chāḍite*—to give up; *nā*—not; *pāre*—are able.

TRANSLATION

This wonderful preparation has to be taken aurally. If one takes it, he becomes greedy to relish it even further.

TEXT 307

'রসতত্ত্ব-জ্ঞান' হয় ইহার শ্রবণে।
'প্রেমভক্তি' হয় রাধাকৃষ্ণের চরণে ॥ ৩০৭ ॥

'rasa-tattva-jñāna' haya ihāra śravaṇe
'prema-bhakti' haya rādhā-kṛṣṇera caraṇe

SYNONYMS

rasa-tattva-jñāna—transcendental knowledge of the humors of conjugal love of Rādhā and Kṛṣṇa; *haya*—is; *ihāra*—of this; *śravaṇe*—by hearing; *prema-bhakti*—pure love of Godhead; *haya*—becomes possible; *rādhā-kṛṣṇera caraṇe*—at the lotus feet of Rādhā and Kṛṣṇa.

TRANSLATION

By hearing talks between Rāmānanda Rāya and Śrī Caitanya Mahāprabhu, one is enlightened to the transcendental knowledge of the mellows of Rādhā and Kṛṣṇa's pastimes. Thus one can develop unalloyed love for the lotus feet of Rādhā and Kṛṣṇa.

TEXT 308

চৈতন্যের গূঢ়তত্ত্ব জানি ইহা হৈতে।
বিশ্বাস করি' শুন, তর্ক না করিহ চিত্তে ॥ ৩০৮ ॥

caitanyera gūḍha-tattva jāni ihā haite
viśvāsa kari' śuna, tarka nā kariha citte

SYNONYMS

caitanyera—of Lord Śrī Caitanya Mahāprabhu; *gūḍha-tattva*—the confidential truth; *jāni*—we can learn; *ihā haite*—from these talks; *viśvāsa kari'*—having firm faith; *śuna*—hear; *tarka*—arguments; *nā*—not; *kariha*—do; *citte*—within the heart.

TRANSLATION

The author requests every reader to hear these talks with faith and without argument. By studying them in this way, one will be able to understand the confidential truth of Śrī Caitanya Mahāprabhu.

TEXT 309

অলৌকিক লীলা এই পরম নিগূঢ়।
বিশ্বাসে পাইয়ে, তর্কে হয় বহুদূর ॥ ৩০৯ ॥

alaukika līlā ei parama nigūḍha
viśvāse pāiye, tarke haya bahu-dūra

SYNONYMS

alaukika—uncommon; *līlā*—pastimes; *ei*—this; *parama*—most; *nigūḍha*—confidential; *viśvāse*—by faith; *pāiye*—we can get; *tarke*—by argument; *haya*—is; *bahu-dūra*—far away.

TRANSLATION

This part of Śrī Caitanya Mahāprabhu's pastimes is most confidential. One can derive benefit quickly only by faith; otherwise by arguing one will always remain far away.

TEXT 310

শ্রীচৈতন্য-নিত্যানন্দ-অদ্বৈত-চরণ ।
যাঁহার সর্বস্ব, তাঁরে মিলে এই ধন ॥ ৩১০ ॥

śrī-caitanya-nityānanda-advaita-caraṇa
yāṅhāra sarvasva, tāṅre mile ei dhana

SYNONYMS

śrī-caitanya—of Lord Śrī Caitanya Mahāprabhu; *nityānanda*—of Lord Nityānanda; *advaita-caraṇa*—and the lotus feet of Śrī Advaita Prabhu; *yāṅhāra sarva-sva*—whose everything; *tāṅre*—him; *mile*—meets; *ei*—this; *dhana*—treasure.

TRANSLATION

He who has accepted as everything the lotus feet of Śrī Caitanya Mahāprabhu, Nityānanda Prabhu and Advaita Prabhu can attain this transcendental treasure.

PURPORT

Śrī Bhaktisiddhānta Sarasvatī Ṭhākura says that Kṛṣṇa is obtainable for the faithful, but for those who are accustomed to argue, Kṛṣṇa is far, far away. Similarly, these talks between Rāmānanda Rāya and Śrī Caitanya Mahāprabhu can be understood by a person who has firm faith. Those who are not in the disciplic succession, the *asauta-panthīs,* cannot have faith in these talks. They are always doubting and engaging in mental concoctions. These talks cannot be understood by such whimsical people. Transcendental topics remain far, far away from those engaged in mundane arguments. In this regard, the Vedic *mantras* in the *Kaṭha Upaniṣad* (1.2.9) state, *naiṣā tarkeṇa matir āpaneyā proktānyenaiva sujñānāya preṣṭha.* According to the *Muṇḍaka Upaniṣad* (3.2.3), *nāyam ātmā pravacanena labhyo na medhayā na bahunā śrutena / yam evaiṣa vṛṇute tena labhyas tasyaiṣa ātmā vivṛṇute tanūṁ svām.* And according to the *Brahma-sūtra* (2.1.11), *tarkāpratiṣṭhānāt.*

All Vedic literatures declare that transcendental subjects cannot be understood simply by argument or logic. Spiritual matters are far above experimental knowledge. If one is interested in the transcendental loving affairs of Kṛṣṇa, it is only by Kṛṣṇa's mercy that he can understand them. If one tries to understand these transcendental topics simply by using one's material brain substance, the attempt will be futile. It doesn't matter whether one is a *prākṛta-sahajiyā,* a mundane opportunist or a scholar; one's labor to understand these topics by mundane means will ultimately be frustrated. One therefore has to give up all mundane attempts and try to become a pure devotee of Lord Viṣṇu. When a devotee follows the regulative principles, the truth of these talks will be revealed to him. This is confirmed:

ataḥ śrī-kṛṣṇa-nāmādi
na bhaved grāhyam indriyaiḥ
sevonmukhe hi jihvādau
svayam eva sphuraty adaḥ
(*Bhakti-rasāmṛta-sindhu,* 1.2.109)

One cannot understand the holy name of the Lord, His pastimes, form, qualities, and entourage by blunt material senses. However, when the senses are purified by the constant rendering of service, the spiritual truth of the pastimes of Rādhā and Kṛṣṇa are revealed. As confirmed in the *Muṇḍaka Upaniṣad: yam evaiṣa vṛṇute tena labhyas.* Only one who is favored by the Supreme Personality of Godhead can understand the transcendental features of Śrī Caitanya Mahāprabhu.

TEXT 311

রামানন্দ রায়ে মোর কোটী নমস্কার ।
যাঁর মুখে কৈল প্রভু রসের বিস্তার ॥ ৩১১ ॥

rāmānanda rāye mora koṭī namaskāra
yāṅra mukhe kaila prabhu rasera vistāra

SYNONYMS

rāmānanda rāye—unto Śrī Rāmānanda Rāya; *mora*—my; *koṭī*—ten million; *namaskāra*—obeisances; *yāṅra mukhe*—in whose mouth; *kaila*—did; *prabhu*—Śrī Caitanya Mahāprabhu; *rasera vistāra*—the expansion of transcendental mellows.

TRANSLATION

I offer ten million obeisances unto the lotus feet of Śrī Rāmānanda Rāya because from his mouth much spiritual information has been expanded by Śrī Caitanya Mahāprabhu.

TEXT 312

দামোদর-স্বরূপের কড়চা-অনুসারে ।
রামানন্দ-মিলন-লীলা করিল প্রচারে ॥ ৩১২ ॥

dāmodara-svarūpera kaḍacā-anusāre
rāmānanda-milana-līlā karila pracāre

SYNONYMS

dāmodara-svarūpera—of Svarūpa Dāmodara Gosvāmī; *kaḍacā*—with the notebooks; *anusāre*—in accordance; *rāmānanda-milana-līlā*—the pastimes of the meeting with Rāmānanda; *karila*—have done; *pracāre*—distribution.

TRANSLATION

I have tried to preach the pastimes of Lord Śrī Caitanya Mahāprabhu's meeting with Rāmānanda Rāya in accordance with the notebooks of Śrī Svarūpa Dāmodara.

PURPORT

At the end of every chapter, the author admits the value of the disciplic succession. He never claims to have written this transcendental literature by carrying out research work. He simply admits his indebtedness to the notes taken by Svarūpa Dāmodara, Raghunātha dāsa Gosvāmī and other authoritative persons. This is the way of describing transcendental literatures, which are never meant for so-called scholars and research workers. The process is *mahājano yena gataḥ sa panthāḥ:* one has to strictly follow great personalities and *ācāryas. Ācāryavān puruṣo veda*: one who has the favor of the *ācārya* knows everything. This statement made by Kavirāja Gosvāmī is very valuable for all pure devotees. Sometimes the *prākṛta-sahajiyās* claim that they have heard the truth from their *guru.* However, one cannot have transcendental knowledge simply by hearing from a *guru* who is not bona fide. The *guru* must be bona fide, and he must have heard from his bona fide *guru.* Only then will his message be accepted as bona fide. This is confirmed in *Bhagavad-gītā:*

śrī bhagavān uvāca
imaṁ vivasvate yogaṁ
proktavān aham avyayam
vivasvān manave prāha
manur ikṣvākave 'bravīt

"The Blessed Lord said: I instructed this imperishable science of *yoga* to the sun-god, Vivasvān, and Vivasvān instructed it to Manu, the father of mankind, and Manu in turn instructed it to Ikṣvāku." (Bg. 4.1)

In this way the message is transmitted in the bona fide spiritual disciplic succession from bona fide spiritual master to bona fide student. Śrīla Kavirāja Gosvāmī therefore as usual concludes this chapter by reasserting his faith in the lotus feet of the six Gosvāmīs. Thus he is able to set forth this transcendental literature, *Caitanya-caritāmṛta.*

TEXT 313

শ্রীরূপ-রঘুনাথ-পদে যার আশ ।
চৈতন্যচরিতামৃত কহে কৃষ্ণদাস ॥ ৩১৩ ॥

śrī-rūpa-raghunātha-pade yāra āśa
caitanya-caritāmṛta kahe kṛṣṇadāsa

SYNONYMS

śrī-rūpa—Śrīla Rūpa Gosvāmī; *raghunātha*—Śrīla Raghunātha dāsa Gosvāmī; *pade*—at the lotus feet; *yāra*—whose; *āśa*—expectation; *caitanya-caritāmṛta*—the book named *Caitanya-caritāmṛta*; *kahe*—describes; *kṛṣṇa-dāsa*—Śrīla Kṛṣṇadāsa Kavirāja Gosvāmī.

TRANSLATION

Praying at the lotus feet of Śrī Rūpa and Śrī Raghunātha, always desiring their mercy, I, Kṛṣṇadāsa, narrate Śrī Caitanya-caritāmṛta, following in their footsteps.

Thus end the Bhaktivedanta purports to the Śrī Caitanya-caritāmṛta, Madhya-līlā, *Eighth Chapter, describing the talks between Śrī Caitanya Mahāprabhu and Rāmānanda Rāya.*

CHAPTER 9

Lord Śrī Caitanya Mahāprabhu's Travels to the Holy Places

A summary of the Ninth Chapter is given by Śrīla Bhaktivinoda Ṭhākura. After leaving Vidyānagara, Śrī Caitanya Mahāprabhu visited such places of pilgrimage as Gautamī-gaṅgā, Mallikārjuna, Ahovala-nṛsiṁha, Siddhavaṭa, Skanda-kṣetra, Trimaṭha, Vṛddhakāśī, Bauddha-sthāna, Tripati, Trimalla, Pānā-nṛsiṁha, Śiva-kāñcī, Viṣṇu-kāñcī, Trikāla-hastī, Vṛddhakola, Śiyālī-bhairavī, Kāverī-tīra and Kumbhakarṇa-kapāla.

Finally the Lord went to Śrī Raṅga-kṣetra, where He converted a *brāhmaṇa* named Vyeṅkaṭa Bhaṭṭa, who, along with his family, became a devotee of Kṛṣṇa. After leaving Śrī Raṅga, Caitanya Mahāprabhu reached Ṛṣabha-parvata, where He met Paramānanda Purī, who later arrived at Jagannātha Purī. Lord Śrī Caitanya Mahāprabhu then proceeded farther, arriving at Setubandha Rāmeśvara. At Śrī Śaila-parvata, the Lord met Lord Śiva and his wife Durgā in the dress of a *brāhmaṇa* and *brāhmaṇī.* From there He went to Kāmakoṣṭhī-purī and later arrived at southern Mathurā. A *brāhmaṇa* devotee of Lord Rāmacandra talked with Him. Then the Lord took His bath in the River Kṛtamālā. On the hill known as Mahendra-śaila, the Lord saw Paraśurāma. Then the Lord went to Setubandha and took His bath at Dhanus-tīrtha. He also visited Rāmeśvara, where He collected some papers connected with Sītādevī, whose illusory form was kidnapped by Rāvaṇa. The Lord next visited the places known as Pāṇḍya-deśa, Tāmraparṇī, Nayatripadī, Ciyaḍatalā, Tilakāñcī, Gajendra-mokṣaṇa, Pānāgaḍi, Cāmtāpura, Śrī Vaikuṇṭha, Malaya-parvata and Kanyākumārī. The Lord then met the Bhaṭṭathāris at Mallāra-deśa and saved Kālā Kṛṣṇadāsa from their clutches. The Lord also collected *Brahma-saṁhitā,* Fifth Chapter, on the banks of the Payasvinī River. He then visited Payasvinī, Śṛṅgavera-purī-maṭha and Matsya-tīrtha. At the village of Uḍupī, He saw the Gopāla installed by Śrī Madhvācārya. He then defeated the Tattvavādīs in śāstric conversation. The Lord next visited Phalgu-tīrtha, Tritakūpa, Pañcāpsarā, Sūrpāraka and Kolāpura. At Śrī Raṅgapurī the Lord received news of Śaṅkarāraṇya's disappearance. He then went to the banks of the Kṛṣṇaveṇvā River, where He collected from among the Vaiṣṇava *brāhmaṇas* a book written by Bilvamaṅgala, *Kṛṣṇa-karṇāmṛta.* The Lord then visited Tāptī, Māhiṣmatī-pura, Narmadā-tīra and Ṛṣyamūka-parvata. He entered Daṇḍakāraṇya and liberated the seven palm trees. From there He visited a place known as Pampā-sarovara and visited Pañcavaṭī, Nāsika, Brahmagiri and also the source of the Godāvarī River,

Kuśāvarta. Thus the Lord visited almost all the holy places in South India. He finally returned to Jagannātha Purī by taking the same route, after visiting Vidyānagara again.

TEXT 1

নানামতগ্রাহগ্রস্তান্ দাক্ষিণাত্যজনদ্বিপান্ ।
কৃপারিণা বিমুচ্যৈতান্ গৌরশ্চক্রে স বৈষ্ণবান্ ॥১॥

nānā-mata-grāha-grastān
dākṣiṇātya-jana-dvipān
kṛpāriṇā vimucyaitān
gauraś cakre sa vaiṣṇavān

SYNONYMS

nānā-mata—by various philosophies; *grāha*—like crocodiles; *grastān*—captured; *dākṣiṇātya-jana*—the inhabitants of South India; *dvipān*—like elephants; *kṛpā-ariṇā*—by His disc of mercy; *vimucya*—liberating; *etān*—all these; *gauraḥ*—Śrī Caitanya Mahāprabhu; *cakre*—converted; *saḥ*—He; *vaiṣṇavān*—to the Vaiṣṇava cult.

TRANSLATION

Lord Śrī Caitanya Mahāprabhu converted the inhabitants of South India. These people were as strong as elephants, but they were under the clutches of the crocodiles of various philosophies—such as the Buddhist, Jaina and Māyāvāda philosophies. By His disc of mercy, the Lord converted all of them into Vaiṣṇavas, devotees of the Lord.

PURPORT

Herein it is stated that the Lord delivered the Gajendra, the elephant, who was being attacked by crocodiles. When Śrī Caitanya Mahāprabhu visited southern India, almost all the residents were under the claws of crocodiles presenting Buddhist, Jaina and Māyāvāda philosophy. Although Kavirāja Gosvāmī states that these people were as strong as elephants, they were actually under the clutches of death because they were being attacked by the crocodiles of various philosophies. However, Śrī Caitanya Mahāprabhu saved the elephant from the clutches of the crocodiles by His mercy.

TEXT 2

জয় জয় শ্রীচৈতন্য জয় নিত্যানন্দ ।
জয়াদ্বৈতচন্দ্র জয় গৌরভক্তবৃন্দ ॥ ২ ॥

jaya jaya śrī-caitanya jaya nityānanda
jayādvaita-candra jaya gaura-bhakta-vṛnda

SYNONYMS

jaya jaya—all glories; *śrī-caitanya*—to Lord Caitanya Mahāprabhu; *jaya*—all glories; *nityānanda*—unto Nityānanda Prabhu; *jaya advaita-candra*—all glories to Advaita Prabhu; *jaya*—all glories; *gaura-bhakta-vṛnda*—to the devotees of Lord Śrī Caitanya Mahāprabhu.

TRANSLATION

All glories to Lord Śrī Caitanya Mahāprabhu! All glories to Lord Nityānanda Prabhu! All glories to Śrī Advaita Prabhu! And all glories to the devotees of Śrī Caitanya Mahāprabhu!

TEXT 3

দক্ষিণগমন প্রভুর অতি বিলক্ষণ ।
সহস্র সহস্র তীর্থ কৈল দরশন ॥ ৩ ॥

dakṣiṇa-gamana prabhura ati vilakṣaṇa
sahasra sahasra tīrtha kaila daraśana

SYNONYMS

dakṣiṇa-gamana—touring in South India; *prabhura*—of the Lord; *ati*—very; *vilakṣaṇa*—extraordinary; *sahasra sahasra*—thousands of thousands; *tīrtha*—holy places; *kaila*—did; *daraśana*—visit.

TRANSLATION

Śrī Caitanya Mahāprabhu's tour of South India was certainly very extraordinary because He visited many thousands of places of pilgrimage there.

TEXT 4

সেই সব তীর্থ স্পর্শি' মহাতীর্থ কৈল ।
সেই ছলে সেই দেশের লোক নিস্তারিল ॥ ৪ ॥

sei saba tīrtha sparśi' maha-tīrtha kaila
sei chale sei deśera loka nistārila

SYNONYMS

sei saba—all those; *tīrtha*—holy places; *sparśi'*—touching; *mahā-tīrtha*—into great places of pilgrimage; *kaila*—made them; *sei chale*—under that plea; *sei deśera*—of those countries; *loka*—the people; *nistārila*—He delivered.

TRANSLATION

When the Lord visited all those holy places, He converted many thousands of residents. Thus many people were delivered. Simply by touching the holy places, He made them into great places of pilgrimage.

PURPORT

It is said: *tīrthī-kurvanti tīrthāni.* A *tīrtha,* or holy place, is a place where great saintly personalities visit or reside. Although the holy places were already places of pilgrimage, they were all purified by Śrī Caitanya Mahāprabhu's visit. Many people go to these holy places and leave their sinful activities there, thus becoming free from contamination. When these contaminations pile up, they are counteracted by the visit of great personalities like Śrī Caitanya Mahāprabhu and His strict followers. Many kinds of patients come to a hospital, which may be infected by many types of disease. Actually the hospital is always infected, but the expert physician keeps the hospital sterilized by his expert presence and management. Similarly, places of pilgrimage are always infected by the sins left by the sinners who go there, but when a personality like Śrī Caitanya Mahāprabhu visits such a place, all contaminations vanish.

TEXT 5

সেই সব তীর্থের ক্রম কহিতে না পারি ।
দক্ষিণ-বামে তীর্থ-গমন হয় ফেরাফেরি ॥ ৫ ॥

sei saba tīrthera krama kahite nā pāri
dakṣiṇa-vāme tīrtha-gamana haya pherāpheri

SYNONYMS

sei saba—all those; *tīrthera*—of holy places; *krama*—the chronological order; *kahite*—to tell of; *nā pāri*—I am unable; *dakṣiṇa-vāme*—left and right; *tīrtha-gamana*—visiting the holy places; *haya*—is; *pherāpheri*—going and coming back.

TRANSLATION

I cannot chronologically record all the places of pilgrimage visited by Lord Śrī Caitanya Mahāprabhu. I can only summarize everything by saying that the Lord visited all holy places right and left, coming and going.

TEXT 6

অতএব নাম-মাত্র করিয়ে গণন ।
কহিতে না পারি তার যথা অনুক্রম ॥ ৬ ॥

ataeva nāma-mātra kariye gaṇana
kahite nā pāri tāra yathā anukrama

SYNONYMS

ataeva—therefore; *nāma-mātra*—only as a token record; *kariye gaṇana*—I count; *kahite*—to tell; *nā pāri*—I am unable; *tāra*—of that; *yathā*—as; *anukrama*—chronological order.

TRANSLATION

Because it is impossible for me to record all these places in chronological order, I simply make a token gesture of recording them.

TEXTS 7-8

পূর্ব্ববৎ পথে যাইতে যে পায় দরশন ।
যেই গ্রামে যায়, সে গ্রামের যত জন ॥ ৭ ॥
সবেই বৈষ্ণব হয়, কহে 'কৃষ্ণ' 'হরি' ।
অন্য গ্রাম নিস্তারয়ে সেই 'বৈষ্ণব' করি' ॥ ৮ ॥

pūrvavat pathe yāite ye pāya daraśana
yei grāme yāya, se grāmera yata jana

sabei vaiṣṇava haya, kahe 'kṛṣṇa' 'hari'
anya grāma nistāraye sei 'vaiṣṇava' kari'

SYNONYMS

pūrva-vat—as done previously; *pathe*—on the way; *yāite*—while going; *ye*—anyone who; *pāya*—gets; *daraśana*—audience; *yei*—which; *grāme*—in the village; *yāya*—Lord Śrī Caitanya Mahāprabhu goes; *se*—that; *grāmera*—of the village; *yata*—all; *jana*—people; *sabei*—all of them; *vaiṣṇava haya*—become devotees; *kahe*—say; *kṛṣṇa hari*—the holy names of Lord Kṛṣṇa and Hari; *anya grāma*—other villages; *nistāraye*—delivers; *sei*—He; *vaiṣṇava*—devotees; *kari'*—making.

TRANSLATION

As previously stated, all the residents of the villages visited by Lord Caitanya became Vaiṣṇavas and began to chant Hari and Kṛṣṇa. In this way, in all the villages visited by the Lord, everyone became a Vaiṣṇava, a devotee.

PURPORT

The holy names of Kṛṣṇa and Hari, or the chanting of the Hare Kṛṣṇa *mahā-mantra,* are so spiritually powerful that even today, as our preachers go to remote parts of the world, people immediately begin chanting Hare Kṛṣṇa. Śrī Caitanya Mahāprabhu was the Supreme Personality of Godhead Himself. There cannot be anyone who can compare to Him or His potencies. However, because we are following in His footsteps and are also chanting the Hare Kṛṣṇa *mahā-mantra,* the effect is almost as potent as during the time of Lord Caitanya Mahāprabhu. Our preachers mainly belong to European and American countries, yet by the grace of Lord Caitanya they have tremendous success wherever they go to open branches. Indeed, everywhere people are very seriously chanting Hare Kṛṣṇa, Hare Kṛṣṇa, Kṛṣṇa Kṛṣṇa, Hare Hare/ Hare Rāma, Hare Rāma, Rāma Rāma, Hare Hare.

TEXT 9

দক্ষিণ দেশের লোক অনেক প্রকার ।
কেহ জ্ঞানী, কেহ কর্মী, পাষণ্ডী অপার ॥ ৯ ॥

dakṣiṇa deśera loka aneka prakāra
keha jñānī, keha karmī, pāṣaṇḍī apāra

SYNONYMS

dakṣiṇa deśera—of South India; *loka*—people; *aneka*—many; *prakāra*—varieties; *keha*—someone; *jñānī*—philosophical speculator; *keha*—someone; *karmī*—fruitive worker; *pāṣaṇḍī*—nondevotees; *apāra*—innumerable.

TRANSLATION

In South India there were many types of people. Some were philosophical speculators, and some were fruitive workers, but in any case there were innumerable nondevotees.

TEXT 10

সেই সব লোক প্রভুর দর্শনপ্রভাবে ।
নিজ-নিজ-মত ছাড়ি' হইল বৈষ্ণবে ॥ ১০ ॥

sei saba loka prabhura darśana-prabhāve
nija-nija-mata chāḍi' ha-ila vaiṣṇave

SYNONYMS

sei saba loka—all those people; *prabhura*—of Lord Śrī Caitanya Mahāprabhu; *darśana-prabhāve*—by the influence of His visit; *nija-nija*—their own; *mata*—opinion; *chāḍi'*—giving up; *ha-ila*—became; *vaiṣṇave*—devotees.

TRANSLATION

By the influence of Śrī Caitanya Mahāprabhu, all these people abandoned their own opinions and became Vaiṣṇavas, devotees of Kṛṣṇa.

TEXT 11

বৈষ্ণবের মধ্যে রাম-উপাসক সব ।
কেহ 'তত্ত্ববাদী', কেহ হয় 'শ্রীবৈষ্ণব' ॥ ১১ ॥

vaiṣṇavera madhye rāma-upāsaka saba
keha 'tattvavādī', keha haya 'śrī-vaiṣṇava'

SYNONYMS

vaiṣṇavera madhye—amongst Vaiṣṇavas; *rāma-upāsaka saba*—all worshipers of Lord Śrī Rāmacandra; *keha*—someone; *tattva-vādī*—followers of Madhvācārya; *keha*—someone; *haya*—is; *śrī-vaiṣṇava*—devotees following the disciplic succession of Śrī Rāmānujācārya.

TRANSLATION

At the time, all the South Indian Vaiṣṇavas were worshipers of Lord Rāmacandra. Some were Tattvavādīs, and some were followers of Rāmānujācārya.

PURPORT

Śrīla Bhaktisiddhānta Sarasvatī Ṭhākura points out that Tattvavādī refers to the followers of Śrīla Madhvācārya. To distinguish his disciplic succession from the Māyāvādī followers of Śaṅkarācārya, Śrīla Madhvācārya named his party the Tattvavāda. Impersonal monists are always attacked by these Tattvavādīs, who attempt to defeat their philosophy of impersonalism. Generally, they establish the supremacy of the Supreme Personality of Godhead. Actually the disciplic succession of Madhvācārya is known as the Brahma-Vaiṣṇava sect; that is the sect coming down from Lord Brahmā. Consequently the Tattvavādīs, or followers of Madhvācārya, do not accept the incident of Lord Brahmā's illusion, which is recorded in the Tenth Canto of *Śrīmad-Bhāgavatam*. Śrīla Madhvācārya has purposefully avoided commenting on that portion of *Śrīmad-Bhāgavatam* in which *brahma-mohana*, the illusion of Lord Brahmā, is mentioned. Śrīla Mādhavendra Purī was one of the *ācāryas* in the Tattvavāda disciplic succession, and he established the ultimate goal of transcendentalism to be attainment of pure devotional service, love of Godhead. Those Vaiṣṇavas belonging to the Gauḍīya-sampradāya, the disciplic succession following Śrī Caitanya Mahāprabhu, are distinct from the Tattvavādīs, although they belong to the same Tattvavāda *sampradāya*. The followers of Śrī Caitanya Mahāprabhu are therefore known as the Madhva-Gauḍīya-sampradāya.

The word *pāṣaṇḍī* refers to those who are opposed to pure devotional service. In particular, these are the Māyāvādīs, the impersonalists. A definition of *pāṣaṇḍī* is given in the *Hari-bhakti-vilāsa* (1.73), wherein it is stated:

yas tu nārāyaṇaṁ devaṁ
brahma-rudrādi-daivataiḥ
samatvenaiva vīkṣeta
sa pāṣaṇḍī bhaved dhruvam

A *pāṣaṇḍī* is one who thinks that the Supreme Lord Nārāyaṇa, the Personality of Godhead, is on the same level with the demigods headed by Lord Brahmā and Lord Śiva. The devotee never considers Lord Nārāyaṇa to be on the same platform with Lord Brahmā and Lord Śiva. The Madhvācārya-sampradāya and Rāmānuja-sampradāya are mainly worshipers of Lord Rāmacandra, although the Śrī Vaiṣṇavas are supposed to be worshipers of Lord Nārāyaṇa and Lakṣmī and the Tattvavādīs are supposed to be worshipers of Lord Kṛṣṇa. At present, in most of the monasteries belonging to the Madhva-sampradāya, Lord Rāmacandra is worshiped.

In the book known as *Adhyātma-rāmāyaṇa*, there are statements in Chapters Twelve to Fifteen about the worship of the Deities Śrī Rāmacandra and Sītā. There it is stated that during Lord Rāmacandra's time, there was a *brāhmaṇa* who took a vow refusing to accept breakfast until he saw Lord Rāmacandra. Sometimes, due to business, Lord Rāmacandra was absent from His capital for a full week and could not be seen by citizens during that time. Because of his vow, the *brāhmaṇa* could not take even a drop of water during that week. Later, after eight or nine days, when the *brāhmaṇa* could see Lord Rāmacandra personally, he would break his fast. Upon observing the *brāhmaṇa's* rigid vow, Lord Śrī Rāmacandra ordered

His younger brother Lakṣmaṇa to deliver a pair of Sītā-Rāma Deities to the *brāhmaṇa.* The *brāhmaṇa* received the Deities from Śrī Lakṣmaṇajī and worshiped them faithfully as long as he lived. At the time of his death, he delivered the Deities to Śrī Hanumānjī, who, for many years, hung Them around his neck and served Them with all devotion. After many years, when Hanumānjī departed on the hill known as Gandha-mādana, he delivered the Deities to Bhīmasena, one of the Pāṇḍavas, and Bhīmasena brought Them to his palace, where he kept Them very carefully. The last king of the Pāṇḍavas, Kṣemakānta, worshiped the Deities in that palace. Later, the same Deities were kept in the custody of the kings of Orissa known as Gajapatis. One of the *ācāryas,* known as Narahari Tīrtha, who was in the disciplic succession of Madhvācārya, received these Deities from the King of Orissa.

It may be noted that these particular Deities of Rāma and Sītā have been worshiped from the time of King Ikṣvāku. Indeed, they were worshiped by the royal princes even before the appearance of Lord Rāmacandra. Later, during Lord Rāmacandra's presence, the Deities were worshiped by Lakṣmaṇa. It is said that just three months before his disappearance, Śrī Madhvācārya received these Deities and installed them in the Uḍupī temple. Since then the Deities have been worshiped by the Madhvācārya-sampradāya at that monastery. As far as the Śrī Vaiṣṇavas are concerned, beginning with Rāmānujācārya, they also worshiped Deities of Sītā-Rāma. Sītā-Rāma Deities are also being worshiped in Tirupati and other places. From the Śrī Rāmānuja-sampradāya there is another branch known as Rāmānandī or Rāmāt, and the followers of that branch also worship Deities of Sītā-Rāma very rigidly. The Rāmānuja-sampradāya Vaiṣṇavas prefer the worship of Lord Rāmacandra to Rādhā-Kṛṣṇa.

TEXT 12

সেই সব বৈষ্ণব মহাপ্রভুর দর্শনে ।
কৃষ্ণ-উপাসক হৈল, লয় কৃষ্ণনামে ॥ ১২ ॥

sei saba vaiṣṇava mahāprabhura darśane
kṛṣṇa-upāsaka haila, laya kṛṣṇa-nāme

SYNONYMS

sei saba—all those; *vaiṣṇava*—devotees; *mahāprabhura*—of Śrī Caitanya Mahāprabhu; *darśane*—by seeing; *kṛṣṇa-upāsaka*—devotees of Lord Kṛṣṇa; *haila*—became; *laya*—took; *kṛṣṇa-nāme*—the holy name of Lord Kṛṣṇa.

TRANSLATION

After meeting Śrī Caitanya Mahāprabhu, all those different Vaiṣṇavas became devotees of Kṛṣṇa and began chanting the Hare Kṛṣṇa mahā-mantra.

TEXT 13

রাম ! রাঘব ! রাম ! রাঘব ! রাম ! রাঘব ! পাহি মাম্ ।
কৃষ্ণ ! কেশব ! কৃষ্ণ ! কেশব ! কৃষ্ণ ! কেশব ! রক্ষ মাম্ ॥ ১৩ ॥

rāma! rāghava! rāma! rāghava! rāma! rāghava! pāhi mām
kṛṣṇa! keśava! kṛṣṇa! keśava! kṛṣṇa! keśava! rakṣa mām

SYNONYMS

rāma—O Rāma; *rāghava*—descendant of Raghu; *pāhi*—please protect; *mām*—me; *kṛṣṇa*—O Kṛṣṇa; *keśava*—killer of Keśī; *rakṣa*—protect; *mām*—me.

TRANSLATION

"O Lord Rāmacandra, descendant of Mahārāja Raghu, kindly protect me! O Lord Kṛṣṇa, killer of the Keśī demon, kindly protect me!"

TEXT 14

এই শ্লোক পথে পড়ি' করিলা প্রয়াণ ।
গৌতমী-গঙ্গায় যাই' কৈল গঙ্গাস্নান ॥ ১৪ ॥

ei śloka pathe paḍi' karilā prayāṇa
gautamī-gaṅgāya yāi' kaila gaṅgā-snāna

SYNONYMS

ei śloka—this Sanskrit verse; *pathe*—on the way; *paḍi'*—reciting; *karilā*—did; *prayāṇa*—going; *gautamī-gaṅgāya*—to the bank of the Gautamī-gaṅgā; *yāi'*—going; *kaila*—did; *gaṅgā-snāna*—bathing in the Ganges.

TRANSLATION

While walking on the road, Śrī Caitanya Mahāprabhu used to chant this Rāma Rāghava mantra. Chanting in this way, He arrived at the banks of the Gautamī-gaṅgā and took His bath there.

PURPORT

The Gautamī-gaṅgā is another branch of the River Godāvarī. Formerly a great sage named Gautama Ṛṣi used to live on the bank of this river opposite the city of Rājamahendri, and consequently this branch was called the Gautamī-gaṅgā.

Śrīla Bhaktivinoda Ṭhākura says that Śrīla Kavirāja Gosvāmī has recorded the names of the holy places visited by Śrī Caitanya Mahāprabhu but that there is no chronological order of the places visited. However, there is a notebook of Govinda dāsa's containing a chronological order and references to geographical positions. Śrīla Bhaktivinoda Ṭhākura requests the readers to refer to that book. According to Govinda dāsa, Śrī Caitanya Mahāprabhu went to Trimanda from the Gautamī-gaṅgā. From there He went to Ḍhuṇḍirāma-tīrtha, another place of pilgrimage. According to this book, after visiting Gautamī-gaṅgā, Śrī Caitanya Mahāprabhu went to Mallikārjuna-tīrtha.

TEXT 15

মল্লিকার্জুন-তীর্থে যাই' মহেশ দেখিল।
তাহাঁ সব লোকে কৃষ্ণনাম লওয়াইল ॥ ১৫ ॥

mallikārjuna-tīrthe yāi' maheśa dekhila
tāhāṅ saba loke kṛṣṇa-nāma laoyāila

SYNONYMS

mallikārjuna-tīrthe—to the holy place known as Mallikārjuna; *yāi'*—going; *maheśa*—the deity of Lord Śiva; *dekhila*—He saw; *tāhāṅ*—there; *saba loke*—all the people; *kṛṣṇa-nāma*—Lord Kṛṣṇa's holy name; *laoyāila*—He induced to chant.

TRANSLATION

Śrī Caitanya Mahāprabhu then went to Mallikārjuna-tīrtha and saw the deity of Lord Śiva there. He also induced all the people to chant the Hare Kṛṣṇa mahā-mantra.

PURPORT

Mallikārjuna is also known as Śrī Śaila. It is situated about seventy miles south of Karṇula on the right bank of the Kṛṣṇā River. There are great walls all around the village, and within the walls resides the deity known as Mallikārjuna. It is a deity of Lord Śiva and is one of the Jyotirliṅgas.

TEXT 16

রামদাস মহাদেবে করিল দরশন।
অহোবল-নৃসিংহেরে করিলা গমন ॥ ১৬ ॥

rāmadāsa mahādeve karila daraśana
ahovala-nṛsiṁhere karilā gamana

SYNONYMS

rāma-dāsa—Rāmadāsa; *mahā-deve*—of Mahādeva; *karila*—did; *daraśana*—seeing; *ahovala-nṛsiṁhere*—to Ahovala-nṛsiṁha; *karilā*—did; *gamana*—going.

TRANSLATION

There he saw Lord Mahādeva [Śiva], the servant of Lord Rāma. He then went to Ahovala-nṛsiṁha.

TEXT 17

নৃসিংহ দেখিয়া তাঁরে কৈল নতি-স্তুতি ।
সিদ্ধবট গেলা যাহাঁ মূর্তি সীতাপতি ॥ ১৭ ॥

nṛsiṁha dekhiyā tāṅre kaila nati-stuti
siddhavaṭa gelā yāhāṅ mūrti sītāpati

SYNONYMS

nṛsiṁha dekhiyā—after seeing the Lord Nṛsiṁha Deity; *tāṅre*—unto Him; *kaila*—did; *nati-stuti*—offering of various prayers; *siddha-vaṭa*—to Siddhavaṭa; *gelā*—He went; *yāhāṅ*—where; *mūrti*—the Deity; *sītā-pati*—Lord Rāmacandra.

TRANSLATION

After seeing the Ahovala-nṛsiṁha Deity, Caitanya Mahāprabhu offered many prayers unto the Lord. He then went to Siddhavaṭa, where He saw the Deity of Rāmacandra, the Lord of Sītādevī.

PURPORT

This Siddhavaṭa is ten miles east of the village Kuḍāpā. It is also known as Sidhauṭa. Previously this place was also known as southern Benares. There is a great banyan tree there, and it is therefore known as Siddhavaṭa. *Vaṭa* means banyan tree.

TEXT 18

রঘুনাথ দেখি' কৈল প্রণতি স্তবন ।
তাহাঁ এক বিপ্র প্রভুর কৈল নিমন্ত্রণ ॥ ১৮ ॥

raghunātha dekhi' kaila praṇati stavana
tāhāṅ eka vipra prabhura kaila nimantraṇa

SYNONYMS

raghu-nātha dekhi'—after seeing Lord Rāmacandra, the descendant of Mahārāja Raghu; *kaila*—offered; *praṇati*—obeisances; *stavana*—prayers; *tāhāṅ*—there; *eka*—one; *vipra*—*brāhmaṇa; prabhura*—to Lord Śrī Caitanya Mahāprabhu; *kaila*—did; *nimantraṇa*—invitation.

TRANSLATION

After seeing the Deity of Lord Rāmacandra, the descendant of King Raghu, the Lord offered His prayers and obeisances. Then a brāhmaṇa invited the Lord to take lunch.

TEXT 19

সেই বিপ্র রামনাম নিরন্তর লয়।
'রাম' 'রাম' বিনা অন্য বাণী না কহয় ॥ ১৯ ॥

sei vipra rāma-nāma nirantara laya
'rāma' 'rāma' vinā anya vāṇī nā kahaya

SYNONYMS

sei vipra—that *brāhmaṇa; rāma-nāma*—the holy name of Lord Rāmacandra; *nirantara*—constantly; *laya*—chants; *rāma rāma*—the holy names Rāma Rāma; *vinā*—without; *anya*—other; *vāṇī*—vibration; *nā*—does not; *kahaya*—speak.

TRANSLATION

That brāhmaṇa constantly chanted the holy name of Rāmacandra. Indeed, but for chanting Lord Rāmacandra's holy name, that brāhmaṇa did not speak a word.

TEXT 20

সেই দিন তাঁর ঘরে রহি' ভিক্ষা করি'।
তাঁরে কৃপা করি' আগে চলিলা গৌরহরি ॥ ২০ ॥

sei dina tāṅra ghare rahi' bhikṣā kari'
tāṅre kṛpā kari' āge calilā gaurahari

SYNONYMS

sei dina—on that day; *tāṅra ghare*—the house of that *brāhmaṇa; rahi'*—staying; *bhikṣā kari'*—accepting *prasāda; tāṅre*—unto him; *kṛpā kari'*—showing mercy; *āge*—ahead; *calilā*—departed; *gaura-hari*—Lord Śrī Caitanya Mahāprabhu.

TRANSLATION

That day, Lord Caitanya remained there and accepted prasāda at his house. After bestowing mercy upon him in this way, the Lord proceeded ahead.

TEXT 21

স্কন্দক্ষেত্র-তীর্থে কৈল স্কন্দ দরশন ।
ত্রিমঠ আইলা, তাহাঁ দেখি' ত্রিবিক্রম ॥ ২১ ॥

skanda-kṣetra-tīrthe kaila skanda daraśana
trimaṭha āilā, tāhāṅ dekhi' trivikrama

SYNONYMS

skanda-kṣetra-tīrthe—in the holy place known as Skanda-kṣetra; *kaila*—did; *skanda daraśana*—visiting Lord Skanda (Kārttikeya, son of Lord Śiva); *trimaṭha*—at Trimaṭha; *āilā*—arrived; *tāhāṅ*—there; *dekhi'*—seeing; *trivikrama*—a form of Lord Viṣṇu, Trivikrama.

TRANSLATION

At the holy place known as Skanda-kṣetra, Lord Śrī Caitanya Mahāprabhu visited the temple of Skanda. From there He went to Trimaṭha, where He saw the Viṣṇu Deity Trivikrama.

TEXT 22

পুনঃ সিদ্ধবট আইলা সেই বিপ্র-ঘরে ।
সেই বিপ্র কৃষ্ণনাম লয় নিরন্তরে ॥ ২২ ॥

punaḥ siddhavaṭa āilā sei vipra-ghare
sei vipra kṛṣṇa-nāma laya nirantare

SYNONYMS

punaḥ—again; *siddha-vaṭa*—to the place known as Siddhavaṭa; *āilā*—returned; *sei*—that; *vipra-ghare*—in the house of the *brāhmaṇa; sei vipra*—that *brāhmaṇa; kṛṣṇa-nāma*—the holy name of Lord Kṛṣṇa; *laya*—chants; *nirantare*—constantly.

TRANSLATION

After visiting the temple of Trivikrama, the Lord returned to Siddhavaṭa, where He again visited the house of the brāhmaṇa, who was now constantly chanting the Hare Kṛṣṇa mahā-mantra.

TEXT 23

ভিক্ষা করি' মহাপ্রভু তাঁরে প্রশ্ন কৈল ।
"কহ বিপ্র, এই তোমার কোন্ দশা হৈল ॥ ২৩ ॥

bhikṣā kari' mahāprabhu tāṅre praśna kaila
"kaha vipra, ei tomāra kon daśā haila

SYNONYMS

bhikṣā kari'—after accepting lunch; *mahāprabhu*—Śrī Caitanya Mahāprabhu; *tāṅre*—unto him; *praśna kaila*—asked a question; *kaha vipra*—My dear *brāhmaṇa* friend, please say; *ei*—this; *tomāra*—your; *kon*—what; *daśā*—situation; *haila*—became.

TRANSLATION

After finishing His lunch there, Śrī Caitanya Mahāprabhu asked the brāhmaṇa, "My dear friend, kindly tell Me what your position is now.

TEXT 24

পূর্বে তুমি নিরন্তর লৈতে রামনাম।
এবে কেনে নিরন্তর লও কৃষ্ণনাম॥" ২৪ ॥

pūrve tumi nirantara laite rāma-nāma
ebe kene nirantara lao kṛṣṇa-nāma"

SYNONYMS

pūrve—formerly; *tumi*—you; *nirantara*—constantly; *laite*—used to chant; *rāma-nāma*—the holy name of Lord Rāmacandra; *ebe*—now; *kene*—why; *nirantara*—constantly; *lao*—you chant; *kṛṣṇa-nāma*—the holy name of Kṛṣṇa.

TRANSLATION

"Formerly you were constantly chanting the holy name of Lord Rāma. Why are you now constantly chanting the holy name of Kṛṣṇa?"

TEXT 25

বিপ্র বলে,—এই তোমার দর্শন-প্রভাবে।
তোমা দেখি' গেল মোর আজন্ম স্বভাবে॥ ২৫ ॥

vipra bale, ——ei tomāra darśana-prabhāve
tomā dekhi' gela mora ājanma svabhāve

SYNONYMS

vipra bale—the *brāhmaṇa* replied; *ei*—this; *tomāra darśana-prabhāve*—by the influence of Your visit; *tomā dekhi'*—after seeing You; *gela*—went; *mora*—my; *ā-janma*—from childhood; *sva-bhāve*—nature.

TRANSLATION

The brāhmaṇa replied, "This is all due to Your influence, sir. After seeing You, I have lost the long practice of my life.

TEXT 26

বাল্যাবধি রামনাম-গ্রহণ আমার ।
তোমা দেখি' কৃষ্ণনাম আইল একবার ॥ ২৬ ॥

bālyāvadhi rāma-nāma-grahaṇa āmāra
tomā dekhi' kṛṣṇa-nāma āila eka-bāra

SYNONYMS

bālya-avadhi—since the days of my childhood; *rāma-nāma-grahaṇa*—chanting the holy name of Lord Rāmacandra; *āmāra*—my; *tomā dekhi'*—after seeing You; *kṛṣṇa-nāma*—the holy name of Lord Kṛṣṇa; *āila*—came; *eka-bāra*—once only.

TRANSLATION

"From my childhood I have been chanting the holy name of Lord Rāmacandra, but after seeing You I began to chant the holy name of Lord Kṛṣṇa.

TEXT 27

সেই হৈতে কৃষ্ণনাম জিহ্বাতে বসিলা ।
কৃষ্ণনাম স্ফুরে, রামনাম দূরে গেলা ॥ ২৭ ॥

sei haite kṛṣṇa-nāma jihvāte vasilā
kṛṣṇa-nāma sphure, rāma-nāma dūre gelā

SYNONYMS

sei haite—since that time; *kṛṣṇa-nāma*—the holy name of Lord Kṛṣṇa; *jihvāte*—on the tongue; *vasilā*—was seated tightly; *kṛṣṇa-nāma*—the holy name of Lord Kṛṣṇa; *sphure*—automatically comes; *rāma-nāma*—the holy name of Lord Rāmacandra; *dūre*—far away; *gelā*—went.

TRANSLATION

"Since then, the holy name of Kṛṣṇa has been tied to my tongue. Indeed, when I chant the holy name of Kṛṣṇa, the holy name of Lord Rāmacandra goes far away.

TEXT 28

বাল্যকাল হৈতে মোর স্বভাব এক হয়।
নামের মহিমা-শাস্ত্র করিয়ে সঞ্চয় ॥ ২৮ ॥

bālya-kāla haite mora svabhāva eka haya
nāmera mahimā-śāstra kariye sañcaya

SYNONYMS

bālya-kāla haite—from my childhood; *mora*—my; *sva-bhāva*—practice; *eka*—one; *haya*—there is; *nāmera*—of the holy name; *mahimā*—concerning the glories; *śāstra*—the revealed scriptures; *kariye sañcaya*—I collect.

TRANSLATION

"From my childhood I have been practicing this chanting and have been collecting the glories of the holy name from revealed scriptures.

TEXT 29

রমন্তে যোগিনোঽনন্তে সত্যানন্দে চিদাত্মনি।
ইতি রামপদেনাসৌ পরং ব্রহ্মাভিধীয়তে ॥ ২৯ ॥

ramante yogino 'nante
satyānande cid-ātmani
iti rāma-padenāsau
paraṁ brahmābhidhīyate

SYNONYMS

ramante—take pleasure; *yoginaḥ*—transcendentalists; *anante*—in the unlimited; *satya-ānande*—real pleasure; *cit-ātmani*—in spiritual existence; *iti*—thus; *rāma*—Rāma; *padena*—by the word; *asau*—He; *param*—supreme; *brahma*—truth; *abhidhīyate*—is called.

TRANSLATION

" 'The Supreme Absolute Truth is called Rāma because the transcendentalists take pleasure in the unlimited true pleasure of spiritual existence.'

PURPORT

This is the eighth verse of the *Śatanāma-stotra* of Lord Rāmacandra, which is found in the *Padma Purāṇa*.

TEXT 30

কৃষির্ভূবাচকঃ শব্দো ণশ্চ নির্বৃতিবাচকঃ।
তয়োরৈক্যং পরং ব্রহ্ম কৃষ্ণ ইত্যভিধীয়তে ॥ ৩০ ॥

kṛṣir bhū-vācakaḥ śabdo
ṇaś ca nirvṛti-vācakaḥ
tayor aikyaṁ paraṁ brahma
kṛṣṇa ity abhidhīyate

SYNONYMS

kṛṣiḥ—the verbal root *kṛṣ; bhū*—attractive existence; *vācakaḥ*—signifying; *śabdaḥ*—word; *ṇaḥ*—the syllable *ṇa*; *ca*—and; *nirvṛti*—spiritual pleasure; *vācakaḥ*—indicating; *tayoḥ*—of both; *aikyam*—amalgamation; *param*—supreme; *brahma*—Absolute Truth; *kṛṣṇaḥ*—Lord Kṛṣṇa; *iti*—thus; *abhidhīyate*—is called.

TRANSLATION

" 'The word "kṛṣ" is the attractive feature of the Lord's existence, and "ṇa" means spiritual pleasure. When the verb "kṛṣ" is added to the affix "ṇa," it becomes Kṛṣṇa, which indicates the Absolute Truth.'

PURPORT

This is a verse from the *Udyoga-parva* (71.4) of the *Mahābhārata.*

TEXT 31

পরংব্রহ্ম দুইনাম সমান হইল।
পুনঃ আর শাস্ত্রে কিছু বিশেষ পাইল॥ ৩১ ॥

paraṁ brahma dui-nāma samāna ha-ila
punaḥ āra śāstre kichu viśeṣa pāila

SYNONYMS

param brahma—the Absolute Truth; *dui-nāma*—two names (Rāma and Kṛṣṇa); *samāna*—on an equal level; *ha-ila*—were; *punaḥ*—again; *āra*—further; *śāstre*—in revealed scripture; *kichu*—some; *viśeṣa*—specification; *pāila*—is found.

TRANSLATION

"As far as the holy names of Rāma and Kṛṣṇa are concerned, they are on an equal level, but for further advancement we receive some specific information from revealed scriptures.

TEXT 32

রাম রামেতি রামেতি রমে রামে মনোরমে।
সহস্রনামভিস্তুল্যং রামনাম বরাননে ॥ ৩২ ॥

rāma rāmeti rāmeti
rame rāme manorame
sahasra-nāmabhis tulyaṁ
rāma-nāma varānane

SYNONYMS

rāma—Rāma; *rāma*—Rāma; *iti*—thus; *rāma*—Rāma; *iti*—thus; *rame*—I enjoy; *rāme*—in the holy name of Rāma; *manaḥ-rame*—most beautiful; *sahasra-nāmabhiḥ*—with the one thousand names; *tulyam*—equal; *rāma-nāma*—the holy name of Rāma; *vara-ānane*—O lovely-faced woman.

TRANSLATION

"Lord Śiva addressed his wife Durgā as Varānanā and explained, 'I chant the holy name of Rāma, Rāma, Rāma and thus enjoy this beautiful sound. This holy name of Rāmacandra is equal to one thousand holy names of Lord Viṣṇu.'

PURPORT

This is a verse from the *Bṛhad-viṣṇu-sahasranāma-stotra* (72.335) in the *Uttara-khaṇḍa* of the *Padma Purāṇa.*

TEXT 33

সহস্রনাম্নাং পুণ্যানাং ত্রিরাবৃত্ত্যা তু যৎ ফলম্।
একাবৃত্ত্যা তু কৃষ্ণস্য নামৈকং তৎ প্রযচ্ছতি ॥ ৩৩ ॥

sahasra-nāmnāṁ puṇyānāṁ
trir-āvṛttyā tu yat phalam
ekāvṛttyā tu kṛṣṇasya
nāmaikaṁ tat prayacchati

SYNONYMS

sahasra-nāmnām—of one thousand names; *puṇyānām*—holy; *triḥ-āvṛttyā*—by thrice chanting; *tu*—but; *yat*—which; *phalam*—result; *eka-āvṛttyā*—by one repetition; *tu*—but; *kṛṣṇasya*—of Lord Kṛṣṇa; *nāma*—holy name; *ekam*—only one; *tat*—that result; *prayacchati*—gives.

TRANSLATION

" 'The pious results derived from chanting the thousand holy names of Viṣṇu three times can be attained by only one repetition of the holy name of Kṛṣṇa.'

PURPORT

This verse from the *Brahmāṇḍa Purāṇa* is found in the *Laghu-bhāgavatāmṛta* (1.354), by Rūpa Gosvāmī. For every three times one chants the holy name of Rāma, one can attain the same results simply by chanting the name of Kṛṣṇa once.

TEXT 34

এই বাক্যে কৃষ্ণনামের মহিমা অপার।
তথাপি লইতে নারি, শুন হেতু তার ॥ ৩৪ ॥

ei vākye kṛṣṇa-nāmera mahimā apāra
tathāpi la-ite nāri, śuna hetu tāra

SYNONYMS

ei vākye—in this statement; *kṛṣṇa-nāmera*—of the holy name of Kṛṣṇa; *mahimā*—glories; *apāra*—unlimited; *tathāpi*—still; *la-ite*—to chant; *nāri*—I am unable; *śuna*—just hear; *hetu*—the reason; *tāra*—of that.

TRANSLATION

"According to the statement of the śāstras, the glories of the holy name of Kṛṣṇa are unlimited. Still I could not chant His holy name. Please hear the reason for this.

TEXT 35

ইষ্টদেব রাম, তাঁর নামে সুখ পাই।
সুখ পাঞা রামনাম রাত্রিদিন গাই ॥ ৩৫ ॥

iṣṭa-deva rāma, tāṅra nāme sukha pāi
sukha pāñā rāma-nāma rātri-dina gāi

SYNONYMS

iṣṭa-deva—my worshipable Lord; *rāma*—Lord Śrī Rāmacandra; *tāṅra nāme*—in His holy name; *sukha pāi*—I get happiness; *sukha pāñā*—getting such transcendental happiness; *rāma-nāma*—the holy name of Lord Rāma; *rātri-dina*—day and night; *gāi*—I chant.

TRANSLATION

"My worshipable Lord has been Lord Rāmacandra, and by chanting His holy name I received happiness. Because I received such happiness, I chanted the holy name of Lord Rāma day and night.

TEXT 36

তোমার দর্শনে যবে কৃষ্ণনাম আইল।
তাহার মহিমা তবে হৃদয়ে লাগিল ॥ ৩৬ ॥

tomāra darśane yabe kṛṣṇa-nāma āila
tāhāra mahimā tabe hṛdaye lāgila

SYNONYMS

tomāra darśane—by meeting You; *yabe*—when; *kṛṣṇa-nāma*—the holy name of Kṛṣṇa; *āila*—appeared; *tāhāra*—His; *mahimā*—glories; *tabe*—at that time; *hṛdaye*—in the heart; *lāgila*—became fixed.

TRANSLATION

"By Your appearance, Lord Kṛṣṇa's holy name also appeared, and at that time the glories of Kṛṣṇa's name awoke in my heart."

TEXT 37

সেই কৃষ্ণ তুমি সাক্ষাৎ—ইহা নির্ধারিল।
এত কহি' বিপ্র প্রভুর চরণে পড়িল ॥ ৩৭ ॥

sei kṛṣṇa tumi sākṣāt—ihā nirdhārila
eta kahi' vipra prabhura caraṇe paḍila

SYNONYMS

sei—that; *kṛṣṇa*—the Personality of Godhead, Kṛṣṇa; *tumi*—You; *sākṣāt*—directly; *ihā*—this; *nirdhārila*—ascertained; *eta kahi'*—saying this; *vipra*—the *brāhmaṇa; prabhura*—of Lord Caitanya Mahāprabhu; *caraṇe*—at the lotus feet; *paḍila*—fell down.

TRANSLATION

The brāhmaṇa concluded, "Sir, You are that Lord Kṛṣṇa Himself. This is my ascertainment." Saying this, the brāhmaṇa fell down at the lotus feet of Śrī Caitanya Mahāprabhu.

TEXT 38

তাঁরে কৃপা করি' প্রভু চলিলা আর দিনে ।
বৃদ্ধকাশী আসি' কৈল শিব-দরশনে ॥ ৩৮ ॥

tāṅre kṛpā kari' prabhu calilā āra dine
vṛddhakāśī āsi' kaila śiva-daraśane

SYNONYMS

tāṅre—unto him; *kṛpā kari'*—showing mercy; *prabhu*—Lord Śrī Caitanya Mahāprabhu; *calilā*—traveled; *āra dine*—the next day; *vṛddhakāśī*—to Vṛddhakāśī; *āsi'*—coming; *kaila*—did; *śiva-daraśane*—visiting Lord Śiva's temple.

TRANSLATION

After showing mercy to the brāhmaṇa, Lord Śrī Caitanya Mahāprabhu left the next day and arrived at Vṛddhakāśī, where He visited the temple of Lord Śiva.

PURPORT

Vṛddhakāśī's present name is Vṛddhācalam. It is situated in the southern Ārkaṭa district on the bank of the River Maṇimukha. This place is also known as Kālahasti-pura. Lord Śiva's temple there was worshiped for many years by Govinda, the cousin of Rāmānujācārya.

TEXT 39

তাহাঁ হৈতে চলি' আগে গেলা এক গ্রামে ।
ব্রাহ্মণ-সমাজ তাহাঁ, করিল বিশ্রামে ॥ ৩৯ ॥

tāhāṅ haite cali' āge gelā eka grāme
brāhmaṇa-samāja tāhāṅ, karila viśrāme

SYNONYMS

tāhāṅ haite—from there; *cali'*—going; *āge*—forwards; *gelā*—went; *eka*—one; *grāme*—to a village; *brāhmaṇa-samāja*—assembly of *brāhmaṇas*; *tāhāṅ*—there; *karila viśrāme*—He rested.

TRANSLATION

Śrī Caitanya Mahāprabhu then left Vṛddhakāśī and proceeded further ahead. In one village He saw that most of the residents were brāhmaṇas, and He took His rest there.

TEXT 40

প্রভুর প্রভাবে লোক আইল দরশনে।
লক্ষার্বুদ লোক আইসে না যায় গণনে ॥ ৪০॥

prabhura prabhāve loka āila daraśane
lakṣārbuda loka āise nā yāya gaṇane

SYNONYMS

prabhura—of Lord Śrī Caitanya Mahāprabhu; *prabhāve*—by the influence; *loka*—people; *āila*—came; *daraśane*—to see Him; *lakṣa-arbuda*—many millions; *loka*—persons; *āise*—came; *nā*—not; *yāya gaṇane*—can be counted.

TRANSLATION

Due to the influence of Lord Caitanya Mahāprabhu, many millions of men came just to see Him. Indeed, the assembly was so unlimited that its members could not be counted.

TEXT 41

গোসাঞির সৌন্দর্য দেখি' তাতে প্রেমাবেশ।
সবে 'কৃষ্ণ' কহে, 'বৈষ্ণব' হৈল সর্বদেশ ॥ ৪১ ॥

gosāñira saundarya dekhi' tāte premāveśa
sabe 'kṛṣṇa' kahe, 'vaiṣṇava' haila sarva-deśa

SYNONYMS

gosāñira—of the Lord; *saundarya*—the beauty; *dekhi'*—seeing; *tāte*—in that; *prema-āveśa*—ecstatic love; *sabe*—everyone; *kṛṣṇa kahe*—uttered the holy name of Kṛṣṇa; *vaiṣṇava*—Vaiṣṇava devotees; *haila*—became; *sarva-deśa*—everyone.

TRANSLATION

The Lord's bodily features were very beautiful, and in addition He was always in the ecstasy of love of Godhead. Simply by seeing Him, everyone began chanting the holy name of Kṛṣṇa, and thus everyone became a Vaiṣṇava devotee.

TEXT 42

তার্কিক-মীমাংসক, যত মায়াবাদিগণ।
সাংখ্য, পাতঞ্জল, স্মৃতি, পুরাণ, আগম ॥ ৪২ ॥

tārkika-mīmāṁsaka, yata māyāvādi-gaṇa
sāṅkhya, pātañjala, smṛti, purāṇa, āgama

SYNONYMS

tārkika—logicians; *mīmāṁsaka*—followers of *mīmāṁsā* philosophy; *yata*—all; *māyāvādi-gaṇa*—followers of Śaṅkarācārya; *sāṅkhya*—followers of Kapila; *pātañjala*—followers of mystic *yoga; smṛti*—supplementary Vedic literatures; *purāṇa—Purāṇas; āgama*—the *tantra-śāstras.*

TRANSLATION

There are many kinds of philosophers. Some are logicians who follow Gautama or Kaṇāda. Some follow the mīmāṁsā philosophy of Jaimini. Some follow the Māyāvāda philosophy of Śaṅkarācārya, and others follow Kapila's sāṅkhya philosophy or the mystic yoga system of Patañjali. Some follow the smṛti-śāstra composed of twenty religious scriptures, and others follow the Purāṇas and the tantra-śāstra. In this way there are many different types of philosophers.

TEXT 43

নিজ-নিজ-শাস্ত্রোদ্গ্রাহে সবাই প্রচণ্ড।
সর্ব মত দুষি' প্রভু করে খণ্ড খণ্ড ॥ ৪৩ ॥

nija-nija-śāstrodgrāhe sabāi pracaṇḍa
sarva mata duṣi' prabhu kare khaṇḍa khaṇḍa

SYNONYMS

nija-nija—their own; *śāstra*—of the scripture; *udgrāhe*—to establish the conclusion; *sabāi*—all of them; *pracaṇḍa*—very powerful; *sarva*—all; *mata*—opinions; *duṣi'*—condemning; *prabhu*—Śrī Caitanya Mahāprabhu; *kare*—does; *khaṇḍa khaṇḍa*—breaking to pieces.

TRANSLATION

All of these adherents of various scriptures were ready to present the conclusions of their respective scriptures, but Śrī Caitanya Mahāprabhu broke all their opinions to pieces and established His own cult of bhakti based on the Vedas, Vedānta, the Brahma-sūtra and the philosophy of acintya-bhedābheda-tattva.

TEXT 44

সর্বত্র স্থাপয় প্রভু বৈষ্ণবসিদ্ধান্তে।
প্রভুর সিদ্ধান্ত কেহ না পারে খণ্ডিতে ॥ ৪৪ ॥

sarvatra sthāpaya prabhu vaiṣṇava-siddhānte
prabhura siddhānta keha nā pāre khaṇḍite

SYNONYMS

sarvatra—everywhere; *sthāpaya*—establishes; *prabhu*—Śrī Caitanya Mahāprabhu; *vaiṣṇava-siddhānte*—the conclusion of the Vaiṣṇavas; *prabhura*—of Lord Śrī Caitanya Mahāprabhu; *siddhānta*—conclusion; *keha*—anyone; *nā pāre*—is not able; *khaṇḍite*—to defy.

TRANSLATION

Śrī Caitanya Mahāprabhu established the devotional cult everywhere. No one could defeat Him.

TEXT 45

হারি' হারি' প্রভুমতে করেন প্রবেশ ।
এইমতে 'বৈষ্ণব' প্রভু কৈল দক্ষিণ দেশ ॥ ৪৫ ॥

hāri' hāri' prabhu-mate karena praveśa
ei-mate 'vaiṣṇava' prabhu kaila dakṣiṇa deśa

SYNONYMS

hāri' hāri'—being defeated; *prabhu-mate*—into the cult of Śrī Caitanya Mahāprabhu; *karena praveśa*—enter; *ei-mate*—in this way; *vaiṣṇava*—Vaiṣṇava devotees; *prabhu*—Lord Śrī Caitanya Mahāprabhu; *kaila*—made; *dakṣiṇa*—South India; *deśa*—country.

TRANSLATION

Being thus defeated by Lord Śrī Caitanya Mahāprabhu, all these philosophers and their followers entered into His cult. In this way Lord Caitanya made South India into a country of Vaiṣṇavas.

TEXT 46

পাষণ্ডী আইল যত পাণ্ডিত্য শুনিয়া ।
গর্ব করি' আইল সঙ্গে শিষ্যগণ লঞা ॥ ৪৬ ॥

pāṣaṇḍī āila yata pāṇḍitya śuniyā
garva kari' āila saṅge śiṣya-gaṇa lañā

SYNONYMS

pāṣaṇḍī—nonbelievers; *āila*—came there; *yata*—all; *pāṇḍitya*—erudition; *śuniyā*—hearing; *garva kari'*—with great pride; *āila*—came there; *saṅge*—with; *śiṣya-gaṇa*—disciples; *lañā*—taking.

TRANSLATION

When the nonbelievers heard of the erudition of Śrī Caitanya Mahāprabhu, they came to Him with great pride, bringing their disciples with them.

TEXT 47

বৌদ্ধাচার্য মহাপণ্ডিত নিজ নবমতে ।
প্রভুর আগে উদ্‌গ্রাহ করি' লাগিলা বলিতে ॥ ৪৭ ॥

bauddhācārya mahā-paṇḍita nija nava-mate
prabhura āge udgrāha kari' lāgilā balite

SYNONYMS

bauddha-ācārya—the leader in Buddhist philosophy; *mahā-paṇḍita*—greatly learned scholar; *nija*—own; *nava*—nine; *mate*—philosophical conclusions; *prabhura āge*—before Lord Śrī Caitanya Mahāprabhu; *udgrāha*—argument; *kari'*—making; *lāgilā*—began; *balite*—to speak.

TRANSLATION

One of them was the leader of a Buddhist cult and was a very learned scholar. To establish their nine philosophical conclusions, he came before the Lord and began to speak.

TEXT 48

যদ্যপি অসম্ভাষ্য বৌদ্ধ অযুক্ত দেখিতে ।
তথাপি বলিলা প্রভু গর্ব খণ্ডাইতে ॥ ৪৮ ॥

yadyapi asambhāṣya bauddha ayukta dekhite
tathāpi balilā prabhu garva khaṇḍāite

SYNONYMS

yadyapi—although; *asambhāṣya*—not fit for discussion; *bauddha*—followers of Buddha's philosophy; *ayukta*—not fit; *dekhite*—to see; *tathāpi*—still; *balilā*—spoke; *prabhu*—Lord Śrī Caitanya Mahāprabhu; *garva*—pride; *khaṇḍāite*—to diminish.

TRANSLATION

Although the Buddhists are unfit for discussion and should not be seen by Vaiṣṇavas, Caitanya Mahāprabhu spoke to them just to decrease their false pride.

TEXT 49

তর্ক-প্রধান বৌদ্ধশাস্ত্র 'নব মতে'।
তর্কেই খণ্ডিল প্রভু, না পারে স্থাপিতে ॥ ৪৯ ॥

tarka-pradhāna bauddha-śāstra 'nava mate'
tarkei khaṇḍila prabhu, nā pāre sthāpite

SYNONYMS

tarka-pradhāna—argumentative; *bauddha-śāstra*—scriptures of the Buddhist cult; *nava mate*—in nine basic principles; *tarkei*—by argument; *khaṇḍila*—refuted; *prabhu*—Śrī Caitanya Mahāprabhu; *nā*—not; *pāre*—can; *sthāpite*—establish.

TRANSLATION

The scriptures of the Buddhist cult are chiefly based on argument and logic, and they contain nine chief principles. Because Śrī Caitanya Mahāprabhu defeated them in their argument, they could not establish their cult.

PURPORT

Śrīla Bhaktivinoda Ṭhākura states that according to the Buddhist cult there are two ways of understanding philosophy. One is called *hīnāyana*, and the other is called *mahāyana*. Along this path, there are nine principles. (1) The creation is eternal; therefore there is no need to accept a creator. (2) This cosmic manifestation is false. (3) "I am" is the truth. (4) There is repetition of birth and death. (5) Lord Buddha is the only source of understanding the truth. (6) The principle of *nirvāṇa*, or annihilation, is the ultimate goal. (7) The philosophy of Buddha is the only philosophical path. (8) The *Vedas* are compiled by human beings. (9) Pious activities, showing mercy to others and so on are advised.

No one can attain the Absolute Truth by argument. One may be very expert in logic, and another person may be even more expert in the art of argument. Because there is so much word jugglery in logic, one can never come to the real conclusion about the Absolute Truth by argument. The followers of Vedic principles understand this. However, it is seen here that Śrī Caitanya Mahāprabhu defeated the Buddhist philosophy by argument. Those who are preachers in ISKCON will certainly meet many people who believe in intellectual arguments. Most of these people do not believe in the authority of the *Vedas*. Nevertheless, they accept intellectual speculation and argument. Therefore the preachers of Kṛṣṇa consciousness should be prepared to defeat others by argument, just as Śrī Caitanya Mahāprabhu did. In this verse it is clearly said, *tarkei khaṇḍila prabhu*. Lord Śrī Caitanya Mahāprabhu put forward such a strong argument that they could not counter Him to establish their cult.

Their first principle is that the creation is always existing, but if this is the case, there can be no theory of annihilation. The Buddhists maintain that annihilation or dissolution is the highest truth. If the creation is eternally existing, there is no question of dissolution or annihilation. This argument is not very strong because by practical experience we see that material things have a beginning, a middle and an end. The ultimate aim of the Buddhist philosophy is to dissolve the body. This is proposed because the body has a beginning. Similarly, the entire cosmic manifestation is also a gigantic body, but if we accept the fact that it is always existing, there can be no question of annihilation. Therefore the attempt to annihilate everything in order to attain zero is an absurdity. By our own practical experience we have to accept the beginning of creation, and when we accept the beginning, we must accept a creator. Such a creator must possess an all-pervasive body, as pointed out by *Bhagavad-gītā:*

sarvataḥ pāṇi-pādaṁ tat
sarvato 'kṣi-śiro-mukham
sarvataḥ śrutimal loke
sarvam āvṛtya tiṣṭhati

"Everywhere are His hands and legs, His eyes and faces, and He hears everything. In this way the Supersoul exists." (Bg. 13.14)

The Supreme Person must be present everywhere. His body existed before the creation; otherwise He could not be the creator. If the Supreme Person is a created being, there can be no question of a creator. The conclusion is that the cosmic manifestation is certainly created at a certain time, and the creator existed before the creation; therefore the creator is not a created being. The creator is Paraṁ Brahman, or the Supreme Spirit. Matter is not only subordinate to spirit but is actually created on the basis of spirit. When the spirit soul enters the womb of a mother, the body is created by material ingredients supplied by the mother. Everything is created in the material world, and consequently there must be a creator who is the Supreme Spirit and who is distinct from matter. It is confirmed in *Bhagavad-gītā* that the material energy is inferior and that the spiritual energy is the living entity. Both inferior and superior energies belong to a supreme person.

The Buddhists argue that the world is false, but this is not valid. The world is temporary, but it is not false. As long as we have the body, we must suffer the pleasures and pains of the body, even though we are not the body. We may not take these pleasures and pains very seriously, but they are factual nonetheless. We cannot actually say that they are false. If the bodily pains and pleasures are false, the creation would be false also, and consequently no one would take very much interest in it. The conclusion is that the material creation is not false or imaginary, but it is temporary.

The Buddhists maintain that the principle "I am" is the Ultimate Truth, but this excludes the individuality of "I" and "you." If there is no "I" and "you," or individuality, there is no possibility of argument. The Buddhist philosophy depends on argument, but there can be no argument if one simply depends on "I am." There must be a "you," or another person also. The philosophy of duality—the existence of the individual soul and the Supersoul—must be there. This is confirmed in the Second Chapter of *Bhagavad-gītā,* wherein the Lord says:

na tv evāhaṁ jātu nāsaṁ
na tvaṁ neme janādhipāḥ
na caiva na bhaviṣyāmaḥ
sarve vayam ataḥ param

"Never was there a time when I did not exist, nor you, nor all these kings; nor in the future shall any of us cease to be." (Bg. 2.12)

We existed in the past in different bodies, and after the annihilation of this body, we shall exist in another body. The principle of the soul is eternal, and it exists in this body or in another body. Even in this lifetime we experience existence in a child's body, a youth's body, a man's body and an old body. After the annihilation of the body, we acquire another body. The Buddhist cult also accepts the philosophy of transmigration, but the Buddhists do not properly explain the next birth. There are 8,400,000 species of life, and our next birth may be in any one of them; therefore this human body is not guaranteed.

According to the Buddhist's fifth principle, Lord Buddha is the only source for the attainment of knowledge. We cannot accept this, for Lord Buddha rejected the principles of Vedic knowledge. One must accept a principle of standard knowledge because one cannot attain the Absolute Truth simply by intellectual speculation. If everyone is an authority, or if everyone accepts his own intelligence as the ultimate criterion—as is presently fashionable—the scriptures will be interpreted in many different ways, and everyone will claim his own philosophy supreme. This has become a very great problem, and everyone is interpreting scripture in his own way and setting up his own basis of authority. *Yata mata tata pāṭha.* Now everybody and anybody is trying to establish his own theory as the Ultimate Truth. The Buddhists theorize that annihilation, or *nirvāṇa,* is the ultimate goal. Annihilation applies to the body, but the spirit soul transmigrates from one body to another. If this were not the case, how can so many multifarious bodies come into existence? If the next birth is a fact, the next bodily form is also a fact. As soon as we accept a material body, we must accept the fact that that body will be annihilated and that we will have to accept another body. If all material bodies are doomed to annihilation, we must obtain a nonmaterial body, or a spiritual body, if we wish the next birth to be anything but false. How the spiritual body is attained is explained in *Bhagavad-gītā:*

janma karma ca me divyam
evaṁ yo vetti tattvataḥ
tyaktvā dehaṁ punar janma
naiti mām eti so 'rjuna

"One who knows the transcendental nature of My appearance and activities does not, upon leaving the body, take his birth again in this material world, but attains My eternal abode, O Arjuna." (Bg. 4.9)

This is the highest perfection by which one can transcend the transmigration of material bodies and return home, back to Godhead. It is not that existence becomes void or zero: Existence continues, but if we positively want to annihilate the material body, we have to accept a spiritual body; otherwise there can be no eternality for the soul.

We cannot accept the theory that the Buddhist philosophy is the only way, for there are so many defects in that philosophy. A perfect philosophy is one that has no defects, and that is Vedānta philosophy. No one can point out any defects in Vedānta philosophy, and therefore we can conclude that Vedānta is the supreme philosophical way of understanding the truth. According to the Buddhist cult, the *Vedas* are compiled by ordinary human beings. If this were the case, they would not be authoritative. From Vedic literatures we understand that shortly after the creation, Lord Brahmā was instructed in the *Vedas*. It is not that the *Vedas* were created by Brahmā, although Brahmā is the original person in the universe. If Brahmā did not create the *Vedas,* but he is acknowledged as the first created being, wherefrom did Vedic knowledge come to Brahmā? Obviously the *Vedas* did not come from an ordinary person born in this material world. According to *Śrīmad-Bhāgavatam, tene brahma hṛdā ya ādi-kavaye:* after the creation, the Supreme Person imparted Vedic knowledge within the heart of Brahmā. There was no person in the beginning of the creation other than Brahmā, yet he did not compile the *Vedas;* therefore the conclusion is that the *Vedas* were not compiled by any created being. Vedic knowledge was given by the Supreme Personality of Godhead, who created this material world. This is also accepted by Śaṅkarācārya, although Śaṅkarācārya is not a Vaiṣṇava.

It is stated that mercy is one of the qualities of a Buddhist, but mercy is a relative thing. We show our mercy to a subordinate or to one who is suffering more than ourselves. However, if there is a superior person present, the superior person cannot be the object of our mercy. Rather, we are objects for the mercy of the superior person. Therefore showing compassion and mercy is a relative activity. It is not the Absolute Truth. Apart from this, we also must know what actual mercy is. To give a sick man something forbidden for him to eat is not mercy. Rather, it is cruelty. Unless we know what mercy really is, we may create an undesirable situation. If we wish to show real mercy, we will preach Kṛṣṇa consciousness in order to revive the lost consciousness of human beings, the living entity's original consciousness. Since the Buddhist philosophy does not admit the existence of the spirit soul, the so-called mercy of the Buddhists is defective.

TEXT 50

বৌদ্ধাচার্য 'নব প্রশ্ন' সব উঠাইল ।
দৃঢ় যুক্তি-তর্কে প্রভু খণ্ড খণ্ড কৈল ॥ ৫০ ॥

bauddhācārya 'nava praśna' saba uṭhāila
dṛḍha yukti-tarke prabhu khaṇḍa khaṇḍa kaila

SYNONYMS

bauddha-ācārya—the teacher of the Buddhist cult; *nava praśna*—nine different types of questions; *saba*—all; *uṭhāila*—raised; *dṛḍha*—strong; *yukti*—argument; *tarke*—with logic; *prabhu*—Lord Śrī Caitanya Mahāprabhu; *khaṇḍa khaṇḍa kaila*—broke into pieces.

TRANSLATION

The teacher of the Buddhist cult set forth nine principles, but Śrī Caitanya Mahāprabhu broke them to pieces with His strong logic.

TEXT 51

দার্শনিক পণ্ডিত সবাই পাইল পরাজয় ।
লোকে হাস্য করে, বৌদ্ধ পাইল লজ্জা-ভয় ॥ ৫১ ॥

dārśanika paṇḍita sabāi pāila parājaya
loke hāsya kare, bauddha pāila lajjā-bhaya

SYNONYMS

dārśanika—philosophical speculators; *paṇḍita*—scholars; *sabāi*—all of them; *pāila parājaya*—were defeated; *loke*—people in general; *hāsya kare*—laugh; *bauddha*—the Buddhists; *pāila*—got; *lajjā*—shame; *bhaya*—fear.

TRANSLATION

All mental speculators and learned scholars were defeated by Śrī Caitanya Mahāprabhu, and when the people began to laugh, the Buddhist philosophers felt both shame and fear.

PURPORT

These philosophers were all atheists, for they did not believe in the existence of God. Atheists may be very expert in mental speculation and may be so-called great philosophers, but they can be defeated by a Vaiṣṇava firmly situated in his conviction and God consciousness. Following in the footsteps of Śrī Caitanya Mahāprabhu, all the preachers engaged in the service of ISKCON should be very expert in putting forward strong arguments and defeating all types of atheists.

TEXT 52

প্রভুকে বৈষ্ণব জানি' বৌদ্ধ ঘরে গেল ।
সকল বৌদ্ধ মিলি' তবে কুমন্ত্রণা কৈল ॥ ৫২ ॥

prabhuke vaiṣṇava jāni' bauddha ghare gela
sakala bauddha mili' tabe kumantraṇā kaila

SYNONYMS

prabhuke—Lord Śrī Caitanya Mahāprabhu; *vaiṣṇava jāni'*—knowing to be a Vaiṣṇava; *bauddha*—the Buddhists; *ghare gela*—returned home; *sakala bauddha*—all the Buddhists; *mili'*—coming together; *tabe*—thereafter; *ku-mantraṇā*—plot; *kaila*—made.

TRANSLATION

The Buddhists could understand that Lord Śrī Caitanya Mahāprabhu was a Vaiṣṇava, and they returned home very unhappy. Later, however, they began to plot against the Lord.

TEXT 53

অপবিত্র অন্ন এক থালিতে ভরিয়া ।
প্রভু-আগে নিল 'মহাপ্রসাদ' বলিয়া ॥ ৫৩ ॥

apavitra anna eka thālite bhariyā
prabhu-āge nila 'mahā-prasāda' baliyā

SYNONYMS

apavitra—polluted; *anna*—food; *eka*—one; *thālite*—plate; *bhariyā*—filling; *prabhu-āge*—in front of Lord Śrī Caitanya Mahāprabhu; *nila*—brought; *mahā-prasāda baliyā*—calling it *mahā-prasāda.*

TRANSLATION

Having made their plot, the Buddhists brought a plate of untouchable food before Lord Śrī Caitanya Mahāprabhu and called it mahā-prasāda.

PURPORT

The word *apavitra anna* refers to food that is unacceptable for a Vaiṣṇava. In other words, a Vaiṣṇava cannot accept any food offered by an *avaiṣṇava* in the name of *mahā-prasāda.* This should be a principle for all Vaiṣṇavas. When asked, "What is the behavior of a Vaiṣṇava?" Śrī Caitanya Mahāprabhu replied, "A Vaiṣṇava must avoid the company of an *avaiṣṇava* [*asat*]." The word *asat* refers to an *avaiṣṇava,* that is, one who is not a Vaiṣṇava. *Asat-saṅga-tyāga,* —— *ei vaiṣṇava-ācāra* (Cc. *Madhya* 22.87). A Vaiṣṇava must be very strict in this respect and should not at all cooperate with an *avaiṣṇava.* If an *avaiṣṇava* offers food in the name of *mahā-prasāda,* it should not be accepted. Such food cannot be *prasāda* because an *avaiṣṇava* cannot offer anything to the Lord. Sometimes preachers in the Kṛṣṇa consciousness movement have to accept food in a home where the householder is an *avaiṣṇava;* however, if this food is offered to the Deity, it can be taken. Ordinary food cooked by an *avaiṣṇava* should not be accepted by a Vaiṣṇava. Even if an *avaiṣṇava* cooks food without fault, he cannot offer it to Lord Viṣṇu, and it cannot be accepted as *mahā-prasāda.* According to *Bhagavad-gītā:*

patraṁ puṣpaṁ phalaṁ toyaṁ
yo me bhaktyā prayacchati
tad ahaṁ bhakty-upahṛtam
aśnāmi prayatātmanaḥ

"If one offers Me with love and devotion a leaf, a flower, fruit or water, I will accept it." (Bg. 9.26)

Kṛṣṇa can accept anything offered by His devotee with devotion. An *avaiṣṇava* may be a vegetarian and a very clean cook, but because he cannot offer the foodstuff to Viṣṇu, the food he cooks cannot be accepted as *mahā-prasāda.* It is better that a Vaiṣṇava abandon such food as untouchable.

TEXT 54

হেনকালে মহাকায় এক পক্ষী আইল ।
ঠোঁটে করি' অন্নসহ থালি লঞা গেল ॥ ৫৪ ॥

hena-kāle mahā-kāya eka pakṣī āila
ṭhoṅṭe kari' anna-saha thāli lañā gela

SYNONYMS

hena-kāle—at this time; *mahā-kāya*—having a large body; *eka*—one; *pakṣī*—bird; *āila*—appeared there; *ṭhoṅṭe kari'*—by the beak; *anna-saha*—with food; *thāli*—the plate; *lañā*—taking; *gela*—went away.

TRANSLATION

When the contaminated food was offered to Śrī Caitanya Mahāprabhu, a very large bird appeared on the spot, picked up the plate in its beak and flew away.

TEXT 55

বৌদ্ধগণের উপরে অন্ন পড়ে অমেধ্য হৈয়া ।
বৌদ্ধাচার্যের মাথায় থালি পড়িল বাজিয়া ॥ ৫৫ ॥

bauddha-gaṇera upare anna paḍe amedhya haiyā
bauddhācāryera māthāya thāli paḍila bājiyā

SYNONYMS

bauddha-gaṇera—all the Buddhists; *upare*—upon; *anna*—the food; *paḍe*—began to fall down; *amedhya*—untouchable; *haiyā*—being; *bauddha-ācāryera*—of the teacher of the Buddhists; *māthāya*—on the head; *thāli*—the plate; *paḍila*—fell down; *bājiyā*—making a great sound.

TRANSLATION

Indeed, the untouchable food fell upon the Buddhists, and the large bird dropped the plate on the head of the chief Buddhist teacher. When it fell on his head, it made a big sound.

TEXT 56

তেরছে পড়িল থালি,—মাথা কাটি' গেল ।
মূর্চ্ছিত হঞা আচার্য ভূমিতে পড়িল ॥ ৫৬ ॥

terache paḍila thāli,——māthā kāṭi' gela
mūrcchita hañā ācārya bhūmite paḍila

SYNONYMS

terache—at an angle; *paḍila*—fell down; *thāli*—the plate; *māthā*—the head; *kāṭi'*—cutting; *gela*—went; *mūrcchita*—unconscious; *hañā*—becoming; *ācārya*—the teacher; *bhūmite*—on the ground; *paḍila*—fell down.

TRANSLATION

The plate was made of metal, and when its edge hit the head of the teacher, it cut him, and the teacher immediately fell to the ground unconscious.

TEXT 57

হাহাকার করি' কান্দে সব শিষ্যগণ ।
সবে আসি' প্রভু-পদে লইল শরণ ॥ ৫৭ ॥

hāhākāra kari' kānde saba śiṣya-gaṇa
sabe āsi' prabhu-pade la-ila śaraṇa

SYNONYMS

hāhā-kāra—a roaring sound; *kari'*—making; *kānde*—cry; *saba*—all; *śiṣya-gaṇa*—disciples; *sabe*—all of them; *āsi'*—coming; *prabhu-pade*—to the lotus feet of Lord Caitanya Mahāprabhu; *la-ila*—took; *śaraṇa*—shelter.

TRANSLATION

When the teacher fell unconscious, his Buddhist disciples cried aloud and ran to the lotus feet of Śrī Caitanya Mahāprabhu for shelter.

TEXT 58

তুমি ত' ঈশ্বর সাক্ষাৎ, ক্ষম অপরাধ ।
জীয়াও আমার গুরু, করহ প্রসাদ ॥ ৫৮ ॥

tumi ta' īśvara sākṣāt, kṣama aparādha
jīyāo āmāra guru, karaha prasāda

SYNONYMS

tumi—You; *ta'*—indeed; *īśvara*—the Supreme Personality of Godhead; *sākṣāt*—directly; *kṣama*—please excuse; *aparādha*—offense; *jīyāo*—bring back to consciousness; *āmāra*—our; *guru*—spiritual master; *karaha*—do; *prasāda*—this mercy.

TRANSLATION

They all prayed to Lord Śrī Caitanya Mahāprabhu, addressing Him as the Supreme Personality of Godhead Himself and saying, "Sir, please excuse our offense. Please have mercy upon us and bring our spiritual master back to life."

TEXT 59

প্রভু কহে,—সবে কহ 'কৃষ্ণ' 'কৃষ্ণ' 'হরি'।
গুরুকর্ণে কহ কৃষ্ণনাম উচ্চ করি' ॥ ৫৯ ॥

prabhu kahe,——sabe kaha 'kṛṣṇa' 'kṛṣṇa' 'hari'
guru-karṇe kaha kṛṣṇa-nāma ucca kari'

SYNONYMS

prabhu kahe—Lord Śrī Caitanya Mahāprabhu said; *sabe*—all of you; *kaha*—chant; *kṛṣṇa kṛṣṇa hari*—the holy names of Lord Kṛṣṇa and Hari; *guru-karṇe*—near the ear of your spiritual master; *kaha*—chant; *kṛṣṇa-nāma*—the holy name of Lord Kṛṣṇa; *ucca kari'*—very loudly.

TRANSLATION

The Lord then replied to the Buddhist disciples: "You should all chant the names of Kṛṣṇa and Hari very loudly near the ear of your spiritual master.

TEXT 60

তোমা-সবার 'গুরু' তবে পাইবে চেতন।
সব বৌদ্ধ মিলি' করে কৃষ্ণসঙ্কীর্তন ॥ ৬০ ॥

tomā-sabāra 'guru' tabe pāibe cetana
saba bauddha mili' kare kṛṣṇa-saṅkīrtana

SYNONYMS

tomā-sabāra—all of you; *guru*—the spiritual master; *tabe*—then; *pāibe*—will get; *cetana*—consciousness; *saba bauddha*—all the Buddhist disciples; *mili'*—coming together; *kare*—do; *kṛṣṇa-saṅkīrtana*—chanting of the Hare Kṛṣṇa *mantra.*

TRANSLATION

"By this method your spiritual master will regain his consciousness." Following Śrī Caitanya Mahāprabhu's advice, all the Buddhist disciples began to chant the holy name of Kṛṣṇa congregationally.

TEXT 61

গুরু-কর্ণে কহে সবে 'কৃষ্ণ' 'রাম' 'হরি'।
চেতন পাঞা আচার্য বলে 'হরি' 'হরি' ॥ ৬১ ॥

guru-karṇe kahe sabe 'kṛṣṇa' 'rāma' 'hari'
cetana pāñā ācārya bale 'hari' 'hari'

SYNONYMS

guru-karṇe—into the ear of the spiritual master; *kahe*—they said; *sabe*—all together; *kṛṣṇa rāma hari*—the holy names of the Lord, Kṛṣṇa, Rāma and Hari; *cetana*—consciousness; *pāñā*—getting; *ācārya*—the teacher; *bale*—chanted; *hari hari*—the name of Lord Hari.

TRANSLATION

When all the disciples chanted the holy names Kṛṣṇa, Rāma and Hari, the Buddhist teacher regained consciousness and immediately began to chant the holy name of Lord Hari.

PURPORT

Śrī Bhaktisiddhānta Sarasvatī Ṭhākura comments that all the Buddhist disciples were actually initiated by Śrī Caitanya Mahāprabhu to chant the holy name of Kṛṣṇa, and when they chanted, they actually became different persons. At that time they were not Buddhists or atheists but Vaiṣṇavas. Consequently they immediately accepted Śrī Caitanya Mahāprabhu's order. Their original Kṛṣṇa consciousness was revived, and they were immediately able to chant Hare Kṛṣṇa and begin worshiping the Supreme Lord Viṣṇu.

It is the spiritual master who delivers the disciple from the clutches of *māyā* by initiating him into the chanting of the Hare Kṛṣṇa *mahā-mantra.* In this way a sleeping human being can revive his consciousness by chanting Hare Kṛṣṇa, Hare Kṛṣṇa, Kṛṣṇa Kṛṣṇa, Hare Hare/ Hare Rāma, Hare Rāma, Rāma Rāma, Hare Hare. In other words, the spiritual master awakens the sleeping living entity to his original consciousness so that he can worship Lord Viṣṇu. This is the purpose of *dīkṣā,* or initiation. Initiation means receiving the pure knowledge of spiritual consciousness.

One point to note in this regard is that the spiritual master of the Buddhists did not initiate his disciples. Rather, his disciples were initiated by Śrī Kṛṣṇa Caitanya Mahāprabhu, and they in turn were able to initiate their so-called spiritual master. This is the *paramparā* system. The so-called spiritual master of the Buddhists was actually in the position of a disciple, and after his disciples were initiated by Śrī Caitanya Mahāprabhu, they acted as his spiritual masters. This was possible only because the disciples of the Buddhist *ācārya* received the mercy of Lord Śrī Caitanya Mahāprabhu. Unless one is favored by Śrī Caitanya Mahāprabhu in the disciplic succession, one cannot act as a spiritual master. We should take the instructions of Śrī Caitanya Mahāprabhu, the spiritual master of the whole universe, to understand how one becomes a spiritual master and a disciple.

TEXT 62

কৃষ্ণ বলি' আচার্য প্রভুরে করেন বিনয়।
দেখিয়া সকল লোক হইল বিস্ময়॥ ৬২॥

kṛṣṇa bali' ācārya prabhure karena vinaya
dekhiyā sakala loka ha-ila vismaya

SYNONYMS

kṛṣṇa bali'—chanting the holy name of Kṛṣṇa; *ācārya*—the so-called spiritual master of the Buddhists; *prabhure*—unto Lord Śrī Caitanya Mahāprabhu; *karena*—does; *vinaya*—submission; *dekhiyā*—seeing this; *sakala loka*—all the people; *ha-ila*—became; *vismaya*—astonished.

TRANSLATION

When the spiritual master of the Buddhists began to chant the holy name of Kṛṣṇa and submitted to Lord Śrī Caitanya Mahāprabhu, all the people who were gathered there were astonished.

TEXT 63

এইরূপে কৌতুক করি' শচীর নন্দন।
অন্তর্ধান কৈল, কেহ না পায় দর্শন॥ ৬৩॥

ei-rūpe kautuka kari' śacīra nandana
antardhāna kaila, keha nā pāya darśana

SYNONYMS

ei-rūpe—in this way; *kautuka kari'*—making fun; *śacīra nandana*—the son of mother Śacī; *antardhāna kaila*—disappeared; *keha*—anyone; *nā*—does not; *pāya*—get; *darśana*—audience.

TRANSLATION

Śrī Caitanya Mahāprabhu, the son of Śacīdevī, then suddenly and strangely disappeared from everyone's sight, and it was impossible for anyone to find Him.

TEXT 64

মহাপ্রভু চলি' আইলা ত্রিপতি-ত্রিমল্লে।
চতুর্ভুজ মূর্তি দেখি' ব্যেঙ্কটাদ্রে্য চলে॥ ৬৪॥

mahāprabhu cali' āilā tripati-trimalle
catur-bhuja mūrti dekhi' vyeṅkaṭādrye cale

SYNONYMS

mahāprabhu—Lord Śrī Caitanya Mahāprabhu; *cali' āilā*—arrived by walking; *tripati-trimalle*—at the holy places named Tripati and Trimalla; *catuḥ-bhuja*—four-handed; *mūrti*—Deity; *dekhi'*—seeing; *vyeṅkaṭa-adrye*—to the holy place Vyeṅkaṭa Hill; *cale*—began to proceed.

TRANSLATION

Śrī Caitanya Mahāprabhu next arrived at Tirupati and Trimalla, where He saw a four-handed Deity. Then He next proceeded toward Vyeṅkaṭa Hill.

PURPORT

Śrīla Bhaktisiddhānta Sarasvatī Ṭhākura has actually described the chronological order of Lord Caitanya Mahāprabhu's visit. The Tirupati temple is sometimes called Tirupaṭura. It is situated on the northern side of Ārkaṭa in the district of Candragiri. It is a famous holy place of pilgrimage. In pursuance of His name, Vyeṅkaṭeśvara, the four-handed Lord Viṣṇu, the Deity of Bālājī, with His potencies named Śrī and Bhū, is located on Vyeṅkaṭa Hill, about eight miles from Tirupati. This Vyeṅkaṭeśvara Deity is in the form of Lord Viṣṇu, and the place where He is situated is known as Vyeṅkaṭa-kṣetra. There are many temples in southern India, but this Bālājī temple is especially opulent. A great fair is held there in the months of September and October. There is a railway station called Tirupati on the southern railway. Nimna-tirupati is located in the valley of the Vyeṅkaṭa Hill. There are several temples there also, among which are Govindarāja and the Deity of Lord Rāmacandra.

TEXT 65

ত্রিপতি আসিয়া কৈল শ্রীরাম দরশন ।
রঘুনাথ-আগে কৈল প্রণাম স্তবন ॥ ৬৫ ॥

tripati āsiyā kaila śrī-rāma daraśana
raghu-nātha-āge kaila praṇāma stavana

SYNONYMS

tripati āsiyā—coming to Tripati; *kaila śrī-rāma daraśana*—visited the temple of Rāmacandra; *raghu-nātha-āge*—before Lord Rāmacandra; *kaila*—did; *praṇāma*—obeisances; *stavana*—offering prayers.

TRANSLATION

After arriving at Tripati, Lord Śrī Caitanya Mahāprabhu visited the temple of Lord Rāmacandra. He offered His prayers and obeisances before Rāmacandra, the descendant of King Raghu.

TEXT 66

স্বপ্রভাবে লোক-সবার করাঞা বিস্ময়।
পানা-নৃসিংহে আইলা প্রভু দয়াময় ॥ ৬৬ ॥

sva-prabhāve loka-sabāra karāñā vismaya
pānā-nṛsiṁhe āilā prabhu dayā-maya

SYNONYMS

sva-prabhāve—by His own influence; *loka-sabāra*—of all the people; *karāñā*—inducing; *vismaya*—astonishment; *pānā-nṛsiṁhe*—to the Lord named Pānā-nṛsiṁha; *āilā*—came; *prabhu*—Lord Śrī Caitanya Mahāprabhu; *dayā-maya*—the most merciful.

TRANSLATION

Everywhere Śrī Caitanya Mahāprabhu went, His influence astonished everyone. He next arrived at the temple of Pānā-nṛsiṁha. The Lord is so merciful.

PURPORT

This Pānā-nṛsiṁha, or Pānākal-narasiṁha, is located in the district of Kṛṣṇā in the hills known as Maṅgalagiri, about seven miles from a city known as Vejaoyādā. One must climb six hundred steps to reach the temple. It is said that when the Lord is offered food with syrup here, He does not take more than half. Within this temple is a conchshell presented by the late king of Tāñjor, and it is said that this shell was used by Lord Kṛṣṇa Himself. During the month of March, a great fair takes place in this temple.

TEXT 67

নৃসিংহে প্রণতি-স্তুতি প্রেমাবেশে কৈল।
প্রভুর প্রভাবে লোক চমৎকার হৈল ॥ ৬৭ ॥

nṛsiṁhe praṇati-stuti premāveśe kaila
prabhura prabhāve loka camatkāra haila

SYNONYMS

nṛsiṁhe—unto Lord Nṛsiṁha; *praṇati-stuti*—obeisances and prayers; *prema-āveśe*—in ecstatic love; *kaila*—offered; *prabhura*—of the Lord; *prabhāve*—by the influence; *loka*—the people; *camatkāra haila*—were astonished.

TRANSLATION

In great ecstatic love, Śrī Caitanya Mahāprabhu offered obeisances and prayers unto Lord Nṛsiṁha. The people were astonished to see Lord Caitanya's influence.

TEXT 68

শিবকাঞ্চী আসিয়া কৈল শিব দরশন ।
প্রভাবে 'বৈষ্ণব' কৈল সব শৈবগণ ॥ ৬৮ ॥

śiva-kāñcī āsiyā kaila śiva daraśana
prabhāve 'vaiṣṇava' kaila saba śaiva-gaṇa

SYNONYMS

śiva-kāñcī—to the holy place named Śiva-kāñcī; *āsiyā*—coming; *kaila*—did; *śiva daraśana*—visiting the temple of Lord Śiva; *prabhāve*—by His influence; *vaiṣṇava kaila*—turned into Vaiṣṇavas; *saba*—all; *śaiva-gaṇa*—the devotees of Lord Śiva.

TRANSLATION

Arriving at Śiva-kāñcī, Caitanya Mahāprabhu visited the deity of Lord Śiva. By His influence, He converted all the devotees of Lord Śiva into Vaiṣṇavas.

PURPORT

This Śiva-kāñcī is also known as Kañjibhirām, or the Benares of southern India. In Śiva-kāñcī there are hundreds of symbolic representations of Lord Śiva, as well as a temple that is supposed to be very, very old.

TEXT 69

বিষ্ণুকাঞ্চী আসি' দেখিল লক্ষ্মী-নারায়ণ ।
প্রণাম করিয়া কৈল বহুত স্তবন ॥ ৬৯ ॥

viṣṇu-kāñcī āsi' dekhila lakṣmī-nārāyaṇa
praṇāma kariyā kaila bahuta stavana

SYNONYMS

viṣṇu-kāñcī—to the holy place named Viṣṇu-kāñcī; *āsi'*—coming; *dekhila*—the Lord saw; *lakṣmī-nārāyaṇa*—the Deity of Lord Nārāyaṇa with mother Lakṣmī, the goddess of fortune; *praṇāma kariyā*—after offering obeisances; *kaila*—made; *bahuta stavana*—many prayers.

TRANSLATION

The Lord then visited a holy place known as Viṣṇu-kāñcī. He saw there Lakṣmī-Nārāyaṇa Deities, and He offered His respects and many prayers to please Them.

PURPORT

Viṣṇu-kāñcī is situated about five miles away from Kañjibhirām. It is here that Lord Varadarāja, another form of Lord Viṣṇu, resides. There is also a big lake known as Ananta-sarovara.

TEXT 70

প্রেমাবেশে নৃত্য-গীত বহুত করিল।
দিন-দুই রহি' লোকে 'কৃষ্ণভক্ত' কৈল ॥ ৭০ ॥

premāveśe nṛtya-gīta bahuta karila
dina-dui rahi' loke 'kṛṣṇa-bhakta' kaila

SYNONYMS

prema-āveśe—in ecstatic love; *nṛtya-gīta*—dancing and chanting; *bahuta*—much; *karila*—performed; *dina-dui*—for two days; *rahi'*—staying; *loke*—the people in general; *kṛṣṇa-bhakta*—devotees of Lord Kṛṣṇa; *kaila*—made.

TRANSLATION

When Śrī Caitanya Mahāprabhu stayed at Viṣṇu-kāñcī for two days, He danced and performed kīrtana in ecstasy. When all the people saw Him, they were converted into devotees of Lord Kṛṣṇa.

TEXT 71

ত্রিমলয় দেখি' গেলা ত্রিকালহস্তি-স্থানে।
মহাদেব দেখি' তাঁরে করিল প্রণামে ॥ ৭১ ॥

trimalaya dekhi' gelā trikāla-hasti-sthāne
mahādeva dekhi' tāṅre karila praṇāme

SYNONYMS

trimalaya dekhi'—after seeing Trimalaya; *gelā*—went; *tri-kāla-hasti-sthāne*—to the place named Trikāla-hastī; *mahā-deva*—Lord Śiva; *dekhi'*—seeing; *tāṅre*—unto him; *karila praṇāme*—offered obeisances.

TRANSLATION

After visiting Trimalaya, Caitanya Mahāprabhu went to see Trikāla-hastī. It was there that He saw Lord Śiva and offered him all respects and obeisances.

PURPORT

Trikāla-hastī is situated about twenty-two miles northeast of Tirupati. On its northern side is a river known as Suvarṇa-mukhī. The temple of Trikāla-hastī is located on the southern side of the river. The place is generally known as Śrī Kālahastī or Kālahastī and is famous for its temple of Lord Śiva. There he is called Vāyuliṅga-śiva.

TEXT 72

পক্ষিতীর্থ দেখি' কৈল শিব দরশন ।
বৃদ্ধকোল-তীর্থে তবে করিলা গমন ॥ ৭২ ॥

pakṣi-tīrtha dekhi' kaila śiva daraśana
vṛddhakola-tīrthe tabe karilā gamana

SYNONYMS

pakṣi-tīrtha dekhi'—after visiting the place known as Pakṣi-tīrtha; *kaila*—did; *śiva daraśana*—visiting the temple of Lord Śiva; *vṛddhakola-tīrthe*—to the holy place known as Vṛddhakola; *tabe*—then; *karilā gamana*—went.

TRANSLATION

At Pakṣi-tīrtha, Lord Śrī Caitanya Mahāprabhu visited the temple of Lord Śiva. Then He went to the Vṛddhakola place of pilgrimage.

PURPORT

This Pakṣi-tīrtha is also called Tirukāḍi-kuṇḍam and is located nine miles southeast of Ciṁlipaṭ. It has a five-hundred-foot elevation and is situated in a chain of hills known as Vedagiri or Vedācalam. There is a temple of Lord Śiva there, and the deity is known as Vedagirīśvara. It is said that two birds come there daily to receive food from the temple priest, and it is claimed that these birds have been coming since time immemorial.

TEXT 73

শ্বেতবরাহ দেখি, তাঁরে নমস্করি'।
পীতাম্বর-শিব-স্থানে গেলা গৌরহরি ॥ ৭৩ ॥

śveta-varāha dekhi, tāṅre namaskari'
pītāmbara-śiva-sthāne gelā gaurahari

SYNONYMS

śveta-varāha—the white boar incarnation; *dekhi*—seeing; *tāṅre*—unto Him; *namaskari'*—offering respect; *pīta-ambara*—dressed with yellow garments; *śiva-sthāne*—to the temple of Lord Śiva; *gelā*—went; *gaura-hari*—Lord Śrī Caitanya Mahāprabhu.

TRANSLATION

At Vṛddhakola, Lord Śrī Caitanya Mahāprabhu visited the temple of Śveta-varāha, the white boar. After offering Him respects, the Lord visited the temple of Lord Śiva, wherein the deity is dressed with yellow garments.

PURPORT

The temple of the white boar incarnation is situated at Vṛddhakola. The temple is made of stone and is located about one mile south of an oasis known as Bali-pīṭham. There is a Deity of the white boar incarnation, above whose head Śeṣa Nāga serves as an umbrella. The deity of Lord Śiva is known as Pītāmbara, and is also known as Cidāmbaram. This temple is located twenty-six miles south of Kuḍālora, and the deity there is also known as Ākāśaliṅga. The deity is in the form of Lord Śiva. This temple is situated on about thirty-nine acres of land, and all this land is surrounded by a wall sixty feet high.

TEXT 74

শিয়ালী ভৈরবী দেবী করি' দরশন।
কাবেরীর তীরে আইলা শচীর নন্দন ॥ ৭৪ ॥

śiyālī bhairavī devī kari' daraśana
kāverīra tīre āilā śacīra nandana

SYNONYMS

śiyālī bhairavī—Śiyālī-bhairavī; *devī*—goddess; *kari' daraśana*—visiting; *kāverīra tīre*—on the bank of the River Kāverī; *āilā*—came; *śacīra nandana*—the son of mother Śacī.

TRANSLATION

After visiting the temple of Śiyālī-bhairavī [another form of the goddess Durgā], Śrī Caitanya Mahāprabhu, the son of mother Śacī, went to the bank of the River Kāverī.

PURPORT

Śiyālī-bhairavī is located in the Tāñjor district, about forty-eight miles east of Tāñjor City. There is a very celebrated temple of Lord Śiva there and also a very large lake. It is said that one small boy, a devotee of Lord Śiva, came to that temple, and the goddess Durgā, known as Bhairavī, gave him her breast to suck. After visiting this temple, Śrī Caitanya Mahāprabhu went to the bank of the River Kāverī via the district of Tricinapallī. The Kāverī is mentioned in *Śrīmad-Bhāgavatam* (11.5.40) as a very pious river.

TEXT 75

গো-সমাজে শিব দেখি' আইলা বেদাবন ।
মহাদেব দেখি' তাঁরে করিলা বন্দন ॥ ৭৫ ॥

go-samāje śiva dekhi' āilā vedāvana
mahādeva dekhi' tāṅre karilā vandana

SYNONYMS

go-samāje—at the place named Go-samāja; *śiva dekhi'*—seeing the deity of Lord Śiva; *āilā vedāvana*—He arrived at Vedāvana; *mahā-deva dekhi'*—seeing Lord Śiva; *tāṅre*—unto him; *karilā vandana*—offered prayers.

TRANSLATION

The Lord then visited a place known as Go-samāja, where He saw Lord Śiva's temple. He then arrived at Vedāvana, where He saw another deity of Lord Śiva and offered him prayers.

PURPORT

Go-samāja is a place of pilgrimage for the devotees of Lord Śiva. It is very important and is located next to Vedāvana.

TEXT 76

অমৃতলিঙ্গ-শিব দেখি' বন্দন করিল ।
সব শিবালয়ে শৈব 'বৈষ্ণব' হইল ॥ ৭৬ ॥

amṛtaliṅga-śiva dekhi' vandana karila
saba śivālaye śaiva 'vaiṣṇava' ha-ila

SYNONYMS

amṛta-liṅga-śiva—the Lord Śiva deity named Amṛtaliṅga; *dekhi'*—seeing; *vandana karila*—offered obeisances; *saba śiva-ālaye*—in all the temples of Lord Śiva; *śaiva*—devotees of Lord Śiva; *vaiṣṇava ha-ila*—became devotees of Lord Kṛṣṇa.

TRANSLATION

Seeing the Śiva deity named Amṛtaliṅga, Lord Caitanya Mahāprabhu offered His obeisances. Thus He visited all the temples of Lord Śiva and converted the devotees of Lord Śiva into Vaiṣṇavas.

TEXT 77

দেবস্থানে আসি' কৈল বিষ্ণু দরশন ।
শ্রী-বৈষ্ণবের সঙ্গে তাহাঁ গোষ্ঠী অনুক্ষণ ॥ ৭৭ ॥

deva-sthāne āsi' kaila viṣṇu daraśana
śrī-vaiṣṇavera saṅge tāhāṅ goṣṭhī anukṣaṇa

SYNONYMS

deva-sthāne—to the place known as Deva-sthāna; *āsi'*—coming; *kaila*—did; *viṣṇu daraśana*—visiting the temple of Lord Viṣṇu; *śrī-vaiṣṇavera saṅge*—with the Vaiṣṇavas in the disciplic succession of Rāmānuja; *tāhāṅ*—there; *goṣṭhī*—discussion; *anukṣaṇa*—always.

TRANSLATION

At Deva-sthāna, Caitanya Mahāprabhu visited the temple of Lord Viṣṇu, and there He talked with the Vaiṣṇavas in the disciplic succession of Rāmānujācārya. These Vaiṣṇavas are known as Śrī Vaiṣṇavas.

TEXT 78

কুম্ভকর্ণ-কপালে দেখি' সরোবর ।
শিব-ক্ষেত্রে শিব দেখে গৌরাঙ্গসুন্দর ॥ ৭৮ ॥

kumbhakarṇa-kapāle dekhi' sarovara
śiva-kṣetre śiva dekhe gaurāṅga-sundara

SYNONYMS

kumbhakarṇa-kapāle—at Kumbhakarṇa-kapāla; *dekhi'*—after seeing; *sarovara*—the lake; *śiva-kṣetre*—at Śiva-kṣetra; *śiva*—Lord Śiva; *dekhe*—sees; *gaurāṅga-sundara*—Lord Śrī Caitanya Mahāprabhu.

TRANSLATION

At Kumbhakarṇa-kapāla, Śrī Caitanya Mahāprabhu saw a great lake and then the holy place named Śiva-kṣetra, where a temple of Lord Śiva is located.

PURPORT

Kumbhakarṇa is the name of the brother of Rāvaṇa. At the present moment the city of Kumbhakoṇam is situated twenty miles northeast of the city of Tāñjor. There are twelve temples of Lord Śiva located at Kumbhakoṇam as well as four Viṣṇu temples and one temple to Lord Brahmā. Śiva-kṣetra, within the city of Tāñjor, is situated near a big lake known as Śiva-gaṅgā. There is a large temple to Lord Śiva there known as Bṛhatīśvara-śiva-mandira.

TEXT 79

পাপনাশনে বিষ্ণু কৈল দরশন ।
শ্রীরঙ্গক্ষেত্রে তবে করিলা গমন ॥ ৭৯ ॥

pāpa-nāśane viṣṇu kaila daraśana
śrī-raṅga-kṣetre tabe karilā gamana

SYNONYMS

pāpa-nāśane—at the place named Pāpanāśana; *viṣṇu*—Lord Viṣṇu; *kaila*—did; *daraśana*—visiting; *śrī-raṅga-kṣetre*—to the holy place named Śrī Raṅga-kṣetra; *tabe*—then; *karilā*—did; *gamana*—departure.

TRANSLATION

After visiting the holy place named Śiva-kṣetra, Caitanya Mahāprabhu arrived at Pāpanāśana and there saw the temple of Lord Viṣṇu. Then He finally reached Śrī Raṅga-kṣetra.

PURPORT

According to some, the place known as Pāpanāśana was located eight miles southwest of Kumbhakoṇam. Others say that in the district of Tinebheli there is a city known as Pālamakoṭā. Twenty miles west of there is a holy place known as

Pāpanāśana near the river named Tāmraparṇī. Śrī Raṅga-kṣetra is a very famous place. Near Tricinapallī is a river named Kāverī, or Kolirana. A city known as Śrī Raṅgam is located on this river in the district of Tāñjor about ten miles west of Kumbhakoṇam. The Śrī Raṅga temple is the largest in India, and there are seven walls surrounding it. There are also seven roads leading to Śrī Raṅga. The ancient names of these roads are the road of Dharma, the road of Rājamahendra, the road of Kulaśekhara, the road of Ālināḍana, the road of Tiruvikrama, the Tirubiḍi road of Māḍamāḍi-gāisa, and the road of Aḍa-iyāvala-indāna. The temple was founded before the reign of Dharmavarma, who reigned before Rājamahendra. Many celebrated kings like Kulaśekhara, and others such as Ālabandāru, resided in the temple of Śrī Raṅgam. Yāmunācārya, Śrī Rāmānuja, Sudarśanācārya and others also supervised this temple.

The incarnation of the goddess of fortune known as Godādevī, who was one of the twelve liberated persons known as *divya-sūris,* was married to the Deity, Lord Śrī Raṅganātha. Later she entered into the body of the Lord. An incarnation of Kārmuka, Tirumaṅga (one of the Ālovaras), acquired some money by stealing, and built the fourth boundary wall of Śrī Raṅgam. It is said that in the year 289 of the age of Kali, the Ālovara of the name Toṇḍaraḍippaḍi was born. While engaged in devotional service, he became victim to a prostitute, and Śrī Raṅganātha, seeing His devotee so degraded, sent one of His servants with a golden plate to that prostitute. When the golden plate was discovered missing from the temple, there was a search, and it was found in the prostitute's house. When the devotee saw Raṅganātha's mercy upon this prostitute, his mistake was rectified. He then prepared the third boundary wall of Raṅganātha temple and cultivated a *tulasī* garden there.

There was also a celebrated disciple of Rāmānujācārya's known as Kūreśa. Śrī Rāmapillāi was the son of Kūreśa, and his son was Vāgvijaya Bhaṭṭa, whose son was Vedavyāsa Bhaṭṭa, or Śrī Sudarśanācārya. When Sudarśanācārya was an old man, the Mohammedens attacked the temple of Raṅganātha and killed about twelve hundred Śrī Vaiṣṇavas. At that time the Deity Raṅganātha was transferred to the temple of Tirupati in the kingdom of Vijaya-nagara. The governor of Giṅgi, Goppaṇārya, brought Śrī Raṅganātha from the temple of Tirupati to a place known as Siṁha-brahma, where the Lord was situated for three years. In the year 1293 Śaka the Deity was again reinstalled in the Raṅganātha temple. On the eastern wall of the Raṅganātha temple is an inscription written by Vedānta-deśika relating how Raṅganātha was returned to the temple.

TEXT 80

কাবেরীতে স্নান করি' দেখি' রঙ্গনাথ ।
স্তুতি-প্রণতি করি' মানিলা কৃতার্থ ॥ ৮০ ॥

kāverīte snāna kari' dekhi' raṅganātha
stuti-praṇati kari' mānilā kṛtārtha

SYNONYMS

kāverīte—in the river known as Kāverī; *snāna kari'*—after bathing; *dekhi'*—visiting; *raṅga-nātha*—the Raṅganātha temple; *stuti*—prayers; *praṇati*—obeisances; *kari'*—offering; *mānilā*—thought Himself; *kṛta-artha*—very successful.

TRANSLATION

After bathing in the River Kāverī, Śrī Caitanya Mahāprabhu saw the temple of Raṅganātha and offered His ardent prayers and obeisances. Thus He felt Himself successful.

TEXT 81

প্রেমাবেশে কৈল বহুত গান নর্তন ।
দেখি' চমৎকার হৈল সব লোকের মন ॥ ৮১ ॥

premāveśe kaila bahuta gāna nartana
dekhi' camatkāra haila saba lokera mana

SYNONYMS

prema-āveśe—in the ecstasy of love; *kaila*—did; *bahuta*—various; *gāna*—songs; *nartana*—dancing; *dekhi'*—seeing which; *camatkāra*—astonished; *haila*—were; *saba*—all; *lokera*—of persons; *mana*—minds.

TRANSLATION

In the temple of Raṅganātha, Śrī Caitanya Mahāprabhu chanted and danced in ecstatic love of Godhead. Seeing His performance, everyone was struck with wonder.

TEXT 82

শ্রী-বৈষ্ণব এক,—'ব্যেঙ্কট ভট্ট' নাম ।
প্রভুরে নিমন্ত্রণ কৈল করিয়া সম্মান ॥ ৮২ ॥

śrī-vaiṣṇava eka,——'vyeṅkaṭa bhaṭṭa' nāma
prabhure nimantraṇa kaila kariyā sammāna

SYNONYMS

śrī-vaiṣṇava eka—one devotee belonging to the Rāmānuja-sampradāya; *vyeṅkaṭa bhaṭṭa*—Vyeṅkaṭa Bhaṭṭa; *nāma*—named; *prabhure*—unto Lord

Caitanya Mahāprabhu; *nimantraṇa*—invitation; *kaila*—did; *kariyā*—offering; *sammāna*—great respect.

TRANSLATION

One Vaiṣṇava known as Vyeṅkaṭa Bhaṭṭa then invited Śrī Caitanya Mahāprabhu to his home with great respect.

PURPORT

Śrī Vyeṅkaṭa Bhaṭṭa was a Vaiṣṇava *brāhmaṇa* and an inhabitant of Śrī Raṅga-kṣetra. He belonged to the disciplic succession of Śrī Rāmānujācārya. Śrī Raṅga is one of the places of pilgrimage in the province of Tāmila-deśa. The inhabitants of that province do not retain the name Vyeṅkaṭa. It is therefore supposed that Vyeṅkaṭa Bhaṭṭa did not belong to that province, although he may have been residing there for a very long time. Vyeṅkaṭa Bhaṭṭa was in a branch of the Rāmānuja-sampradāya known as Baḍagala-i. He had a brother in the Rāmānuja-sampradāya known as Śrīpāda Prabodhānanda Sarasvatī. The son of Vyeṅkaṭa Bhaṭṭa was later known in the Gauḍīya-sampradāya as Gopāla Bhaṭṭa Gosvāmī, and he established the Rādhāramaṇa temple in Vṛndāvana. More information about him may be found in a book known as *Bhakti-ratnākara* (1.100) by Narahari Cakravartī.

TEXT 83

নিজ-ঘরে লঞা কৈল পাদপ্রক্ষালন ।
সেই জল লঞা কৈল সবংশে ভক্ষণ ॥ ৮৩ ॥

nija-ghare lañā kaila pāda-prakṣālana
sei jala lañā kaila sa-vaṁśe bhakṣaṇa

SYNONYMS

nija-ghare—to his own home; *lañā*—bringing; *kaila*—did; *pāda-prakṣālana*—washing of the feet; *sei jala*—that water; *lañā*—taking; *kaila*—did; *sa-vaṁśe*—with all the family members; *bhakṣaṇa*—drinking.

TRANSLATION

Śrī Vyeṅkaṭa Bhaṭṭa took Śrī Caitanya Mahāprabhu to his home. After he washed the Lord's feet, all the members of his family drank the water.

TEXT 84

ভিক্ষা করাঞা কিছু কৈল নিবেদন ।
চাতুর্মাস্য আসি' প্রভু, হৈল উপসন্ন ॥ ৮৪ ॥

bhikṣā karāñā kichu kaila nivedana
cāturmāsya āsi' prabhu, haila upasanna

SYNONYMS

bhikṣā karāñā—after offering lunch; *kichu*—some; *kaila*—did; *nivedana*—submission; *cāturmāsya*—the period of Cāturmāsya; *āsi'*—coming; *prabhu*—my Lord; *haila upasanna*—has already arrived.

TRANSLATION

After offering lunch to the Lord, Vyeṅkaṭa Bhaṭṭa submitted that the period of Cāturmāsya had already arrived.

TEXT 85

চাতুর্মাস্যে কৃপা করি' রহ মোর ঘরে ।
কৃষ্ণকথা কহি' কৃপায় উদ্ধার' আমারে ॥ ৮৫ ॥

cāturmāsye kṛpā kari' raha mora ghare
kṛṣṇa-kathā kahi' kṛpāya uddhāra' āmāre

SYNONYMS

cāturmāsye—during this period of Cāturmāsya; *kṛpā kari'*—being merciful; *raha*—please stay; *mora ghare*—at my place; *kṛṣṇa-kathā*—topics of Lord Kṛṣṇa; *kahi'*—speaking; *kṛpāya*—by Your mercy; *uddhāra' āmāre*—kindly deliver me.

TRANSLATION

Vyeṅkaṭa Bhaṭṭa said, "Please be merciful to me and stay at my house during Cāturmāsya. Speak about Lord Kṛṣṇa's pastimes and kindly deliver me by Your mercy."

TEXT 86

তাঁর ঘরে রহিলা প্রভু কৃষ্ণকথা-রসে ।
ভট্টসঙ্গে গোঙাইল সুখে চারি মাসে ॥ ৮৬ ॥

tāṅra ghare rahilā prabhu kṛṣṇa-kathā-rase
bhaṭṭa-saṅge goṅāila sukhe cāri māse

SYNONYMS

tāṅra ghare—in his home; *rahilā*—stayed; *prabhu*—Lord Śrī Caitanya Mahāprabhu; *kṛṣṇa-kathā-rase*—enjoying the transcendental mellow of discussing Lord Kṛṣṇa's pastimes; *bhaṭṭa-saṅge*—with Vyeṅkaṭa Bhaṭṭa; *goṅāila*—passed; *sukhe*—in happiness; *cāri māse*—four months.

TRANSLATION

Śrī Caitanya Mahāprabhu remained at the house of Vyeṅkaṭa Bhaṭṭa for four continuous months. The Lord passed His days in great happiness, enjoying the transcendental mellow of discussing Lord Kṛṣṇa's pastimes.

TEXT 87

কাবেরীতে স্নান করি' শ্রীরঙ্গ দর্শন ।
প্রতিদিন প্রেমাবেশে করেন নর্তন ॥ ৮৭ ॥

kāverīte snāna kari' śrī-raṅga darśana
prati-dina premāveśe karena nartana

SYNONYMS

kāverīte—in the river known as Kāverī; *snāna kari'*—taking a bath; *śrī-raṅga darśana*—visiting the temple of Śrī Raṅga; *prati-dina*—every day; *prema-āveśe*—in great happiness; *karena*—does perform; *nartana*—dancing.

TRANSLATION

While there, Śrī Caitanya Mahāprabhu took His bath in the River Kāverī and visited the temple of Śrī Raṅga. Every day the Lord also danced in ecstasy.

TEXT 88

সৌন্দর্যাদি প্রেমাবেশ দেখি, সর্বলোক ।
দেখিবারে আইসে, দেখে, খণ্ডে দুঃখ-শোক ॥ ৮৮ ॥

saundaryādi premāveśa dekhi, sarva-loka
dekhibāre āise, dekhe, khaṇḍe duḥkha-śoka

SYNONYMS

saundarya-ādi—the beauty of the body, etc.; *prema-āveśa*—His ecstatic love; *dekhi*—seeing; *sarva-loka*—all men; *dekhibāre*—to see; *āise*—come there; *dekhe*—and see; *khaṇḍe duḥkha-śoka*—are relieved from all unhappiness and distress.

TRANSLATION

The beauty of Lord Caitanya's body and His ecstatic love of God were witnessed by everyone. Many people used to come see Him, and as soon as they saw Him, all their unhappiness and distress vanished.

TEXT 89

লক্ষ লক্ষ লোক আইল নানা-দেশ হৈতে।
সবে কৃষ্ণনাম কহে প্রভুকে দেখিতে ॥ ৮৯ ॥

lakṣa lakṣa loka āila nānā-deśa haite
sabe kṛṣṇa-nāma kahe prabhuke dekhite

SYNONYMS

lakṣa lakṣa—many hundreds of thousands; *loka*—of people; *āila*—came there; *nānā-deśa*—different countries; *haite*—from; *sabe*—all of them; *kṛṣṇa-nāma kahe*—chant the Hare Kṛṣṇa *mahā-mantra; prabhuke*—the Lord; *dekhite*—seeing.

TRANSLATION

Many hundreds of thousands of people from various countries came to see the Lord, and after seeing Him, they all chanted the Hare Kṛṣṇa mahā-mantra.

TEXT 90

কৃষ্ণনাম বিনা কেহ নাহি কহে আর।
সবে কৃষ্ণভক্ত হৈল,—লোকে চমৎকার ॥ ৯০ ॥

kṛṣṇa-nāma vinā keha nāhi kahe āra
sabe kṛṣṇa-bhakta haila,—loke camatkāra

SYNONYMS

kṛṣṇa-nāma vinā—without chanting the Hare Kṛṣṇa *mahā-mantra; keha*—anyone; *nāhi*—does not; *kahe*—speak; *āra*—anything else; *sabe*—all of them; *kṛṣṇa-bhakta*—Lord Kṛṣṇa's devotees; *haila*—became; *loke*—the people; *camatkāra*—astonished.

TRANSLATION

Indeed, they did not chant anything but the Hare Kṛṣṇa mahā-mantra, and all of them became Lord Kṛṣṇa's devotees. Thus the general populace was astonished.

TEXT 91

শ্রীরঙ্গক্ষেত্রে বৈসে যত বৈষ্ণব-ব্রাহ্মণ।
এক এক দিন সবে কৈল নিমন্ত্রণ ॥ ৯১ ॥

śrī-raṅga-kṣetre vaise yata vaiṣṇava-brāhmaṇa
eka eka dina sabe kaila nimantraṇa

SYNONYMS

śrī-raṅga-kṣetre—in Śrī Raṅga-kṣetra; *vaise*—residing; *yata*—all; *vaiṣṇava-brāhmaṇa*—Vaiṣṇava *brāhmaṇas*; *eka eka dina*—every day; *sabe*—all of them; *kaila nimantraṇa*—invited the Lord.

TRANSLATION

All the Vaiṣṇava brāhmaṇas residing in Śrī Raṅga-kṣetra invited the Lord to their homes every day.

TEXT 92

এক এক দিনে চাতুর্মাস্য পূর্ণ হৈল ।
কতক ব্রাহ্মণ ভিক্ষা দিতে না পাইল ॥ ৯২ ॥

eka eka dine cāturmāsya pūrṇa haila
kataka brāhmaṇa bhikṣā dite nā pāila

SYNONYMS

eka eka dine—day by day; *cāturmāsya*—the period of Cāturmāsya; *pūrṇa haila*—became filled; *kataka brāhmaṇa*—some of the *brāhmaṇas*; *bhikṣā dite*—to offer Him lunch; *nā*—did not; *pāila*—get the opportunity.

TRANSLATION

Each day the Lord was invited by a different brāhmaṇa, but some of them did not get the opportunity to offer Him lunch because the period of Cāturmāsya came to an end.

TEXT 93

সেই ক্ষেত্রে রহে এক বৈষ্ণব-ব্রাহ্মণ ।
দেবালয়ে আসি' করে গীতা আবর্তন ॥ ৯৩ ॥

sei kṣetre rahe eka vaiṣṇava-brāhmaṇa
devālaye āsi' kare gītā āvartana

SYNONYMS

sei kṣetre—in that holy place; *rahe*—there was; *eka*—one; *vaiṣṇava-brāhmaṇa*—a *brāhmaṇa* following the Vaiṣṇava cult; *deva-ālaye*—in the temple; *āsi'*—coming; *kare*—does; *gītā*—of *Bhagavad-gītā*; *āvartana*—recitation.

TRANSLATION

In the holy place of Śrī Raṅga-kṣetra, a brāhmaṇa Vaiṣṇava used to visit the temple daily and recite the entire text of Bhagavad-gītā.

TEXT 94

অষ্টাদশাধ্যায় পড়ে আনন্দ-আবেশে ।
অশুদ্ধ পড়েন, লোক করে উপহাসে ॥ ৯৪ ॥

aṣṭādaśādhyāya paḍe ānanda-āveśe
aśuddha paḍena, loka kare upahāse

SYNONYMS

aṣṭādaśa-adhyāya—eighteen chapters; *paḍe*—reads; *ānanda-āveśe*—in great ecstasy; *aśuddha paḍena*—could not pronounce the text correctly; *loka*—people in general; *kare*—do; *upahāse*—joking.

TRANSLATION

The brāhmaṇa regularly read the eighteen chapters of Bhagavad-gītā in great transcendental ecstasy, but because he could not pronounce the words correctly, people used to joke about him.

TEXT 95

কেহ হাসে, কেহ নিন্দে, তাহা নাহি মানে ।
আবিষ্ট হঞা গীতা পড়ে আনন্দিত-মনে ॥ ৯৫ ॥

keha hāse, keha ninde, tāhā nāhi māne
āviṣṭa hañā gītā paḍe ānandita-mane

SYNONYMS

keha hāse—someone laughs; *keha ninde*—someone criticizes; *tāhā*—that; *nāhi māne*—he does not care for; *āviṣṭa hañā*—being in great ecstasy; *gītā paḍe*—reads *Bhagavad-gītā*; *ānandita*—in great happiness; *mane*—his mind.

TRANSLATION

Due to his incorrect pronunciation, people sometimes criticized him and laughed at him, but he did not care. He was full of ecstasy due to reading Bhagavad-gītā and was personally very happy.

TEXT 96

পুলকাশ্রু, কম্প, স্বেদ,—যাবৎ পঠন ।
দেখি' আনন্দিত হৈল মহাপ্রভুর মন ॥ ৯৬ ॥

pulakāśru, kampa, sveda,——yāvat paṭhana
dekhi' ānandita haila mahāprabhura mana

SYNONYMS

pulaka—standing of the hairs of the body; *aśru*—tears; *kampa*—trembling; *sveda*—perspiration; *yāvat*—during; *paṭhana*—the reading of the book; *dekhi'*—seeing this; *ānandita*—very happy; *haila*—became; *mahāprabhura*—of Śrī Caitanya Mahāprabhu; *mana*—the mind.

TRANSLATION

While reading the book, the brāhmaṇa experienced transcendental bodily transformations. His hair stood on end, tears welled in his eyes, and his body trembled and perspired as he read. Seeing this, Śrī Caitanya Mahāprabhu became very happy.

PURPORT

Although the *brāhmaṇa* could not pronounce the words very well due to illiteracy, he still experienced ecstatic symptoms while reading *Bhagavad-gītā*. Śrī Caitanya Mahāprabhu was very pleased to observe these symptoms, and this indicates that the Supreme Personality of Godhead is pleased by devotion, not by erudite scholarship. Even though the words were imperfectly pronounced, Śrī Caitanya Mahāprabhu, Lord Kṛṣṇa Himself, did not think this very serious. Rather, the Lord was pleased by the *bhāva* (devotion). In *Śrīmad-Bhāgavatam* (1.5.11) this is confirmed:

tad-vāg-visargo janatāgha-viplavo
yasmin prati-ślokam abaddhavaty api
nāmāny anantasya yaśo 'ṅkitāni yat
śṛṇvanti gāyanti gṛṇanti sādhavaḥ

"On the other hand, that literature which is full of descriptions of the transcendental glories of the name, fame, forms and pastimes of the unlimited Supreme Lord is a different creation, full of transcendental words directed toward bringing about a revolution in the impious lives of this world's misdirected civilization. Such transcendental literatures, even though imperfectly composed, are heard, sung and accepted by purified men who are thoroughly honest."

The purport to this verse may be considered for further information on this subject.

TEXT 97

মহাপ্রভু পুছিল তাঁরে, শুন, মহাশয় ।
কোন্ অর্থ জানি' তোমার এত সুখ হয় ॥ ৯৭ ॥

mahāprabhu puchila tāṅre, śuna, mahāśaya
kon artha jāni' tomāra eta sukha haya

SYNONYMS

mahāprabhu—Śrī Caitanya Mahāprabhu; *puchila*—inquired; *tāṅre*—from him; *śuna*—please hear; *mahā-āśaya*—My dear sir; *kon*—what; *artha*—meaning; *jāni'*—knowing; *tomāra*—your; *eta*—so great; *sukha*—happiness; *haya*—is.

TRANSLATION

Śrī Caitanya Mahāprabhu asked the brāhmaṇa, "My dear sir, why are you in such ecstatic love? Which portion of Bhagavad-gītā gives you such transcendental pleasure?"

TEXT 98

বিপ্র কহে,—মূর্খ আমি, শব্দার্থ না জানি ।
শুদ্ধাশুদ্ধ গীতা পড়ি, গুরু-আজ্ঞা মানি' ॥ ৯৮ ॥

vipra kahe,——mūrkha āmi, śabdārtha nā jāni
śuddhāśuddha gītā paḍi, guru-ājñā māni'

SYNONYMS

vipra kahe—the *brāhmaṇa* replied; *mūrkha āmi*—I am illiterate; *śabda-artha*—the meaning of the words; *nā jāni*—I do not know; *śuddha-aśuddha*—sometimes correct and sometimes not correct; *gītā*—*Bhagavad-gītā*; *paḍi*—I read; *guru-ājñā*—the order of my spiritual master; *māni'*—accepting.

TRANSLATION

The brāhmaṇa replied, "I am illiterate and therefore do not know the meaning of the words. Sometimes I read Bhagavad-gītā correctly and sometimes incorrectly, but in any case I am doing this in compliance with the orders of my spiritual master."

PURPORT

This is a good example of a person who had become so successful that he was able to capture the attention of Śrī Caitanya Mahāprabhu even while reading *Bhagavad-gītā* incorrectly. His spiritual activities did not depend on material things such as correct pronunciation. Rather, his success depended on strictly following the instructions of his spiritual master.

yasya deve parā bhaktir
yathā deve tathā gurau
tasyaite kathitā hy arthāḥ
prakāśante mahātmanaḥ

"Only unto those great souls who have implicit faith in both the Lord and the spiritual master are all the imports of Vedic knowledge automatically revealed." (*Śvet. Up.* 6.23)

Actually the meaning of the words of *Bhagavad-gītā* or *Śrīmad-Bhāgavatam* are revealed to one strictly following the orders of the spiritual master. They are also revealed to one who has equal faith in the Supreme Personality of Godhead. In other words, being faithful to both Kṛṣṇa and the spiritual master is the secret of success in spiritual life.

TEXT 99

অর্জুনের রথে কৃষ্ণ হয় রজ্জুধর ।
বসিয়াছে হাতে তোত্র শ্যামল সুন্দর ॥ ৯৯ ॥

arjunera rathe kṛṣṇa haya rajju-dhara
vasiyāche hāte totra śyāmala sundara

SYNONYMS

arjunera—of Arjuna; *rathe*—in the chariot; *kṛṣṇa*—Lord Kṛṣṇa; *haya*—is; *rajju-dhara*—holding the reins; *vasiyāche*—He was sitting there; *hāte*—in the hand; *totra*—a bridle; *śyāmala*—blackish; *sundara*—very beautiful.

TRANSLATION

The brāhmaṇa continued, "Actually I only see a picture of Lord Kṛṣṇa sitting on a chariot as Arjuna's charioteer. Taking the reins in His hands, He appears very beautiful and blackish.

TEXT 100

অর্জুনেরে কহিতেছেন হিত-উপদেশ ।
তাঁরে দেখি' হয় মোর আনন্দ-আবেশ ॥ ১০০ ॥

arjunere kahitechena hita-upadeśa
tāṅre dekhi' haya mora ānanda-āveśa

SYNONYMS

arjunere—unto Arjuna; *kahitechena*—He is speaking; *hita-upadeśa*—good instruction; *tāṅre*—Him; *dekhi'*—seeing; *haya*—there is; *mora*—my; *ānanda*—transcendental happiness; *āveśa*—ecstasy.

TRANSLATION

"When I see the picture of Lord Kṛṣṇa sitting in a chariot and instructing Arjuna, I am filled with ecstatic happiness.

TEXT 101

যাবৎ পড়োঁ, তাবৎ পাঙ তাঁর দরশন ।
এই লাগি' গীতা-পাঠ না ছাড়ে মোর মন ॥ ১০১ ॥

yāvat paḍoṅ, tāvat pāṅa tāṅra daraśana
ei lāgi' gītā-pāṭha nā chāḍe mora mana

SYNONYMS

yāvat—as long as; *paḍoṅ*—I read; *tāvat*—so long; *pāṅa*—I get; *tāṅra*—His; *daraśana*—audience; *ei lāgi'*—for this reason; *gītā-pāṭha*—reading *Bhagavad-gītā*; *nā chāḍe*—does not quit; *mora mana*—my mind.

TRANSLATION

"As long as I read Bhagavad-gītā, I simply see the Lord's beautiful features. It is for this reason that I am reading Bhagavad-gītā, and my mind cannot be distracted from this."

TEXT 102

প্রভু কহে,—গীতা-পাঠে তোমারই অধিকার ।
তুমি সে জানহ এই গীতার অর্থ-সার ॥ ১০২ ॥

prabhu kahe,——gītā-pāṭhe tomāra-i adhikāra
tumi se jānaha ei gītāra artha-sāra

SYNONYMS

prabhu kahe—the Lord replied; *gītā-pāṭhe*—in reading *Bhagavad-gītā*; *tomāra-i adhikāra*—you have the proper authority; *tumi*—you; *se*—that; *jānaha*—know; *ei*—this; *gītāra*—of *Bhagavad-gītā*; *artha-sāra*—the real purport.

TRANSLATION

Śrī Caitanya Mahāprabhu told the brāhmaṇa, "Indeed, you are an authority in the reading of Bhagavad-gītā. Whatever you know constitutes the real purport of Bhagavad-gītā."

PURPORT

According to the *śāstras*: *bhaktyā bhāgavataṁ grāhyaṁ na buddhyā na ca ṭīkayā.* One should understand *Bhagavad-gītā* and *Śrīmad-Bhāgavatam* by hearing them from a real devotee. One cannot understand them simply by erudite scholarship or sharp intelligence. It is also said:

gītādhītā ca yenāpi
bhakti-bhāvena cetasā
veda-śāstra-purāṇāni
tenādhītāni sarvaśaḥ

To one who reads *Bhagavad-gītā* with faith and devotion, the essence of Vedic knowledge is revealed. According to the *Śvetāśvatara Upaniṣad* (6.23):

yasya deve parā bhaktir
yathā deve tathā gurau
tasyaite kathitā hy arthāḥ
prakāśante mahātmanaḥ

All Vedic literatures are to be understood with faith and devotion, not by mundane scholarship. We therefore present *Bhagavad-gītā As It Is.* There are many so-called scholars and philosophers who read *Bhagavad-gītā* in a scholarly way. They simply waste their time and mislead those who read their commentaries.

TEXT 103

এত বলি' সেই বিপ্রে কৈল আলিঙ্গন ।
প্রভু-পদ ধরি' বিপ্র করেন রোদন ॥ ১০৩ ॥

eta bali' sei vipre kaila āliṅgana
prabhu-pada dhari' vipra karena rodana

SYNONYMS

eta bali'—saying this; *sei vipre*—that *brāhmaṇa; kaila āliṅgana*—He embraced; *prabhu-pada*—the lotus feet of Lord Śrī Caitanya Mahāprabhu; *dhari'*—catching; *vipra*—the *brāhmaṇa*; *karena*—does; *rodana*—crying.

TRANSLATION

After saying this, Lord Caitanya Mahāprabhu embraced the brāhmaṇa, and the brāhmaṇa, catching the lotus feet of the Lord, began to cry.

TEXT 104

তোমা দেখি' তাহা হৈতে দ্বিগুণ সুখ হয়।
সেই কৃষ্ণ তুমি,—হেন মোর মনে লয় ॥ ১০৪ ॥

tomā dekhi' tāhā haite dvi-guṇa sukha haya
sei kṛṣṇa tumi,——hena mora mane laya

SYNONYMS

tomā dekhi'—by seeing You; *tāhā haite*—than the vision of Lord Kṛṣṇa; *dvi-guṇa*—twice as much; *sukha*—happiness; *haya*—there is; *sei kṛṣṇa*—that Lord Kṛṣṇa; *tumi*—You are; *hena*—such; *mora*—my; *mane*—in the mind; *laya*—takes.

TRANSLATION

The brāhmaṇa said, "Upon seeing You, my happiness is doubled. I take it that You are the same Lord Kṛṣṇa."

TEXT 105

কৃষ্ণস্ফূর্ত্যে তাঁর মন হঞাছে নির্মল।
অতএব প্রভুর তত্ত্ব জানিল সকল ॥ ১০৫ ॥

kṛṣṇa-sphūrtye tāṅra mana hañāche nirmala
ataeva prabhura tattva jānila sakala

SYNONYMS

kṛṣṇa-sphūrtye—by revelation of Lord Kṛṣṇa; *tāṅra*—his; *mana*—mind; *hañāche*—did become; *nirmala*—purified; *ataeva*—therefore; *prabhura*—of Lord Śrī Caitanya Mahāprabhu; *tattva*—truth; *jānila*—could understand; *sakala*—all.

TRANSLATION

The brāhmaṇa's mind was purified by the revelation of Lord Kṛṣṇa, and therefore he could understand the truth of Śrī Caitanya Mahāprabhu in all details.

TEXT 106

তবে মহাপ্রভু তাঁরে করাইল শিক্ষণ ।
এই বাত্ কাহাঁ না করিহ প্রকাশন ॥ ১০৬ ॥

tabe mahāprabhu tāṅre karāila śikṣaṇa
ei vāt kāhāṅ nā kariha prakāśana

SYNONYMS

tabe—then; *mahāprabhu*—Śrī Caitanya Mahāprabhu; *tāṅre*—unto the *brāhmaṇa*; *karāila*—made; *śikṣaṇa*—instruction; *ei vāt*—this version; *kāhāṅ*—anywhere; *nā*—do not; *kariha*—do; *prakāśana*—revelation.

TRANSLATION

Śrī Caitanya Mahāprabhu then taught the brāhmaṇa very thoroughly and requested him not to disclose the fact that He was Lord Kṛṣṇa Himself.

TEXT 107

সেই বিপ্র মহাপ্রভুর বড় ভক্ত হৈল ।
চারি মাস প্রভু-সঙ্গ কভু না ছাড়িল ॥ ১০৭ ॥

sei vipra mahāprabhura baḍa bhakta haila
cāri māsa prabhu-saṅga kabhu nā chāḍila

SYNONYMS

sei vipra—that *brāhmaṇa*; *mahāprabhura*—of Śrī Caitanya Mahāprabhu; *baḍa*—big; *bhakta*—devotee; *haila*—became; *cāri māsa*—for four months; *prabhu-saṅga*—association of the Lord; *kabhu*—at any time; *nā*—did not; *chāḍila*—give up.

TRANSLATION

That brāhmaṇa became a great devotee of Śrī Caitanya Mahāprabhu, and for four continuous months he did not give up the Lord's company.

TEXT 108

এইমত ভট্টগৃহে রহে গৌরচন্দ্র ।
নিরন্তর ভট্ট-সঙ্গে কৃষ্ণকথানন্দ ॥ ১০৮ ॥

ei-mata bhaṭṭa-gṛhe rahe gauracandra
nirantara bhaṭṭa-saṅge kṛṣṇa-kathānanda

SYNONYMS

ei-mata—in this way; *bhaṭṭa-gṛhe*—in the house of Vyeṅkaṭa Bhaṭṭa; *rahe*—remained; *gaura-candra*—Śrī Caitanya Mahāprabhu; *nirantara*—constantly; *bhaṭ-ṭa-saṅge*—with Vyeṅkaṭa Bhaṭṭa; *kṛṣṇa-kathā-ānanda*—the transcendental bliss of talking about Kṛṣṇa.

TRANSLATION

Śrī Caitanya Mahāprabhu remained at the house of Vyeṅkaṭa Bhaṭṭa and constantly talked about Lord Kṛṣṇa. In this way He was very happy.

TEXT 109

'শ্রী-বৈষ্ণব' ভট্ট সেবে লক্ষ্মী-নারায়ণ ।
তাঁর ভক্তি দেখি' প্রভুর তুষ্ট হৈল মন ॥ ১০৯ ॥

śrī-vaiṣṇava' bhaṭṭa seve lakṣmī-nārāyaṇa
tāṅra bhakti dekhi' prabhura tuṣṭa haila mana

SYNONYMS

śrī-vaiṣṇava—a devotee of the Rāmānuja-sampradāya; *bhaṭṭa*—Vyeṅkaṭa Bhaṭ-ṭa; *seve*—used to worship; *lakṣmī-nārāyaṇa*—the Deities of Lord Nārāyaṇa and the goddess of fortune, Lakṣmī; *tāṅra*—his; *bhakti*—devotion; *dekhi'*—seeing; *prabhura*—of Lord Śrī Caitanya Mahāprabhu; *tuṣṭa*—happy; *haila*—became; *mana*—the mind.

TRANSLATION

Being a Vaiṣṇava in the Rāmānuja-sampradāya, Vyeṅkaṭa Bhaṭṭa worshiped the Deity of Lakṣmī and Nārāyaṇa. Seeing his pure devotion, Śrī Caitanya Mahāprabhu was very satisfied.

TEXT 110

নিরন্তর তাঁর সঙ্গে হৈল সখ্যভাব ।
হাস্য-পরিহাসে দুঁহে সখ্যের স্বভাব ॥ ১১০ ॥

nirantara tāṅra saṅge haila sakhya-bhāva
hāsya-parihāse duṅhe sakhyera svabhāva

SYNONYMS

nirantara—constantly; *tāṅra saṅge*—being associated with him; *haila*—there was; *sakhya-bhāva*—a friendly relationship; *hāsya*—laughing; *parihāse*—joking; *duṅhe*—both of them; *sakhyera*—of fraternity; *sva-bhāva*—nature.

TRANSLATION

Constantly associating with one another, Śrī Caitanya Mahāprabhu and Vyeṅkaṭa Bhaṭṭa gradually developed a friendly relationship. Indeed, sometimes they laughed and joked together.

TEXT 111

প্রভু কহে,—ভট্ট, তোমার লক্ষ্মী-ঠাকুরাণী।
কান্ত-বক্ষঃস্থিতা, পতিব্রতা-শিরোমণি ॥ ১১১॥

prabhu kahe,——bhaṭṭa, tomāra lakṣmī-ṭhākurāṇī
kānta-vakṣaḥ-sthitā, pativratā-śiromaṇi

SYNONYMS

prabhu kahe—Lord Śrī Caitanya Mahāprabhu said; *bhaṭṭa*—My dear Bhaṭṭācārya; *tomāra*—your; *lakṣmī-ṭhākurāṇī*—goddess of fortune; *kānta*—of her husband, Nārāyaṇa; *vakṣaḥ-sthitā*—situated on the chest; *pati-vratā*—chaste woman; *śiromaṇi*—the topmost.

TRANSLATION

Śrī Caitanya Mahāprabhu told Bhaṭṭācārya, "Your worshipable goddess of fortune, Lakṣmī, always remains on the chest of Nārāyaṇa, and she is certainly the most chaste woman in the creation.

TEXT 112

আমার ঠাকুর কৃষ্ণ—গোপ, গো-চারক।
সাধ্বী হঞা কেনে চাহে তাঁহার সঙ্গম ॥ ১১২ ॥

āmāra ṭhākura kṛṣṇa——gopa, go-cāraka
sādhvī hañā kene cāhe tāṅhāra saṅgama

SYNONYMS

āmāra ṭhākura—My worshipable Deity; *kṛṣṇa*—Lord Kṛṣṇa; *gopa*—cowherd; *go-cāraka*—a tender of cows; *sādhvī hañā*—being so chaste; *kene*—why; *cāhe*—wants; *tāṅhāra*—His; *saṅgama*—association.

TRANSLATION

"However, my Lord is Lord Śrī Kṛṣṇa, a cowherd boy who is engaged in tending cows. Why is it that Lakṣmī, being such a chaste wife, wants to associate with My Lord?

TEXT 113

এই লাগি' সুখভোগ ছাড়ি' চিরকাল ।
ব্রত-নিয়ম করি' তপ করিল অপার ॥ ১১৩ ॥

ei lāgi' sukha-bhoga chāḍi' cira-kāla
vrata-niyama kari' tapa karila apāra

SYNONYMS

ei lāgi'—for this reason; *sukha-bhoga*—the enjoyment of Vaikuṇṭha; *chāḍi'*—giving up; *cira-kāla*—for a long time; *vrata-niyama*—vows and regulative principles; *kari'*—accepting; *tapa*—austerity; *karila apāra*—performed unlimitedly.

TRANSLATION

"Just to associate with Kṛṣṇa, Lakṣmī abandoned all transcendental happiness in Vaikuṇṭha and for a long time accepted vows and regulative principles and performed unlimited austerities."

TEXT 114

কস্যানুভাবোঽস্য ন দেব বিদ্মহে,তবাঙ্ঘ্রি রেণুস্পরশাধিকারঃ।
যদ্বাঞ্ছয়া শ্রীর্ললনাচরত্তপো, বিহায় কামান্ সুচিরং ধৃতব্রতা॥ ১১৪ ॥

kasyānubhāvo 'sya na deva vidmahe
tavāṅghri-reṇu-sparaśādhikāraḥ
yad-vāñchayā śrīr lalanācarat tapo
vihāya kāmān suciraṁ dhṛta-vratā

SYNONYMS

kasya—of what; *anubhāvaḥ*—a result; *asya*—of the serpent (Kāliya); *na*—not; *deva*—O Lord; *vidmahe*—we know; *tava aṅghri*—of Your lotus feet; *reṇu*—of the dust; *sparaśa*—for touching; *adhikāraḥ*—qualification; *yat*—which; *vāñchayā*—by desiring; *śrīḥ*—the goddess of fortune; *lalanā*—the topmost woman; *acarat*—performed; *tapaḥ*—austerity; *vihāya*—giving up; *kāmān*—all desires; *su-ciram*—for a long time; *dhṛta*—a law upheld; *vratā*—as a vow.

TRANSLATION

Caitanya Mahāprabhu then said, " 'O Lord, we do not know how the serpent Kāliya attained such an opportunity to be touched by the dust of Your lotus feet. Even the goddess of fortune, for this end, performed austerities for centuries, giving up all other desires and taking austere vows. Indeed, we do not know how the serpent Kāliya got such an opportunity.' "

PURPORT

This is a quotation from *Śrīmad-Bhāgavatam* (10.16.36) spoken by the wives of the Kāliya serpent.

TEXT 115

ভট্ট কহে, কৃষ্ণ-নারায়ণ— একই স্বরূপ ।
কৃষ্ণেতে অধিক লীলা-বৈদগ্ধ্যাদিরূপ ॥ ১১৫ ॥

bhaṭṭa kahe, kṛṣṇa-nārāyaṇa——eka-i svarūpa
kṛṣṇete adhika līlā-vaidagdhyādi-rūpa

SYNONYMS

bhaṭṭa kahe—Vyeṅkaṭa Bhaṭṭa said; *kṛṣṇa-nārāyaṇa*—Kṛṣṇa and Nārāyaṇa; *eka-i svarūpa*—one and the same; *kṛṣṇete*—in Lord Kṛṣṇa; *adhika*—more; *līlā*—pastimes; *vaidagdhya-ādi-rūpa*—sportive nature.

TRANSLATION

Vyeṅkaṭa Bhaṭṭa then said, "Lord Kṛṣṇa and Lord Nārāyaṇa are one and the same, but the pastimes of Kṛṣṇa are more relishable due to their sportive nature.

TEXT 116

তার স্পর্শে নাহি যায় পতিব্রতা-ধর্ম ।
কৌতুকে লক্ষ্মী চাহেন কৃষ্ণের সঙ্গম ॥ ১১৬ ॥

tāra sparśe nāhi yāya pativratā-dharma
kautuke lakṣmī cāhena kṛṣṇera saṅgama

SYNONYMS

tāra sparśe—by the touching of Kṛṣṇa by Lakṣmī; *nāhi*—does not; *yāya*—disappear; *pati-vratā-dharma*—the vow of chastity; *kautuke*—in great fun; *lakṣmī*—the goddess of fortune; *cāhena*—wants; *kṛṣṇera*—of Lord Kṛṣṇa; *saṅgama*—association.

TRANSLATION

"Since Kṛṣṇa and Nārāyaṇa are both the same personality, Lakṣmī's association with Kṛṣṇa does not break her vow of chastity. Rather, it was in great fun that the goddess of fortune wanted to associate with Lord Kṛṣṇa."

PURPORT

This is an answer to Lord Śrī Caitanya Mahāprabhu's question, and from this we can understand that Vyeṅkaṭa Bhaṭṭa knew the truth. He told Śrī Caitanya Mahāprabhu that Nārāyaṇa is a form of Kṛṣṇa associated with transcendental opulence. Although Kṛṣṇa is two-armed and Nārāyaṇa four-armed, there is no difference in the person. They are one and the same. Nārāyaṇa is as beautiful as Kṛṣṇa, but Kṛṣṇa's pastimes are more sportive. It is not that the sportive pastimes of Kṛṣṇa make Him different from Nārāyaṇa. Lakṣmī's desiring to associate with Kṛṣṇa was perfectly natural. In other words, it is understandable that a chaste woman wants to associate with her husband in all his different dresses. Therefore one should not criticize Lakṣmī for wanting to associate with Kṛṣṇa.

TEXT 117

সিদ্ধান্ততস্ত্বভেদেঽপি শ্রীশ-কৃষ্ণস্বরূপয়োঃ ।
রসেনোৎকৃষ্যতে কৃষ্ণরূপমেষা রসস্থিতিঃ ॥ ১১৭ ॥

siddhāntatas tv abhede 'pi
śrīśa-kṛṣṇa-svarūpayoḥ
rasenotkṛṣyate kṛṣṇa-
rūpam eṣā rasa-sthitiḥ

SYNONYMS

siddhāntataḥ—in reality; *tu*—but; *abhede*—no difference; *api*—although; *śrī-īśa*—of the husband of Lakṣmī, Nārāyaṇa; *kṛṣṇa*—of Lord Kṛṣṇa; *svarūpayoḥ*—between the forms; *rasena*—by transcendental mellows; *utkṛṣyate*—is superior; *kṛṣṇa-rūpam*—the form of Lord Kṛṣṇa; *eṣā*—this; *rasa-sthitiḥ*—reservoir of pleasure.

TRANSLATION

Vyeṅkaṭa Bhaṭṭa continued, "'According to transcendental realization, there is no difference between the forms of Nārāyaṇa and Kṛṣṇa. Yet in Kṛṣṇa there is a special transcendental attraction due to the conjugal mellow, and consequently He surpasses Nārāyaṇa. This is the conclusion of transcendental mellows.'

PURPORT

This verse quoted by Vyeṅkaṭa Bhaṭṭa is also found in *Bhakti-rasāmṛta-sindhu* (1.2.59).

TEXT 118

কৃষ্ণসঙ্গে পতিব্রতা-ধর্ম নহে নাশ ।
অধিক লাভ পাইয়ে, আর রাসবিলাস ॥ ১১৮ ॥

kṛṣṇa-saṅge pativratā-dharma nahe nāśa
adhika lābha pāiye, āra rāsa-vilāsa

SYNONYMS

kṛṣṇa-saṅge—in the association of Lord Kṛṣṇa; *pati-vratā*—of chastity; *dharma*—vow; *nahe*—is not; *nāśa*—lost; *adhika*—more; *lābha*—profit; *pāiye*—I get; *āra*—also; *rāsa-vilāsa*—the enjoyment in the *rāsa* dance.

TRANSLATION

"The goddess of fortune considered that her vow of chastity would not be damaged by her relationship with Kṛṣṇa. Rather, by associating with Kṛṣṇa she could enjoy the benefit of the rāsa dance."

TEXT 119

বিনোদিনী লক্ষ্মীর হয় কৃষ্ণে অভিলাষ ।
ইহাতে কি দোষ, কেনে কর পরিহাস ॥ ১১৯ ॥

vinodinī lakṣmīra haya kṛṣṇe abhilāṣa
ihāte ki doṣa, kene kara parihāsa

SYNONYMS

vinodinī—the enjoyer; *lakṣmīra*—of the goddess of fortune; *haya*—there is; *kṛṣṇe*—for Lord Kṛṣṇa; *abhilāṣa*—desire; *ihāte*—in this; *ki*—what; *doṣa*—fault; *kene*—why; *kara*—You do; *parihāsa*—joking.

TRANSLATION

Vyeṅkaṭa Bhaṭṭa further explained, "Mother Lakṣmī, the goddess of fortune, is also an enjoyer of transcendental bliss; therefore if she wanted to enjoy herself with Kṛṣṇa, what fault is there? Why are You joking so about this?"

TEXT 120

প্রভু কহে,—দোষ নাহি, ইহা আমি জানি ।
রাস না পাইল লক্ষ্মী, শাস্ত্রে ইহা শুনি ॥ ১২০ ॥

prabhu kahe,——doṣa nāhi, ihā āmi jāni
rāsa nā pāila lakṣmī, śāstre ihā śuni

SYNONYMS

prabhu kahe—the Lord replied; *doṣa nāhi*—there is no fault; *ihā āmi jāni*—this I know; *rāsa nā pāila lakṣmī*—Lakṣmī, the goddess of fortune, could not join the *rāsa* dance; *śāstre ihā śuni*—we get this information from revealed scriptures.

TRANSLATION

Lord Caitanya Mahāprabhu replied, "I know that there is no fault on the part of the goddess of fortune, but still she could not enter into the rāsa dance. We hear this from revealed scriptures.

TEXT 121

নায়ং শ্রিয়োঽঙ্গ উ নিতান্তরতেঃ প্রসাদঃ
স্বর্যোষিতাং নলিনগন্ধরুচাং কুতোঽন্যাঃ ।
রাসোৎসবেঽস্য ভুজদণ্ডগৃহীতকণ্ঠ-
লব্ধাশিষাং য উদগাদ্‌ব্রজসুন্দরীণাম্ ॥ ১২১ ॥

nāyaṁ śriyo 'ṅga u nitānta-rateḥ prasādaḥ
svar-yoṣitāṁ nalina-gandha-rucāṁ kuto 'nyāḥ
rāsotsave 'sya bhuja-daṇḍa-gṛhīta-kaṇṭha-
labdhāśiṣāṁ ya udagād vraja-sundarīṇām

SYNONYMS

na—not; *ayam*—this; *śriyaḥ*—of the goddess of fortune; *aṅge*—on the chest; *u*—alas; *nitānta-rateḥ*—one who is very intimately related; *prasādaḥ*—the favor; *svaḥ*—of the heavenly planets; *yoṣitām*—of women; *nalina*—of the lotus flower; *gandha*—having the aroma; *rucām*—and bodily luster; *kutaḥ*—much less; *anyāḥ*—others; *rāsa-utsave*—in the festival of the *rāsa* dance; *asya*—of Lord Śrī Kṛṣṇa; *bhuja-daṇḍa*—by the arms; *gṛhīta*—embraced; *kaṇṭha*—their necks; *labdha-āśiṣām*—who achieved such a blessing; *yaḥ*—which; *udagāt*—became manifest; *vraja-sundarīṇām*—of the beautiful *gopīs,* the transcendental girls.

TRANSLATION

" 'When Lord Śrī Kṛṣṇa was dancing with the gopīs in the rāsa-līlā, He put His arms around their necks and embraced them. This transcendental favor was never granted to the goddess of fortune or other consorts in the spiritual

world. Nor was such a thing ever imagined by the most beautiful girls from the heavenly planets, girls whose bodily luster and aroma exactly resemble lotus flowers. And what to speak of worldly women who may be very, very beautiful by material estimation?'

PURPORT

This is a verse from *Śrīmad-Bhāgavatam* (10.47.60).

TEXT 122

লক্ষ্মী কেনে না পাইল, ইহার কি কারণ।
তপ করি' কৈছে কৃষ্ণ পাইল শ্রুতিগণ ॥ ১২২ ॥

lakṣmī kene nā pāila, ihāra ki kāraṇa
tapa kari' kaiche kṛṣṇa pāila śruti-gaṇa

SYNONYMS

lakṣmī—the goddess of fortune; *kene*—why; *nā*—did not; *pāila*—get; *ihāra*—of this; *ki*—what; *kāraṇa*—cause; *tapa kari'*—undergoing severe austerities; *kaiche*—how; *kṛṣṇa*—Lord Kṛṣṇa; *pāila*—attained; *śruti-gaṇa*—Vedic authorities.

TRANSLATION

"But can you tell me why the goddess of fortune, Lakṣmī, could not enter the rāsa dance? The authorities of Vedic knowledge could enter the dance and associate with Kṛṣṇa.

TEXT 123

নিভৃতমরুন্মনোঽক্ষদৃঢ়যোগযুজো হৃদি য-
ন্মুনয় উপাসতে তদরয়োঽপি যযুঃ স্মরণাৎ।
স্ত্রিয় উরগেন্দ্র-ভোগভুজদণ্ডবিষক্ত-ধিয়ো
বয়মপি তে সমাঃ সমদৃশোঽঙ্ঘ্রিসরোজসুধাঃ ॥ ১২৩ ॥

nibhṛta-marun-mano 'kṣa-dṛḍha-yoga-yujo hṛdi yan-
munaya upāsate tad arayo 'pi yayuḥ smaraṇāt
striya uragendra-bhoga-bhuja-daṇḍa-viṣakta-dhiyo
vayam api te samāḥ samadṛśo 'ṅghri-saroja-sudhāḥ

SYNONYMS

nibhṛta—controlled; *marut*—the life air; *manaḥ*—the mind; *akṣa*—the senses; *dṛḍha*—strong; *yoga*—in the mystic *yoga* process; *yujaḥ*—who are engaged;

hṛdi—within the heart; *yat*—who; *munayaḥ*—the great sages; *upāsate*—worship; *tat*—that; *arayaḥ*—the enemies; *api*—also; *yayuḥ*—obtain; *smaraṇāt*—from remembering; *striyaḥ*—the *gopīs;* *vraga-indra*—of serpents; *bhoga*—like the bodies; *bhuja*—the arms; *daṇḍa*—like rods; *viṣakta*—fastened to; *dhiyaḥ*—whose minds; *vayam api*—we also; *te*—Your; *samāḥ*—equal to them; *sama-dṛśaḥ*—having the same ecstatic emotions; *aṅghri-saroja*—of the lotus feet; *sudhāḥ*—the nectar.

TRANSLATION

" 'Great sages, by practicing the mystic yoga system and controlling the breath, conquer the mind and senses. Thus engaging in mystic yoga and seeing the Supersoul within their hearts, they ultimately enter into impersonal Brahman, along with the enemies of the Supreme Personality of Godhead. However, the damsels of Vraja, the gopīs, want to embrace Kṛṣṇa and His arms, which are like serpents. Being attracted by the beauty of Kṛṣṇa, the gopīs ultimately tasted the nectar of the lotus feet of the Lord. The Upaniṣads have also tasted the nectar of His lotus feet by following in the footsteps of the gopīs.' "

PURPORT

This verse is from *Śrīmad-Bhāgavatam* (10.87.23).

TEXT 124

শ্রুতি পায়, লক্ষ্মী না পায়, ইথে কি কারণ ।
ভট্ট কহে,—ইহা প্রবেশিতে নারে মোর মন ॥১২৪॥

śruti pāya, lakṣmī nā pāya, ithe ki kāraṇa
bhaṭṭa kahe,——ihā praveśite nāre mora mana

SYNONYMS

śruti pāya—the Vedic authorities got admission; *lakṣmī nā pāya*—and the goddess of fortune could not get admission; *ithe ki kāraṇa*—what must be the reason for this; *bhaṭṭa kahe*—Vyeṅkaṭa Bhaṭṭa replied; *ihā*—this; *praveśite*—to enter; *nāre*—is not able; *mora*—my; *mana*—mind.

TRANSLATION

Having been asked by Caitanya Mahāprabhu why the goddess of fortune could not enter into the rāsa dance whereas the authorities on Vedic knowledge could, Vyeṅkaṭa Bhaṭṭa replied, "I cannot enter into the mysteries of this behavior."

TEXT 125

আমি জীব,—ক্ষুদ্রবুদ্ধি, সহজে অস্থির ।
ঈশ্বরের লীলা—কোটিসমুদ্র-গম্ভীর ॥ ১২৫ ॥

āmi jīva,——kṣudra-buddhi, sahaje asthira
īśvarera līlā——koṭi-samudra-gambhīra

SYNONYMS

āmi jīva—I am an ordinary living being; *kṣudra-buddhi*—possessing limited intelligence; *sahaje asthira*—very easily agitated; *īśvarera līlā*—the pastimes of the Lord; *koṭi-samudra*—as millions of oceans; *gambhīra*—as deep.

TRANSLATION

Vyeṅkaṭa Bhaṭṭa then admitted, "I am an ordinary human being. Since my intelligence is very limited and I am easily agitated, my mind cannot enter within the deep ocean of the pastimes of the Lord.

TEXT 126

তুমি সাক্ষাৎ সেই কৃষ্ণ, জান নিজকর্ম ।
যারে জানাহ, সেই জানে তোমার লীলামর্ম ॥ ১২৬॥

tumi sākṣāt sei kṛṣṇa, jāna nija-karma
yāre jānāha, sei jāne tomāra līlā-marma

SYNONYMS

tumi—You; *sākṣāt*—directly; *sei*—that; *kṛṣṇa*—the Supreme Personality of Godhead; *jāna*—You know; *nija-karma*—Your activities; *yāre jānāha*—and unto whom You make it known; *sei*—that person; *jāne*—knows; *tomāra*—Your; *līlā-marma*—the purport of the pastimes.

TRANSLATION

"You are the Supreme Personality of Godhead Kṛṣṇa Himself. You know the purpose of Your activities, and the person whom You enlighten can also understand Your pastimes."

PURPORT

The Supreme Personality of Godhead Kṛṣṇa and His pastimes cannot be understood by blunt material senses. One has to purify the senses by rendering transcendental loving service unto the Lord. When the Lord is pleased and reveals

Himself, one can understand the transcendental form, name, qualities and pastimes of the Lord. This is confirmed in the *Kaṭha Upaniṣad* (2.23) and in the *Muṇḍaka Upaniṣad* (3.2.3): *yam evaiṣa vṛṇute tena labhyas tasyaiṣa ātmā vivṛṇute tanūṁ svām.* "Anyone who is favored by the Supreme Personality of Godhead can understand His transcendental name, qualities, form and pastimes."

TEXT 127

প্রভু কহে,—কৃষ্ণের এক স্বভাব বিলক্ষণ ।
স্বমাধুর্যে সর্ব চিত্ত করে আকর্ষণ ॥ ১২৭ ॥

prabhu kahe,——kṛṣṇera eka svabhāva vilakṣaṇa
sva-mādhurye sarva citta kare ākarṣaṇa

SYNONYMS

prabhu kahe—the Lord replied; *kṛṣṇera*—of Lord Kṛṣṇa; *eka*—one; *sva-bhāva*—characteristic; *vilakṣaṇa*—specific; *sva-mādhurye*—His conjugal love; *sarva*—all; *citta*—hearts; *kare*—does; *ākarṣaṇa*—attraction.

TRANSLATION

The Lord replied, "Lord Kṛṣṇa has a specific characteristic. He attracts everyone's heart by the mellow of His personal conjugal love.

TEXT 128

ব্রজলোকের ভাবে পাইয়ে তাঁহার চরণ ।
তাঁরে ঈশ্বর করি' নাহি জানে ব্রজজন ॥ ১২৮ ॥

vraja-lokera bhāve pāiye tāṅhāra caraṇa
tāṅre īśvara kari' nāhi jāne vraja-jana

SYNONYMS

vraja-lokera—of the inhabitants of Goloka Vṛndāvana; *bhāve*—in the ecstasy; *pāiye*—one gets; *tāṅhāra*—Lord Kṛṣṇa's; *caraṇa*—lotus feet; *tāṅre*—unto Him; *īśvara*—the Supreme Person; *kari'*—accepting; *nāhi*—do not; *jāne*—know; *vraja-jana*—the inhabitants of Vrajabhūmi.

TRANSLATION

"By following in the footsteps of the inhabitants of the planet known as Vrajaloka or Goloka Vṛndāvana one can attain the shelter of the lotus feet of Śrī Kṛṣṇa. However, in that planet the inhabitants do not know that Lord Kṛṣṇa is the Supreme Personality of Godhead.

TEXT 129

কেহ তাঁরে পুত্র-জ্ঞানে উদুখলে বান্ধে।
কেহ সখা-জ্ঞানে জিনি' চড়ে তাঁর কান্ধে ॥ ১২৯ ॥

keha tāṅre putra-jñāne udukhale bāndhe
keha sakhā-jñāne jini' caḍe tāṅra kāndhe

SYNONYMS

keha—someone; *tāṅre*—Him; *putra-jñāne*—by accepting as a son; *udukhale*—to a big mortar; *bāndhe*—ties; *keha*—someone; *sakhā-jñāne*—by accepting as a friend; *jini'*—conquering; *caḍe*—gets up; *tāṅra*—His; *kāndhe*—on the shoulder.

TRANSLATION

"There someone may accept Him as a son and sometimes bind Him to a grinding mortar. Someone else may accept Him as an intimate friend and, attaining victory over Him, playfully mount His shoulders.

TEXT 130

'ব্রজেন্দ্রনন্দন' বলি' তাঁরে জানে ব্রজজন।
ঐশ্বর্যজ্ঞানে নাহি কোন সম্বন্ধ-মানন ॥ ১৩০ ॥

'vrajendra-nandana' bali' tāṅre jāne vraja-jana
aiśvarya-jñāne nāhi kona sambandha-mānana

SYNONYMS

vrajendra-nandana—the son of Nanda Mahārāja, the King of Vrajabhūmi; *bali'*—as; *tāṅre*—Him; *jāne*—know; *vraja-jana*—the inhabitants of Vrajabhūmi; *aiśvarya-jñāne*—in opulence; *nāhi*—there is not; *kona*—any; *sambandha*—relationship; *mānana*—regarding.

TRANSLATION

"The inhabitants of Vrajabhūmi know Kṛṣṇa as the son of Mahārāja Nanda, the King of Vrajabhūmi, and they consider that there can be no relationship with the Lord in the rasa of opulence.

TEXT 131

ব্রজলোকের ভাবে যেই করয়ে ভজন।
সেই জন পায় ব্রজে ব্রজেন্দ্রনন্দন ॥ ১৩১ ॥

vraja-lokera bhāve yei karaye bhajana
sei jana pāya vraje vrajendra-nandana

SYNONYMS

vraja-lokera—of the inhabitants of Vrajabhūmi; *bhāve*—in the ecstasy; *yei*—anyone who; *karaye*—does; *bhajana*—worship; *sei jana*—that person; *pāya*—attains; *vraje*—in Vraja; *vrajendra-nandana*—Lord Kṛṣṇa, the son of Mahārāja Nanda.

TRANSLATION

"One who worships the Lord by following in the footsteps of the inhabitants of Vrajabhūmi attains the Lord and gets to know Him as He is known in the transcendental planet of Vraja. There He is known as the son of Mahārāja Nanda."

PURPORT

The inhabitants of Vrajabhūmi, or Goloka Vṛndāvana, know Kṛṣṇa as the son of Mahārāja Nanda. They do not accept Him as the Supreme Personality of Godhead. The Lord is the supreme maintainer of everyone and the chief personality among all personalities. In Vrajabhūmi Kṛṣṇa is certainly the central point of love, but no one knows Him there as the Supreme Personality of Godhead. Rather, a person may know Him as a friend, son, lover or master. In any case, the center is Kṛṣṇa. The inhabitants of Vrajabhūmi are related to the Lord in servitude, friendship, paternal love and conjugal love. A person engaged in devotional service may accept any one of these transcendental relationships, which are known as mellows. One who is in the perfectional stage may return home, back to Godhead, and attain his pure spiritual identity.

TEXT 132

নায়ং সুখাপো ভগবান্ দেহিনাং গোপিকাসুতঃ ।
জ্ঞানিনাং চাত্মভূতানাং যথা ভক্তিমতামিহ ॥ ১৩২ ॥

nāyaṁ sukhāpo bhagavān
dehināṁ gopikā-sutaḥ
jñānināṁ cātma-bhūtānāṁ
yathā bhaktimatām iha

SYNONYMS

na—not; *ayam*—this Lord Śrī Kṛṣṇa; *sukha-āpaḥ*—easily available; *bhagavān*—the Supreme Personality of Godhead; *dehinām*—for materialistic persons who have accepted the body as the self; *gopikā-sutaḥ*—the son of mother Yaśodā; *jñāninām*—for persons addicted to mental speculation; *ca*—and; *ātma-bhūtānām*—for persons performing severe austerities and penances; *yathā*—as; *bhaktimatām*—for persons engaged in spontaneous devotional service; *iha*—in this world.

TRANSLATION

Caitanya Mahāprabhu then quoted, "'The Supreme Personality of Godhead, Kṛṣṇa, the son of mother Yaśodā, is accessible to those devotees engaged in spontaneous loving service, but He is not as easily accessible to mental speculators, to those striving for self-realization by severe austerities and penances, or to those who consider the body to be the same as the self.'

PURPORT

This verse, also given in *Madhya-līlā* 8.227, is quoted from *Śrīmad-Bhāgavatam* (10.9.21).

TEXT 133

শ্রুতিগণ গোপীগণের অনুগত হঞা ।
ব্রজেশ্বরীসুত ভজে গোপীভাব লঞা ॥ ১৩৩ ॥

śruti-gaṇa gopī-gaṇera anugata hañā
vrajeśvarī-suta bhaje gopī-bhāva lañā

SYNONYMS

śruti-gaṇa—the authorities of Vedic hymns; *gopī-gaṇera*—of the *gopīs*; *anugata hañā*—following in the footsteps; *vrajeśvarī-suta*—the son of mother Yaśodā; *bhaje*—worship; *gopī-bhāva*—the ecstasy of the *gopīs*; *lañā*—accepting.

TRANSLATION

"The authorities in Vedic literatures known as śruti-gaṇa worshiped Lord Kṛṣṇa in the ecstasy of the gopīs and followed in their footsteps.

PURPORT

The authorities in Vedic literature known as *śruti-gaṇa* desired to enter into Lord Śrī Kṛṣṇa's *rāsa* dance; therefore they began to worship the Lord in the ecstasy of the *gopīs*. In the beginning, however, they were unsuccessful. When they could not enter the dance simply by thinking of Kṛṣṇa in the ecstasy of the *gopīs*, they actually accepted bodies like those of the *gopīs*. They even took birth in Vrajabhūmi just like the *gopīs* and consequently became engrossed in the ecstasy of the *gopīs'* love. In this way they were allowed to enter into the *rāsa-līlā* dance of the Lord.

TEXT 134

বাহ্যান্তরে গোপীদেহ ব্রজে যবে পাইল।
সেই দেহে কৃষ্ণসঙ্গে রাসক্রীড়া কৈল ॥ ১৩৪ ॥

bāhyāntare gopī-deha vraje yabe pāila
sei dehe kṛṣṇa-saṅge rāsa-krīḍā kaila

SYNONYMS

bāhya-antare—externally and internally; *gopī-deha*—the body of a *gopī*; *vraje*—in Vrajabhūmi; *yabe*—when; *pāila*—they got; *sei dehe*—in that body; *kṛṣṇa-saṅge*—with Kṛṣṇa; *rāsa-krīḍā*—pastimes of the *rāsa* dance; *kaila*—performed.

TRANSLATION

"The personified authorities on the Vedic hymns acquired bodies like those of the gopīs and took birth in Vrajabhūmi. In those bodies they were allowed to enter into the Lord's rāsa-līlā dance.

TEXT 135

গোপজাতি কৃষ্ণ, গোপী—প্রেয়সী তাঁহার।
দেবী বা অন্য স্ত্রী কৃষ্ণ না করে অঙ্গীকার ॥ ১৩৫ ॥

gopa-jāti kṛṣṇa, gopī——preyasī tāṅhāra
devī vā anya strī kṛṣṇa nā kare aṅgīkāra

SYNONYMS

gopa-jāti—belonging to the cowherd community; *kṛṣṇa*—Lord Kṛṣṇa; *gopī*—the damsels of Vrajabhūmi, the *gopīs*; *preyasī*—dearmost; *tāṅhāra*—His; *devī*—the wives of the demigods; *vā*—or; *anya*—other; *strī*—women; *kṛṣṇa*—Lord Kṛṣṇa; *nā*—does not; *kare*—do; *aṅgīkāra*—acceptance.

TRANSLATION

"Lord Kṛṣṇa belongs to the cowherd community, and the gopīs are the dearmost lovers of Kṛṣṇa. Although the wives of the denizens of the heavenly

planets are most opulent within the material world, neither they nor any other women in the material universe can acquire Kṛṣṇa's association.

TEXT 136

লক্ষ্মী চাহে সেই দেহে কৃষ্ণের সঙ্গম ।
গোপিকা-অনুগা হঞা না কৈল ভজন ॥ ১৩৬ ॥

lakṣmī cāhe sei dehe kṛṣṇera saṅgama
gopikā-anugā hañā nā kaila bhajana

SYNONYMS

lakṣmī—the goddess of fortune; *cāhe*—wants; *sei*—that; *dehe*—in the body; *kṛṣṇera saṅgama*—the association of Kṛṣṇa; *gopikā*—of the *gopīs*; *anugā*—follower; *hañā*—becoming; *nā*—did not; *kaila*—perform; *bhajana*—worship.

TRANSLATION

"The goddess of fortune, Lakṣmī, wanted to enjoy Kṛṣṇa and at the same time retain her spiritual body in the form of Lakṣmī. However, she did not follow in the footsteps of the gopīs in her worship of Kṛṣṇa.

TEXT 137

অন্য দেহে না পাইয়ে রাসবিলাস ।
অতএব 'নায়ং' শ্লোক কহে বেদব্যাস ॥ ১৩৭ ॥

anya dehe nā pāiye rāsa-vilāsa
ataeva 'nāyaṁ' śloka kahe veda-vyāsa

SYNONYMS

anya dehe—in a body other than those of the *gopīs*; *nā*—not; *pāiye*—one gets; *rāsa-vilāsa*—the pastimes of the *rāsa* dance; *ataeva*—therefore; *nāyam*—beginning with the word *nāyam*; *śloka*—the Sanskrit verse; *kahe*—says; *veda-vyāsa*—Dvaipāyana Vedavyāsa.

TRANSLATION

"Vyāsadeva, the supreme authority on Vedic literature, composed a verse beginning 'nāyaṁ sukhāpo bhagavān' because no one can enter into the rāsa-līlā dance in any body other than the bodies of the gopīs."

PURPORT

This verse confirms a verse of *Bhagavad-gītā* (9.25):

yānti deva-vratā devān
pitṝn yānti pitṛ-vratāḥ
bhūtāni yānti bhūtejyā
yānti mad-yājino 'pi mām

"Those who worship the demigods will take birth among the demigods; those who worship ghosts and spirits will take birth among such beings; those who worship ancestors go the ancestors; and those who worship Me will live with Me."

Only when one regains his original spiritual body can one enter into the spiritual kingdom. As far as the *rāsa-līlā* pastimes of the Lord are concerned, it is futile to attempt to imitate the Lord's dances within the material world. One has to attain a spiritual body like the *gopīs* to enter into the pastimes of *rāsa-līlā*. In the *nāyaṁ sukhāpo* verse, the devotees are referred to as *bhaktimat,* that is, they are fully engaged in devotional service and are devoid of material contamination. Simply by artificially imitating Kṛṣṇa's *rāsa-līlā* dance or artificially thinking oneself Kṛṣṇa and dressing oneself up like a *sakhī,* one cannot enter into His *rāsa-līlā* dance. Kṛṣṇa's *rāsa-līlā* dance is completely spiritual. It has nothing to do with material contamination; therefore no one can enter into the pastimes by artificial material means. That is the instruction of this verse.

TEXT 138

পূর্বে ভট্টের মনে এক ছিল অভিমান ।
'শ্রীনারায়ণ' হয়েন স্বয়ং-ভগবান্ ॥ ১৩৮ ॥

pūrve bhaṭṭera mane eka chila abhimāna
'śrī-nārāyaṇa' hayena svayaṁ-bhagavān

SYNONYMS

pūrve—before this; *bhaṭṭera*—of Vyeṅkaṭa Bhaṭṭa; *mane*—in the mind; *eka*—one; *chila*—there was; *abhimāna*—an impression; *śrī-nārāyaṇa*—the form of the Lord as Nārāyaṇa; *hayena*—is; *svayam*—personally; *bhagavān*—the Supreme Personality of Godhead.

TRANSLATION

Before this explanation was given by Śrī Caitanya Mahāprabhu, Vyeṅkaṭa Bhaṭṭa thought that Śrī Nārāyaṇa was the Supreme Personality of Godhead.

TEXT 139

তাঁহার ভজন সর্বোপরি-কক্ষা হয় ।
'শ্রী-বৈষ্ণবে'র ভজন এই সর্বোপরি হয় ॥ ১৩৯ ॥

tāṅhāra bhajana sarvopari-kakṣā haya
'śrī-vaiṣṇave'ra bhajana ei sarvopari haya

SYNONYMS

tāṅhāra bhajana—worship of Nārāyaṇa; *sarva-upari*—topmost; *kakṣā*—department; *haya*—is; *śrī-vaiṣṇavera*—of the followers of Rāmānujācārya; *bhajana*—worship; *ei*—this; *sarva-upari haya*—is the topmost.

TRANSLATION

Thinking in this way, Vyeṅkaṭa Bhaṭṭa believed that worship of Nārāyaṇa was the supreme form of worship, superior to all other processes of devotional service, for it was followed by the Śrī Vaiṣṇava disciples of Rāmānujācārya.

TEXT 140

এই তাঁর গর্ব প্রভু করিতে খণ্ডন ।
পরিহাসদ্বারে উঠায় এতেক বচন ॥ ১৪০ ॥

ei tāṅra garva prabhu karite khaṇḍana
parihāsa-dvāre uṭhāya eteka vacana

SYNONYMS

ei—this; *tāṅra*—his (Vyeṅkaṭa Bhaṭṭa's); *garva*—pride; *prabhu*—Lord Caitanya Mahāprabhu; *karite khaṇḍana*—to curb; *parihāsa-dvāre*—by joking; *uṭhāya*—raises; *eteka*—so many; *vacana*—words.

TRANSLATION

Śrī Caitanya Mahāprabhu had understood this misconception of Vyeṅkaṭa Bhaṭṭa, and to correct it the Lord talked so much in a joking way.

TEXT 141

প্রভু কহে,—ভট্ট, তুমি না করিহ সংশয় ।
'স্বয়ং-ভগবান্' কৃষ্ণ এই ত' নিশ্চয় ॥ ১৪১ ॥

prabhu kahe,——bhaṭṭa, tumi nā kariha saṁśaya
'svayaṁ-bhagavān' kṛṣṇa ei ta' niścaya

SYNONYMS

prabhu kahe—the Lord said; *bhaṭṭa*—My dear Vyeṅkaṭa Bhaṭṭa; *tumi*—you; *nā kariha*—do not do; *saṁśaya*—doubt; *svayam-bhagavān*—the Supreme Personality of Godhead; *kṛṣṇa*—is Lord Kṛṣṇa; *ei ta' niścaya*—this is the conclusion.

TRANSLATION

The Lord then continued, "My dear Vyeṅkaṭa Bhaṭṭa, please do not continue doubting. Lord Kṛṣṇa is the Supreme Personality of Godhead, and this is the conclusion of Vedic literatures.

TEXT 142

কৃষ্ণের বিলাস-মূর্তি - শ্রীনারায়ণ ।
অতএব লক্ষ্মী-আদ্যের হরে তেঁহ মন ॥ ১৪২ ॥

kṛṣṇera vilāsa-mūrti——śrī-nārāyaṇa
ataeva lakṣmī-ādyera hare teṅha mana

SYNONYMS

kṛṣṇera—of Lord Kṛṣṇa; *vilāsa-mūrti*—form for enjoyment; *śrī-nārāyaṇa*—Lord Nārāyaṇa; *ataeva*—therefore; *lakṣmī-ādyera*—of the goddess of fortune and her followers; *hare*—attracts; *teṅha*—He (Lord Nārāyaṇa); *mana*—the mind.

TRANSLATION

"Lord Nārāyaṇa, the opulent form of Kṛṣṇa, attracts the mind of the goddess of fortune and her followers.

TEXT 143

এতে চাংশকলাঃ পুংসঃ কৃষ্ণস্তু ভগবান্ স্বয়ম্ ।
ইন্দ্রারিব্যাকুলং লোকং মৃড়য়ন্তি যুগে যুগে ॥ ১৪৩ ॥

ete cāṁśa-kalāḥ puṁsaḥ
kṛṣṇas tu bhagavān svayam
indrāri-vyākulaṁ lokaṁ
mṛḍayanti yuge yuge

SYNONYMS

ete—these; *ca*—and; *aṁśa*—plenary portions; *kalāḥ*—parts of plenary portions; *puṁsaḥ*—of the *puruṣa-avatāras*; *kṛṣṇaḥ*—Lord Kṛṣṇa; *tu*—but; *bhagavān*—the Supreme Personality of Godhead; *svayam*—Himself; *indra-ari*—the enemies of Lord Indra; *vyākulam*—full of; *lokam*—the world; *mṛḍayanti*—make happy; *yuge yuge*—at the right time in each age.

TRANSLATION

" 'All these incarnations of Godhead are either plenary portions or parts of the plenary portions of the puruṣa-avatāras. But Kṛṣṇa is the Supreme Per-

sonality of Godhead Himself. In every age He protects the world through His different features when the world is disturbed by the enemies of Indra.'

PURPORT

This is a verse from *Śrīmad-Bhāgavatam* (1.3.28).

TEXT 144

নারায়ণ হৈতে কৃষ্ণের অসাধারণ গুণ ।
অতএব লক্ষ্মীর কৃষ্ণে তৃষ্ণা অনুক্ষণ ॥ ১৪৪ ॥

nārāyaṇa haite kṛṣṇera asādhāraṇa guṇa
ataeva lakṣmīra kṛṣṇe tṛṣṇā anukṣaṇa

SYNONYMS

nārāyaṇa haite—over and above Nārāyaṇa; *kṛṣṇera*—of Lord Kṛṣṇa; *asādhāraṇa guṇa*—uncommon qualities; *ataeva*—therefore; *lakṣmīra*—of the goddess of fortune; *kṛṣṇe*—unto Kṛṣṇa; *tṛṣṇā*—desire; *anukṣaṇa*—always.

TRANSLATION

"Because Kṛṣṇa has four extraordinary qualities not possessed by Lord Nārāyaṇa, the goddess of fortune, Lakṣmī, always desires His company.

PURPORT

Lord Nārāyaṇa has sixty transcendental qualities. Over and above these, Kṛṣṇa has four extraordinary transcendental qualities absent in Lord Nārāyaṇa. These four qualities are: (1) wonderful pastimes that are compared to an ocean; (2) association in the circle of supreme devotees in conjugal love (the *gopīs*); (3) Lord Kṛṣṇa's playing on the flute whose vibration attracts the three worlds; (4) Lord Kṛṣṇa's extraordinary beauty, which surpasses the beauty of the three worlds. Lord Kṛṣṇa's beauty is unequaled and unsurpassed.

TEXT 145

তুমি যে পড়িলা শ্লোক, সে হয় প্রমাণ ।
সেই শ্লোকে আইসে 'কৃষ্ণ—স্বয়ং ভগবান্' ॥ ১৪৫ ॥

tumi ye paḍilā śloka, se haya pramāṇa
sei śloke āise 'kṛṣṇa——svayaṁ bhagavān'

SYNONYMS

tumi—you; *ye*—which; *paḍilā*—have recited; *śloka*—verse; *se*—that; *haya*—is; *pramāṇa*—evidence; *sei śloke*—in that verse; *āise kṛṣṇa*—Kṛṣṇa is; *svayam bhagavān*—the Supreme Personality of Godhead.

TRANSLATION

"You have recited the śloka beginning with 'siddhāntatas tv abhede 'pi.' That very verse is evidence that Kṛṣṇa is the Supreme Personality of Godhead.

TEXT 146

সিদ্ধান্ততস্ত্বভেদেঽপি শ্রীশ-কৃষ্ণস্বরূপয়োঃ ।
রসেনোৎকৃষ্যতে কৃষ্ণরূপমেষা রসস্থিতিঃ ॥ ১৪৬ ॥

siddhāntatas tv abhede 'pi
śrīśa-kṛṣṇa-svarūpayoḥ
rasenotkṛṣyate kṛṣṇa-
rūpam eṣā rasa-sthitiḥ

SYNONYMS

siddhāntataḥ—in reality; *tu*—but; *abhede*—no difference; *api*—although; *śrī-īśa*—of the husband of Lakṣmī, Nārāyaṇa; *kṛṣṇa*—of Lord Kṛṣṇa; *svarūpayoḥ*—between the forms; *rasena*—by transcendental mellows; *utkṛṣyate*—is superior; *kṛṣṇa-rūpam*—the form of Lord Kṛṣṇa; *eṣā*—this; *rasa-sthitiḥ*—the reservoir of pleasure.

TRANSLATION

" 'According to transcendental realization, there is no difference between the forms of Kṛṣṇa and Nārāyaṇa. Yet in Kṛṣṇa there is a special transcendental attraction due to the conjugal mellow, and consequently He surpasses Nārāyaṇa. This is the conclusion of transcendental mellows.'

PURPORT

This is a verse from *Bhakti-rasāmṛta-sindhu* (1.2.59).

TEXT 147

'স্বয়ং ভগবান্ 'কৃষ্ণ' হরে লক্ষ্মীর মন ।
গোপিকার মন হরিতে নারে 'নারায়ণ' ॥ ১৪৭ ॥

svayaṁ bhagavān 'kṛṣṇa' hare lakṣmīra mana
gopikāra mana harite nāre 'nārāyaṇa'

SYNONYMS

svayam bhagavān—the Supreme Personality of Godhead; *kṛṣṇa*—is Lord Kṛṣṇa; *hare*—attracts; *lakṣmīra*—of the goddess of fortune; *mana*—the mind; *gopikāra*—of the *gopīs*; *mana*—the minds; *harite*—to attract; *nāre*—is not able; *nārāyaṇa*—Lord Nārāyaṇa.

TRANSLATION

"The Supreme Personality of Godhead, Kṛṣṇa, attracts the mind of the goddess of fortune, but Lord Nārāyaṇa cannot attract the minds of the gopīs. This proves the superexcellence of Kṛṣṇa.

TEXT 148

নারায়ণের কা কথা, শ্রীকৃষ্ণ আপনে ।
গোপিকারে হাস্য করাইতে হয় 'নারায়ণে' ॥ ১৪৮ ॥

nārāyaṇera kā kathā, śrī-kṛṣṇa āpane
gopikāre hāsya karāite haya 'nārāyaṇe'

SYNONYMS

nārāyaṇera—of Lord Nārāyaṇa; *kā kathā*—what to speak; *śrī-kṛṣṇa*—Lord Śrī Kṛṣṇa; *āpane*—Himself; *gopikāre*—the *gopīs*; *hāsya karāite*—to make them jubilant; *haya*—becomes; *nārāyaṇe*—in the form of Nārāyaṇa.

TRANSLATION

"To say nothing of Lord Nārāyaṇa personally, Lord Kṛṣṇa Himself appeared as Nārāyaṇa just to play a joke on the gopīs.

TEXT 149

'চতুর্ভুজ-মূর্তি' দেখায় গোপীগণের আগে ।
সেই 'কৃষ্ণে' গোপিকার নহে অনুরাগে ॥ ১৪৯ ॥

'catur-bhuja-mūrti' dekhāya gopī-gaṇera āge
sei 'kṛṣṇe' gopikāra nahe anurāge

SYNONYMS

catuḥ-bhuja-mūrti—four-handed form; *dekhāya*—exhibits; *gopī-gaṇera*—of the *gopīs*; *āge*—in front; *sei kṛṣṇe*—unto that Kṛṣṇa; *gopikāra*—of the *gopīs*; *nahe*—not; *anurāge*—attraction.

TRANSLATION

"Although Kṛṣṇa assumed the four-armed form of Nārāyaṇa, He could not attract the serious attention of the gopīs in ecstatic love.

TEXT 150

গোপীনাং পশুপেন্দ্রনন্দনজুষো ভাবস্য কস্তাং কৃতী
বিজ্ঞাতুং ক্ষমতে দুরূহপদবীসঞ্চারিণঃ প্রক্রিয়াম্ ।
আবিষ্কুর্বতি বৈষ্ণবীমপি তনুং তস্মিন্ ভুজৈর্জিষ্ণুভি-
র্যাসাং হন্ত চতুর্ভিরদ্ভুতরুচিং রাগোদয়ঃ কুঞ্চতি ॥ ১৫০ ॥

gopīnāṁ paśupendra-nandana-juṣo bhāvasya kas tāṁ kṛtī
vijñātuṁ kṣamate durūha-padavī-sañcāriṇaḥ prakriyām
āviṣkurvati vaiṣṇavīm api tanuṁ tasmin bhujair jiṣṇubhir
yāsāṁ hanta caturbhir adbhuta-ruciṁ rāgodayaḥ kuñcati

SYNONYMS

gopīnām—of the gopīs; *paśupendra-nandana-juṣaḥ*—of the service of the son of Vraja's King, Mahārāja Nanda; *bhāvasya*—ecstatic; *kaḥ*—what; *tām*—that; *kṛtī*—learned man; *vijñātum*—to understand; *kṣamate*—is able; *durūha*—very difficult to understand; *padavī*—the position; *sañcāriṇaḥ*—which provokes; *prakriyām*—activity; *āviṣkurvati*—He manifests; *vaiṣṇavīm*—of Viṣṇu; *api*—certainly; *tanum*—the body; *tasmin*—in that; *bhujaiḥ*—with arms; *jiṣṇubhiḥ*—very beautiful; *yāsām*—of whom (the *gopīs*); *hanta*—alas; *caturbhiḥ*—four; *adbhuta*—wonderfully; *rucim*—beautiful; *rāga-udayaḥ*—the evoking of ecstatic feelings; *kuñcati*—cripples.

TRANSLATION

" 'Once Lord Śrī Kṛṣṇa playfully manifested Himself as Nārāyaṇa with four victorious hands and a very beautiful form. When the gopīs saw this exalted form, however, their ecstatic feelings abated. A learned scholar, therefore, cannot understand the gopīs' ecstatic feelings, which are firmly centered upon the original form of Lord Kṛṣṇa as the son of Nanda Mahārāja. The wonderful feelings of the gopīs in ecstatic parama-rasa with Kṛṣṇa constitute the greatest mystery of spiritual life.' "

PURPORT

This is a verse spoken by Nārada Muni in *Lalita-mādhava-nāṭaka* (6.14), a drama written by Śrīla Rūpa Gosvāmī. This verse clarifies the verse *siddhāntatas tv abhede 'pi,* which Kavirāja Gosvāmī quotes from *Bhakti-rasāmṛta-sindhu.* Lord Caitanya Mahāprabhu Himself spoke it to Vyeṅkaṭa Bhaṭṭa. The verse was quoted by Lord Caitanya long before *Bhakti-rasāmṛta-sindhu* was composed, and in this regard Śrīla Bhaktivinoda Ṭhākura points out that all these verses were current at the time and were quoted by devotees long before *Bhakti-rasāmṛta-sindhu* was composed.

TEXT 151

এত কহি' প্রভু তাঁর গর্ব চূর্ণ করিয়া।
তাঁরে সুখ দিতে কহে সিদ্ধান্ত ফিরাইয়া॥ ১৫১ ॥

eta kahi' prabhu tāṅra garva cūrṇa kariyā
tāṅre sukha dite kahe siddhānta phirāiyā

SYNONYMS

eta kahi'—saying this; *prabhu*—Lord Śrī Caitanya Mahāprabhu; *tāṅra*—his (of Vyeṅkaṭa Bhaṭṭa); *garva*—pride; *cūrṇa kariyā*—smashing into pieces; *tāṅre*—unto him; *sukha dite*—to give happiness; *kahe*—says; *siddhānta phirāiyā*—turning the whole conversation.

TRANSLATION

In this way Lord Śrī Caitanya Mahāprabhu deflated the pride of Vyeṅkaṭa Bhaṭṭa, but just to make him happy again, He spoke as follows.

TEXT 152

দুঃখ না ভাবিহ, ভট্ট, কৈলুঁ পরিহাস।
শাস্ত্রসিদ্ধান্ত শুন, যাতে বৈষ্ণব-বিশ্বাস॥ ১৫২ ॥

duḥkha nā bhāviha, bhaṭṭa, kailuṅ parihāsa
śāstra-siddhānta śuna, yāte vaiṣṇava-viśvāsa

SYNONYMS

duḥkha—unhappiness; *nā*—do not; *bhāviha*—bear; *bhaṭṭa*—My dear Vyeṅkaṭa Bhaṭṭa; *kailuṅ parihāsa*—I was simply making a joke; *śāstra-siddhānta*—the conclusion of the revealed scriptures; *śuna*—hear; *yāte*—in which; *vaiṣṇava-viśvāsa*—the faith of the Vaiṣṇavas.

TRANSLATION

The Lord pacified Vyeṅkaṭa Bhaṭṭa by saying, "Actually whatever I have said is by way of jest. Now you can hear from Me the conclusion of the śāstras, in which every Vaiṣṇava devotee has firm faith.

TEXT 153

কৃষ্ণ-নারায়ণ, যৈছে একই স্বরূপ ।
গোপী-লক্ষ্মী-ভেদ নাহি হয় একরূপ ॥ ১৫৩ ॥

kṛṣṇa-nārāyaṇa, yaiche eka-i svarūpa
gopī-lakṣmī-bheda nāhi haya eka-rūpa

SYNONYMS

kṛṣṇa-nārāyaṇa—Lord Kṛṣṇa and Lord Nārāyaṇa; *yaiche*—as; *eka-i*—one; *svarūpa*—form; *gopī*—the *gopīs*; *lakṣmī*—the goddess of fortune; *bheda*—difference; *nāhi*—there is not; *haya*—there is; *eka-rūpa*—one form.

TRANSLATION

"There is no difference between Lord Kṛṣṇa and Lord Nārāyaṇa, for They are of the same form. Similarly, there is no difference between the gopīs and the goddess of fortune, for they also are of the same form.

TEXT 154

গোপীদ্বারে লক্ষ্মী করে কৃষ্ণসঙ্গাস্বাদ ।
ঈশ্বরত্বে ভেদ মানিলে হয় অপরাধ ॥ ১৫৪ ॥

gopī-dvāre lakṣmī kare kṛṣṇa-saṅgāsvāda
īśvaratve bheda mānile haya aparādha

SYNONYMS

gopī-dvāre—through the *gopīs*; *lakṣmī*—the goddess of fortune; *kare*—does; *kṛṣṇa-saṅga-āsvāda*—tasting the sweetness of the association of Lord Kṛṣṇa; *īśvaratve*—in the Supreme Personality of Godhead; *bheda*—difference; *mānile*—if one considers; *haya*—there is; *aparādha*—offense.

TRANSLATION

"The goddess of fortune enjoys the association of Kṛṣṇa through the gopīs. One should not make distinctions between the forms of the Lord, for such conceptualizing is offensive.

TEXT 155

এক ঈশ্বর—ভক্তের ধ্যান-অনুরূপ ।
একই বিগ্রহে করে নানাকার রূপ ॥ ১৫৫ ॥

eka īśvara——bhaktera dhyāna-anurūpa
eka-i vigrahe kare nānākāra rūpa

SYNONYMS

eka īśvara—the Lord is one; *bhaktera*—of the devotees; *dhyāna*—meditation; *anurūpa*—according to; *eka-i*—one; *vigrahe*—in form; *kare*—exhibits; *nānā-ākāra*—different; *rūpa*—forms.

TRANSLATION

"There is no difference between the transcendental forms of the Lord. Different forms are manifest due to different attachments of different devotees. Actually the Lord is one, but He appears in different forms just to satisfy His devotees.

PURPORT

In *Brahma-saṁhitā* (5.33) it is stated:

advaitam acyutam anādim ananta-rūpam
ādyaṁ purāṇa-puruṣaṁ nava-yauvanaṁ ca

The Lord is *advaita,* without differentiation. There is no difference between the forms of Kṛṣṇa, Rāma, Nārāyaṇa and Viṣṇu. All of them are one. Sometimes foolish people ask whether when we chant "Rāma" in the Hare Kṛṣṇa *mantra* we refer to Lord Rāmacandra or Lord Balarāma. If a devotee says that the name Rāma in the Hare Kṛṣṇa *mahā-mantra* refers to Balarāma, a foolish person may become angry because to him the name Rāma refers to Lord Rāmacandra. Actually there is no difference between Balarāma and Lord Rāma. It doesn't matter if one chants Hare Rāma referring to Balarāma or Lord Rāmacandra, for there is no difference between Them. However, it is offensive to think that Balarāma is superior to Lord Rāmacandra or vice versa. Neophyte devotees do not understand this śāstric conclusion, and consequently they unneccesarily create an offensive situation. Śrī Caitanya Mahāprabhu clarifies this in a very lucid way: *īśvaratve bheda mānile haya aparādha.* It is offensive for one to differentiate between the forms of the Lord. On the other hand, one should not think that the forms of the Lord are the same as the forms of the demigods. This is certainly offensive. As confirmed by the *Vaiṣṇava-tantra*:

yas tu nārāyaṇaṁ devaṁ
brahma-rudrādi-daivataiḥ
samatvenaiva vīkṣeta
sa pāṣaṇḍī bhaved dhruvam

"A *pāṣaṇḍī* is one who considers the great demigods such as Lord Brahmā and Lord Śiva equal to the Supreme Personality of Godhead, Nārāyaṇa." (*Hari-bhakti-vilāsa* 1.117) The conclusion is that we should not differentiate between the forms of the Lord. However, we should not equate the forms of the Lord with the forms of demigods or human beings. For instance, sometimes foolish *sannyāsīs* equate *daridra-nārāyaṇa* with Nārāyaṇa, and this is certainly offensive. To think of the body of the Lord as material is also offensive. Unless one is instructed by a bona fide spiritual master, he cannot perfectly understand these different forms. *Brahma-saṁhitā* confirms, *vedeṣu durlabham adurlabham ātma-bhaktau.* One cannot understand the differences between the forms of the Lord simply by academic study or by reading Vedic literature. One must learn from a realized devotee. Only then can one learn how to distinguish between one form of the Lord and another. The conclusion is that there is no difference between the forms of the Lord, but there is a difference between His forms and those of the demigods.

TEXT 156

মণির্যথা বিভাগেন নীলপীতাদিভির্যুতঃ ।
রূপভেদমবাপ্নোতি ধ্যানভেদাত্তথাচ্যুতঃ ॥ ১৫৬ ॥

maṇir yathā vibhāgena
nīla-pītādibhir yutaḥ
rūpa-bhedam avāpnoti
dhyāna-bhedāt tathācyutaḥ

SYNONYMS

maṇiḥ—jewel, specifically the jewel known as *vaidūrya; yathā*—as; *vibhāgena*—separately; *nīla*—blue; *pīta*—yellow; *ādibhiḥ*—and with other colors; *yutaḥ*—joined; *rūpa-bhedam*—difference of form; *avāpnoti*—gets; *dhyāna-bhedāt*—by different types of meditation; *tathā*—similarly; *acyutaḥ*—the infallible Supreme Personality of Godhead.

TRANSLATION

" 'When the jewel known as vaidūrya touches other materials, it appears to be separated into different colors. Consequently the forms also appear different. Similarly, according to the meditational ecstasy of the devotee, the Lord, who is known as Acyuta [infallible], appears in different forms, although He is essentially one.' "

PURPORT

This is a verse quoted form *Śrī Nārada-pañcarātra.*

TEXT 157

ভট্ট কহে,—কাহাঁ আমি জীব পামর ।
কাহাঁ তুমি সেই কৃষ্ণ,—সাক্ষাৎ ঈশ্বর ॥ ১৫৭ ॥

bhaṭṭa kahe,——kāhāṅ āmi jīva pāmara
kāhāṅ tumi sei kṛṣṇa,——sākṣāt īśvara

SYNONYMS

bhaṭṭa kahe—Vyeṅkaṭa Bhaṭṭa said; *kāhāṅ*—whereas; *āmi*—I; *jīva*—an ordinary living being; *pāmara*—fallen; *kāhāṅ*—whereas; *tumi*—You; *sei kṛṣṇa*—the same Supreme Personality of Godhead, Kṛṣṇa; *sākṣāt īśvara*—directly the Lord.

TRANSLATION

Vyeṅkaṭa Bhaṭṭa then said, "I am an ordinary fallen living entity, but You are Kṛṣṇa, the Supreme Personality of Godhead Himself.

TEXT 158

অগাধ ঈশ্বর-লীলা কিছুই না জানি ।
তুমি যেই কহ, সেই সত্য করি' মানি ॥ ১৫৮ ॥

agādha īśvara-līlā kichui nā jāni
tumi yei kaha, sei satya kari' māni

SYNONYMS

agādha—unfathomable; *īśvara-līlā*—pastimes of the Lord; *kichui*—anything; *nā jāni*—I do not know; *tumi*—You; *yei*—whatever; *kaha*—say; *sei satya*—that is right; *kari' māni*—I accept.

TRANSLATION

"The transcendental pastimes of the Lord are unfathomable, and I do not know anything about them. Whatever You say I accept as the truth.

PURPORT

This is the way to understand the truth about the Supreme Personality of Godhead. After hearing *Bhagavad-gītā*, Arjuna said very much the same thing:

sarvam etad ṛtaṁ manye
yan māṁ vadasi keśava

na hi te bhagavan vyaktiṁ
vidur devā na dānavāḥ

"O Kṛṣṇa, I totally accept as truth all that You have told me. Neither the gods nor demons, O Lord, know Thy personality." (Bg. 10.14)

Vyeṅkaṭa Bhaṭṭa says very much the same thing to Śrī Caitanya Mahāprabhu. It is not possible to understand the truth about the pastimes of the Lord simply by using our own logic, argument and academic education. We must receive bona fide information from the Supreme Personality of Godhead, just as Arjuna received information when Kṛṣṇa spoke *Bhagavad-gītā.* We have to accept *Bhagavad-gītā* or any other Vedic literature in good faith. These Vedic literatures are the only source of knowledge. We must understand that we cannot comprehend the Absolute Truth by the speculative process.

TEXT 159

মোরে পূর্ণ কৃপা কৈল লক্ষ্মী-নারায়ণ।
তাঁর কৃপায় পাইনু তোমার চরণ-দরশন॥ ১৫৯॥

more pūrṇa kṛpā kaila lakṣmī-nārāyaṇa
tāṅra kṛpāya pāinu tomāra caraṇa-daraśana

SYNONYMS

more—unto me; *pūrṇa*—complete; *kṛpā*—mercy; *kaila*—did; *lakṣmī-nārāyaṇa*—the Deity of mother goddess of fortune and Nārāyaṇa; *tāṅra kṛpāya*—by Their mercy; *pāinu*—I have gotten; *tomāra*—Your; *caraṇa-daraśana*—vision of the lotus feet.

TRANSLATION

"I have been engaged in the service of Lakṣmī-Nārāyaṇa, and it is due to Their mercy that I have been able to see Your lotus feet.

TEXT 160

কৃপা করি' কহিলে মোরে কৃষ্ণের মহিমা।
যাঁর রূপ-গুণৈশ্বর্যের কেহ না পায় সীমা॥ ১৬০ ॥

kṛpā kari' kahile more kṛṣṇera mahimā
yāṅra rūpa-guṇaiśvaryera keha nā pāya sīmā

SYNONYMS

kṛpā kari'—showing causeless mercy; *kahile*—You have spoken; *more*—unto me; *kṛṣṇera*—of Lord Kṛṣṇa; *mahimā*—the glories; *yāṅra*—whose; *rūpa-guṇa-*

aiśvaryera—of forms, qualities and opulence; *keha*—anyone; *nā*—not; *pāya*—gets; *sīmā*—the limit.

TRANSLATION

"Out of Your causeless mercy You have told me of the glories of Lord Kṛṣṇa. No one can reach the end of the opulence, qualities and forms of the Lord.

TEXT 161

এবে সে জানিনু কৃষ্ণভক্তি সর্বোপরি ।
কৃতার্থ করিলে, মোরে কহিলে কৃপা করি' ॥ ১৬১ ॥

ebe se jāninu kṛṣṇa-bhakti sarvopari
kṛtārtha karile, more kahile kṛpā kari'

SYNONYMS

ebe—now; *se*—that; *jāninu*—I understand; *kṛṣṇa-bhakti*—devotional service to Lord Kṛṣṇa; *sarva-upari*—above all; *kṛta-artha*—successful; *karile*—You have made; *more*—unto me; *kahile*—You have spoken; *kṛpā kari'*—by Your causeless mercy.

TRANSLATION

"I can now understand that devotional service unto Kṛṣṇa is the supreme form of worship. Out of Your causeless mercy You have made my life successful simply by explaining the facts."

TEXT 162

এত বলি' ভট্ট পড়িলা প্রভুর চরণে ।
কৃপা করি' প্রভু তাঁরে কৈলা আলিঙ্গনে ॥ ১৬২ ॥

eta bali' bhaṭṭa paḍilā prabhura caraṇe
kṛpā kari' prabhu tāṅre kailā āliṅgane

SYNONYMS

eta bali'—saying this; *bhaṭṭa*—Vyeṅkaṭa Bhaṭṭa; *paḍilā*—fell down; *prabhura caraṇe*—at the lotus feet of the Lord; *kṛpā kari'*—showing him mercy; *prabhu*—Lord Śrī Caitanya Mahāprabhu; *tāṅre*—unto him; *kailā*—did; *āliṅgane*—embracing.

TRANSLATION

After saying this, Vyeṅkaṭa Bhaṭṭa fell down before the lotus feet of the Lord, and the Lord, out of His causeless mercy, embraced him.

TEXT 163

চাতুর্মাস্য পূর্ণ হৈল, ভট্ট-আজ্ঞা লঞা ।
দক্ষিণ চলিলা প্রভু শ্রীরঙ্গ দেখিয়া ॥ ১৬৩ ॥

cāturmāsya pūrṇa haila, bhaṭṭa-ājñā lañā
dakṣiṇa calilā prabhu śrī-raṅga dekhiyā

SYNONYMS

cāturmāsya—the period of Cāturmāsya; *pūrṇa haila*—became completed; *bhaṭṭa-ājñā lañā*—taking permission from Vyeṅkaṭa Bhaṭṭa; *dakṣiṇa*—south; *calilā*—proceeded; *prabhu*—Śrī Caitanya Mahāprabhu; *śrī-raṅga dekhiyā*—visiting Śrī Raṅga.

TRANSLATION

When the period of Cāturmāsya was completed, Śrī Caitanya Mahāprabhu took permission to leave Vyeṅkaṭa Bhaṭṭa, and after visiting Śrī Raṅga, proceeded further towards southern India.

TEXT 164

সঙ্গেতে চলিলা ভট্ট, না যায় ভবনে ।
তাঁরে বিদায় দিলা প্রভু অনেক যতনে ॥ ১৬৪ ॥

saṅgete calilā bhaṭṭa, nā yāya bhavane
tāṅre vidāya dilā prabhu aneka yatane

SYNONYMS

saṅgete—along with Him; *calilā*—began to go; *bhaṭṭa*—Vyeṅkaṭa Bhaṭṭa; *nā yāya bhavane*—does not return to his home; *tāṅre*—unto him; *vidāya dilā*—gave farewell; *prabhu*—Śrī Caitanya Mahāprabhu; *aneka yatane*—with great endeavor.

TRANSLATION

Vyeṅkaṭa Bhaṭṭa did not want to return home but also wanted to go with the Lord. It was with great endeavor that Śrī Caitanya Mahāprabhu bade him farewell.

TEXT 165

প্রভুর বিয়োগে ভট্ট হৈল অচেতন ।
এই রঙ্গলীলা করে শচীর নন্দন ॥ ১৬৫ ॥

prabhura viyoge bhaṭṭa haila acetana
ei raṅga-līlā kare śacīra nandana

SYNONYMS

prabhura viyoge—on account of separation from Śrī Caitanya Mahāprabhu; *bhaṭṭa*—Vyeṅkaṭa Bhaṭṭa; *haila*—became; *acetana*—unconscious; *ei*—this; *raṅga-līlā*—pastime at Śrī Raṅga-kṣetra; *kare*—does; *śacīra nandana*—the son of mother Śacī.

TRANSLATION

When He did so, Vyeṅkaṭa Bhaṭṭa fell down unconscious. Such are the pastimes of Lord Śrī Caitanya Mahāprabhu, the son of mother Śacī, at Śrī Raṅga-kṣetra.

Thus end the Bhaktivedanta purports to the Śrī Caitanya-caritāmṛta, Madhya-līlā, *Ninth Chapter, First Part, describing Lord Śrī Caitanya Mahāprabhu's travels to the holy places.*

CONTINUED IN THE NEXT VOLUME.

References

The statements of *Śrī Caitanya-caritāmṛta* are all confirmed by standard Vedic authorities. The following authentic scriptures are quoted in this book on the pages listed. Numerals in bold type refer the reader to *Śrī Caitanya-caritāmṛta's* translations. Numerals in regular type are references to its purports.

Adhyātma-rāmāyaṇa, 296-297

Ādi Purāṇa, 243-245

Amṛta-pravāha-bhāṣya (Bhaktivinoda Ṭhākura), 1, 29, 49, 79-80, 113, 122, 220

Anubhāṣya (Bhaktisiddhānta Sarasvatī), 118, 120

Bhagavad-gītā, 30, 32-33, 35, **64-**65, 97, 103-104, 110, 111-112, **114-**115, **117, 119,** 140, 141, **144,** 171-172, 173, 174-175, 176, 213, 232, 255, 265, 272, 276, 287, 316, 317, 318, 321, **343-348,** 367, 378-379

Bhakti-rasāmṛta-sindhu (Rūpa Gosvāmī), 122, 133-134, **136,** 175, **178, 203, 204-205, 224,** 267, 286, 355, **371**

Bhakti-ratnākara (Narahari Cakravartī), 338

Brahma-saṁhitā, **169,** 172, 174, **190,** 264, 376, 377

Bṛhad-bhāgavatāmṛta (Sanātana Gosvāmī), 247

Bṛhad-vāmana Purāṇa, 244

Bṛhan-nāradīya Purāṇa, 243

Caitanya-candrāmṛta (Prabodhānanda Sarasvatī), 18, 245

Garuḍa Purāṇa, 242, 243

Gīta-govinda (Jayadeva Gosvāmī), **152, 179**

Govinda-līlāmṛta (Kṛṣṇadāsa Kavirāja), **200, 218, 221**

Hari-bhakti-vilāsa (Sanātana Gosvāmī), 163, 377

Itihāsa-samuccaya, 243

Glossary

A

Ācārya—a spiritual master who teaches by his own example.
Acyuta—the infallible Lord.
Adhikārī—one who knows the science of Kṛṣṇa and is engaged in His service.
Adhīra—restless ecstasy of love for Kṛṣṇa.
Advaita—without differentiation.
Ahaṅghrahopāsanā—a Māyāvādī's worship of his own body as the Supreme.
Akhila-rasāmṛta-mūrti—the transcendental form of attraction for all kinds of devotees.
Aparādha—an offense.
Apavitra-anna—food that is unacceptable for a Vaiṣṇava.
Aprākṛta—the spiritual or anti-material world.
Amṛtatva—eternal life.
Artha—economic development.
Āśramas—the spiritual orders of life.
Āśraya—the worshiper.
Avaiṣṇava—one who is not a Vaiṣṇava.

B

Bhakti—love of God; purified service of the senses of the Lord by one's own senses.
Bhakti-śakti—the spiritual potency which is the essence of the pleasure potency and the eternity potency.
Bhajanānandī—a Vaiṣṇava who is not interested in preaching work.
Bhāva—the preliminary stage of transcendental love of God.
Brahma-bhūta—state of being freed from material contamination; characterized by transcendental happiness and engagement in the service of the Lord.
Brahma-jñānī—an impersonalist scholar.
Brahma-vidyā—transcendental knowledge.
Brāhmaṇas—the intelligent class of men.

C

Caitanya—spiritual force.
Caitya-guru—the spiritual master within.
Caṇḍālas—dog-eaters.

D

Dāsya-rasa—loving relationship with Kṛṣṇa in servitorship.

Dharma—the capacity to render service, which is the essential quality of a living being.

Dhīra—ecstasy of sober love for Kṛṣṇa.

Dīkṣā—spiritual initiation.

Dīkṣā-guru—the spiritual master who initiates according to the regulations of the *śāstras.*

G

Gāyatrī—that which delivers one from material entanglement.

Gopīs—the transcendental girls of Vrajabhūmi.

Goṣṭhyānandī—a Vaiṣṇava who is interested in spreading Kṛṣṇa consciousness.

Guṇātīta—*See: Nirguṇa.*

Guru—spiritual master.

H

Hlādinī—Kṛṣṇa's pleasure potency.

J

Jñānīs—mental speculators who simply try to understand what is spirit and what is matter.

K

Kacchapī-vīṇā—the stringed instrument of Rādhārāṇī.

Kāma—sense gratification.

Karma-tyāga—renunciation of family life to take up Kṛṣṇa consciousness.

Karmīs—fruitive workers whose only aim is sense gratification.

Kṛṣṇa-kathā—topics about Kṛṣṇa.

Kṣatriyas—the ruling and administrative class of men.

L

Līlā—pastimes.

M

Madana—Cupid.

Mādhurya-rasa—relationship with Kṛṣṇa in conjugal love.

Mahā-bhāgavata—a devotee in the highest stage of devotional life.

Mahābhāva—highest perfectional stage of love of God.

Mahāmāyā—the superintendent of the material world.
Mahā-paṇḍita—a very learned person.
Mahā-prasāda—remnants of foodstuff offered on the plate of the Deity.
Mamatā—the feeling of oneness between the servitor and the served in devotional service.
Mokṣa—liberation.

N

Neti neti—the process of the *jñānīs:* "This is not spirit, this is not Brahman."
Nirguṇa—uncontaminated by the three modes of material nature.
Nirvāṇa—the end of the process of materialistic life.

P

Paramparā—the chain of disciplic succession beginning with Kṛṣṇa Himself.
Pāṣaṇḍī—one who thinks that Nārāyaṇa is on the same level with the demigods.
Patita-pāvana—Lord Caitanya, the deliverer of all fallen souls.
Paugāṇḍa—the age from five to ten years.
Premā—unalloyed love of God.
Prema-bhakti—loving service to Kṛṣṇa without expectation of reward or return.

R

Rādhā-kuṇḍa—the bathing place of Śrīmatī Rādhārāṇī.
Rāgānugā-bhakti—devotional service in spontaneous love for Kṛṣṇa.
Rasa—relationship between the Lord and the living entities.
Rasābhāsa—an overlapping of transcendental mellows.
Rūpānugas—followers of Śrīla Rūpa Gosvāmī.

S

Sac-cid-ānanda—eternal existence, knowledge and bliss.
Sādhana-bhakti—devotional service in practice.
Sahajiyās—a class of so-called devotees who try to imitate the Lord's pastimes.
Sajātīya—a person within the intimate circle of the Lord.
Sakhī—one who expands the conjugal love of Kṛṣṇa and His enjoyment among the *gopīs*.
Sakhya-prema—love of God in friendship.
Samvit—the Supreme Lord's aspect of cognizance.
Sandhinī—the Supreme Lord's aspect of eternal existence.
Śānta-rasa—relationship with Kṛṣṇa in the mood of awe and veneration.

Śāstras—revealed scriptures.
Siddha-deha—a perfected spiritual body.
Śikṣā-guru—the spiritual master who gives instructions for elevation.
Smārtas—nondevotee followers of Vedic rituals.
Śṛṅgāra-rasa—*See: Mādhurya-rasa.*
Śruti-gaṇa—the authorities in Vedic literatures.
Strī—a woman.
Śūdras—the laboring or servant class of men.
Svarūpa-gata—the stage of understanding Kṛṣṇa in truth while still maintaining some material connection.
Svarūpa-siddhi—the perfection of one's eternal relationship with the Supreme Lord.

T

Tāruṇyāmṛta—the nectar of youth.
Tattvavādīs—the followers of Madhvācārya.
Tilaka—sacred clay markings on the body of a Vaiṣṇava.
Tīrtha—a holy place where great saintly personalities reside.

V

Vaiśyas—the agricultural and mercantile class of men.
Varṇas—the four social orders of life: *brāhmaṇa, kṣatriya, vaiśya, śudra.*
Vartma-pradarśaka-guru—the one who first gives information about spiritual life.
Vastu-gata—the stage of being completely uncontaminated by the material body and mind.
Vātsalya-rasa—loving relation of a devotee to Kṛṣṇa as His parent.
Vidhi-mārga—worshiping the Lord with regulative principles.
Vijātīya—one who is outside of devotional service.
Vipra—a *brāhmaṇa.*
Viṣaya—the object of worship.
Viṣayī—one who is interested only in material sense gratification.
Viśrambha—devotional service devoid of a respectful attitude toward the Lord.
Viśuddha-sattva—the platform of unalloyed goodness.
Vivarta—sorrow and confusion due to unfulfillment of material desires.

Y

Yogamāyā—the spiritual or internal energy of the Lord.

Bengali Pronunciation Guide

BENGALI DIACRITICAL EQUIVALENTS AND PRONUNCIATION

Vowels

অ a   আ ā   ই i   ঈ ī   উ u   ঊ ū   ঋ ṛ

ৠ ṝ   এ e   ঐ ai   ও o   ঔ au

ং ṁ *(anusvāra)*   ঁ ṅ *(candra-bindu)*   ঃ ḥ *(visarga)*

Consonants

Gutterals:	ক ka	খ kha	গ ga	ঘ gha	ঙ ṅa
Palatals:	চ ca	ছ cha	জ ja	ঝ jha	ঞ ña
Cerebrals:	ট ṭa	ঠ ṭha	ড ḍa	ঢ ḍha	ণ ṇa
Dentals:	ত ta	থ tha	দ da	ধ dha	ন na
Labials:	প pa	ফ pha	ব ba	ভ bha	ম ma
Semivowels:	য ya	র ra	ল la	ব va	
Sibilants:	শ śa	ষ ṣa	স sa	হ ha	

Vowel Symbols

The vowels are written as follows after a consonant:

া ā   ি i   ী ī   ু u   ূ ū   ৃ ṛ   ৄ ṝ   ে e   ৈ ai   ো o   ৌ au

For example: কা kā   কি ki   কী kī   কু ku   কূ kū   কৃ kṛ

কৄ kṝ   কে ke   কৈ kai   কো ko   কৌ kau

The letter *a* is implied after a consonant with no vowel symbol.

The symbol *virāma* (্) indicates that there is no final vowel. ক্ k

The letters above should be pronounced as follows:

a –like the *o* in h*o*t; sometimes like the *o* in go; final *a* is usually silent.
ā –like the *a* in f*a*r.
i, ī –like the *ee* in m*ee*t.
u, ū –like the *u* in r*u*le.
ṛ –like the *ri* in *ri*m.
ṝ –like the *ree* in *ree*d.
e –like the *ai* in p*ai*n; rarely like *e* in b*e*t.
ai –like the *oi* in b*oi*l.
o –like the *o* in g*o*.
au –like the *ow* in *ow*l.
ṁ –*(anusvāra)* like the *ng* in so*ng*.
ḥ –*(visarga)* a final *h* sound like in Ah.
ṅ –*(candra-bindu)* a nasal *n* sound like in the French word *bon*.
k –like the *k* in *k*ite.
kh –like the *kh* in Ec*kh*art.
g –like the *g* in *g*ot.
gh –like the *gh* in bi*g-h*ouse.
ṅ –like the *n* in ba*n*k.
c –like the *ch* in *ch*alk.
ch –like the *chh* in mu*ch-h*aste.
j –like the *j* in *j*oy.
jh –like the *geh* in colle*ge-h*all.
ñ –like the *n* in bu*n*ch.
ṭ –like the *t* in *t*alk.
ṭh –like the *th* in ho*t-h*ouse.
ḍ –like the *d* in *d*awn.
ḍh –like the *dh* in goo*d-h*ouse.
ṇ –like the *n* in *gn*aw.
t–as in *t*alk but with the tongue against the the teeth.
th–as in ho*t-h*ouse but with the tongue against the teeth.
d–as in *d*awn but with the tongue against the teeth.
dh–as in goo*d-h*ouse but with the tongue against the teeth.
n–as in *n*or but with the tongue against the teeth.
p –like the *p* in *p*ine.
ph –like the *ph* in *ph*ilosopher.
b –like the *b* in *b*ird.
bh –like the *bh* in ru*b-h*ard.
m –like the *m* in *m*other.
y –like the *j* in *j*aw. য
y –like the *y* in *y*ear. য়
r –like the *r* in *r*un.
l –like the *l* in *l*aw.
v –like the *b* in *b*ird or like the *w* in d*w*arf.
ś, ṣ –like the *sh* in *sh*op.
s –like the *s* in *s*un.
h–like the *h* in *h*ome.

This is a general guide to Bengali pronunciation. The Bengali transliterations in this book accurately show the original Bengali spelling of the text. One should note, however, that in Bengali, as in English, spelling is not always a true indication of how a word is pronounced. Tape recordings of His Divine Grace A.C. Bhaktivedanta Swami Prabhupāda chanting the original Bengali verses are available from the International Society for Krishna Consciousness, 3959 Landmark St., Culver City, California 90230.

Index of Bengali and Sanskrit Verses

This index constitutes a complete alphabetical listing of the first and third line of each four-line verse and both lines of each two-line verse in *Śrī Caitanya-caritāmṛta*. In the first column the transliteration is given, and in the second and third columns respectively the chapter-verse references and page number for each verse are to be found.

B

C

G

H

I

J

K

L

M

R

T

General Index

Numerals in bold type indicate references to *Śrī Caitanya-caritāmṛta's* verses. Numerals in regular type are references to its purports.

A

Absolute Truth
 brāhmaṇa knows, 98
 called Rāma, **305**
 impersonal realization of transcendental, 143
 Kṛṣṇa indicates, **306**
 not attainable by argument, 315
 understanding sense activities of, 207
 See also: Kṛṣṇa
Ācāryas
 have analyzed types of love of God, 135
 one must follow, 287
 sometimes disregard social etiquette, 14
 See also: Spiritual master
Ācāryavān puruṣo veda
 verse quoted, 287
Acintya-bhedābheda-tattva
 philosophy of as basis of *bhakti* cult, **312**
Acyuta
 Kṛṣṇa known as, **377**
Adhikārīs
 gṛhasthas known as, 30-31
Adhyātma-rāmāyaṇa
 cited on Deities of Rāma and Sītā, 296-297
Ādi Purāṇa
 quoted on glory of a devotee, 243
 quoted on glory of *gopīs,* 244-245
Advaita Ācārya
 Caitanya taken to house of against His will, **9**
 initiated by Mādhavendra Purī, 163
Advaitam acyutam anādim ananta
 verses quoted, 376
Adyāpi ca muni-śreṣṭhā
 verses quoted, 243
Ahaṅghrahopāsanā
 defined, 217
Ahovala-nṛsiṁha
 visited by Caitanya, **300**
Akhila-rasāmṛta-mūrti
 Kṛṣṇa known as, 178
Ālālanātha
 devotees followed Caitanya to, **38**
Ambarīṣa Mahārāja
 protected from Durvāsā Muni, **125**-126
Amṛtaliṅga
 as deity of Śiva, **334**
 Sārvabhauma instructed Gopīnātha Ācārya on path to, **28**
Amṛta-pravāha-bhāṣya
 cited on devotional service, 122
 cited on Rāmānanda Rāya instrucing Caitanya, 162
 cited on spiritual potency, 49
 cited on Vidyānagara, 29
 quoted on Rādhā as creeper of love of God, 220
 quoted on satisfying the Lord, 113
 Seventh Chapter summarized in, 1
 summary of Eighth Chapter in, 79-80
Ānanda-cin-maya-rasa
 verses quoted, 174
Antavat tu phalaṁ teṣaṁ tad
 verses quoted, 141
Anubhāṣya
 cited on mixed devotional service, 118, 120
Anugrahāya bhūtānāṁ mānuṣaṁ
 verses quoted, 248
Anyābhilāṣitā-śūnyaṁ jñāna
 verses quoted, 122
Aprākṛta-madana
 Kṛṣṇa known as, 173
Āra kabe nitāi-cāṅdera karuṇā
 verses quoted, 170
Arjuna
 Kṛṣṇa's offer to, 104
 Mahā-Viṣṇu addressed Kṛṣṇa and, **180-181**
 receives information from Kṛṣṇa, 379

E

O

P

Y